Principles of the philosophy of religion

PHILOSOPHIA RELIGIONIS

The series *Philosophia Religionis* consists of studies in the field of the philosophy of religion. It is not restricted to any particular *Weltanschauung*, nor to any specific philosophical currents or methods. It is open for Dutch and foreign contributions of a strictly scientific character.

PRINCIPLES
of the
PHILOSOPHY
of
RELIGION

by

H.G. Hubbeling

Van Gorcum 1987

Assen/Maastricht, The Netherlands
Wolfeboro, New Hampshire 03894-2069, U.S.A.

Library of Congress Cataloguing-in-Publication Data

Hubbeling, Hubertus Gezinus.

   Principles of the philosophy of religion.

   (Philosophia religionis; vol. 25)
   Bibliography: p. 248
   Includes index.
   1. Religion-Philosophy. I. Title. II. Series:
Philosophia religionis; 25.
Bl51.H8896 1987 220'.1 87-2142

ISBN 90-232-2272-5

Printed in The Netherlands by Van Gorcum, Assen

Preface

The author of the present book, my late husband, did not live to see its publication. While it was still uncertain at what time it would go to the press, he suddenly died on 7 October 1986. Although it is most regrettable that everything could not be settled during his lifetime, it is gratifying that, thanks to financial support from the Netherlands Organization for the Advancement of Pure Research (Z.W.O.), publication is now possible. On behalf of my late husband I want to express my gratitude to all those who helped in some way or other to bring this about.

The day-to-day worries of academic life make it difficult for scholars to find the time needed for writing books. Therefore, the author appreciated it very much when the staff of the department of Systematic Theology of the Theological Faculty of Groningen University offered him the opportunity to take sabbatical leave to write this book. In it he tried to bring together the results of his research over the past years. He intended to dedicate the book to the members of his staff: dr. R. Veldhuis, mr. A.F. Sanders, dr. I.D. de Beaufort, mr. H.J. Siebrand and mr. M.E. Carvallo.

After my husband's death someone had to be charged with the final preparations for publication. I am very grateful to dr. R. Veldhuis for all his editorial work.

Finally, I think I act along my husband's lines when I also mention our two daughters. He was grateful to see them grow up to be independent and open-minded persons. Their interest in what he was doing and their critical attitude stimulated him in his life and work.

J. Hubbeling-Drent

NOTE FROM THE EDITOR

Professor Hubbeling wrote most of the present book during a sabbatical leave in 1984. After the completion of the manuscript he made some minor corrections and added a few details. However, the final revision of the text, which he apparently put off until the moment of publication would be known, could not be carried out by himself because of his untimely death. When I was asked to take the responsibility for publication, I was grateful that I could render this small service to my former teacher and friend, whose death I deplore deeply. I realized that it was difficult to know exactly what he himself would have wanted to change in the final revision. It goes without saying that I refrained as much as possible from interfering in the contents and the style of the book, but some corrections were necessary. First, I adopted quite a few suggestions made primarily by professor C.J. Labuschagne and afterwards by professor J. Kemp for the improvement of the English of the text. I am very grateful for their assistance. Moreover, I corrected some small errors that had escaped the author's notice and I removed a few needless repetitions. Finally, a few bibliographical references were added.

I want to extend my thanks to Frank Blaakmeer and Wim B. Drees, and particularly to Andy F. Sanders, for their advice and their help with the proofreading. Thanks are due to Pieter J. Huiser who made the indices.

Ruurd Veldhuis

Table of contents

1
Concepts and Problems

1.1 *Philosophy and theology*

In this book a survey of the various problems and methods in philosophy of religion will be presented. Philosophy of religion is a discipline which may be considered a part of philosophy, but it is also possible to give it a place within theology. I shall treat it as a part of philosophy, although I shall also consider authors who take a theological position. As we shall see, the borders between philosophy and theology cannot always be drawn sharply. The following provisional criterion for distinguishing between theology and philosophy may be given: in a philosophical argument a reference to revelation is not permitted, whereas in theology one may refer to revelation as an argument. This is not only true for Christian or Jewish philosophy of religion, but also for the other kinds of philosophy of religion. One may e.g. refer to the Upanishads, the Koran, the Bible, the Old and New Testament, etc., or even to some sacred tradition which is valid in a given religion. None of these arguments can be valid in a philosophical argumentation, because here only rational arguments are permitted.

Of course, the distinction is not so simple as might seem at first sight, because what is understood by 'rational' may vary from author to author. A clear-cut definition of 'rational' and 'reason' cannot be given. For that matter we shall see that there are different philosophical systems, varying insofar as a broader or stricter concept of 'rational' is used. We shall consider this point in detail in our treatise. Here it may be sufficient to point out that one may distinguish between a scientific philosophy and one based on a given   ld view. For example, one might refer to religious experience. Naturally, such a reference exceeds the limits of science, but as long as one tries to give a rational foundation for such a trespass one remains within the borders of philosophy.

Before going further we must first explain a few terms. By 'science' and 'scientific' we understand not the natural sciences but also what is known on the continent as 'Geisteswissenschaft' and 'geisteswissenschaftlich', viz. all that is treated in the non-natural sciences, i.e. the arts and humanities. Now it might be clear that there are not always strict borders between philosophical systems based on a certain world view and theological systems. One may base one's reference to revelation, for example, on religious experience. But there still remains a fundamental difference between a philosophical and a theological (dogmatic) treatise, in that in the former a rational foundation will always be given. The statements in Scripture, the Upanishads, the Koran, etc., are never taken for granted without further examination. A Church authority is never a starting point for an argumentation. All statements in any book of revelation or of an ecclesiastical or religious authority are open to criticism and investigation.

In theology, however, a book of revelation or a treatise written by an ecclesiastical or religious authority may be considered to be a source and criterion of truth. Theology is also a discipline in which one operates with a scientific method, and its students do not accept without criticism and investigation everything brought forward by the ecclesiastical authorities. But some tradition and some revelation must always constitute the foundation of this discipline. The student of theology may criticize the less essential parts of a book of revelation by referring to the more important parts of that book. He may also criticize ecclesiastical authorities by referring to Scripture, or he may oppose one religious tradition with the help of another. But there must always be some tradition, some authority or some written or oral revelation on which theology as a discipline bases its doctrine.

In philosophy things are different. Here every revelation, tradition and authority is subjected to a rational investigation and to criticism. This investigation and criticism may be more or less strict, but there will always be a rational argument. Many theologians, for example, those from the Barthian school, reject such a critical and philosophical investigation in advance. I agree that such an investigation ought not to take place in theology (dogmatics), but in the present book we are concerned with a philosophical discipline, and things are therefore different. The advantage of our approach is that non-believers also can share, to a greater or lesser extent, the presuppositions and starting-points of our argument. And therefore there are better opportunities for discussion and argumentation. As we shall see, one of the main purposes of our treatise is to offer the best possible arguments for the various viewpoints.

1.2 *Various concepts of philosophy of religion*

In 'Philosophy *of Religion*' one may regard the adjunct '*of religion*' as the equivalent of an objective genitive or of a subjective genitive. If we consider it to be the equivalent of an objective genitive, 'philosophy of religion' is a rational investigation of the various religions and religious phenomena. If, on the other hand, we regard it as a subjective genitive, 'philosophy of religion' refers to the various philosophical implications which the different religions and religious beliefs may have. Obviously, this may lead to a great variety of questions and problems. For example:

1. What is religion? What makes a statement or action a religious state-

ment or action? In a more traditional way this question could be formulated as the problem of the *essence* of religion. In order to answer this question philosophy of religion makes use of material collected and classified by science of religion. The problem as such, i.e. looking for the 'essence' of religion, certainly belongs to science of religion too. Dutch Catholic philosophers of religion (Bellon, Dupré, Möller) combine in their work philosophy and science of religion. As a rule protestant philosophers of religion refrain from doing this, but I myself want to base philosophy of religion on the material provided by science of religion.

2. What logical rules are valid for religious statements or what is their logical status? This problem is a subject of the logic of religion, a discipline which has been founded by Bocheński.

3. The question of the truth of religious statements is in my opinion the central problem of the philosophy of religion. Philosophy of religion distinguishes itself from science of religion precisely on this point. Science of religion does not ask for the truth or falseness of religious institutions or statements, it just describes and explains them. Philosophy of religion, then, may be characterized as follows:
Philosophy of religion = science of religion + the investigation of truth or falsity.
It is possible to put the question of truth and falsity in a philosophical way, so that no reference to revelation is permitted in order to solve this question. In this book we shall try to remain within the limits of a philosophical, rational discipline. I shall, however, take 'reason' and 'rational' in a broad sense, distinguishing between the various senses by means of logic.

4. It is also possible to approach the problem of truth and falsity from a dogmatic point of view. In that case philosophy of religion becomes a part of dogmatics, specifically that part in which the discussion with other religions and various philosophical theories is conducted. We may find an example of such a philosophy of religion in the work of the Swiss theologian Emil Brunner.

5. What is the ethical, aesthetic or religious value of the various religious statements? Do they promote the social and psychological integration of man? The task of answering these questions is shared by the philosophy of religion with the sociology and psychology of religion. It would be interesting to ask what political and social ideas and actions are implied by the various religions. The Buddhism of Sri Lanka (Ceylon) and Thailand has developed an interesting theory of tolerance, which has as a consequence that in these countries all religions are promoted by the state. On the other hand there are great differences between the political attitudes in Vietnamese and Thai Buddhism. The former is much more militant than the latter. However, on practical grounds I will refrain from entering into these questions.

3

6. What is the logical status of theological statements? The difference between this problem and that mentioned in 2 above is that there the logical status of *religious* statements is treated and here the status of *theological* statements.

For practical reasons the questions mentioned in 2 and 3 are in the centre of our investigations. I shall not only defend my own opinion with respect to the truth of certain religious statements, but I shall also try to find the best possible arguments for other positions. Moreover I shall not make decisions as a consequence of a particular philosophical position, but shall base the arguments on logic and on religious experience.

1.3 *Definitions*

Various definitions of philosophy and theology are possible. The definition one chooses depends on the purpose of one's investigations. In this book I shall be primarily concerned with the epistemological foundation of the philosophy of religion. Therefore we give the following definition:

Both philosophy and religion try to give an answer to the most fundamental questions of life, such as 'Does God Exist?' 'What is the meaning of life?' 'What is happiness?' 'Is there eternal life?', etc. The difference between philosophy and theology lies in the fact that theology refers to revelation, whereas philosophy acknowledges only the authority of reason. Theology is the critical reflexion on one's own religion, which is presented as a logically ordered system. In the foundation of this system it is permitted to refer to revelation and/or ecclesiastical or other traditional authorities. Philosophy of religion tries to give a critical evaluation of the various religious convictions on rational grounds. The most important part of philosophy of religion is the philosophical doctrine of God, i.e. a doctrine of God based on reason. As I said, rational thinking is not unequivocal. Therefore various philosophical systems are possible and there are various systems of the philosophy of religion. They differ from each other in that various concepts of reason and various sources of experience are among the constituents of these systems.

To an approach like this many objections have been raised. I shall return to them later (3.3).

1.4 *Relation of philosophy and religion*

Before we continue our exposition of the problems and methods of the philosophy of religion we must first consider the relation between philosophy (of religion) and religion more carefully. One could formulate this problem as that of the relation between reason and faith. The answers given here by the various authors differ. Even in putting the question various approaches are possible.

1.4.1 *Philosophy and religions considered as two systems of statemens*

If we consider for a moment philosophy and religion as two systems of statements, the following positions are possible:

(i)   *Faith (religion) and philosophy coincide.* That means that philosophy teaches the same doctrines as faith (theology) or, in other words, everything that is taught in dogmatics can be proved by reason. But a difference in emphasis is still possible.

    (a) Religion can be considered to be more fundamental and more important than philosophy. The reason which proves the doctrines of dogmatics is considered to be a reason 'enlightened by faith'. This is the position of Anselm.

    (b) It is also possible to emphasize reason more strongly than religion. From a rational point of view religion might be regarded as a less adequate representation of truth than reason, though emotionally religion might be richer. This is more or less the position of Hegel.

(ii)   *Faith (religion) and philosophy coincide only partially.* This means that only some dogmas of religion can be proved by reason. This is the position of Thomas Aquinas.

(iii)   *Faith (religion) and philosophy are completely separated.* This means that none of the doctrines of theology (faith) can be proved by reason. But this position too may have different variants.

    (a) Faith is central and philosophy has only a subordinate place. This is the position of the Swiss theologians Barth and Brunner, but also of Schleiermacher. There are, of course, differences between the three in that in Barth's view philosophy has only the task of analysing certain concepts, but has no right to bring forward metaphysical propositions, whereas Schleiermacher clearly offers a kind of metaphysics.

    (b) Faith has a subordinate position and philosophy is central. We may find this view in the philosophies of Kant and Spinoza.

The positions indicated above are expounded more extensively in the course of our treatise. Here we have only given the various positions in outline.

1.4.2 *The function of philosophy in relation to religion*

Though the approach given in 1.4.1 is the common one, others are also possible. One might ask what the task and function of philosophy (reason) are with respect to religion (faith), as M.J. Charlesworth has done. There are the following possibilities:

(i)   *Philosophy refutes religion.* This means that reasons discloses that religious doctrines are false. It unmasks religion as an ill-conceived activity, not so much by refuting metaphysically or scientifically the religious doctrines as by exposing the psychological (Freud) or social (Marx) roots of religion.

(ii) *Philosophy cannot refute religion, neither can it by any means serve as a preparation for faith.* At most it can analyse human concepts which are also used in dogmatics. We may find this position in Karl Barth's work.

(iii) *Philosophy cannot prove religious doctrine, but it may serve as a preparation for religion.* Here also reason cannot by any means prove the religious doctrines, but it may facilitate man's road towards the acceptance of faith. It may show the shortcomings of reason and the necessity for man to look elsewhere for an answer to the questions of life (Pascal, Kierkegaard, Brunner). It may also take its starting-point in morality and show that God belongs to the postulates of morality (Kant).

(iv) *Philosophy may provide faith with an apologetics.* In Christian, Islamic and Jewish philosophies of religion this is a very common position: Anselm, Thomas Aquinas, Avicenna, Maimonides. Their ways differ, however, in that – as we have already seen above – the degree in which dogmatic doctrines might be proved, differs.

(v)   *Philosophy is faith in another form.* Philosophy presents the same doctrines as faith (theology), but whereas faith puts them forward in the form of an emotional representation, philosophy gives the true rational expression. We may find this position in Hegel's work.

2

Religious knowledge and the problem of verification

2.1 *General philosophical orientation*

It is very important for a philosopher to ascertain the right starting-point for his philosophical investigations. With what questions should he start? What should stand in the centre of his consideration?

(i) One might start with *man*, and nowadays this is a very usual starting-point in continental philosophy. But even this may be done in various ways. We could consider man as a member of society, and it might be obvious that in this case the social relations of man with his fellow-men and with his environment remain in the centre of philosophical research. One might consider these relations as the foundation of the other activities of man: knowing, believing, etc. But even if we take this anthropological starting-point, we are not obliged to consider man primarily as a social being. We may also choose man in general for our starting-point. That does not mean that we shall regard man as an autonomous being without relations with his fellow-men and his environment. From a modern point of view such a position is dated. Man stands in relation to his fellowmen and to his environment by means of thousands of threads. But a difference of emphasis is still possible. We might develop an anthropological point of view in which society has no logical priority over the individual. The social relations may not be the foundation of man's other activities, but the latter may support the former. One may start with man as a knowing, moral and emotional being who establishes relations with his fellow-men, etc.

(ii) This starting-point in man was, however, not the first starting-point taken in Western philosophy. Greek philosophy started with considerations about the fundamental constituents of the *world*. The first Greek philosophers of nature looked for what was to be considered the constant element in all the processes of change. What was the permanent, fundamental constituent, the essence or *archè* of all beings? Change is only possible if there remains something that is to be changed, that is, if there is something that remains constant. First the Greeks indicated something in the world as the essence of all things: water (Thales), air (Anaximenes), etc. Soon more complicated concepts were formed: *apeiron*, the indefinable, which has no qualifications (Anaximander). An atomic theory was devised also (Democritus). Only with the arrival of the Sophists on the philosophical scene man became the focus of attention and Socrates, despite all his objections against the Sophists, adhered to this approach.

(iii) But other approaches are certainly possible. If man wants to found his approach on the highest conceivable being it is natural to start with *God*. In Indian philosophy this is a very common approach. In Western philosophy also we may find God as the beginning of all philosophy. This is not necessarily an indication of a religious philosophy, because Spinoza too has put God in the centre or beginning of his philosophy. In Spinoza's work this is a philosophical conception of God and not a religious one.

(iv) Now we have already three possible starting-points: man, world and *God*. So we could try to find a common denominator of these three approaches. This might be done in the following way. Of all three it can be said that they *are*, in other words, they are *beings*. We shall not argue here that it is self-evident that God is, or that his existence can be proved; we shall come to this in the next chapter. The only thing we are saying now is that if God is, he has something in common with man and the world, and that is that he *is*. Therefore many philosophers have taken *being* as the starting-point of philosophy (ontology). And one cannot deny that there is some plausibility in this approach.

(v) But objections might be raised against all these approaches. In order to bring forward a certain element as the starting-point of one's philosophical investigations, one must bring forward some arguments in favour of that position. One must *know* that this position is right and that the arguments are valid. That means one must take epistemology as the foundation of philosophy, though not in the sense that one takes as a starting-point the *actual* way in which man discovers truth. This might be considered a variant of the anthropological approach. Here the point is how we *ought* to attain knowledge.

(vi) But now an even more fundamental approach turns up. In order to gain true knowledge, it is necessary to know how to argue and how to find valid arguments. Thus, *logic* might be considered the true foundation for philosophy.

(vii) Can we do logic without presupposing language? In logic, for example, negation is a fundamental concept. Now, how do we know of negation if we do not know in advance how to use the word 'not' or 'no' in language?

(viii) In all the preceding approaches a philosopher is considered to be a man only contemplating the world from a certain point of view. But is this not a wrong picture? Is man not primarily an active being trying to attain certain objectives? Even his knowledge serves some purpose. Are not *values*, therefore, more fundamental than all the other concepts? And does it not follow that ethics or axiology (the doctrine of values) should be our starting-point in philosophy?

(ix) Marxists do not like to speak about values as the starting-point of philosophy, but they take a similar position in that they teach the priority of *praxis* over theory or, in other words, the priority of practical over theoretical philosophy.

All these positions (and even more are known!) have been taken in the history of philosophical thought. Some of them are related to each other. Thus the differences between (v), (vi) and (vii) are not fundamental and may be considered variants within the same approach. On the other hand (i) and (viii) or (i) and (ix) may easily go together.

Should we not decide definitely which approach is the best, or perhaps even the only possible one? If we could demonstrate that a certain approach is presupposed by all the others, then we would have our most fundamental starting-point! Let us try to prove that some starting-point has priority over the others. We might reason in the following way:

PROPOSITION I: *In every philosophical statement man is presupposed. Therefore one should start with man and thus take an anthropological starting-point.*

PROOF: In every statement about the world, being, God, logical rules, etc., human categories are used. In every proposition man, who thinks and knows, is presupposed. We need not necessarily presuppose a specific individual being, but if we think all human beings away, we cannot think of any proposition being formed, uttered, etc. One could, of course, conceive of God as a being without human beings and still forming certain propositions. But *we* on our part cannot speak about God without using human concepts and therefore even theology starts with God's revelation to *man*. Thus, even theology has an anthropological foundation. With these considerations our proposition may be proved.

This might seem manifest at first sight, but another proposition might also be established:

PROPOSITION II: Every philosophical statement presupposes the validity of logical laws. Therefore logic should be the starting-point in philosophy.

PROOF: One can easily prove that our *proposition I* presupposes *proposition II*. For adherents of *proposition I* must at least presuppose that their proposition is true and that its opposite is false. Otherwise *proposition I* cannot be the most fundamental proposition. But in doing so they already presuppose one of the fundamental laws in logic, namely the law of non-contradiction.

This is manifest also. But what shall we do now? For we might even 'prove' other propositions in which respectively all the starting-points are 'proved' to be the most fundamental ones. They seem to be all equally true and this again seems to be logically contradictory, but this is not so. For in a logical contradiction the two contradicting propositions must be taken to be true at the same time and within the same conceptual framework. If I say that someone has dark hair, I do not exclude that the same person can have grey hair later in his life. If at time t_1 the statement p is true and at time t_{1+i}

9

the statement non-p is true then there is no contradiction. Thus the moment of time is important. The same is true with respect to the point of view with regard to the proposition. If I say that a certain book is to the right of my typewriter and a person sitting opposite to me says that it is to the left, then there is no contradiction, because our points of view are different. The same goes for our conceptual frameworks. If in science there are two seemingly contradictory theories about the movement of light, i.e. the theory of waves and the theory of particles, there is no contradiction, because they are formed within different conceptual frameworks and corroborated by different experiments. In science one speaks about the complementarity of the two theories. All the starting-points seem to presuppose each other. None of them can claim to be the absolute starting-point.

Let us for a moment consider our two propositions. *Proposition I* is a more material, more concrete proposition, whereas *proposition II* is a more formal, abstract proposition. But may one not say: the concrete world (man etc.) is more important than all these systems of logic? Certainly, if one takes a more material, more concrete position. But if one takes a more formal position and looks primarily for criteria of truth, the priorities change. In a formal framework logic has the priority, in a more concrete framework man (or the world) may have the priority.

Whether one takes a more concrete or a more abstract position is a matter of choice. This illustrates the fact that in philosophy making decisions is important! As in a philosophy with an anthropological starting-point a chapter on logic must occur and in a philosophy with logic at its base a chapter on anthropology is indispensable, these decisions might after all not be so important, and I am indeed quite convinced that they are not. But although this might theoretically be true, in practice we see that the choice of a starting-point *is* important and that philosophies with an anthropological starting-point usually lead to results that differ from those with an epistemological starting-point.

Now W. Härle has made an interesting proposal to finding the most fundamental position. He is of the opinion that all the approaches at least presuppose the use of signs and that we should therefore take our starting-point in semiotics, the doctrine of signs. This certainly appeals to me, but I am afraid that this position is not definitive either, for all the arguments in favour of it presuppose a formal, abstract approach. Moreover the same arguments, which defenders of an anthropological approach have put forward against the logical starting-point (that there is no use of logic without the presence of human thinking, etc.) may be adduced here too. Perhaps one may say that the semiotic approach is more fundamental than the other abstract, formal approaches (using the epistemological, logical or linguistic starting-point). But even this is not convincing. For the use of signs presupposes correct operating with *identical* and *different* signs, in other words it presupposes perhaps both language and logic, and it presupposes at least the validity of the fundamental logical laws of identity and difference.

We are faced here with the question whether mathematics is more fundamental than logic or *vice versa*. In a so-called Lindenbaum-algebra, which belongs to the theory of (half-)groups, systems of propositional logic appear as applications (models) of a more abstract theory, so that one might argue that logic is based on mathematics. But in mathematics too, the well-known fundamental logical laws of identity and non-contradiction are presupposed. In view of this one might be tempted to think that logic is, after all, the most fundamental starting-point, and I am certainly inclined to do so. But here all the arguments in favour of *proposition I* return, and even in a formal, abstract approach the 'fundamental' logical laws turn out to be not so fundamental as they at first sight appear, for in certain axiom-systems of logic they appear as derived theorems. One cannot evade the fact that the many possible starting-points seem to lie in a circle. I wish it were otherwise!

For the purpose of the present book, however, we must make adecision. On practical and personal grounds I choose an epistemological starting-point with an emphasis on logic, because we are concerned here with the philosophy of religion, and in our cultural situation the question of the *truth* of the various religious beliefs is most fundamental and indispensable. Besides logic, the results of science of religion are also very important for our study, because we are investigating the meaning and truth of religious convictions.

As a model of presentation of these convictions we take the linguistic model of statements. We shall therefore investigate what the meaning and the truth value of certain religious statements are. I choose this model, because statements are more easily accessible than attitudes, actions or states of consciousness. I do not assert that religion is nothing but a set of statements. What I introduce here is a model of presentation, nothing more. Other approaches are certainly possible. The advantage of the approach used here is, as said above, that we face the problems of our time that are much disputed, i.e. those connected with the question of the *truth* of religious beliefs. Hence our epistemological approach.

On the other hand we do not confine ourselves to purely epistemological questions or to the problems of sense and meaning. A disadvantage of many Kantian and analytical approaches is that one does not do more than prepare the tools without using them. Grinding knives is boring if one has nothing to cut. I have tried to avoid this situation. I am convinced that certain metaphysical statements are possible, because logic is valid in all possible worlds. In this I follow rather a Leibnizian (and Spinozistic) tradition than a Humean or Kantian one. H. Scholz tried to present a metaphysics as a strict science along these lines, but modern philosophers of mathematics (Kripke) nowadays also operate from this position. A defence of this approach will be given later.

11

It is, however, not my intention to try to convert the reader to Christianity, although my personal beliefs are expressed in the present book. Philosophy of religion is no substitute for apologetics. It is the task of philosophy of religion to reflect critically on the various religious convictions and to find the best possible arguments for the various fundamental religious statements. It is then up to the reader to make his choice. Without choosing one cannot do philosophy, let alone philosophy of religion!

2.2 *General epistemology. Various systems of logical empiricism*

The reader realizes that philosophy of religion has to deal with many problems which we cannot discuss at length in this book. We have to make a choice, and on practical grounds I shall confine myself mainly to the problems of Western philosophies of religion. Christian religion will, therefore, be in the centre of our investigations, but as far as possible we shall also consider other religions. Further we shall, as said above, pay special attention to the epistemological problems. Before considering the problems of religious knowledge we have to reflect on the problems of epistemology in general. We shall deal with these problems insofar as we need them in our later expositions.

As to general epistemology, there are many theories and standpoints. We want to make as few decisions as possible here in order to present an approach that may commend itself to a great number of different schools. Therefore we shall not investigate the ways in which we receive our knowledge, for this belongs to cognitive psychology, a field in which most of the problems arise. We shall confine ourselves to indicating what sources of knowledge there are. Here also many differences occur, but they can at least be defined in an exact manner. The purpose of every philosophy, and certainly that of philosophy of religion, is to show the presuppositions of every interesting theory and argumentation. Thus it is our task to indicate what the presuppositions of the various religious convictions are and on what (hidden) argumentations they are founded.

Certainly, faith and religion are psychologically and sociologically not founded on argument, but if the question of truth or falsehood arises, arguments figure prominently. Philosophy of religion cannot decide conclusively which religious or atheistic statements are true and which are false, because all presuppositions may be disputed. But philosophy of religion can indicate the various presuppositions on which the manifold argumentations are founded. In this way philosophy of religion can help people to make a rational choice. I shall try to be as objective as possible, and also to adduce the best possible arguments for positions to which I myself do not subscribe.

It is generally acknowledged that man has two major sources of knowledge, *viz.* thinking (logic) and experience. Sometimes only one of them was considered to be the real and relevant source of knowledge. In the older forms of empiricism, the opinion was held that logical rules and laws were nothing but generalized experience. This point of view is refuted by modern insights. Logical and mathematical laws are not proved or refuted by empirical means. In rationalism, in its older forms, it was thought that experience was only a means to stimulate thinking in its operations. Truth was said to be found by reason alone and not by experience. But in the light of modern science such a position cannot be maintained.

Therefore we have to accept both sources as genuine sources of knowledge. Of course, here we have the interesting problem as to how the two can go together, but we shall leave this problem aside and simply take the two sources as two irreducible ways of getting knowledge. Further we presuppose that 'pure' experience is impossible. For example, I never see an ashtray without any operation of thought. With my senses alone I see only colours and forms and even in order to identify colours and forms I need logical operations, but to identify a certain set of colours and forms as an ashtray I need an operation of my mind. I need to interpret them in such a way that I can say: 'I see an ashtray'.

Experience is never without interpretation. But there are stages in the processes of interpretation. I interpret certain sets of colours and forms as a group of ashtrays. Next I interpret certain ashtrays as e.g. big, small, circular, etc. Then I may interpret them as useful, worthless, ugly, beautiful, etc. On every occasion, what is interpreted at one stage might be 'raw material' for the next interpretation.

Now we shall consider the two sources of knowledge more carefully. There is more than one kind of experience. We have common sense experience, moral, religious, aesthetic experience, etc. This is nothing new. Whether these various sources of experience lead to knowledge is a matter of dispute. That common sense experience will be a source of true statements, if certain precautions are taken, is commonly accepted. Modern science might be seen as based on logic (mathematics) and methodically used common sense experience.

The question is, however, whether moral and aesthetic statements are true statements, i.e. whether the question of the truth or falsity of such statements can meaningfully be raised. We shall discuss this problem later. For the moment we may state that it is obvious that these sources of experience are not so great a problem for epistemology as the other source, namely religious experience. Whether this leads to genuine knowledge is rightly a matter of doubt and dispute. But that there are various sources of *experience* is a well-known fact.

New in our times is the fact that modern logic has discovered that there are various systems of *logic* too. So rational thinking is not an unequivocal concept. It is a wide-spread misunderstanding that there is only one kind of logic. There are, however, more or less strict systems in logic. There is a variety of axioms and rules of inference. In the stricter systems fewer axioms and/or rules of inference are valid and therefore one can prove fewer theorems in these systems. In the less strict systems there are more axioms and/or rules of inference and therefore more theorems can be proved in them. It is not true that in the less strict systems one can prove theorems that logically contradict theorems of the stricter systems. In the less strict systems one can prove theorems that are *unprovable* in the stricter systems. I shall explain this more in detail, but for a more fundamental treatment the reader is invited to consult the textbooks on logic.

First we shall consider the difference between *axiom* and *rule*. Axioms are statements (propositions) that form the basis of a logical system without further proof. Their truth is taken for granted within the system. Rules are directions for operations with the statements. With their help we can, from certain proved statements or axioms, infer other, new, statements. A well-known rule e.g. is *modus ponendo ponens*: if p is true and p implies q, then q is true. Here p and q are variables for statements, which refer to states of affairs. In logical signs:

p
p → q
―――――
q   [→ sign for implication]

The *axioms* of logic are themselves *logical* axioms. But this is not true with regard to the other sciences. In Euclidean geometry the following axiom is true: 'The shortest connection between two points is the straigth line'. This is, of course, a geometrical, not a logical axiom. But the *rules* are always logical rules. *Modus ponens* is also a rule in the proofs of the Euclidean geometrical system. And this is also valid for the other scientific systems. With the help of axioms and some (logical) rules the various scientific systems are constructed.

We have said above that there are stricter and less strict logical systems. We shall only consider those that are relevant from a practical point of view. Then the most strict system is that of intuitionistic or constructivistic logic. In this logic one makes use of another concept of negation than the one used in classical logic. This becomes manifest in that in classical logic the negation of the negation of a statement is equivalent to the statement, but in constructivistic logic it is not. Thus, in classical logic the following always true':

(1) p ⟷ ∼ ∼ p

(i.e. p is equivalent to the negation of the negation of p). [⟷ sign for equivalence; ∼ sign for negation]

This axiom is not true in constructivistic of intuitionistic logic. This does not mean that the contradictory opposite of (1) is true in intuitionistic logic. It means only that this axiom is not true or derivable in this kind of logic. Or, formulated a little more precisely, in intuitionistic logic (1') is true, but (1") is not.

(1') $p \rightarrow \sim \sim p$

(1") $\sim \sim p \rightarrow p$

A terminological explanation in passing: in logic a distinction is made between 'derivability' and 'truth'. A statement is said be derivable in a system, if it can be inferred from the axioms of the system with the help of the rules of inference which are valid in the system. A statement is said to be true, if it refers to a real state of affairs and a logical theorem is said to be true, if it refers to a state of affairs that is present in all possible worlds.

Other definitions are also possible. Sometimes one makes the same distinction by speaking about, respectively, the syntax and the semantics of the system. Properly speaking one should say that a statement is valid in a a system, if one refers to the syntax, and that it is true, if one refers to the semantics of the system. What is valid is at the same time true, but the reverse is not always true. Gödel has proved that not every true statement can be proved. In our exposition, however, we confine ourselves to those logical systems in which what is true is at the same time provable (derivable).

In intuitionistic logic the proof with the help of a reduction to the contradiction (*reductio ad absurdum*) has only limited validity. This has to do with what has been said above. If we suppose p hypothetically and infer from this hypothesis a contradiction, then we may conclude to non-p. But in intuitionistic logic the reverse is not permitted. If we suppose non-p hypothetically, and we infer from this hypothesis a contradiction, then we may conclude that non-non-p ($\sim \sim p$), but not that p, because as we have seen above, from $\sim \sim p$ we cannot conclude that p in intuitionistic logic. Such a conclusion is permitted in classical logic, but not in intuitionistic or constructivistic logic. All this makes demonstrations in intuitionistic logic more difficult than in classical logic. What is demonstrable in intuitionistic logic, is also derivable in classical logic, but the reverse is not true. Suppose, for example, we want to demonstrate the existence of God by an indirect proof. We suppose by means of a hypothesis that God does not exist. Should we succeed in inferring a contradiction from this hypothesis then we are allowed to conclude to the existence of God in classical logic, but not in intuitionistic logic, where a direct demonstration is always required if we want to prove a positive statement. There is a connection between what is said above and the fact that in classical logic (unlike intuitionistic logic) the law of excluded middle is valid: 'Of the two statements, p and non-p, one is always true':

(2) p v ~ p

The logic we have considered until now, is a form of extensional logic. It is called extensional, because it assumes the validity of the principle of extensionality: 'Two equivalent statements may replace each other'. E.g. in classical logic we may replace the variable p by ~ ~ p without changing the truth value of the original formula. There are, however, systems of logic, where this is not the case. For example 'London' is equivalent to 'the capital of Great Britain' and thus in the statement

(3) London lies on the river Thames

we may replace 'London' by 'the capital of Great Britain' without changing the truth value of the statement:

(3') The capital of Great Britain lies on the river Thames.

But if we add to (3) the words 'Mr A knows' we may not replace 'London' by its equivalent, for we are not sure whether Mr A also knows that London is the capital of Great Britain.

(4) Mr A knows that London lies on the river Thames.

(4') Mr A knows that the capital of Great Britain lies on the river Thames.

The truth values of (4) and (4') need not be the same. We have to do here with epistemic logic and this is a system of logic in which the principle of extensionality is no longer valid. We call such systems intensional systems of logic. Besides epistemic logic, particularly modal logic and deontic logic belong to intensional logic. Modal logic contains axioms and rules of inference in which words such as 'necessary', 'possible', 'contingent' occur, to which also 'probable' may be added. Deontic logic contains axioms and rules of inference in which words such as 'obligatory', 'permitted', 'morally indifferent' figure, to which also 'morally desirable' may be added. Here too the principle of extensionality is not valid. For example (5) is true:

(5) It is logically (arithmetically) necessary that $1 + 1 = 2$.

Now the number of moons around Mars is equivalent to 2, but statement (5') is not true:

(5′) It is logically necessary that $1 + 1 =$ the number of moons around Mars.

For it is not logically necessary that the number of moons around Mars is 2!

Now also in modal and deontic logic various systems are possible in which more or fewer theorems can be derived depending on the axioms and/or rules of inference which constitute the system. In a stricter system fewer theorems can be derived and vice versa. I shall not make use of these systems in this book except in the appendices. The main point is to keep in mind that there are more or less strict systems in logic, because it is very important to determine the strictness of the system in which we try to prove certain religious statements.

We have seen that there is a variety of experiences and also of logical systems. If we combine the two, we get a great variety of philosophical systems, differing from each other in that they might be more or less strict with respect to experience and/or logic. One cannot prove that only one kind of system is permissible. Of course, the more strict a system is, the better it is from a scientific point of view, but a system must be adapted to the field of investigation. In mathematics constructivistic (intuitionistic) logic is often to be preferred to classical logic, but in physics this system is too strict. There we need classical logic and mathematics in order to prove the usual physical laws. The philosopher has to choose a certain system and the only thing one may require from him is that the indicates the system in which he argues. Now this is seldom done explicitly, but in the work of a good philosopher one can infer his system from the way he argues.

I myself make use of the following two systems:

1. A relatively strict system which is called the standard system, because it is the usual system in science. This system is based on common sense experience (systematized in scientific experience), classical logic, to which also classical modal logic may be added (technically: the system S_5) and the multifold validity of the a priori rule *ex nihilo nihil fit* (out of nothing nothing occurs) (the negative formulation of the principle of sufficient reason, *principium rationis sufficientis*). I speak of the multifold validity of this principle, because I believe it is not only valid within certain scientific systems, but also in the foundation of these systems, or in the relation of these systems to each other. I shall discuss this more extensively later on.

This system is strong enough to give a cosmological argument for the existence of God, as we shall see. It is, however, too strict to give a more complete and interesting system of the philosophy of religion, because it does not permit references to religious experience. We shall therefore accept a less strict system for the completion of our system of philosophy of religion after we have laid our foundation with the help of a strict system. We should remember that stricter systems than our standard system are possible, but the standard system is a respectable one from a scientific point of view.

2. To complete scientific philosophy of religion I make use of a less strict system, in which more can be proved. I supplement the standard system by adding moral, aesthetic and religious experience as cognitive sources. Thus I construct a second, less strict system. The concept of religious experience must be taken in a broad sense. It comprises more than only religious feelings. Religious experience may also include a reference to religious intuition, and may finally give a foundation for a reference to revelation. In the course of this book some further qualifications will be necessary, for instance, whether or not we are willing to accept reference to parapsychological data (ESP, etc.).

These two systems are from a scientific point of view respectable. Also the method of first laying a foundation with the help of a strict system and then completing it with the help of a less strict system, seems justifiable to me. If the existence of God has been proved, a reference to religious experience is certainly plausible.

But besides these two systems which have a 'respectable' status from a scientific point of view, there are other logical systems, called dialectical logic, which are more doubtful and are not accepted in science, but may have a certain degree of plausibility in philosophy. Previously, some of these dialectical systems were universally acknowledged, and with their help the existence of God could easily be proved. The interesting aspect of the modern revival of the proofs of God's existence is that they can be exhibited now in a much stricter system than in the traditional proofs. In the present book these dialectical systems are not used, but there might be fields in which they have to be used, and therefore I shall at least say a few things about them.

(1) We may call the first system the *dialectic* (or the dialectical logic) *of the infinite or the absolute*. In this system a rule of inference is used, which has a certain plausibility, but is not (universally) valid according to modern insight. We refer here to the rule of inference in which a conclusion from the finite to the infinite or from the relative to the absolute is permitted. For example, in this system the following line of reasoning is permitted: 'There are various degrees of certainty. That means that one statement is more certain than another. But in order to measure these various degrees of certainty, one ought to presuppose an absolute degree of certainty by which we can attain the degree of certainty of the various statements. Therefore an absolute degree of certainty must be accepted'.

A classical example of this way of reasoning we may find in the fourth way of Thomas Aquinas: 'The fourth way is based on the gradation observed in things. Some things are found to be more good, more true, more noble, and so on, and other things less. But such comparative terms describe varying degrees of approximation to a superlative; e.g. things are hotter and hotter the nearer they approach what is hottest. Something therefore is the truest and best and most noble of things, and hence the most fully in being; for Aristotle says that the truest things are things most fully in being. Now when many things possess some property in common, the one most fully possessing it causes it in the others: fire, to use Aristotle's example, the hottest of all things, causes all other things to be not. There is something therefore that causes in all other things their being, their goodness, and whatever other perfection they have. And this we call "God" '. Arguments like these have undeniably a certain degree of plausibility. As a universal rule this dialectical rule of inference cannot be accepted, but in some contexts it may be valid (*vide* Appendix 8).

(2) In the second place there is a *dialectic of polarity*. We may find this in Pythagoreanism, in the philosophies of the Far East (China, Japan), in Goethe and others. The world is conceived here as consisting of indissoluble polarities: warm versus cold, North versus South, male versus female, Yang versus Yin, etc. This principle of polarity plays a great role in the religions of China, Japan and Indonesia, and in many 'primitive' religions, as we shall see. It is also an important principle in aesthetics, but in science it is not valid.

(3) In the third place there is the *dialectic of synthesis*, which may also be called Hegelian dialectic. The processes in the world and the ideas that reflect these processes proceed *via* contradictions, which are – in contrast to the polarities of the dialectic mentioned under (2) – brought into a new synthesis. We find this form of dialectic in Fichte and Hegel and in Marxism. Every thesis is followed by an antithesis, and thesis and antithesis are united in a new synthesis. In Marxism this Hegelian dialectics has been taken over, but it was put on its feet, i.e. it was transformed from a dialectics of ideas into a dialectic of history and of the economic forces operating in history.

Dialectic, however, is controversial in Marxism. Engels defines it as the most universal law in nature and he mentions three principal characteristics: (i) sudden shift of quantity into quality and vice versa; (ii) penetration of the polar contradictions into each other and changing into each other in the long run; (iii) development through contradictions or the negation of the negation – a spiral form of development. Stalin dropped this negation of the negation and taught only a development through contradictions and the shift of quantity into quality. He also taught the universal validity of dialectics in nature and society. Later Marxists have restored the doctrine of the negation of the negation, i.e. the synthesis after thesis and antithesis. Only Mao maintained the indissolubility of the contradictions. In this he remained in the dialectics referred to under (2). There might even be – in the case of Mao – some influence of traditional Chinese thought.

Besides the points mentioned above, which may be considered characteristic for Marxist dialectic (i.e. mainly: the development through contradictions, the negation of the negation or the emerging of a new synthesis

19

and the unity of nature and society), we find in Hegelian dialectics also the point that (iv) the concrete elements in reality can never be fully subsumed under a general abstract rule. A concrete element always adds something new to the characteristics comprised the abstract rule. In this way in the synthesis a concrete (as opposed to abstract) generality is achieved; (v) all finite elements must be interpreted in the light of the whole. From the last characteristic it may be clear that this (Hegelian) dialectic of the synthesis presupposes the dialectic of the infinity so that in Hegelian philosophy, as a consequence, the existence of God can be proved (in contradistinction to Kant). Hegel himself emphasizes that this proof has no abstract validity, but can only be established in the concrete performance of thought.

Even in Marxist philosophy the dialectic of infinity is sometimes used in such a way that, paradoxically, God's existence can be proved here too. But as we shall see in our next chapter, the 'proofs of God's existence' do not prove God in His proper divine sense, but only as an *ens necessarium* (a necessary being), a *prima causa* (a first cause), etc., and these concepts must be interpreted further. Marxism might interpret them as referring to matter that is dialectically qualified.

A form of dialectic that is related to that of Hegel, but less pronounced and with fewer characteristics, is that of the process philosophy of Whitehead. Here the concept of *prehension* plays an important role. In the process of the world every new state of affairs 'prehends' the preceding states of affairs, i.e. it selects some elements, takes them over and transforms them into a new configuration.

In science dialectic is hardly used, especially not in its Hegelian-Marxist variant, be it that the Whiteheadian variant is more plausible, but in aesthetics, the historical sciences and philosophy it does play a role. The important point is that in processes in science every new state of affairs is conceived as wholly determined by the immediately preceding state of affairs, whereas more remote states of affairs are of no importance (Marcus process). To give an example: if an aeroplane is about to make a landing, it is important to know its velocity, its direction towards the location of the airfield, etc. It is of no importance to know with what velocity it has started its flight, etc. The states of affairs of the plane that are remote from the moment of landing are of no importance.

Where they *are* important we are dealing with a dialectical process and here Hegelian-Marxist, or at least Whiteheadian, dialectic comes in. Remote states of affairs still have their influence in history. Sometimes it is said that classical logic has to do with statics and dialectical logic with dynamics, but this is not true, since in science there are many dynamic processes where we have no need for dialectical logic, *viz.* the Marcus processes as we have seen above. On the other hand we need a kind of dialectic in aesthetics, even where there is no process. In a painting or in a piece of architecture a criterion of 'harmony' is sometimes used, an equilibrium of opposing colours, forms, etc. that cannot be fully explained by classical logic.

But classical logic is stricter than dialectical logic, and one should try to achieve as much as possible within the stricter systems. The possibilities of devising a logic of change that remains within the boundaries of classical logic are by no means exhausted and the same can be said of the application of logic to aesthetics. It must be admitted, however, that until now a completely satisfying system of concepts, which covers all the aspects of change and development and remains within the bounds of classical logic, has not yet been developed. The same goes for aesthetics and some other sciences. We on our part shall try to remain as long as possible within the bounds of classical logic, as this is the stricter system. In our next section we shall briefly discuss the question why this is necessary, i.e. why a stricter system is to be preferred to a less strict system.

2.3 *Some aspects of the philosophy of science*

2.3.1 *A model of language systems*

In order to acquire a better insight into the structure of science we shall give the following *model*, taking scientific activity as a kind of arranging of language statements. It is not an explanatory model that pretends to explain facts in nature and elsewhere, but a kind of simplifying model, within which the explanatory theories can be developed and tested. It is common practice in science to test certain theories in a simplified model, in which the irrelevant aspect of the phenomena are not taken into account. If we have, for example, two experiments in physics, and one is made one hour later than the other, we take it for granted that the temperature is the same, although in an absolute sense this is not the case. A model of water works is built in order to test water currents, and so on. In the same way the following model is a simplification of scientific investigation, but what is left out is irrelevant to our purpose.

The reader is, however, by no means obliged to accept this model. He may make another one. The only thing claimed here is that the *relevant parts* of any other model may be translated into the following model. This model is only used to acquire a better insight into the problems of scientific investigation. It also makes it easier for us to discuss the problems that arise.

Note, however, that what is said elsewhere in this book about logical and empirical presuppositions is independent of the language model. It has its validity, whatever the use and validity of the latter may be.

I shall now develop the model of language systems as a means of talking more concretely about the problems that concern us. In every language system we first have a vocabulary: this consists of the words of the system.

Then we have rules (criteria) for constructing well-formed formulae. These are the basic meaningful statements of our language systems. Next we need criteria (rules) for deciding which statements are basically true and which are not. Let me illustrate this with an example.

In arithmetic the vocabulary is formed by the numbers, among which we may distinguish between natural, rational, real numbers, etc. In addition we need a set of operational signs such as '+', '−', '×', ':', '=', etc. The set of numbers and the set of operational signs form the vocabulary of our arithmetical language system. Now we need rules to decide which statements are meaningful and which are not. On the basis of these rules we can say that '3 + 2 = 5' is meaningful; so is '10 + 11 = 101'. The latter statement is false in our decimal arithmetical system, yet not meaningless. A statement like '4++=-5+' would be meaningless in ordinary arithmetic. It is very important to distinguish meaningful and meaningless statements on the one hand and true and false statements on the other hand.

After having established the criteria by which we may distinguish between meaningful and meaningless statements, we lay down criteria by which we may decide which statements are true and which are false. On the ground of these criteria we may determine that '3 + 2 = 5' is a true and that '10 + 11 = 101' is a false statement in our decimal arithmetical system. How much all this is based on convention is shown by the fact that '10 + 11 = 101' is false in our decimal system, but not in the digital arithmetical system, where '10 + 11 = 101' is the equivalent of '2 + 3 = 5' in the decimal system.

So far we have shown how to determine which are the basic meaningful and which the basic true statements in our language system. These statements are thus the primitive or elementary statements of our language system. In scientific language systems it is necessary to look for principles of arranging the primitive statements, so that with the help of these principles we may acquire an optimal ordering of these primitive basic statements. These latter principles of arranging are usually called hypotheses. They cannot be laid down by convention, in contradistinction to the basic primitive statements.

By 'optimal order' we understand the arranging of primitive statements with the help of a minimum number of principles of arrangement (i.e. a minimum number of hypotheses). These principles of arrangement must arrange a maximum number of primitive statements, and the deduction of the primitive statements from the principles of arrangement must be as simple as possible (i.e. the strictest possible from of logic must be used). With the concept of *optimal order* I have given the *(meta-)principle of economy in science*, a fundamental principle of all theory and science. This principle of economy thus consists of three constituents:

(i)   A minimum of principles of arrangement (a minimum of hypotheses);

(ii)   A deduction as simple as possible (i.e. the strictest possible system of logic);

(iii)   A maximal arrangement of primitive statements.

That the principle of economy is fundamental in science can be easily explained. It is, for example, more fundamental than the principle that a scientific theory must be able to produce predictions. We can show this in the following rather trivial way. Suppose we want to explain some phenomena in astronomy. Suppose that an astronomical theory A, consisting of a set of hypotheses, $p_1, p_2, p_3 \ldots \ldots p_n$, explains all these phenomena. We are, moreover, able to predict some unknown phenomena with the help of this set of hypotheses which are confirmed by later observations. Now if predictive power were the fundamental criterion of a scientific theory instead of the principle of economy, then we could construct a competing theory B, consisting of the same set of hypotheses as theory A, to which, however, are added some unnecessary hypotheses, $p_{n+1} \ldots \ldots p_{n+m}$, for example we could contrive the unnecessary hypothesis that somewhere in the galactic universe there are mountains made of green cheese. Now the predictive power of theory B is not less than that of theory A. Theory B only produces some predictions that cannot be verified or refuted. All the predictions of theory A, however, are also predicted by theory B. If predictive power were the fundamental criterion we could not decide between A and B. By the principle of economy, however, we must decide for theory A. The predictive power has shown itself to be a useful criterion in scientific theory, but it is a derived criterion, because it has shown itself to be helpful in acquiring an optimal order of arranging.

The structure of language systems given so far is abstract enough to cover all the scientific systems. As the fundamental structure is the same in all sciences, this is an argument in favour of our use of the term science as applying to both the natural sciences and the humanities and arts. This may sound a little awkward to the English reader, accustomed as he is to the restriction of the term 'science' to natural science, but we cannot avoid extending the scope of this concept, because in our view there is no *fundamental* difference between natural science and human sciences.

We speak of *arranging* the elementary statements in order to include as many scientific activities as possible. Arranging may consist in describing the elementary statements, but also in explaining them, etc.

Taking the principle of economy as the fundamental scientific criterion allows us to maintain that disciplines such as theology and philosophy also use a scientific method. In philosophical theology, for example, one can try to demonstrate that 'God' is necessary as a principle of arrangement to acquire an optimal order to all the data of our reason and our experience. Even dogmatic theology can fulfil the requirements of our language systems. For example, one may consider the statements of Scripture as primitive statements and try to show that the principle of the Trinity is necessary for the arranging of these statements. The doctrine of the Trinity as such does not occur in Scripture, but one may try to defend it as a hypothesis. Opponents may attempt to show that the acceptance of this principle is unnecessary. There are as a matter of fact many language systems in theology, differing from each other according to the primitive statements accepted in the system. The structural unity of all sciences does not, of course, exclude many important differences among them. Before returning to this question I shall first address myself to some questions concerning the proposed model of language systems.

We have pointed out that the statement '10 + 11 = 101' is false in one arithmetic system and true in another. This is true for all statements with respect to the various language systems. Further: what is meaningless in one system need not be so in another. In arithmetic a statement like '3 is red' is meaningless, but in a language system consisting in classifying painting-colours in which every colour correlates with a certain number the statement '3 is red' makes good sense. The sentence 'God has created the world' is meaningless in the language system of the natural sciences, but it is not so in (philosophical)theology. The statement 'water boils at 100 degrees centigrade' is meaningless as a logical theorem, but it is not meaningless in physics.

Further: what is a primitive statement in one system need not be so in another. For example, the move 'p-k4' ('e2 - e4' in continental notation) is elementary in the language system of chess. But for the calligrapher, who wants to render these signs into calligraphy, 'p-k4' is no longer an elementary statement.

We have stated above that the basic elementary statements are 'true by convention'. Many may object to this, arguing that in this way all truth becomes relative. This, however, is not the case. The theory only says that *within a certain language system* the truth of certain elementary statements is no longer discussed. They are fixed by convention. But in another language system these statements can be discussed and their truth can be critically examined. For example: the statement 'That is a book' is a primitive (elementary) statement in the language system of our daily life, but also in that of physics.

The difficult philosophical problem of perception is not discussed in these language systems. One might say that the physiological side of the problem of perception is discussed in physics. But this does not touch the philosophical side of the problem, because in physics too we rely on our perceptions. Their truth is not discussed in physics. But in spite of the fact that the truth of perception is presupposed in many language systems, its truth is challenged in others, such as philosophy.

The model of language systems says that certain primitive statements are true by convention in a certain language system, only because their truth is no longer challenged within that particular system. This does not mean that their truth was accepted arbitrarily. People may be 'forced' to accept certain primitive statements, such as 'That is a book', because they are self-evident within a certain language system. However, although primitive statements in one language system may be critically examined in another, we cannot continue this process ad infinitum. Finally we must take some primitive statements for granted, in the same way as we must accept some inference rules as valid. That we must make some fundamental choices does not mean that we make these choices arbitrarily. We may be forced to do so by deep convictions.

2.3.2 *Classification of the sciences according to their method*

We have seen that with the help of the model of language systems a fundamental unity in the various disciplines can be shown in that they all observe the principle of economy; at least they can all do so. This unity of method does not exclude a great diversity of variants. We shall now briefly address ourselves to this problem and make a classification of the different disciplines according to their various methods. The variants in method emerge according to the variety of the ways of acquiring and supplying the primitive statements and according to the variety of their ways of inference.

First, notice that there is a considerable difference between those sciences that use exclusively a deductive method, such as logic, mathematics, etc., and the other sciences and theories that always use a combination of deduction and induction. It is very important for the structure of a science to know what the nature of the elementary facts is and consequently which primitive statements express these elementary facts. In some sciences these elementary facts can be extended *ad libitum*, at least in principle, by means of experiments. This is the case in the natural sciences. Here we find the so-called methodological circle of the empirical sciences in its purest form: observation (which produces the elementary statements (facts) of the language system) – guess (i.e. to contrive hypotheses and theoretical concepts by means of inductive rules, by means of abduction or by means of a more or less brilliant flash of thought) – prediction (i.e. to predict from these hypotheses and theoretical concepts new facts using deductive rules) – check (i.e. to verify these predictions with the help of observations). Thus an optimal arrangement is obtained. There are, however, sciences, particularly human sciences such as psychology, sociology, etc., in which the objects, i.e. the people investigated, react to the investigation. Nobody starts a second test unchanged. Although therefore, in principle, there is no difference between natural sciences and human sciences, in that both use the same logical and empirical methods, the latter have their special problems, because the people investigated change during the investigation and react to it.

Second, we have the large group of historical sciences, to which also historical natural sciences, such as astronomy (partly), geology, etc. belong. Here the given facts expressed by the primitive statements must be discovered and cannot be obtained *ad libitum* by making experiments. Therefore these facts cannot be increased in accordance with our wishes. However, we can at least look for new sources of information with the help of historical and archaeological investigations.

This is no longer the case in the sciences we shall refer to presently. In these systems the rules and the criteria of other language systems are studied (epistemology, foundations of sciences); or the given facts (elementary statements) are provided by the results of other sciences. These statements can also be arranged by the method of optimal arrangement sketched above. This is done, for example, in inductive metaphysics that is not based on a particular world view. In this group of sciences too their scientific character is guaranteed by the scientific character of the given facts (statements) and the scientific method of the optimal arrangement. We have a different situation in those disciplines that still use the latter method, but do not obtain their elementary statements in a way that is free from any world view. They gather their elementary statements with the help of a particular world view and religious experience. This is the case in disciplines such as speculative philosophy, theology, etc. One may be reluctant to call these disciplines scientific, but at least they *do* use a scientific method and therefore I think they are scientific. Thus we get the following survey:

Theoretical disciplines (they all seek an optimal arrangement)

1.   Deductive disciplines (logic; mathematics);
2.   Inductive-deductive disciplines;
2.1 The given facts (elementary statements) can be increased *ad libitum* with the help of experiments (natural sciences);
2.2 The objects react to the investigation (human sciences);
2.3 The given facts (elementary statements) cannot be increased *ad libitum*, but they can be found in a direct, scientific way (historical sciences);
2.4 The given facts (elementary statements) can only be increased indirectly, because the discipline is built upon other disciplines (scientific inductive metaphysics) or studies the criteria and foundations of the other disciplines (epistemology, foundations of sciences);
2.5 The given facts (elementary statements) are obtained with the help of a world view and religious experience (speculative philosophy; theology).

Of the disciplines that interest us in this book, theology clearly belongs to the group mentioned above under 2.5, philosophy of religion belongs partly under 2.4 (our basic system I) and partly under 2.5 (the extension of the basic system with religious experience, i.e. system II). Science of religion, however, belongs partly to the group mentioned under 2.2, partly to the group mentioned under 2.3. Its elementary statements are traced by means of ordinary historical methods, such as the investigation of religious documents, ancient descriptions, etc. Modern methods of social sciences are also employed, particularly, though not exclusively, in the study of living religions. Many questions as to the appropriate method can be raised here, but there is certainly no need to refer to the world view of the investigator as a source of knowledge or a criterion of truth.

2.3.3 *Logic and experience. Science of religion and philosophy of religion*

Science of religion need not resort to logical systems stronger (and less strict) than classical logic. Hegelian dialectic on the whole easily leads to subjective applications and should be avoided as much as possible. As a partly historical discipline, science of religion cannot profit from the development of modern logic to the same degree as other sciences nowadays can (mathematics, linguistics and even metaphysics). But even in science of religion modern logic can give a more substantial contribution than it usually does. It would transcend the limits of this book to go into a more detailed discussion here. I shall only refer to the following point, which concerns not only science of religion, but every historical discipline. In many historical arguments we meet the word 'probable', and even if we do not meet it, it is indirectly presupposed. In mathematics and physics also many processes are only probable, but here we can very often give the exact probability of their truth or outcome. (The latter depends on the kind of probability, a problem into which we shall not enter here.) Because we cannot give the exact degree of probability in historical sciences we are tempted to use this notion without much critical reflexion. Modern logic, however, provides a conceptual apparatus that includes the vagueness of the probability of historical processes, while maintaining a degree of exactness which makes it a useful instrument for avoiding mistakes.

Let us give an example, avoiding all technical details. Suppose that we put forward an historical argument that is built upon a chain of arguments, each of which has a high degree of probability, and that we are not able to give the exact degree of this probability. So a theory of probability in history is needed. There are, of course, historical arguments of which the probability of their being true is so high that the probability of their negation may be neglected. But very often arguments are used the negation of which has at least some, albeit a low, degree of probability. We should realize that in such cases the conclusion usually has a degree of probability that is much less than we would intuitively expect. Let us suppose that we could agree in historical sciences to assign a degree of probability not higher than 0.9 on a scale of probability which runs from 0 to 1, to arguments that are not beyond doubt. We should realize that a chain of four such arguments gives us a probability for the conclusion of at most $0.9 \times 0.9 \times 0.9 \times 0.9 = 0.6561$, which cannot be called probable at all. If we use such arguments carelessly, we do not realize that our conclusion has become no longer probable, because to our 'feeling' the arguments themselves have a high degree of probability, so that we are tempted to suppose that our conclusion has the same degree of probability.

Further examples of the relevance of the logic or calculus of probability for historical sciences may be given: sometimes we reach a conclusion not by a chain of arguments, but by advancing arguments, each of which leads independently to the same conclusion. In this case the conclusion is much more probable than our 'feeling' would indicate. Two independent arguments with an estimated degree of probability of 0.6 yield already a conclusion of 0.84 (the probability that the conclusion is not true is $0.4 \times 0.4 = 0.16$) and four independent arguments with an estimated degree of probability of only 0.4 yield a conclusion with a degree of probability of 0.87 (0.8704) (the probability that the conclusion is not true if $0.6 \times 0.6 \times 0.6 \times 0.6 = 0.1296$). Here we have to do with a so-called cumulative argument, a way of arguing that is much in use today in philosophy of religion (Mitchell, Swinburne).

So far I have presented a rather 'scientific' approach in science of religion (and we shall do the same for philosophy of religion). Many objections could be raised here. We shall discuss the most important ones.

In the first place, the impartial, objective approach presented above is often said to be impossible in historical sciences, because in history the preferences of the investigator cannot be omitted. He might consider himself to be as impartial as possible, but he will always show his own preferences in the selection of his material, in the way he phrases the problems, etc., and in doing so he is subjective and not impartial.

Let us consider more carefully what this 'subjectivism' consists of. Of course, out of the vast number of basic elementary statements of the language system the investigator will choose those which he considers the most important for his investigation. And, naturally, his personal preferences may govern this selection. But the basic statements as such are not subjective and their truth can be checked by any other investigator. Should his selection of the basic statements be incomplete in some relevant aspects, his fellow investigators may correct him in the same way as in other sciences. If we use the scientific method as sketched above, all his theories are corrigible. It may take some time before a tempting theory is refuted, but in principle this is always possible. His potential subjective preferences may be countered by other investigators.

Another and related objection is this. Some investigators of the more hermeneutically orientated schools put forward the thesis that what is really relevant to the investigation is the personal capacity of the investigator to 're-experience' the religious feelings and conceptions expressed in the material he is studying. Contrary to this I deny the necessity for the investigator to have religious experiences himself in order to be a scientist of religion. Of course, some sympathy towards, and interest in, the object studied is fruitful for every investigation. But these psychological presuppositions of the investigation have nothing to do with the methodology of the investigation as such. Every theory (set of hypotheses) should be checked by the basic statements (facts) of our study and not by some sympathetic inner feeling or personal re-experience.

In our opinion such a method is the only way to make real progress in science of religion and to penetrate deeper into its field. And although we have pointed out above that there are differences between the natural, human and historical sciences, they all have a dominating structure in common. As H. Albert has pointed out, there is no need to base historical sciences on a reconstruction of 'inner experiences' of individuals by means of a sympathetic method of understanding (*verstehende Methode*). The latter is, as a specific historical method, very often opposed to the method of looking for general laws in natural sciences (Droysen). Today this opposition is considered obsolete by most methodologists.

I agree, however, with those methodologists who put forward the relative importance of the hermeneutical method with respect to the *inventing* of new hypotheses. The same is true for speculative metaphysics (Albert, Stegmüller et al.) They may inspire investigators to view old problems in a new way. The same goes for incorrect theories. There are fruitful mistakes in science! For example, Marx's and Freud's theories are incorrect as complete systems, but they have functioned as eye openers to powers in human life that had not previously been discovered.

Furthermore, I admit that the great scientific discoveries do not always follow from pure scientific presuppositions, as Kuhn has pointed out. These discoveries require imagination and intuition from the side of the investigator. But this is a matter of inventing hypotheses and not a matter of constructing scientific systems as such. Moreover, Kuhn rightly points out that the conceptual scheme of science reflects the spiritual climate of its time, at least to a certain extent. It is very important to realize that a change in a conceptual scheme produces a different theory. All this, however, can be accounted for in our approach. Changes in conceptual schemes primarily produce different basic statements (basic facts). And thus one gets different theories. However, if different theories proceed from different basic statements, we are not concerned with competing theories, but with theories that are complementary to each other. We may compare such a situation with the two theories of light in physics, where the wave theory and the corpuscular theory are not, strictly speaking, competing theories. The basic facts explained by them differ according to the various experiments. In the same way fruitful conceptual schemes are complementary to each other. Theories based on such schemes are always open to public or intersubjective testing, a possibility that is ruled out, if one resorts to one's 'inner experiences'.

Another objection against out methodological position may be raised on the grounds that the axiomatic and deductive part of our theory of language systems is dominant. But as Bunge has pointed out: '...axiomatics is scientifically valuable because it renders explicit all the assumptions actually employed and so makes it possible to keep them under control'. Moreover, modern logical insight has definitely shown that all inductive procedures are based upon deductive ones. Our methodological position has the advantage of incorporating the merits of the logical positivist methodologies without taking over their positivist metaphysics, and in addition to this it can incorporate the merits of hermeneutics and traditional metaphysics in their proper place, i.e., after we have laid down the base of our philosophy of religion with the help of a stricter system.

The following conclusion may be drawn from our methodological considerations. In science and philosophy of religion we should be as strict as possible. Therefore we should restrict ourselves to classical logic and 'ordinary experience' as long as possible. Only after we have laid down our basic theories in a strict system, we may continue in a less strict system. In our strict system it is possible to prove God's existence, or rather, we can prove in such a system the existence of an *ens necessarium* with the help of the modal logical system S_5, which is the classical variant in the series of modal systems, S_4 being more or less the modal equivalent of the intuitionistic system. (It is customary in modal logic to indicate the strictness of the modal systems by an index number placed below the letter S. The stricter the system, the lower the index number.) Here S_5 is a formalization of the 'classical' system in use since the time of Theophrastus. The proof of the existence of an *ens necessarium* can be given in the system S_5 and in the system S_4 only with some additional premises. The usual interpretation of 'necessary' in this connection is 'what occurs in all conceivably possible worlds', or 'what is true in all conceivably possible worlds'. This *ens necessarium* can be given some content. It can be proved to be good in the sense that it is the ground of all being and increases the 'amount of being'. It has an ego-structure in that it is self-reflexive, etc. We shall discuss all these issues later on. We admit that the proof of a Christian God or the truth of some theses of the Christian faith cannot given in such a strict system.

If one wants to go further and give a more developed philosophy of religion, various ways present themselves. The investigator can make the logical part of his system stronger (less strict) and apply the dialectic of infinity or even Hegelian dialectic. As the latter includes the dialectic of infinity and adds some rules of inference to it, it is stronger (less strict) than the dialectic of infinity. In my view, however, taking recourse to mystical and religious experience is more fruitful than employing doubtful logical systems, because if the existence of God is proved it is plausible that we may experience him, but from his existence it does not follow that doubtful logical systems are valid.

Still it cannot be denied that certain choices are made here, but the reader may see the relevance of indicating exactly what kind of system of philosophy of religion some investigator is using. Very often the presupposed logic and experience are not clearly indicated. Moreover, opponents are often measured by a much stricter standard than the one applied to one's own system! An example of such a fallacy may be found in the work of W. Pannenberg. He criticizes the proofs of God's existence in the traditional way, using classical logic. In his own exposé, however, he uses a kind of Hegelian logic, in which all the allegedly refuted arguments for God's existence are valid again! It should be clear that such a procedure is not acceptable. Philosophers of religion should avoid it and indicate clearly what kind of system they are using. Then at least many misunderstandings would disappear and matters would be discussed in a more scientific way.

In my view a reference to religious experience is fundamental for the construction of an adequate philosophy of religion. Religious experience, more than rational thinking, appeals to the human mind and fills man with joy and confidence in God. Unfortunately, however, religious experience cannot be the only and conclusive ground for our belief. From an epistemological point of view many objections can be raised against truth claims based on religious experience. Therefore, we shall build our philosophy of religion on a stricter, rational (logical) system and after having done so, we shall return to religious experience as a source of religious knowledge.

2.4 *Religious and mystical experience*

2.4.1 *Schleiermacher*

Before we systematically investigate the founding of belief upon religious experience we must first listen to a great classic who defended religious experience as the foundation of religion, viz. Friedrich Schleiermacher. In his view rational thinking is insufficient as a foundation for religion. Schleiermacher separated religion and philosophy: religion should have its own province in the human mind and should not depend on a rational foundation. Neither the intellect not the moral will can lead the human mind to religious belief. His definition of religion in his book *Über die Religion. Reden an die Gebildeten unter ihren Verächtern* (1799) (On Religion. Discourses addressed to the Educated among its Despisers) is famous: 'The essence of religion is neither thinking, nor moral activity, but intuition and sentiment'. This fundamental attitude occurs again in his later work *Glaubenslehre* (the Doctrine of Faith).

According to Schleiermacher devotion is the basis of all ecclesiastical communities, and this consists neither in knowing something, nor in doing something. It is an ascertainment of sentiment or of immediate self-consciousness. In his later work Schleiermacher is less radical, because now also knowledge and doing belong to the sphere of religion, although they do not constitute its essence. The devotional mind only formulates its thoughts in a kind of knowledge and performs certain moral acts. But the real devotional states of mind, such as confidence, repentance, joy in God, etc., are devotional without reference to a certain kind of knowledge or doing. In his later work Schleiermacher sees the essence of religion in the feeling of absolute dependence. In this feeling of absolute dependence we are conscious of our relation to God.

There have been many interpretations of Schleiermacher's view, of which we shall discuss the two most important ones. According to one interpretation, only the devotional states of mind are important for religion, and their truth is of no concern. According to the other interpretation, religion includes something like an intuitive certainty, so that its truth is certainly important, but this truth is never reached with the help of thinking or rational argument. Many arguments can be brought forward in favour of both interpretations. It is also possible to advance the opinion that the first interpretation is applicable to the Schleiermacher of the *Reden* and the second to the Schleiermacher of the *Glaubenslehre*. But the fact that there is nowhere a plain breach in Schleiermacher's thinking can be brought forward against such a view.

The best way to approach Schleiermacher's thinking is, I think, to state that Schleiermacher cares most for the *value* of devotional life, the quality it has, and that the question of truth is of secondary importance to him. In contrast to the dogmatics before his time Schleiermacher did not base his theology on natural theology. He did not try to prove the existence of God or the truth of the Christian faith. On the other hand he evaluated the other religions positively, without giving up his own Christian belief. If the devotional sentiments are most important for him, it may have been obvious to him also that sentiments founded on deep intuitions are at the same time true. 'We omit completely any proof of the truth or the necessity of the Christian faith, and presuppose on the other hand that every Christian does have certainty in himself before he enters into investigations of this kind' (investigations into the doctrine of the Christian faith). This truth of religion, however, is not present in Christianity alone. Schleiermacher feels himself deeply connected with all human beings and with their various religions too. Later scientists of religion, such as Van der Leeuw, followed Schleiermacher in this respect, that they not only describe and explain other religions, but also seek for the content of truth in them. Schleiermacher can be considered as the founding father of the so-called hermeneutic (phenomenological) method of which I shall now give a brief summary.

It is Schleiermacher's main concern to understand the *essence* of a certain religion and not only its accidental phenomena. If we only look for the various elements in religions in a purely quantitative and inductive way, we shall never find the real essence of a religion. Trying to reach it by means of abstract methods, one only finds isolated elements, never the essence of a specific religion. According to Schleiermacher no religion has come to its complete development. It is the task of the investigator to enter into the spirit of a religion and fill in the gaps with sympathetic understanding. Creative imagination and empathy are required to understand religion. Many people mistakenly think that what is common to the adherents of a certain religion constitutes its essence. 'They thought that as so many people belong to the same religion, they should have the same religious ideas and feelings, the same opinions and beliefs, and that precisely these ideas, feelings, etc. should be the essence of their religion'. But according to Schleiermacher all these opinions and ideas constitute only the elements of religion, not its essence. We should not deduce the 'spirit of a religion' (= approximately a synonym of 'essence of a religion') from what is common to its adherents. The reason for this is that there is no fully developed religion: '...you should remember that no religion has been realized completely and that you will not know this religion before... you can make additions to it and determine how this or that phenomenon would have become if the mental horizon of that religion had been large enough'. The investigator of a certain religion should enter into the thoughts and ideas of that religion in order to grasp its essence. Creative imagination and empathy are needed: '...in spiritual matters you cannot reach the original truth in any other way than by an original creative act in yourselves'.

Now all this looks pretty bad in the eyes of any modern empirical philosopher and scientist. If the investigator can only reach the essence of a certain religion by an internal creative act, then there is no objective way to find this essence. Men differ very much among themselves in imagination and creative power. If Schleiermacher were right, then there would be no possibility of studying religion in a scientific way. Every investigator may create a different essence of each religion, and there is no authority to decide who is right.

Already Schleiermacher's essentialistic approach in asking for the essence of religion and for the essence of each religion may seem suspect in the eyes of modern investigators. But in my view it is certainly possible to look for a proper definition of religion in general and for each religion separately. And that is another way of saying that we are looking for the essence of (a particular) religion. Very vaguely formulated, an adequate method of finding such a definition could be summarized by the following steps:

(i)   Indicate what phenomena are to be classified as religious and what not.

(ii)   Look for the characteristics of both the religious and the non-religious phenomena.

(iii)   Find out whether these religious phenomena have some characteristics in common $(a_1......a_n)$ that do not occur in the non-religious phenomena.

(iv)   If some characteristics $(a_1......a_j)$ imply the other characteristics $(a_k......a_n)$ define religion with the help of these 'basic' characteristics $(a_1......a_n)$.

It has turned out that it is very difficult to define religion adequately, but we shall not enter into the details of this discussion here. Probably some disjunctive definition $((a_1......a_d)$ v $(a_c......a_i)$ v $......)$ would be the best one. The difficulty is that such an obvious characteristic as, for example, 'the belief in gods (superhuman beings)' is not sufficient, because not all religions include this belief. On the other hand a belief in some transcendent superhuman reality is indeed characteristic of all religions, but also of many metaphysical systems! So this would be too broad a definition. Therefore, some disjunctive definition will probably be necessary.

A particular religion can be characterized by means of the same method. First, we draw attention to the religious phenomena of that religion, i.e. the common beliefs and practices, which are just those things that Schleiermacher rejects! Many modern students of religion see a particular religion as a particular system of beliefs, values and actions. Then we look for the characteristics that distinguish this religion from other religions and thereupon we try to find the 'basic' ones. Whatever the merits of such a method may be, at least it is clear that some empirical method must be applied in the study of religions. From a modern scientific point of view Schleiermacher's method is dated.

Let us, however, not abandon the problem just like that. It is always worthwhile to enter into a discussion with classic authors, and therefore I suggest to proceed by asking: 'Under what conditions would Schleiermacher's method be correct'? As Schleiermacher's method serves to find the essence of (a certain) religion, we should ask: 'What ought to be characteristic for an essence of a religion so that Schleiermacher is right?' Or in other words: 'What should be the relation between the essence of a religion and its non-essential elements?' I think that Schleiermacher's non-empirical method would be correct, if the essence of religion consists of its real, in contradistinction to its apparent phenomena and/or if it consists of its original, in contradistinction to its later and decadent phenomena and/or if it consists of its normative, in contradistinction to its deduced phenomena.

If the essence of religion were something like this, Schleiermacher's method would be correct. For then the empirical method mentioned above would probably lead us astray. The phenomena we discover might then be the seeming instead of the real ones; they might not correspond to the norm that is valid in the religion in question. We might discover decadent features instead of the inspiring original ones. Our task would clearly be to construct a beautiful whole out of the scattered data. In this connection it is not important whether our constructed whole corresponds in a one-one relation to all the features of the religion in question, but it should represent a beautiful instantiation of that religion, and inspire some of its adherents and those who study it. The criterion for deciding which construction is correct, is not of an empirical, but of an aesthetic nature (possibly also of an ethical (moral) nature, but Schleiermacher himself would not agree with this, because, according to him, religion and ethics are two different things). The construction that conforms to the requirements of certain aesthetic (and perhaps ethical) standards would then be the best.

Because science of religion is concerned with actual religions and not with their ideal types, I do not think that there is much use for Schleiermacher's method in this field. But things are different in philosophy of religion. For in this field ethical and aesthetic questions and criteria play a role and here Schleiermacher may still be a competent and inspiring guide. Within philosophy of religion the truth claims of various religions and philosophical world views are discussed. But then it is not interesting when the discussion is carried out by representatives who defend their religion rather weakly. It is, on the contrary, most interesting if the discussion is carried out by ideal representatives who advance the strongest arguments for their truth claims.

2.4.2 *Epistemological status of religious and mystical experience*

In this section we shall discuss the possibility of a verification of religious statements by refering to religious experience. For the validity of this appeal to religious experience some solid reasons may be brought forward. I propose to call this bringing forward of good reasons to support the validity of religious experience a *justification* of religious experience. In this way *verification* refers to a proof *within* a certain logical-empirical system and *justification* is the proof of the *validity* of a certain logical-empirical system. In this sense I shall try to justify the appeal to religious experience. If the reasons are convincing, the verification of the religious statements themselves takes place within a system in which such an appeal to religious experience is permitted. But we must first try to prove the validity of this appeal in a stricter system.

Nobody will be astonished to hear that it is difficult to allow for religious experience in epistemology. Ordinary experience is acknowledged by everyone. If I say that there is an ashtray infront of me, nobody will deny that seriously, if there is indeed an ashtray in front of me. But if I claim that

I experience God in the beauty of nature, not everybody will agree with me. Religious experience, by contrast to ordinary experience, is not acknowledged by everybody. The same is also true for aesthetic experience. Moral experience is a different matter, although here too sometimes people deny its validity. But it is not the place here to discuss this problem. Many defenders of religious experience have referred to the fact that it often happens that a certain experience is not seen or heard by everyone, and that nevertheless nobody doubts its validity. A blind man, for example, cannot see colours, but nobody doubts that there are colours, not even the blind man himself. We said above that not everyone is susceptible to aesthetic experience. A person without a taste for music cannot experience the beauty of a Beethoven symphony, but one cannot seriously deny that Beethoven's symphonies have musical qualities. In this way it has been maintained that the experience of God in nature, in one's inner feelings, etc., is valid, although there are irreligious people.

This position, however, has been effectively attacked by several scholars, notably by C.B. Martin. He acknowledges that there are persons who have religious experiences. This fact is conceded by almost everyone who opposes the validity of religious experience. But from the fact that a certain person has – or that certain persons have – religious experiences, it does not follow that God exists or that there is a superhuman world. These persons can only claim that they have religious experiences and that these experiences may fill them with joy, confidence, etc., but that is all. There is no room for any more far reaching conclusion. The analogy with the blind man (or the deaf man, etc.) is not valid, because the blind man has many means of ascertaining knowledge about colours. Though his knowledge may be incomplete, he can acquire true and indubitable knowledge about colours. Analogous possibilities are always open to us, in the same way as a deaf man can ascertain whether there are sounds in the room, etc. But in the case of God such a possibility is not available. Here such a method of proving the truth or falsity of certain statements is missing. Martin acknowledges, however, that in the case of aesthetic experiences we have difficulties analogous with religious experiences, and he does not deny out of hand that aesthetic experiences are invalid. According to Martin this fact does not support the truth claims of religious experiences, because no truth claims are made by appeal to aesthetic experiences.

As could be expected, Martin's view has been opposed by various authors. Ferré retorted that Martin's concept of experience was too narrow and that he should have included experiences that transcend ordinary experience; but this is, of course, begging the question. J. Hick concedes that there are difficulties in the concept of religious experience, but according to him there are also difficulties in the concept of ordinary experience. It is something determined by culture. If I say that there is an ashtray in front of me, this is by no means obvious to a Papuan from Irian Jaya or to a man from the Stone Age. Ordinary experience is not simply pure sensation. It is also, and even predominantly so, the interpretation of the data of sensation. The same is true, according to Hick, for religion. Religious faith is an 'experience-as'. We experience something as a symbol of God, his love, etc. Two persons can see the same thing and one of them may interpret it as God's revelation, whereas the other does not see anything of the kind. In the same way G.I. Mavrodes points out that, if ordinary experience had to fulfil the same requirements as religious experience, i.e. that the possibility of errors should be excluded, the result would be an infinite regress. For example, if one wants to verify that there is an ashtray in front of me, one must do so with the help of photographs, but what they show may also be doubted, etc.

Let us look into this discussion more closely. It is correct to say that religious experience is an experience-as, and that this also applies to ordinary experience. But the difference remains that ordinary experience is acknowledged by everyone and religious experience is not. A Papuan can learn to identify a certain object as an ashtray, but whether or not he will interpret certain experiences as religious experiences remains dubious.

To be sure, there is a difference here between religious and mystical experience. In mysticism there are ways and techniques of contemplation that are taught and can be learned, at least to a certain degree. Therefore I should like to use this as a decisive criterion to distinguish between mystical and religious experience. Of course, one can use the concept 'religious experience' in a broad sense so that it includes also mystical experience. But it is better to dintinguish between mystical and non-mystical religious experience or between mystical experience and religious experience in a narrower sense. Mystical experience, then, is that kind of experience in which, with the help of a series of techniques of contemplation such as prayer, yoga, dance, inner observation, etc., one reaches higher stages of consciousness in which the world, life, one's own ego and finally God are experienced more deeply. At last the *unio mystica* is attained, i.e. an intense union with God, which may take various forms. In Buddhism, where in most variants God has disappeared, an analogous state can be attained, called Nirvana. This way to the *unio mystica* turns out to have a conspicuous similarity in many different religions and cultures. The state of *unio mystica* is described in a similar way in the different religions too.

This does not mean that all forms of the *unio mystica* are the same, the contrary. But we may find the various types of the *unio mystica* in all religions and in all cultures. If we are allowed to use a rough and rather sketchy distinction we may say that there is first the *unio mystica* that consists in an intimate union with a personal God. One finds this type mainly in Christianity, Judaism and Islam, but also in Hinduism, Buddhism, the religions of South-East Asia, etc. A second type, in which the soul submerges into an impersonal God, can be found mainly in Hinduism, but it is not unknown in other religions. Finally, a third type can be found, mainly in Buddhism. Here the soul dissolves into a great void. This void is difficult to describe, because it is mostly indicated as a 'filled void' of which nothing more can be said. The various Buddhist schools differ among each other in their concept of the Nirvana. But the void is also a concept in other forms of mysticism.

Non-mystical, 'ordinary', religious experience is, according to many scholars (including Van Baaren and his school), ordinary experience (maybe combined with moral, aesthetic, but at any rate non-religious experience), which is put into a religious context, i.e. into a religious conceptual framework. In this view religious experience is a passing through certain events and feelings, which are interpreted religiously. In a 'formula':

Religious experience = ordinary experience + a religious conceptual framework.

This is shown linguistically by the use of certain religious concepts and certain syntactical particularities (see also 2.9). On the whole I think Van Baaren and his school are right, but this must not be taken to mean that religion can be reduced to ordinary experience. The use of a religious framework can be unavoidable for the believer. We have seen above that every experience can be viewed as an experience-as. Conceptual frameworks are always necessary. It is not a matter of pure arbitrariness whether one interprets certain events and feelings religiously or not. Certain events and feelings have such an overwhelming power that one cannot help interpreting them religiously. Very often believers seem to believe *contre coeur*. Thus, although such experiences are only convincing to those who have them and not to those who do not, their occurrence is evident.

There are two problems here. The information we acquire from the religious experience cannot be confirmed outside this experience (with the exception perhaps of aesthetic experience which we shall discuss later on). In other words, religious experience confirms itself and in science this is very suspect. Hypotheses which confirm themselves are not accepted. But let us not forget that the same is true for ordinary experience as we saw above. This cannot be confirmed outside itself either, and we still have to accept this kind of experience as the basis of our scientific work. Nevertheless the problem of the non-universalisability of religious experience remains: in contradistinction to ordinary experience, religious experience is not universally accepted.

The second problem is that the information given by religious experience is not everywhere exactly the same. Even if it is conceded that religious experience leads to genuine knowledge, how can we explain the existence of so many religious views and opinions? And this is true both for the actual information about facts (God's existence, his properties, etc.) and for the way of salvation, the religious value-system, the prescribed worship and morals.

First we shall make some remarks on the non-universality of religious experience. Robert Oakes has defended religious experience with respect to this objection in the following interesting way. He maintains that metaphysical questions have a logical priority over epistemological ones. Indeed, if this were the case, then the objections from the side of Martin and others would not be relevant. For God is a being *sui generis*, a being of a unique kind, and therefore it is no surprise that such a unique being is only accessible through unique and non-universal experiences. This conclusion would be valid if the metaphysical starting-point had an *absolute* logical priority over the epistemological questions. But this is not so. Of course, as we have seen, one may very well start one's philosophical expositions with metaphysical questions, but this does not mean that they have an absolute priority. We have seen that all philosophical problems lie on a circle. If we have proved God's existence independently from religious experience, Oakes' arguments become more convincing. For if God exists, it is evident that religious experience must have a unique character so that in that case the epistemological objections have lost their power.

One of the disadvantages of religious experience from an epistemological point of view is that it cannot be evoked at will. This is not only true for non-believers, but also for believers. We can say, we will carry out this or that physical or chemical experiment at 1 p.m., but we cannot say we will have our religious experience at 10 a.m. sharp. The same goes for aesthetic experience. The French composer Satie wrote ironically that he passes his day in the following way: '...from 9.08 until 9.16 a.m. inspiration, from 9.17-9.21 a cup of coffee, etc.' I wish this were possible! Then many problems in aesthetics and philosophy of religion would be solved! All this does not mean, however, that religious experience is never confirmed. If certain religious experiences are never confirmed they 'dry out' and religion is given up. We find many complaints in religious literature about God who does not reappear, who seems to have left the faithful, etc. But then, suddenly, the believer gets new hope and confidence and re-experiences God's presence.

Mystical experience, again, has a special position, because to a certain degree it *can* be evoked, at least at the lower stages of the mystical way. The attaining of the *unio mystica* can only be reached by grace according to the majority of mystics. Even logical positivists have treated mystical experiences with more respect than ordinary religious experiences, because one could not deny that they at least partly comply with the standards of scientific research. They can be evoked to a certain degree and they show a greater similarity among themselves than ordinary religious experiences.

K. Nielsen, however, a more or less logical-positivist thinker, distinguishes between what is experienced in mystical experience and its interpretation. The latter is determined by culture and tradition, but it is only here that the transcendent divine world appears. The mystical experience as such, i.e. without its interpretation, can be explained completely in a natural way with the help of Freudian psychology or in other ways.

I agree with Nielsen that we must distinguish between mental sensations as such and their interpretation. Although there are nowhere pure physical or mental sensations, there are stages of interpretation. What may be called basic material at one stage is already interpretation in another stage. Identifying a tree involves interpretation with respect to the basic material of the sensations of form and colours. But the tree on its part is basic material in an aesthetic contemplation, etc. It is right that there is a distinction between *interpretandum* and *interpretatio*. But Nielsen is wrong if the thinks that mystical experience can be reduced to mere natural phenomena with the help of psychoanalysis. As we shall see, everything can be 'explained' with the help of psychoanalysis, even atheism. Truth claims can never be solved in a purely psychological way. Another major objection against this naturalistic reduction of mystical (and religious) experiences is that they very often occur against the wishes and volitions of the believers. Even mystics may have their experiences against their will. (Mostly, however, mystics *seek* their mystical experiences.) As an example I may mention Simone Weil.

All this does not yet amount to a convincing justification of mystical experience; for with this type of experience also, it is true that it is only convincing to those who *have* passed through it and not to those who *have not* yet had this experience. But here too the proofs of God's existence, given independently of mystical experience, may enhance its trustworthiness. What is more, one can refute Nielsen's assertion that the mystical interpretation is completely determined by the cultural and religious tradition of the mystic believer. This is certainly true with regard to the images, the metaphors, etc. that he uses, but it is not true with regard to the fundamental structure of his mystical experience. Whether he experiences God in a personal or in an impersonal way, for example, is independent from this, because both forms of mysticism occur in all religions.

The second problem is the multiplicity of religions. For this Hick has put forward the following interesting solution. He asserts that everybody is entitled to trust his own experiences. Without this confidence we could not attain very much either in daily life or in scientific research. Now in our religious experiences we may be informed about states of affairs, which later turn out to be false, for example, via scientific results. Of course, we are not supposed to stick to such false convictions. Not only in religious experiences, but in our everyday experiences and in our scientific researches errors are possible. We have to correct them. In this way many differences in religion would disappear: all kinds of superstition, astrological knowledge, reports about flying saucers, etc. So only the great fundamental differences between the world-religions would remain. Instead of trying to defend the absoluteness of Christianity in one way or the other, Hick asserts that all religions have a correct, but only partially valid, view of God. Relatively they are all true. We must give up all feeling of Western superiority.

Hick's position is without doubt very attractive, but still not completely satisfactory. The adherents of the various religions may certainly learn from each other; for example, a Christian would not have any difficulty in learning certain meditation techniques from Hinduism or Buddhism. The case is different, however, with respect to the concept of God and the various ways of salvation. If in one religion God is considered to be personal, i.e. as having an ego-structure, and in another religion he is considered to be impersonal, i.e. as having a neutrum-structure, the two views contradict each other. Of course, it is possible to construct the concept of God in such a way that it has both an impersonal and a personal aspect, but in this case one of the two aspects will be dominant and include the other, so that finally a choice is unavoidable. Hick himself is prepared to make such a choice and he chooses plainly in favour of a personal concept of God. This seems to bring him back into the Christian tradition, but he is right in saying that such a personal concept of God is also present in other religions, even in Hinduism and Buddhism.

As we said above, one may to try to transcend the contradiction between a personal and an impersonal conception of God, as for example, Tillich, Albert Schweitzer, P. Smits (Leiden) have tried to do. Interesting is the image used by Smits: God's personality is like the warm Gulf Stream in the cold ocean. In Hinduism Ramakrishna propounded the view that in mystical experience God is sometimes present in a personal, sometimes in an impersonal way. But in the philosophy of religion we cannot leave matters at that: either the personal aspects are the foundation of the impersonal ones or it is the other way round. But from the start it should be clear that God is not personal in the way of human beings, neither is he impersonal in the way of stones, pieces of wood, etc. The question is whether we must construct an ego-structure or a neutrum-structure as an *analogon* to God. Or in modern terms, whether God's consciousness is homomorphical to an egostructure or to a neutrum-structure.

Perhaps a point of still greater difficulty is the question of the different ways of salvation. In the Christian faith the suffering of Jesus Christ is positively evaluated. That suffering has its positive aspects, is something that is not exclusively taught in Christianity. Also in Aeschylus' play 'Agamemnon' the idea occurs that one can learn through suffering. But it is especially in the Jewish and the Christian faiths that it is taught that through suffering man is able to experience the world and God in another and more intensive way than in daily life, provided that he interprets this suffering in the right way. We must learn to see the world and ourselves in the light of eternity, *sub specie aeternitatis*. It is by suffering that man is thrown back on the essential things in his life.

Jaspers's border situations (*Grenzsituationen*), i.e. death, sickness, etc., lead to the acknowledgement of a transcendent world. This suggests a Christian inheritance in his humanistic philosophy. He who has lived through times of war will remember that such things as friendship, love, the beauty of nature, the readiness to help others, were experienced much more intensely than in times of peace, in which we very often do not notice the most important things in life, because we are too much occupied with the hustle and bustle of everyday life, our meetings, diaries, consultations, etc. In times of war people live differently: what is missed with respect to the quantity of life, is gained in quality and intensity.

In Hinduism, however, suffering is interpreted as mere appearance. Its way of salvation exists simply in negating suffering and not, as in the Christian faith, in overcoming suffering through suffering, i.e. by following Jesus Christ in his way of the cross (and resurrection). In Hinduism many techniques have been developed in order to lessen suffering so that it is experienced less intensely (at the price of experiencing life less intensely too). Between these two ways of salvation we have to choose, however difficult it may be. One cannot say that the two ways are equally good and that we must practise both. Hick does not do so either. He obviously chooses for the fundamental truths of Christianity.

From what has been said above it may be obvious that on the stength of religious experience alone one cannot decide on its validity, i.e. whether it is a trustworthy source of truth or not. A rational, logical investigation remains necessary.

Another attempt has been made to establish the legitimacy of an appeal to religious experience. Attention has been drawn to the parallelism between religious and aesthetic experience. Like religious experience, aesthetic experience has its epistemological difficulties, but nobody will deny that aesthetics plays an important role in cultural life. Investigations into the various relations of aesthetics and religion have not yet been developed extensively (in contrast to the many studies on the relation of religion and morals!). Here we shall only speak briefly about the subject, and deal more extensively with the relation between religion and aesthetics later in this book. This, however, may be clear: ethics may be a difficult discipline, aesthetics is even more difficult so that one can hardly expect that scholars would easily be in agreement on such a subject as the relation between religion and aesthetics.

C.B. Martin mentions the analogy between aesthetics and religion, but he does not develop it further . K. Nielsen does the same, but he argues that aesthetic experience does not lead to knowledge of facts and from this he infers that religious experience does not lead to knowledge of facts either. Religious and aesthetic experience are both non-cognitive.

A writer on aesthetics like A. Hofstadter refers to the parallelism to prove just the opposite, *viz.* that aesthetic experience is cognitive just like religious experience. Thus, the analogy between aesthetic and religious experience is asserted by two groups of scholars and denied by two groups. It is defended by those who maintain that both kinds of experience are subjective and non-cognitive. It is also defended by those who hold that they are both cognitive and to a certain degree objective. The analogy is denied by those who assert that only one of the two is cognitive and objective.

I myself am prepared to contend that they are both cognitive to a certain degree. They are, of course, not cognitive in the way of science. Most states of affairs and facts in the world should be ascertained by the way of science. But the various sciences look for particular facts. If it comes to knowledge of matters that concern our world view, to the question as to whether God exists or what the meaning of life is, science alone is not competent. I am prepared to contend that suffering can be overcome by suffering, that we are being attended by a transcendent power, that man attains his happiness only through monogamy and not by sexual licentiousness, etc. But these assertions can never be justified by purely scientific investigations. In order to do so I have to appeal to religious, aesthetic and moral experience, and so must anyone who wants to make decisions in such problems.

Experiences such as these are evident enough to me, but to my regret I notice that many competent and respectable people do not agree. I see an analogy between this and the choice between classical and constructive (intuitionistic) logic. Classical logic is evident enough to me, but I must take note that many scholars do not agree. The views gained by means of aesthetic, religious and moral experience are very often forced upon me against my own wishes and needs, so that the assertion that they are a product of wishful thinking and dreams is not acceptable. However, an appeal to religious experiences is only convincing for those who have had such experiences themselves. Others are entitled to put them aside and doubt their legitimacy. As these experiences have the power to intensify one's life, so that they are strongly convincing, we have the strange situation that they are unconvincing to some and most convincing to others.

2.4.3 *Religion as experience means that religion is a projection*

Justifying of religion only with the help of religious experience without a rational justification as we shall give in the next chapter, runs the risk that one's religion will be interpreted as a projection. The answer to Schleiermacher's position was the rise of projection theories such as those of Feuerbach, Freud, Marx and Nietzsche. Religion is viewed here as a kind of projection. Man is frustrated in his possibilities. He is overwhelmed by powers greater than himself and sees no possibility of overcoming them. He refuses, however, to face his defeat and therefore he imagines a superhuman power that is able to overcome these hostile powers. Nothing is more frustrating than doing nothing in the face of great dangers. But now something can be done. One can pray to gods, try to propitiate them, etc.

The frustration that leads to this projection is different in the works of various authors. Feuerbach thinks that man is frustrated in his struggle with nature. Nature is always stronger than man and therefore he imagines gods for himself. But it might also be economic circumstances (Marx) or sexual frustrations (Freud) which cause man to make projections. In all cases man imagines a God or a kingdom of heaven to get compensation for his being thwarted in his self-realisation.

One should not evaluate these projections only negatively. They might be necessary for some people in order to avoid getting drowned in the sea of life. Sometimes it is asserted that not all religious convictions are a product of projection but only some of them. In this way Karl Barth considered all religions, including Christianity, as projections in so far as they are the product of man. Contrary to these projections, God's revelation in Christ is really trustworthy and true, but this cannot be proved in any way outside revelation. Tillich is of the opinion that orthodox Christianity is a product of frustration and anxiety. An open-minded form of Christianity, on the other hand, is not a projection.

These projection theories are always ambiguous. Of course, one can easily 'prove' that the belief in God is a product of imagination caused by frustration and wishful thinking, but the same thing can be done with atheism. For the science of religion such theories could be interesting, because they bring more insight in the imageries of the various religions. But for philosophy of religion they are less interesting, because they cannot contribute to the study of the question whether the truth claims of certain religious statements are legitimate or not. Of course, one can try to prove that a conception of God is nothing but a product of infantile wishful thinking: 'the young man feels himself not at home in this hostile world; he longs for the security and shelter of his parents' home, which, however, has disappeared for ever. What is more comforting in such a situation than imagining a heavenly home as a compensation? What is more simple than to imagine a mental mechanism that produces images such as a father in heaven, now that the earthly father is no longer accessible?

Of course, nothing is more simple, but such a theory can also work in the other direction. As is well known, man dislikes authorities above him. So the idea of a God above is for most people unbearable. What is more simple than to imagine God out of heaven and out of one's existence? With such arguments nothing can be proved, because everything can be 'proved'. If we want to discuss the truth or falsity of religious statements – and we shall see that many arguments can be brought forward for both positions – references to mental mechanisms and psychoanalysis settle nothing. Particularly with the help of modern logic one can demonstrate that theories of projection, which try to reduce religion to something else, are insufficient and do not prove anything. I shall develop this point further in appendix 5.

2.5 *The rational way*

2.5.1 *The two ways*

We have seen that the appeal to religious experience is epistemologically insufficient to serve as a foundation for a philosophy of religion. With its help one cannot attain good reasons for the belief in God, although it can be convincing for certain persons, because on the mental level it works strongly enough. There is, however, also a rational way which finds its centre in the proofs of God's existence. These proofs underwent a remarkable renaissance lately. This is caused mainly by the rise of modern logic, especially modern modal logic, though other logical and mathematical tools have deepened our insight as well; they made it clear that the so-called refutations of the proofs of God's existence were extremely superficial. This does not mean that the existence of God now has been definitely proved. No proof can be established definitely, for all proofs are carried out within a certain logical-empirical system, and one can always take refuge in a stricter system. It can be shown, however, that the proofs of God's existence can be carried out in a stricter system than previously supposed. In the past it was thought that a proof of God's existence presupposed a dialectical logic, usually at least that of the dialectics of infinity. Nowadays it can be shown that the proof is already valid in a system with classical logic and ordinary experience. And such a system is scientifically highly respectable. The theory of the proofs of God's existence is rather complicated and therefore we shall treat them in a separate chapter.

The proofs of God's existence, however, are insufficient to construct a satisfactory doctrine of God. If we have proved God's existence, an appeal to religious experience is certainly legitimate. For we have seen that if God, a unique being, exists, we should not be astonished that he can be known only through a unique kind of experience, i.e. religious experience. Thus, the epistemological objections against religious experience become less convincing. In a cumulative argumentation (2.3.3) we can construct a philosophical doctrine of God with the help of rational arguments and arguments from experience. Before doing so we first have to consider the views of some great classics who have tried to lay a rational foundation for the belief in God, and also to consider some other attempts to find a basis for the belief in God.

Anselm tried to find a more or less rational foundation for the Christian faith. In this respect he may be considered the 'father of scholasticism'. In his view belief and philosophy coincide, and philosophy has an apologetic function with respect to faith. If we say that faith (belief) and philosophy coincide, this does not mean that for Anselm the two are one and the same thing. It means only, that everything the believer knows through revelation can be proved subsequently with the help of reason. A fundamental dictum in this philosophy is: 'Credo ut intelligam' (I believe so that I may (philosophically) understand). In many respects Anselm follows Augustine and thus he stands in a Platonic-Christian tradition. Among other things this means that Anselm did not accept the idea of an autonomous reason such as was taught later in the Aristotelian tradition by Thomas Aquinas and others. For its activities reason is dependent on a preceding belief. First God must enlighten reason with his grace, otherwise it goes astray. And this is not only true in the case of the supernatural truths, for in this respect the Aristotelians would agree with Anselm. No, this also applies to the natural truths of which the Aristotelians teach that reason can find them without receiving the preceding help of God's grace. Hence, Anselm's dictum that I must believe first in order to understand philosophically. But if I believe, after have received God's grace, my reason is able to understand philosophically the whole of the Christian doctrine, i.e. reason can prove all the dogmas of the Church.

How should we interpret this famous dictum *Credo ut intelligam*? What does *intelligam (intelligere)* mean here? Many interpreters, among whom the great Swiss theologian Karl Barth, interpret 'understanding' here as completely dependent on faith. It says nothing more than what has previously been said by faith. *Intelligere* is the more precise expression of *credere*. In Anselm's view there is no difference between faith and reason, between theology and philosophy. And that means that Anselm is primarily a theologian and that philosophy has nothing to contribute to his system. Now it cannot be denied that our dictum strongly points in the direction of this interpretation. But if we consider Anselm's view more closely, we see that he carefully distinguishes between faith and philosophy and that he applies our distinction: theology refers to revelation and philosophy appeals only to reason and rational arguments. According to Anselm, we must first have knowledge of the Christian doctrine through faith with the help of God's grace and revelation: that God is a triune God, that Christ died for our sins, that there will be an eternal judgment after death, etc. But all these things can be proved afterwards by reason, *remoto Christo* (irrespective of Christ). And in his argumentation Anselm does not refer to Scripture or to any ecclesiastical authority. Unlike Thomas Aquinas, Anselm is of the opinion that all the truths of revelation and Scripture can be proved by philosophy with the help of a rational argumentation irrespective of Christ. In Thomas' view this applies only to a small part of the revealed truths, as we shall see presently.

Anselm has become famous for his ontological argument which will be discussed in our next chapter. In this argument the starting-point is the concept of God, here considered as a being greater than which nothing can be conceived. From this concept alone God's existence is inferred. Anselm advanced this argument in his *Proslogion*. Previously he had adduced some traditional arguments for the existence of God, in particular the cosmological argument in which the existence of God is inferred from the world or from something in the world. Anselm could not bear the thought, however, that in this way God was considered to be dependent for his existence upon something outside himself. He could not rest before he had constructed a proof that started with God and ended with God and, so the story goes, after some sleepless nights he came forward with this famous ontological argument. It starts with (the concept of) God and from this (the existence of) God is inferred in a way that makes Him no longer dependent upon something outside himself. Nobody can deny that the construction of this proof is the work of a genius. It is still discussed by scholars in philosophical theology and metaphysics.

It is remarkable that Anselm put this proof in the framework of a prayer, i.e. he started and ended his book by addressing God. This fact is another argument used by Barth to support his assertion that Anselm is primarily a theologian and has only theological interests. Now I admit that Anselm has the passion of a mystic and a believer, but he was also a great logician, a writer of beautiful Latin, a scholar of a high standard, etc. and he certainly did not use any theological argument in his ontological proof.

Anselm was to such an extent worried about the cosmological argument that he thought this proof unworthy of God. This view is connected with his epistemology. Obviously, Anselm presupposed that there is a certain parallelism between being (reality) and knowing or between the *ordo essendi* and the *ordo cognoscendi*. Thomas Aquinas clearly separated the two. Something can be more fundamental in the realm of being (reality), for example the existence of God, and still be a derived concept in the realm of knowing. Thus, something can be closer to our mind than God's existence, without damaging in any way God's majesty and ontological priority. Anselm sees things differently because of the parallelism mentioned above.

This problem has not yet been solved and is still being discussed. Karl Barth, for example, is of the opinion that in dogmatics the order of the topics to be discussed is of fundamental importance. If we put them in a wrong order, we spoil everything. If we do not start with God in dogmatics, we will never reach him. Therefore, according to Barth, we must start with God and his revelation and not with man, the world or anything else. This view also presupposes the parallelism between being (reality) and knowing. But not all theologians share this view. Brunner, for example, thinks that there is a certain amount of freedom in the arranging of the topics in dogmatics. We are not compelled to start with God. We may also begin with man and his shortcomings (see e.g. Brunner's book *Man in Revolt*). So with respect to this question there are two parties. On the one hand there is the view of Anselm that there is a parallelism between being (reality) and knowing, a view shared by great scholars such as Spinoza, Hegel, Barth and others. On the other hand there is the view that there is no such parallelism, a view shared by Thomas Aquinas, Brunner, Kierkegaard and others. In spite of all my admiration for Anselm and Spinoza I share the latter view. Which is in accordance with our daily experience. We usually know things superfically first before coming to know their deeper and more fundamental causes. It is also in agreement with modern logic, in which one can construct various systems and one is not obliged to stick to *one* set of fundamental axioms only. In any case the burden of proof is on the defenders of parallelism, because it is a theorem which is not self-evident, to say the least. In summary, one may say that Anselm shows us a rational way to God, in which the unity of philosophy and belief (theology) is emphasized with a predominance of the latter. All the dogmas of the church can be proved by reason in a philosophical way.

2.5.3 *Thomas Aquinas*

In Thomas' work too philosophy, insofar as it is philosophical theology, serves to defend the truth to the Christian faith. His philosophy has apologetic features, just as that of Anselm. Still, Thomas stood in another tradition, because he belonged to the Aristotelians. Recent research in Thomas' philosophy, however, has shown that in his work Platonic influences are present. The doctrine of participation plays an important role, i.e. the doctrine that the things of this world participate in the powers of the divine ideas. A great difference between Thomas and Anselm is that according to the former not all the truths of the Christian faith can be proved by reason, although that on the other hand reason can operate without the preceding help of supernatural grace. Some doctrines of the Christian faith *can* be proved, e.g. the existence of God and some of his properties, the immortality of the soul and the validity of natural morality. These are exactly the three great doctrines of the Enlightenment in the 18th century. The specific mysteries of the Christian faith, however, the doctrine of the Trinity, sin, the salvation through Christ, the sacraments, etc., cannot be proved by reason. However, it can be shown that they are without contradictions and that they are thus logically possible.

The truths that can be proved by reason are also revealed in Scripture, because in this way they can be acknowledged by all people and not only by the philosophically minded. Besides, in this way they can be recognized more quickly and with greater certainty. For the relation between the two truths various models have been proposed: (i) One model is that of two concentric circles, in which the larger circle represents the set of revealed truths, which means that it includes all truths. The smaller, inner circle is the circle of the reasonable truths. (ii) A second model is that of a building the lower part of which represents nature, i.e. the truths of reason, and the higher section represents grace, i.e. the truths of revelation. Model (i) gives a better expression of the idea that grace presupposes nature: 'Gratia non tollit, sed praesupponit et perficit naturam'. Thomas, by contrast to the Platonic school, does not to teach any longer that reason needs a preceding enlightenment of grace (the Holy Spirit) in order to do its work properly. Reason can study nature and find natural truths without the help of grace. A certain independence of nature from grace is manifest here. In this respect Thomas was an important forerunner of modern natural science.

The position advanced in the present book has a certain analogy to that of Thomas. We also begin by constructing a basis in a stricter system and then we proceed by extending it into a stronger (less strict) system. The difference is, however, that in this less strict system we still refer to reasonable arguments and to religious experience, and not directly to revelation. Of course, one can try to prove the reliability of revelation in this more extended system and thus establish the legitimacy of an appeal to revelation.

We shall return to Thomas' five proofs of God's existence later. On August 4, 1880 Pope Leo XIII declared the philosophy of Thomas Aquinas the standard of Roman Catholic philosophising. This gave rise to Neo-Thomism, for although some scholars defended the dictum 'Thomas solus sui interpes' (i.e. Thomas is the sole interpreter of himself) the majority of scholars gave a modern re-interpretation of Thomas. In the long run, however, this Neo-Thomism developed into modern trends such as existentialism, phenomenology, analytical philosophy, especially in Western Europe and the USA. In Latin America and Southern Europe Neo-Thomism is still an important spiritual force in Roman Catholic circles. But it never had a monopoly in the Roman Catholic world. In addition to it, or mixed with it, there were trends such as Scotism and Suarezism. Neo-Thomism (like Marxism-Leninism) is one of the philosophical trends with the greatest literary output, so that one cannot say that it is dead!

2.5.4 *Spinoza*

Another great classic philosopher who tried to supply a rational basis for the belief in God was Spinoza. To his mind, however, in contradistinction to Thomas and Anselm, philosophy should no longer be regarded as the servant of theology. Spinoza separated theology and philosophy, giving the latter predominance. Only philosophy can teach us the true doctrine of God whereas Scripture can only teach people obedience, i.e. how to live a morally good life. Reason also teaches man how to live morally well and it does this even better than revelation. In principle the man of reason does not need revelation. However, nobody can live completely in accordance with reason, which means that even for the man of reason Scripture and revelation may be of some use.

For Spinoza God is the centre of philosophy. Without God we cannot know anything. Spinoza's concept of God is, however, purely philosophical. The theological concept of God is only important to those who cannot reason according to philosophical teachings. Not everyone can follow the high speculative thoughts of reason, but all may have a moral foothold in Scripture. With the help of revelation man can live a morally good, harmonious and happy life. Spinoza does not attack religion, on the contrary! One should not interpret his philosophy too intellectually either. He accepted three ways of knowledge.

The first way is that of experience. This leads only to superficial knowledge insofar as it is based on hearsay, daily experience, etc. Scientific experience is more important, but it must be preceded by rational knowledge (the second way). Through rational knowledge man learns the structure of the world and God's work in it. Scientific experience provides reason with its basic material and through it we can learn how individual things have their place in the great rational framework of the universe. Spinoza won eminence in philosophy by using the axiomatic system for constructing a complete philosophy. He was the first and only philosopher to do philosophy in this way. Finally, the third way is the best, but also the most difficult way and few people (including Spinoza himself) are able to use it. It is the way of *scientia intuitiva*, intuitive knowledge. Through it we have immediate knowledge of God, a knowledge which is not vague and uncertain, but clear, distinct and certain.

According to Spinoza everything is in God and follows necessarily from God. God has an infinite number of attributes, of which we know only two, namely extension and cogitation. These attributes are modified and in this way the infinite modes are constituted. The things of this world are finite modes and parts of God's infinite modes. They do not belong to God's attributes.

In this way man is constituted by the finite modes of extension, i.e. his body, and those of cogitation, i.e. his soul. There is no direct influence of the soul on the body or vice versa. There is a parallelism between body and soul, which is based upon a parallelism between the attributes of God who is the one and only substance which exists in and through itself. This substance expresses itself in an infinite number of attributes. Because there are only finite modes of extension and cogitation in this world, we know only these two. The relation between the two has been illustrated in the following way: body and soul are the two faces of one clock.

Although Spinoza presented his system in a clear and rational way with the help of the axiomatic method, he was not a cool rationalist who had no eye for the problems of life. The end of life is for him concrete human happiness, which is gained if man sees himself and the world *sub specie aeternitatis*, i.e. viewed from the vantage point of eternity. If a man has learned to see the things of the world and his life from the perspective of eternity, he knows that everything follows necessarily from God, and in this he will find his acquiescence.

Important is Spinoza's view of the relation between God and the eternal (logical and mathematical) truths. Descartes held the view that God had created these truths so that the logical laws were not valid in every possible world. A world in which the logical laws are different, is possible. For Leibniz on the other hand the logical laws are valid independent of God. The latter has to obey them just like human beings. Spinoza offers the more satisfactory solution: God expresses himself in the eternal truths (the logical and mathematical laws). They are God's thoughts and reveal his being.

An analogous position is taken with respect to the question of the relation between God and the perfect (the good). This problem was discussed by the Thomists and the Scotists. The latter held that something was good because God wills it, whereas the former taught that God wills something because it is good. According to Spinoza good and bad are relative terms, attributed by human beings to certain things and acts. Outside human society there is no good and evil. But he knows of another concept, the perfect, which he identifies with reality. God expresses himself in infinite being (reality), in what is perfect.

On this issue I take sides with Spinoza. If one adopted the Cartesian/ Scotist view, there would be no certainty. Everything could be different at any moment. In addition there would be no certainty of salvation. In this view God's will creates everything and is not directed by anything, not even by God's essence, for in that case we would have the Spinozistic position. This pure arbitrariness in God is unsatisfactory. Moreover, in this view God could have prevented suffering and evil in the world. But it may be equally unsatisfactory to subject God to something outside himself. Spinoza expresses himself more critically about the latter view than about former (Cartesian/Scotist). I agree with Spinoza on this matter, although I realize that my philosophy of religion might (wrongly) be interpreted as Spinozistic. I would like to point out, however, (i) that accepting this position does not mean that I accept the whole of Spinoza's philosophy, as will become clear in the rest of the book; (ii) that the usual 'pantheistic' interpretation of Spinoza is fundamentally wrong. The things of this world are a part of God's infinite modes, they are not a part of God's attributes! So there certainly is a transcendent moment in Spinoza's concept of God.

2.5.5 *Hegel*

Another variant of the rational way to God is presented to us by Hegel. In his system philosophy and religion deal with the same subject-matter but here, in contradistinction to Anselm, philosophy is predominant. Hegel is opposed both to the philosophy and theology of the Enlightenment and to traditional orthodox theology. In Enlightenment philosophy and theology the Christian faith has been deprived of its content. It has been reduced to (i) the doctrine of the existence of God, the creator of the world and preserver of morality, (ii) the doctrine of the immortality of the soul and (iii) the doctrine of natural morality, i.e. one that is based upon reason and natural intuition and not upon revelation. The Enlightenment philosopher thinks only in intellectual terms and has no insight into the deeper dimensions of faith. On the other hand conservative, orthodox Christian theology has lost its relevance for modern man, because it cannot give convincing arguments for its doctrines. An appeal to religious feelings, such as may be found in Schleiermacher, is also rejected by Hegel.

The restoration of the orthodox faith has to be achieved by (Hegelian) philosophy. Both religion and philosophy are representations of the absolute spirit. In religion the absolute appears in the form of an emotional representation which is to be replaced (*aufgehoben*) by the philosophical idea. In this *Aufhebung* (replacement) the religious representation does not disappear completely. It is maintained in some way within the philosophical idea. What is called 'idea' by Hegel should not be interpreted abstractly. Only in the beginning of the system, in logic, is thinking abstract in Hegel's philosophy. But with the help of dialectical logic the abstract concepts are (dialectically) negated. Abstract thought steps outside itself and becomes nature. In the ensuing dialectical process nature is replaced by the spirit (*Geist*), first by the subjective spirit in the human mind, then by the objective spirit in human creations such as law, morality, social institutions. Finally, the process ends in the absolute spirit which manifests itself in art, religion and philosophy. In the philosophical idea the whole preceding process is included. In its final state thinking is no longer abstract, but concrete, i.e. the whole world and all beings are included in the idea.

We cannot go into the many details of the interpretation of Hegel or into the many fine shades of meaning in the various Hegelian concepts. One cannot, however, accuse Hegel of abstract idealism without concrete content and applications. Hegel was very well abreast of the scientific results of his day and he knew how to incorporate them into his system. Of course, many details are dated now and modern Hegelians have to change them in order to maintain the principal features of the system. If one reads Hegel, one discovers – perhaps to one's surprise – that he very often starts with concrete, empirical facts. He wanted, however, to *know* them, i.e. he wanted to grasp their essences and he was not content with only superficial knowledge of the facts as such. He wanted to penetrate into their philosophical ideas.

As we said above, in Hegel's philosophy dialectical logic (dialectic) plays an important role. In this respect he differs significantly from Spinoza, who remains within the borders of classical logic. According to Hegel intellectual thought (*das verstandesmässige Denken*) makes the mistake of considering concepts as unambiguous and closed ideas. In rational thought (*das vernunftmässige Denken*) concepts are considered to be full of inner contradictions. They represent states of affairs in reality which are full of contradictions too. Through these contradictions, i.e. through the negations, dynamics enters into the world. These contradictions strive to dissolve themselves and thus to negate the concept of which they are the constituents. This leads to a new concept which is opposed to the original one. But this concept too is full of contradictions and is therefore negated in its turn (the famous negation of negation, mentioned above). In this way we do not come to the original concept as in classical logic, but to a new concept. In classical logic the negation of the negation of A results in A, but in Hegelian dialectic the negation of the negation of A leads to a new concept B. This dialectic of Hegel is a dialectic both of concepts and of reality (in his philosophy there is also a parallelism between thinking and being!). Negation is in his system the driving force of development and dynamics.

I shall explain this Hegelian dialectic with two examples. First an example taken from the beginning of his system. In philosophy thinking starts with the most abstract thought, *viz.* the concept of being (*das Sein*). Being is conceived as empty in order to enable it to include everything. This emptiness leads to its negation, i.e. the concept of nothingness (*das Nichts*). The negation of nothingness leads to a synthesis of being and nothingness, i.e. to the concept of becoming (*das Werden*). In becoming both being and its negation (nothingness) are included.

The second example will be taken from Hegel's philosophy of law. The negation of law is crime. According to Hegel the negation of crime, i.e. the way in which it is extolled, is punishment. In punishment both law and crime are included. In Hegel's system the triad of thesis – antithesis – synthesis plays a great role, although we have to admit that this *terminology* stems from Fichte and was hardly used by Hegel himself. Not all modern Hegelians have taken over this dialectic. The great Italian Hegelian Croce, who had such an influence on the Marxist Gramsci, (who gave the Italian communist party its unique (Hegelian) features), was no dialectician. Hegelian dialectic may be criticised by modern logic, as we have explained above, but it may be very useful in some fields, as we have also seen.

As for philosophy of religion, Hegel was able to incorporate the religious dogmas into his philosophical thought. We shall consider his treatment of the doctrine of the trinity as an example. According to Hegel it belongs to the essence of though that it has a triune structure. Thinking (consciousness) does not stay in itself, but goes out and puts forward ideas with which it stands in relation. Next, it conceives the unity of these ideas with itself. Thus a triune structure emerges, i.e. the philosophical trinity of the spirit. This trinity of the spirit is presented in theology by means of the image of the trinity of God: God the Father produces the Son (i.e. he himself in another form) and next Father and Son love each other through the Holy Ghost, i.e. God in his active form of connecting himself as Father and as Son.

I think the analogy (homomorphy) between the two structures cannot be denied. The triune structure is not something that is uniquely reserved for God. On the other hand I think there is much more in the doctrine of the trinity than mere imagery or a philosophical concept caught in a theological mirror. Therefore many (orthodox) Christians deeply mistrusted such re-interpretations of their theology. Sometimes even non-Hegelian theologians, whose system showed a certain similarity in structure with Hegel's, for example Karl Barth, were suspected of Hegelianism.

Hegel also introduced the dictum 'God is dead' into philosophy (theology), which became a slogan and featured prominently in later thought. By this dictum, however, Hegel only meant to say that in the time of the Enlightenment the idea of God had lost its meaning in human thought. And since according to Hegel the history of thought reflects the history of reality, God 'died' not only in human consciousness, but also in reality. He rose from the dead in Hegel's philosophy, here he came to life again. Again we meet the triad thesis-antithesis-synthesis: God is present in traditional Christianity, he 'died' (is negated) in the philosophy of the Enlightenment, but in Hegel's philosophy a synthesis of the two occurs.

Of course, this Hegelian construction is rather speculative and I am by no means willing to accept it, but it should be clear that in Hegelian philosophy God certainly did not disappear from the human scene. Nietzsche, however, took over this thought, *viz.* that God died in human consciousness, but he refused to add the thought of a resurrection. In our time some theologians have continued this Nietzschean thought: Vahanian, Altizer, Hamilton, Sölle and others. However, they differ when it comes to lending substance to this concept. What they have in common is the intention to give a new meaning to the concept of God at a time when this term, to say the least, has become questionable. Religion in their view may receive a more secularised meaning. Some refer to Heidegger and adopt his idea of a possible return of God (cf. Sölle). Here the possibility of a new 'resurrection' of God remains open. In some way this is a continuation of Hegel's line of thought.

2.5.6 *Final considerations*

In this section we have considered various attempts to find a rational way towards the acceptance of the belief in God. Sometimes this way even leads to a proof of Christian dogma as a whole (e.g. Anselm, Hegel), sometimes it only leads to a theistic conception of God, which must be worked out later in a system (Thomas), sometimes it is not so obvious what would emerge, a theistic, pan-en-theistic or pantheistic concept of God. Hegel's approach is the least convincing, because he makes use of the dialectical method in a rather doubtful way. Anselm certainly tries to prove too much according to modern thinking. To prove the whole of the Christian faith on pure rational grounds is impossible today. In the next chapter I shall try to give a modern variant of the rational way making use of modern logical insights.

2.6 *The moral way*

In a traditional classification of the human mind one has: (i) the intellect, (ii) the will and (iii) the emotions. One may consider the ways of religious experience and reason as representing respectively more or less the ways of human feeling and intuition (= iii) and those of the intellect (= i). In this section we shall consider the way of the will (ii), which is an approach to establishing the acceptance of God on the basis of morals. This can be done in two ways. One can regard religion as being in a certain continuity with morals, or one can assume a gap between religion and morals.

2.6.1 *Continuity between religion and morals. Kant*

Kant tried to show that every attempt to found religion on a rational basis with the help of theoretical reason (*die theoretische Vernunft*) is in vain. He attempted to show that the traditional proofs of God's existence were not valid. For a long time his attempt was considered to be successful, but nowadays we see a remarkable re-emergence ('resurrection') of the proofs of God's existence. More one this in our next chapter.   Although Kant rejected the traditional rational approach to God, he tried to lay the foundation for another one, *viz.* a moral approach. Human moral consciousness is the starting-point of his discussion. Kant's philosophy can be characterized as carefully designed architectonics. He tried to bring the preceding, more rational continental philosophy and British philosophy, which was more empirical, into a synthesis. All knowledge starts with experience, Kant admits. But according to him it is not founded on experience and empirical findings. It is the task of the 'Critique' to find the constitutive elements within experience with the help of which true knowledge is achieved.

Of course, philosophers before Kant also realised that there is a going together of experience and rational thinking. However, rationalists like Descartes, Spinoza, Geulincx, Malebranche, Leibniz, and others were of the opinion that experiential findings served only to stimulate reason in its proper activities. These experiential findings were only a basis from which reason could discover the eternal rational laws of mind and nature. The empiricists (Bacon, Hobbes, Locke, Berkeley, Hume) were, on the other hand, of the opinion that the task of reason was not that important. Truth had to be found through experience, with the help of experiments. Reason could combine certain findings, make classifications, etc., but that was all. Thinking was not creative as it was for the rationalists.

According to Kant, true and certain knowledge was possible, which was also a common axiom for both the rationalists and the empiricists of his time. The only question was how to achieve it. The basis of his system was the sensations of the human mind. That was a good empirical starting-point. But these sensations were nothing but a chaotic mass without any order. It does not give us any point of orientation. It is human reason which brings shape and order into this chaos. However, it is not the individual human reason that accomplishes this, but human reason in general or consciousness in general, i.e. Kant's famous *Bewusstsein überhaupt*.

First, the forms of perception (*Anschauungsformen*), namely space and time, constitute a whole network of spatial and chronological relations between the sensations. These spatial and chronological relations are not a part of reality as such, but a product of our mind. Formerly people thought that in our perception we adapt ourselves to the things, but according to Kant the things adapt themselves to us, or, more correctly, we adapt the things to ourselves. He calls this the Copernican revolution in his philosophy. However, the spatial and chronological order is not the only order we ascribe to the things. We observe a set of colours and shapes which sometimes cohere, sometimes not. In order to identify such a set as, say, an ashtray we need something more than only our spatial and chronological order. What is perceived, is only certain shapes and colours.

At the same time we add the concept that they cohere. In this way our mind constitutes a second form of order with the help of the categories. Kant deduced these categories from Aristotelian logic in a somewhat arbitrary way. The main categories are substance and causality. The time relation is fundamental in establishing the categories. Only if a set of sensations, brought into a certain order, coheres in time, an opportunity is given to reason to identify this set as an object, i.e. as a substance. If a set of sensations A always precedes a set B, reason interprets this as 'A is the cause of B'. Substantiality and causality cannot be deduced from the pure observation of the sensations. These categories are forced upon the sensations so that experience can be constituted as a way of knowledge. Causality and substance therefore do not exist outside the human mind. They belong to the world of appearances, i.e. the world that exists only in the human mind and not in reality. However, the world of appearances is not the imaginary world of an individual. It is the human world as such. This world is called the *phenomenal world* by Kant (*die phänomenale Welt*). The real world is the world of the thing(s) as such (*das Ding an sich*). It is called the *noumenal world* by Kant and it cannot be known by theoretical reason. The phenomenal world is the basis of our 'objective' knowledge which is therefore in reality intersubjective knowledge. As such it is certain and not based upon an individual choice and preference.

Against this background Kant could refute the traditional arguments for God's existence. In these arguments the concept of causality plays a fundamental role. Since this concept only belongs to the phenomenal world and not to the real, noumenal world, we cannot prove God's existence in the real world with the help of this concept. Likewise the other arguments of the philosophy of Enlightenment could be proved false. The doctrine of the immortality of the soul was established with the help of the argument that in the flow of perceptions and thoughts there was something that remains the same, namely the human soul, which was therefore an indivisible substance. And what is indivisible cannot perish. This argument is based upon the concept of substance, which is only valid in the phenomenal world, and not in the real noumenal world. It exists only in the human mind and not in reality.

Kant, however, did not deny the immortality of the human soul, neither did he deny the existence of God. He proved this with the help of practical reason which pertains to the moral world. Starting-point for his argument was the human moral consciousness. Kant not only believed that morality factually exists, but also that it is justified in producing moral judgments, just as in science true and indubitable knowledge is possible. The only question is: *how* is this possible. The critique of theoretical reason supplies the basis for indubitable scientific knowledge, although at the price of no longer being able to know reality as such. Man only knows (intersubjectively) the phenomenal world, but this knowledge is absolutely certain. In the same way Kant was convinced that in the world of morals an absolutely certain method is possible. Moreover, practical reason has priority over theoretical reason. Thus practical reason can lead us to the real noumenal world. And here God reappears as one of the postulates which are necessary to constitute moral consciousness and behaviour.

Kant made the traditional distinction between an axiom and a postulate. We find this distinction already in the work of Euclid. An axiom is an indubitable truth which is completely evident and accepted by everybody who understands the meaning of the axiom. For example: if two objects A and B are both identical with a third object C, i.e. if A = C and B = C, then A and B are identical too, i.e. A = B. Or take the geometrical axiom of Archimedes: 'The straight line is the shortest connection between two points'. The human mind can see immediately that these axioms are true with the help of some kind of intuition or by other means. A postulate, however, is a supposition which is in itself not evident, but is needed in order to construct the system. An example would be Euclid's postulate of the two parallel lines, i.e. that through a point A outside a certain straight line B, always one, and only one line C can be drawn parallel to line B. (This is a later formulation of this postulate; Euclid himself gave another formula, but we need not go into the details here).

This postulate was not self-evident and for a long time scholars tried to deduce it from the presupposed axioms. But this turned out to be impossible. In the 19th century Gauss, Lobachevski and Bolyai constructed, independently from each other, non-Euclidean geometries. In these it was proved that a geometry in which the postulate of parallels was no longer accepted was consistent with the other Euclidean axioms. In modern logic the distinction between axioms and postulates is no longer made, because the choice of axioms is considered to be arbitrary. Many systems of propositional logic, etc. are possible; although they have different axioms, they are nevertheless equivalent.

Back now to Kant! In his days the distinction between axiom and postulate was still in common use. According to Kant a system of morals requires a number of postulates. These postulates need not be self-evident, but they are necessary in the sense that otherwise no system of morals could be constructed. The first postulate is that of freedom. If I have to act morally, I must be responsible for the acting. Therefore I must not be forced to act in this way, for then I cannot take the resposibility for my deed. In other words, I must act in full freedom. If human beings were fully predetermined, they could not be made responsible for their actions. Hence freedom must be postulated in ethics, that is, the rational reflection on morals.

Kant advocated a rigorous morals of obligation in his ethics. Not only outward obedience is important, but also inner sentiment and intention. Moral man obeys the inward voice of his consciousness, not the outward commands of his superiors. We cannot go into the details of Kant's moral philosophy here. But it is obvious that we cannot always fulfil our moral duties and obligations in life. From the priority of practical reason over theoretical reason we may infer that one day this will be possible, if not in this world, then in another. This other world is the kingdom of heaven and thus Kant formulated the postulate of the immortality of the soul. This doctrine cannot be proved in the traditional way, as we have seen, but it reappears as a postulate of practical reason.

The same is true with regard to the doctrine of the existence of God. In order to let morality gain the victory over the opposing powers it is necessary that there should be a judgment after death in which goodness will prevail. A kingdom of heaven presupposes a protector and preserver of morality. In Kant's view religion is the interpretation of the moral commands as divine commands. Nevertheless Kant maintained the autonomy of morality. Man for himself knows what is morally good. He need not receive moral commands from God. We do not have to do certain things, because God wants us to do them. We must perform our deeds, because we are convinced that they are morally good. If we do certain things in order to get a reward in heaven, our moral behaviour is no longer autonomous, but heteronomous. Then we do not perform our actions with the help of our autonomous practical reason, but because of forces outside ourselves.

Some scholars were of the opinion that Kant, by introducing the postulates of God's existence and the immortality of the human soul, was sliding back into a eudaemonistic ethics. According to eudaemonism, one should do what brings happiness and joy. As far as I can see this criticism is not correct, if we emphasize the priority of practical reason over theoretical reason. The main thing is that good deeds must be performed, which is not completely possible in this world. Kant was not concerned about rewards after death. Virtue had its reward in itself, Kant said in agreement with Spinoza and others (the Stroics, for example). His system is logically consistent.

Kant has still another argument for the existence of God, which is very often neglected. We find this argument in his *Critique of Judgment*. Here Kant first gives a basis for aesthetics to which we will return later on in this book. Next he gives a teleological account of nature. This account is not scientific for if we inquire into nature only for scientific purposes, we shall not see the hand of God in it. But we may observe nature in a different way. We may see unity in variety, just by applying some sort of aesthetic principle to our observations. We then see certain ends and purposes in nature and reason to state that God has created the world. One ought to consider nature *as if* God had created it.

What is the meaning of this 'as if' in Kant's work? In my opinion we are on the right track, if we understand Kant as saying that reason, in order to constitute a complete synthesis of all its data, is urged to look for a final end and ideal, and that it finds this in God. Also in theoretical reason God is needed as a regulative idea. However, accepting God on these grounds is not scientifically well founded, but it is an essential characteristic of the human mind to look at nature in this way.

In Kant's philosophy religion is a continuous with morals. It takes the commands of morality as commands of God. There is no breach between them. It is not the case that religious teaches something different from morals. The same moral commands are valid in religion and in ethics. The God of morals is not different from the God of religion. Putting it in a more theological way: there is no gap between law and gospel. In Kant's view there is a continuous line from morals to religion. If we reflect correctly on our moral teachings we may come to know God's will. In his *Religion within the Limits of Reason* he refers to radical evil in man, which causes man not to do what he morally wills. By some evil force he does what he does not want to do. But even here Kant does not take refuge in God's grace. It is through a revolutionary change of the human will that the right attitude can be gained. Continuity between God and man, not discontinuity, is the last word in Kant's philosophy.

2.6.2 *Discontinuity between religion and morals. Kierkegaard and Brunner*

2.6.2.1 *Kierkegaard*

Although there are differences between Kant and Kierkegaard there are also important similarities. Both have a great moral zeal and in connection with this moral attitude they both emphasize the importance of the individual over against the state, all-embracing systems, etc. Kierkegaard challenges the great system of his day, i.e. Hegel's dialectical system. His discussion with Hegel is based upon several considerations. First, he opposes Hegel with arguments borrowed from the Christian faith. In Hegel's philosophy the great discrepancy between God and man has been neglected. Second, Kierkegaard combats Hegel's dialectic with the help of a stricter logic, i.e. that of Aristotle.

Kierkegaard gives the following ideal type of a human evolution towards faith. Such an evolution proceeds through the following stages: (i) first we have the aesthetic stage. Here man lives the life of an individual for whom pleasure and joy are the highest values. The aesthetic mind refuses to assume any responsibility. He does not acknowledge the universally valid moral commands and requirements. By means of a 'leap' man enters (ii) the moral stage. Here he is willing to assume responsibilities and to live a moral life. Like Kant, Kierkegaard teaches that the moral command has universal validity. In a modern formulation: a moral command is valid everywhere and for all men, provided they are in the same situation and have the same abilities. Moral man does not take a position in opposition to the community, quite the contrary. At the moral stage man acts primarily as a member of the community or society in which he lives. The final stage is (iii) the religious stage. Here man is an individual again as at the aesthetic stage, but he is now willing to assume responsibilities. He is responsible primarily towards God, and no longer towards human beings as at the moral stage.

Kierkegaard's famous example is Abraham's sacrifice (Gen. 22). The command to sacrifice his son was not a universal command. It was only valid for Abraham, a special duty assigned to him alone. From a moral point of view Abraham was a (potential) murderer, but religiously he was a hero of faith. Abraham made the double movement of infinity. He gave up his son Isaac, but that was done already at the moral stage. It is moral resignation. But then Abraham makes the leap of faith: he believes that somehow he may keep Isaac. He cannot yet see how this will happen, but somehow it will happen. That is the confidence and hope of faith.

In his later works Kierkegaard makes an additional distinction in the religious stage: Religion A and Religion B. Religion A is the universal, general religion which is accessible to everyone, religion B is the specific Christian faith. Strictly speaking, religion A belongs more to the second stage (the moral stage) than to the religious stage proper. In his book *Philosophiske Smuler* (Philosophical Fragments) Kierkegaard gives the view of Socrates as an example. He puts Socrates opposite to Christianity. He is a representative of religion A and he does not acquire religion through revelation. Deep in himself he already knows the truth of religion, the truth about God and man. If one speaks of revelation in religion A, one refers to a kind of inner enlightenment and not to a real revelation which changes man's inner attitude. There is no leap from stage (ii), the moral stage, to this stage of religion A. There is only a gradual transition. The person who is the messenger of this revelation is of no importance, he is only the outward occasion which causes man's thoughts to go in the right direction. If in religion A man accepts the truths of that religion, he had them already within himself without knowing them precisely. Knowledge of God is at the same time knowledge of man himself. Like the person who is the incidental cause of revelation, the moment in time at which the right view breaks through is of no importance. The relation God-man is and has always been the same, history is of no importance.

In religion B, however, things are completely different. Here *the moment in time is of decisive significance*. From this hypothesis Kierkegaard is able to deduce the whole of the Christian faith. A remarkable achievement! Kierkegaard demonstrates convincingly that in religion B man's relation to God cannot be the same from eternity to eternity. Man is a sinner, who is in need of salvation. By contrast to the Socratic view the messenger of the revelation is now of decisive importance. The moment in time is unique and cannot be repeated, and there must therefore be a renewal of man which is also unique and which cannot be repeated. That means that the person who is the messenger of this revelation and causes this renewal cannot be an ordinary teacher like Socrates. He must be a creator, i.e. God. There is no longer a gradual transition from one stage to another. There is a breach, a gap between the moral stage and the stage of religion B. This gap cannot be overcome with the help of a Hegelian dialectical process. In Hegel's thinking all the elements of the new stage have their dialectical counterparts in the old stage and there is no real novelty. In Kierkegaard's thinking the gap can only be overcome by a leap, the leap of faith. Only in this way can the moment in time have a decisive significance (see appendix 7).

The stages should not be interpreted as an inner evolution to be experienced by everybody. Nor should we think that if one stage has been passed, it will never return: regression is always possible. These stages are ideal constructions (ideal types) which need not occur exactly in reality. In Kierkegaard's writings many variations within the stages are given, but we cannot go into the details of his splendid analyses. Even Socrates is admired by Kierkegaard in spite of his criticism. In the construction mentioned above Socrates, by the way, is an ideal type also. In other writings Kierkegaard even places Socrates in a special position within the moral stage, by distinghuishing between two moral attitudes. First there is man trying to realize the general obligations which are valid in his society. Here morals are still an external affair. Socrates, however, has already seen the importance of the individual and the relevance of the inner life. For him morality becomes internal. One is reminded here of the difference between Hegel and Kant; Kierkegaard definitely sides with the letter.

For the transition (the leap) from the aesthetic to the moral stage irony plays an important role, and the same is true for humour during the transition from the moral to the religious B stage. Kierkegaard wants to bring human beings to real existence which is different from teaching them a certain doctrine. Christianity cannot be taught and Kierkegaard can only try to persuade people to leap themselves. For this purpose Kierkegaard has to use the so-called indirect communication. Therefore, words have often more than one meaning in Kierkegaard's work. This is especially manifest in his irony and humour. If someone wants to persuade someone else to move from the aesthetic to the moral stage he must speak the language of aesthetical man in order to be understood, but the content of his speech may already be moral. So he speaks in two dimensions of meaning, a characteristic of irony and humour. In this way one can speak aesthetically about morals and morally about religion.

Does Kierkegaard renounce rational thinking in order to reach the stage of Christian faith? Was he a complete irrationalist? There are interpreters of Kierkegaard who say so, for example Shestov. Christian faith is said to be analogous to the acceptance of $2 + 2 = 5$. If this were true, Kierkegaard would be uninteresting for me and for many other scholars. Such an interpretation is, however, in contrast with Kierkegaard's sharp rational analyses. No doubt some arguments in favour of an irrationalist interpretation can be brought forward, especially in his *Frygt og Baeven* (Fear and Trembling), where Kierkegaard asserts that Abraham believed by virtue of the absurd.

According to Kierkegaard, however, even religion B is not identical with a spiritual 'ring of roses'. In *Philosophiske Smuler* he teaches that analysis of the human intellect shows that it transcends itself. Thus, the human intellect pushes man towards transcendence and, finally, to God. This gives a picture which differs from the irrationalist interpretation. We cannot go into details here, but one should not forget that Kierkegaard wrote his philosophical works under a pseudonym and that they do not represent his real opinion. It can be shown that Kierkegaard was nearer to the position defended in the *Philosophiske Smuler* than to that in *Frygt of Baeven*. He said so himself and originally he intended to publish the former under his own name, but changed this plan at the very last moment.

All this does not change the fact that Kierkegaard, in contradistinction to Kant, does not teach a gradual and continuous transition from the stage of morals to the stage of religion. There is a gap between the two which man cannot bridge by using his own power and strength. He needs God's grace.

Kierkegaard is said to be the father of existentialism. In Kierkegaard's and existentialist thought 'existence' means total man, human being conceived as a whole, which transcends his intellect. We find this idea, by the way, already in the works of Schelling and Schleiermacher. Besides some Christian thinkers (G. Marcel, A.E. Loen), many atheists belong to existentialism (Sartre, Merleau Ponty, Camus, Beerling and others). After the second world war existentialism became the expression of the then prevailing pessimism.

According to Sartre man should realize himself. He always projects himself, i.e. he finds himself always confronted with various possibilities and the choice between them. But in choosing between certain possibilities he is always guilty of rejecting certain other, essential and important, possibilities. So man cannot avoid being guilty of not realizing certain possibilities. Man is essentially an incomplete being. God is thought of as a complete being, but this is only a projection of wishful thinking. The great suffering in the world contradicts, according to many existentialists, the concept of a good and almighty God.

Heidegger and Jaspers take a special position in this respect. They are not atheists like Sartre, but they are not Christians in the traditional sense either. Jaspers speaks of the transcendence of God, but he rejects the traditional biblical images and concepts. He reminds one of Plotinus, who speaks about God as the One in the sense of a neutrum, not of a personal being. Heidegger combines existentialism with phenomenology. In his philosophy the Holy and God play a certain role, although a subordinate one. A presence of God in this world, here and now, is rejected by Heidegger. However, I already alluded to the fact that for Heidegger a turn (eine Kehre) is possible. A return of God is not excluded.

2.6.2.2 *E. Brunner*

The two famous Swiss theologians Barth and Brunner were influenced by Kierkegaard; Barth, however, only during a short period, in which he wrote the second edition of his commentary on Paul's letter to the Romans (*Römerbrief*, 2. Aufl.). Later Barth was influenced by Anselm, of whom he gave a theological interpretation (*vide* 2.5.2). Since then he developed other views, fundamentally different from Kierkegaard's and Brunner's. We shall consider him in a separate section.

Brunner plainly continues Kierkegaard's thought, although in a much more systematic and much less poetic form. He was also influenced by the personalist philosophers Buber and Ebner, especially in his later period. On the basis of this personalist philosophy Brunner makes a clear distinction between truths of revelation and faith on the one hand and truths of reason and doctrines on the other hand. The first kind of truth has the structure of an encounter; it has a personal character, constituted in person-to-person relations. Man knows himself to be saved by God in Christ. Here the truths are not doctrinal statements about facts. They are existential truths which change the believers. The latter become other men.

Christian dogmaticians were mistaken in treating the Christian truths as statements about facts, thus turning them into doctrinal truths instead of existential truths. Christian dogmatics was presented as a set of salvational statements. In the traditional Christian doctrine one has only to consent to certain truths and accept them intellectually, for instance, that Christ has risen from the dead. This is wrong, however, for a Christian has to be changed in his inner and outer life. He has to be converted and become dedicated to God. He must live from the encounter with God in Christ. All this sounds highly pietistic, but in contradistinction to traditional Pietism, for Brunner just as for Kierkegaard reason still plays a certain role. Reason can analyse the dichotomy, the breach in human life and man's alienation from his essential self. Brunner discusses all this his book *Man in Revolt (Der Mensch in Widerspruch)*.

The various philosophical trends, empiricism, rationalism, idealism, materialism, etc., pay attention only to one side of human existence. Brunner tries to show that in the Christian faith all human aspects are duly considered. One reaches this Christian faith only by a leap, just as in Kierkegaard's thinking. Man cannot do so on his own strength, he needs the grace of God to accomplish it. But the divine grace starts by bringing about a connection between man's natural knowledge of God and his natural morals. First, without man's formal intellectual qualities such as being able to understand, to think, etc., no belief would be possible. Second, natural man has already a vague feeling of guilt which serves as a point of connection (Anknüpfungspunkt) for the divine grace.

Brunner adopts here a (Lutheran) dialectic of law and gospel. Natural man may already know the moral law independently of the divine revelation. The moral law convinces him of his guilt and he suffers from this feeling of guilt. Such a man is in the moral stage of Kierkegaard or in his Religion A. The preaching of the gospel takes its starting-point in this feeling of guilt. It deepens this feeling into a feeling of sin (instead of only guilt). Sin exists only in the relation with God. Man is unable to atone for his sin, but God in his grace forgives him his sins through Christ. The gospel is the opposite and at the same time the fulfilment of the law. It is the opposite, because there is forgiveness of sins without the sinner paying his debt. God forgives through his grace. On the other hand, the gospel fulfils the law, because it is Christ who fulfils all the requirements of the law. He obeys the law and he pays the debts of the sinner.

The dialectic of law and gospel is the basic structure of Brunner's theology and philosophy. Natural theology teaches a God of Law, a God of requirements, not the God of forgiveness whom we meet in the gospel and therefore in Christian theology only. But there is a gap between law and gospel, for there is no gradual transition from law to gospel, from nature to grace.

2.6.3 Systematic evaluation

We have seen that both in Kant's thinking and in that of Kierkegaard and Brunner a moral stage precedes that of faith, and that the difference between the two is that according to Kant the transition is smooth and continuous and that there is hardly any difference between the two, whereas there is a gap, a breach between the two in Kierkegaard's and Brunner's view. I shall now discuss the question whether it is possible and/ or necessary to try to obtain our concept of God through morals. The general problem of the relation of religion to morals will be treated later on.

How shall we evaluate the transition from morals to religion from an epistemological point of view? Usually scholars are willing to accept Kant's first postulate, *viz.* that freedom is presupposed, but not the other two, *viz.* that there must be a kingdom of heaven and that therefore the soul must be immortal, and that God must exist. Kant presupposed that in the end morals must be fully realized, but is this not simply a matter of wishful thinking? Can there be no universal validity of the moral rules, if they are never fully realized?

Moreover, it may be questioned whether the postulate of freedom is absolutely necessary, for even on a deterministic point of view morality is possible as we can see in systems such as that of Spinoza, Hegel, Marxism, and many logical positivists. One might say: in the moral language game (*vide* 2.7.2) we shall certainly speak of man as if he has a free choice, but this does not change the situation that from a scientific point of view he is viewed as determined. This is also Kant's idea, only formulated in more modern terms (the theory of language games). The fundamental difference between the defenders of free will and the determinists is: May we draw ontological conclusions from the moral language game? We play this latter game as if man were free, but is this really so?

Now a generally accepted axiom is: (i) *'Ought "does not imply" is'* and vice versa: (ii) *'Is "does not imply" ought'*. I think this axiom is valid. If a certain state of affairs *is* true it does not follow from it that this state of affairs *ought* to be so, i.e. that it is morally good, and vice versa, if something *ought* to be the case, it does not necessarily follow that it *is* also true, i.e. that it is indeed the case. The axiom is contradicted only when there are misunderstandings. It is sometimes said that from certain states of affairs certain ought-statements would follow. For example, from the fact that 'God has created my fellow-men after His image' it would follow that I ought to love my fellow-men, treat them with respect, etc. I think this conclusion is correct, but 'God has created my fellow-men after His image' is not a purely indicative statement. It does not refer to a pure fact. 'God', 'God's image' are no valueless words and do not refer to valueless states of affairs. An inference from value statements to ought-statements is certainly plausible.

The 'is' in the axioms (i) and (ii) mentioned above refers to pure facts, i.e. facts which have no specific moral or aesthetic value. Now, the question whether and, if so, how facts are invested with values is a difficult one. A 'Platonic' view is possible, in which it is said that values are in some sence objectively valid, even without human beings ascribing them to certain states of affairs. But still another view is possible, *viz.* that values are given by man and that, apart from man, there are no values. Even adherents of the 'Platonic' view cannot deny that the status of values in reality is different from that of material things, human beings, institutions, etc. Put in terms of Popper, they belong to his third world.

Phrased in the terminology of the Value-school of Neo-Kantianism, i.e. the Baden school (Rickert, Windelband, etc.) one might say that values are valid, in a way analogous to that in which logical laws are valid. A logical law does not have some sort of existence like material objects, human beings, etc. It has, so to speak, a connective or, rather, a relational existence. If certain things are given, certain other things follow from them. The kind of existence of values is different. They refer to states of affairs in an ideal world of which we may wish that they were present in our world. Anyway, even on a 'Platonic' view, one must accept the axioms (i) and (ii) for this world. And thus I believe it is wrong to ascribe ontological status to the moral postulates or, in other words, to hold that they imply certain states of affairs in reality, i.e. in this our world. They may imply certain states of affairs in an ideal world; but does this ideal world exist?

Another defence of the Kantian position may be given by asserting a normative theory of truth (*vide* 3.1.5.6.3). For if something is true, if it satisfies certain standards, then perhaps one can try to demonstrate that the moral postulates are true because they satisfy these standards. But even then difficulties arise. First, Kant himself accepted the axioms (i) and (ii) mentioned above; second, it remains doubtful whether the moral postulates include the postulate of the immortality of the soul and the existence of God. Kant says so, but modern moral philosophers doubt it (in contradistinction to the postulate of freedom). At least it is easier to prove non-determinism in this way than the existence of God. Third, I think that in a normative theory of truth proofs such as the ontological argument are valid, so that the moral argument for God is hardly needed.

2.7 *Absolute autonomy of religion*

Until now we have considered authors who in some way tried to supply a basis for religion, either by appeal to religious experience, by providing rational arguments or by an analysis of morals. Not all the authors were convinced of the necessity to do so: Kierkegaard and Brunner, for example. But they, at least, were of the opinion that reason could pave the way for religion by analysing the human mind and particularly man's moral situation.

The authors we shall discuss here are of the opinion that religion is absolutely autonomous and that it needs no foundation. One might also label them religious 'positivists', but this term might evoke misunderstandings. The authors discussed in this section need not be religious themselves (Wittgenstein, for example, was not specifically a religious man), but they give religion an autonomous place and maintain that there is no need for a foundation. Religion is simply given. Now this being given of religion as a fact can be interpreted in different ways. It can be seen as the phenomenon of the church (Barth), it can be interpreted as a language game (and language games are cultural facts!) (Wittgenstein), and it can be taken as belonging to human symbolic, sacramental life as such (Van der Leeuw). The latter, by the way, sometimes appealed to religious experience, especially in his earlier work. But in his later work he defended the thesis of the autonomy of religion.

2.7.1 *Karl Barth*

Originally Barth and Brunner belonged to the same school, but later on their paths parted. Barth rejected Brunner's (Lutheran) dialectic of law and gospel. He emphasized (particularly in his later periods) the triumph of grace. In his work we do not find anything like Kierkegaard's theory of stages. Barth gives absolute priority to the salvation that is achieved by Christ and distributed to man through the church. It is the life of the church that is the starting-point for Barth's foundation of faith. He does not want to speak of religion, because he interprets religion as the attempt made by man to reach God in his own way and through his own strength. In the present book, however, the term religion does not have this sense.

The salvation through Christ can be gained by man without a preceding knowledge of guilt and a broken heart, as was claimed in the works of Kierkegaard and Brunner, who in this respect follow Luther. According to Barth atheism and unbelief cannot be taken seriously. Barth firmly believes in the predominant superiority of grace. Nothing can withstand it. Belief and unbelief do not lie on the same level. Unbelief is just like evil (*das Böse*), which is identified with non-being or Nothingness (*das Nichtige*), only to be seen as a problem, as a riddle, which appears on the border of God's activities.

In his theology Barth works out a trinitarian approach, which appears throughout his great dogmatics. In his view the concept of the trinity is the fundamental doctrine of the church. We find this concept in the structure of his dogmatics as a whole, but also in every part and detail of it. This structure, in which the whole is reflected in all the component parts, resembles that of Hegelian philosophy.

Another characteristic of his dogmatics is what Barth himself calls an Anselmian feature, i.e. we should start with the reality of the revelation and then investigate its possibility. That is to say, like Anselm we should start with the positive facts of revelation and then place them in a larger frame-work of understanding. For philosophy there is no place in his thought. It may contribute to human thought by making conceptual analyses, but it does not have the task of laying foundations or of studying reality alongside the sciences and theology.

2.7.2 *Wittgenstein*

Wittgenstein was one of the most original thinkers in modern Western philosophy. Although his contributions lay mostly outside philosophy of religion, he made some important contributions to it and he has left behind an interesting school of Wittgensteinian philosophers of religion. In Wittgenstein's work the modern *linguistic turn* took place. The philosophers who preceded Wittgenstein analysed primarily human consciousness. By following the Kantians Barth too was more oriented towards consciousness than towards language, but his theology may be easily transposed into a Wittgensteinian framework of language, as Zuurdeeg has shown. By following Wittgenstein many philosophers nowadays take their starting-point in language.

In his first period, the period of the *Tractatus Logico-Philosophicus*, Wittgenstein claimed that reality is reflected in our language. If our state-ments are to be meaningful, they must – at least in principle – be verifiable. Statements which cannot be verified even in principle are senseless. Hence, not only aesthetic, moral, religious statemens, etc. are senseless, but also those of the *Tractatus* itself belong to the class of senseless statements. Clearly, the meaning of *sense* is different here from its usual meaning. It means 'empirically verifiable' so that senseless means 'not empirically verifiable' and not 'nonsense'. The Vienna Circle, which adopted the fundamental ideas of Wittgenstein's *Tractatus*, however, regarded mathematical, logical and some philosophical statements, such as those of the *Tractatus*, as having sense. In this way it followed another line than Wittgenstein himself.

What is senseless is for Wittgenstein not only not 'nonsense', it is even very important. In a letter to a potential editor of his work Wittgenstein wrote that it consisted of two parts. One part contained what was said in it, the other part what was not said and only shown and the latter was more important than the former. This latter part is what Wittgenstein calls the mystical. It has been a point of discussion for a long time what Wittgenstein meant by the mystical and whether one may interpret this term in a religious way or not. From the text of the *Tractatus* alone it was certainly possible to say that Wittgenstein only meant to state that our thought and language have their limits. But new material from the time of the origins of the *Tractatus* clearly suggests a religious interpretation, provided that one does not identify this with a Christian interpretation. We cannot speak about God. He shows himself, however, in the world and in language.

In a 'Lecture on Ethics' Wittgenstein says that in his life he has been touched by some mysteries about which he cannot speak, and of which he can only give hints. One of these mysteries is the existence of the world: Why is there after all something, and why is there not nothing? A second mystery was the deep certainty that nothing could really hurt him and that he was to be saved by some overwhelming power, whatever might happen to him. These mysteries, however, cannot be expressed in language.

In his later works Wittgenstein adopted a more extended concept of language. Now he acknowledged various language games which are a product of culture. They are forms of life. Among these language games a religious language game is also possible. Wittgenstein indicates that a statement like 'I believe in a last judgment' belongs to another level of language than its negation 'I do not believe in a last judgment'. The first statement includes a whole style and attitude of life, whereas the latter is more or less neutral. This reminds one of Karl Barth, who also does not place belief and unbelief on the same level. Like Barth, Wittgenstein simply claims that the various language games are played, and that this is their only justification. Although Wittgenstein was not a religious person himself, he had, as his biographer Norman Malcolm said, a 'possibility for religion'. He had a deep respect for religion and for religious thinkers like Kierkegaard.

2.7.3 *Gerardus van der Leeuw*

In Van der Leeuw's thought many features of the systems of Barth and Wittgenstein are brought into a synthesis with the thought of Schleiermacher. Religion is founded in the sacramental life of man; thus religion is founded in religion! Van der Leeuw was a man with wide interests. He was a scientist of religion, a philosopher of religion, a theologian, a student of liturgy, aesthetics, especially of music, etc. He admired the 'primitive' religions, and was of the opinion that by losing his original primitivity modern man had lost much of life. We can only give a short outline of his interesting system.

Van der Leeuw has called his method *the phenomenological method*, and not without reason. Still Van der Leeuw was more an intuitive than a methodical thinker. This has its disadvantages, but it has the advantage that not everything brought forward in his thought is connected with his method, which means that, even if the method has become dated, much of the system is still valid and worth considering.

Van der Leeuw's phenomenology should not be identified with the phenomenology of Husserl and his school, but rather with that of Schleiermacher and Dilthey. Van der Leeuw followed these two thinkers in his theory of empathy (*Einfühlung*). We must live through various religious images and thoughts in a sympathetic way, for only then can we interpret them correctly. Of course, such a method is in danger of subjectivism, but it is only in this way that it is possible for us to grasp the kernel, the essence of religious phenomena. Even what is exotic and unusual is not completely unknown to us. In some secret place of our soul we recognize the unfamiliar as also present in ourselves.

This theory of empathy stands more in the tradition of Dilthey than in that of Husserl. In order to understand a phenomenon in the right way, Van der Leeuw makes use of Weber's ideal-typical constructions. Ideal types do not occur in reality, but with the help of such constructions we can better understand the phenomena in reality. If I may formulate Van der Leeuw's intentions in my own words, I should say that, in order better to understand the chaotic reality of religious phenomena, we should focus our attention on a specific part of the material and try to read its code. The test of whether we have understood it or not, consists in the answer to the question whether or not we can read the rest of the material with the help of this code. Can we bring some order into the original chaos or not?

Another aspect of his method was more prominent in his lectures than in his written works. Like Schleiermacher, Van der Leeuw emphasized the origin of a religious phenomenon. The initial intuition of a genius is always more valuable. Later reflection, however unavoidable, spoils the original vigour and spontaneity. On the other hand, like his teacher Kristensen he knew that the origin was often only a germ, which had to develop into maturity; so, if we want to know the Rhine, we should not go to its origin in the Swiss mountains, where it is only a small current. However, if he had to choose between the original religious intuition and later logical reflections Van der Leeuw would prefer the original religious intuition. He mistrusted logical and intellectual thinking. In this respect also he did not stand in the phenomenological tradition of Husserl, who was a good logician!

In passing, I should like to say something in defence of logic here, because many scholars in philosophy of religion have a wrong idea about logic. Logic is the science or the art of drawing correct conclusions. Given certain premises a certain conclusion necessarily follows. But premises are always needed, and nobody can build up a philosophical system based on logic alone. No logician has ever pretended to do so. Like many other scholars of the existentialist school, Van der Leeuw confuses logic and experience. His idea that 'primitive man' thinks non-logically is mistaken. I agree with Van Baaren and other scholars that the so-called 'primitive man' draws his conclusions precisely in the same way as we do. He has different experiences, because he has other needs and therefore views the world differently. He makes other classifications and uses other concepts.

Scientific theology should be logical too. The statement 'Christ has risen from the dead' contradicts not logic, but our ordinary and scientific experience. In the same way the primitive myth that a man can be at two different places at the same time contradicts our experience, not logic. In passing: Van der Leeuw does not use the terms 'primitive man' or 'primitive religion' in a pejorative sense. According to Van der Leeuw man in his origin, in his 'primitive' mood, stands closer to reality and truth than intellectual man. We should become as far as possible primitive again, although this is not completely possible, because we cannot abandon our whole Western heritage. I shall follow Van der Leeuw in this non-pejorative sense of the term 'primitive'.

Van der Leeuw put religious (and all other cultural) phenomena in a certain ideal-typical framework or system. This framework should not be interpreted in an evolutionary sense, but purely as a structural scheme. From a systems theoretical point of view Van der Leeuw's ideas are very interesting. He constructs his system in such a way that he goes from the more simple to the more complicated structures. Or phrased otherwise: he starts with the general structures and proceeds to the structures which have more particular features. Thus, the system becomes gradually more and more specific. The centre of the system is formed by the incarnation of Christ, who sustains the whole. He is the sustaining, upholding power of the system. Thus one can classify the phenomena of the various systems in two ways: either one starts with an 'extensive' point of view and proceeds from the more general to the more specific features, or one starts with an 'intensive' point of view and starts with the specimen that has the most sustaining power. This formulation in terms of systems theory is mine, but it is in accordance with Van der Leeuw's intentions. Moreover, he speaks about two ways in theology himself. Let me give some examples.

In his *Phenomenology of Religion* Van der Leeuw starts with dynamism. Whenever there is a special development of power present, when life shows itself extremely powerful, etc. there is *mana*. Here again Van der Leeuw shows himself to be an adherent of the philosophical views of Dilthey, who presented a vitalist philosophy. To the primitive mind, according to Van der Leeuw, the stream of *life* is the material foundation of all being. This originally purely unqualified power gradually receives its specific shapes and forms. It becomes a law of the world (*Tao; Logos* in Heraclitus, etc.), when considered in a more theoretical form. This originally unqualified power expresses itself in more and more specific forms: holy things (fetishes, amulets), holy stones and trees, holy water and fire, holy animals, etc. At some point a new characteristic appears on the scene, *viz.* the idea that everything is animated (animism). Here we find the sacred dead, the sacred people, above all the king, the priest, the prophet and the saviour. Finally we come to the gods. Note that God arrived relatively late in the history of religions! Here we have angels, demons, the 'Sondergötter' (gods for special occasions), the many gods of polytheism, the high gods, and we end with the father God of creation.

With all this we have sketched the *object of religion*. Phenomenology continues with the subject of religion, the object and the subject in their reciprocal action, the world, the various forms of the different religions, etc. We shall confine ourselves to the theory of the object of religion. It is clear that Van der Leeuw moves from the general to the particular and qualified powers. However, as I said, the whole should not be regarded as a historic evolution, but as a structural framework. The theory does not pretend to conform to historical reality, though it may provide a better understanding of it.

The same scheme can be found in *art*. Van der Leeuw starts with life that is rhythmically caught in dance. The dance is the art of movement. Then drama follows, the art of movement and countermovement. Thus drama is more complicated than dance, i.e. it has more characteristics. The centre of art is formed by the beautiful word. Like Kant, Kierkegaard, Heidegger and others, Van der Leeuw regards poetry as the highest form of art. The plastic and graphic arts, architecture and music are more at the periphery. The whole is sustained by the word incarnate, Jesus Christ: 'All the beauty in heaven and on earth is united in Thee alone'.

Although Van der Leeuw was sometimes tempted into saying that the dance is the oldest form of art, thus resorting to a chronological, evolutionary terminology which he wanted to avoid, we must once more interpret this scheme structurally. The gradual separation of religion and art, however, is an historical event. Out of a state of original unity they gradually diverged. According to Van der Leeuw, there is hope for a future harmony, of which he gives certain indications.

In *theology (dogmatics)* Van der Leeuw advocates a highly original theology of the sacraments. Having treated the various relevant biblical texts he starts with a comparative treatment of the sacraments in the various religions. In the primitive religions man knows that he cannot simply accept life. Thus the sacramental view of life originates. In life man cannot dispose of things and events as he likes. The possibility of life is guaranteed by mobilising the power of things. Thus there is a multitude of sacraments. Any vital activity may be a *sacramentale*: eating, drinking, singing, etc. The church's sacraments emerge from these *sacramentalia* by their special character. The sacraments too are sustained by the incarnation of Christ. Human activities in the service of the sacraments perform an official duty. Even the poet and the artist hold in some way an office in the service of mankind. For they too give life a special qualification. Art is not a matter of leisure; it stands in the service of life in order to promote and sustain it. Here too we find Van der Leeuw's framework: in the stream of life man forms shapes, figures, forms of life and it is only through them that life becomes possible. Man plays his role in life, or, what comes to the same thing, he performs his office.

Liturgy too takes place in the midst of life according to Van der Leeuw. It does not stop at the church door. A pupil of Van der Leeuw expressed the thoughts of his master in the following characteristic way: (Van Ruler) 'The cigar after the service also belongs to the liturgy'. It is true that a Christian's spiritual life with his Lord is concentrated in the sacraments of baptism and the Lord's Supper, but the other forms of life too are shaped in Christ and thus receive a devotional consecration, through which they become part of life's liturgy.

The *spiritual song* and the *church hymn* emerged out of worldly songs, especially their melodies. The Church songs are more qualified, more specific than the worldly ones. They are more orientated towards the Lord, but we have here the same situation as with the sacraments. Out of ordinary life special characteristics emerge which are more directed towards the Lord, but in principle everything belongs to the Lord and is sustained by the power of his incarnation. This general scheme is present in the whole of Van der Leeuw's work. In a stream of general activities a gradual concentration takes place, which has its centre in the incarnation of Christ.

Though Van der Leeuw does not equate symbol and sacrament completely, they are closely related. A symbol is not something unreal, 'symbolic' in the modern sense. On the contrary, it expresses the divine (God, the Holy) and refers to it. A symbol is not something static and substantial. It also takes place, it is a holy activity. For Van der Leeuw every sacrament is a symbol, but not vice versa. A sacrament always includes a certain activity, but there are static symbols: the cross in Christianity, the wheel in Hinduism and Buddhism, etc. These are symbols in a narrower sense, and they are no sacraments.

Van der Leeuw's symbolic and sacramental thinking which pervades his whole work is founded on a specific world view and anthropology, namely a kind of primitive world view in which there is no longer a devaluation of matter and the body. Matter and body too are possibilities, i.e. they have the potential power to transcend the given. In accordance with this Van der Leeuw teaches the resurrection of the body and not the immortality of the soul. He also holds the view that the body is a subject, thus anticipating Merleau-Ponty's well-known ideas.

That we know God or the Holy only by means of symbols and sacramental activities, ensues from the fact that a direct knowledge and experience of God is impossible. There is a development in Van der Leeuw's thought here. Originally he did speak of a direct experience of the presence of God. He was of the opinion that in this way he could solve the difficult problem of the relation between belief and history, i.e. how eternal truths could have an historical foundation. Since historical events are always fluid and uncertain, how can they be – as is taught in the Christian doctrine – the foundation of belief? For the life, death and resurrection of Christ are the centre and heart of the Christian faith.

Many theologians and philosophers have tried to give a satisfactory answer to this question. In his earlier period Van der Leeuw thought that he could refer to the living Christ in our hearts. That experience is the best evidence that the Lord lived in historical reality. No historical proof is necessary. In this way direct knowledge by experience is the foundation of an eternal truth. But later he rejected this position and referred to it as a 'metabasis eis allo genos'. Nowadays one would qualify such a reasoning as a confusion of language games or as a category mistake. Direct experience of the Lord is on a level that differs from that of historical truths. According to the later Van der Leeuw it is only possible to know God indirectly, by means of symbols and sacraments.

In this connection it is also important to emphasize that according to Van der Leeuw's epistemology we never get to know things really by means of a contemplating attitude. Knowing always includes an activity. I do not know a mountain really before I have climbed it. I do not know Einstein's theory of relativity until I can work with it and explain it. Knowing is seeing, acting and speaking. Here Van der Leeuw anticipates Wittgenstein's view in *Philosophical Investigations*, in which the latter maintains a close relation between knowing something and operating with it. In his *Bemerkungen über Frazers Golden Bough* Wittgenstein criticizes Frazer for interpreting primitive religion as a prescientific world view. Frazer did not realize that religion is a kind of living and knowing of its own and not a kind of explanation of the world. This is exactly what Van der Leeuw said! Still the two may never have read each other.

Does man invent sacraments and symbols or does he discover them? Is man passive or active when he takes something as a symbol? Though man is always active, a symbol is never arbitrary, it is always necessary. Here Van der Leeuw refers to Jung's doctrine of archetypes (in his later works). In his subconsciousness man keeps ancient primordial symbols. They receive their form in the cult and rites, but also in myths and fairy tales. Symbols are more or less imposed on man. If man, however, does not open his ears and eyes he does not see the symbolic meaning of the things of the world and of life's events, he will not understand the language of symbols. Although we live in a time that is poor in 'natural' symbols, man needs them and so he invents them. Thus, the forming of symbols man is receptive, but at the same time inventive, and if he receives no stimulus, he creates symbols himself. Van der Leeuw gives many examples of this process, but even mentioning them here would take us too far.

In symbol and sacrament man tries to reach another realm by means of everyday forms and activities (eating, drinking, coitus, speaking, education, etc.). This other realm can be one's own inner self or the world. Further, one can try to establish a relation with the world as if one is its ruler and lord, as in magic, or one can see oneself as a part of a greater whole. Or one may see oneself and the world as being directed by yet another. As a phenomenologist Van der Leeuw merely describes the various ways of a symbolic life, but as a Christian philosopher and theologian he chooses for a view in which rites and liturgy (in life and in worship) have an eschatological meaning and are connected with God's creation and salvation.

Though one cannot adduce intellectual arguments for this choice, it need not be arbitrary. Some rational arguments can be brought forward: man is a never completed and fulfilled being, he is always on his way to a certain end and goal. He can only give a partial sense to his many activities and to the events he experiences. But this giving of a partial sense requires a total, all-embracing sense, which we can find neither in ourselves, nor in the world. A third being appears on the scene: God, my creator. Admittedly, this way of arguing has the structure of the dialectic of the infinity which has its weaknesses, but Van der Leeuw was fully aware of this himself. He never presented his arguments as convincing proofs.

2.7.4 *Evaluation*

However convincing all this may be for the religious and theological mind, it is totally unsatisfactory for philosophy. To say simply that the religious language game is played, or that it is a form of life (Wittgenstein), or a matter of revelation (Barth), or both (Van der Leeuw) is to abstain from any argument, and that can never be a philosophical attitude. We have seen that Van der Leeuw sometimes gives an (unsatisfactory) argumentation, which is not sufficient to provide a foundation for religion, though it lends some support to his choice for Christianity.

Now, we must admit that in philosophy of religion no argument can be completely satisfactory, because we have to start with some premises which can always be doubted. This is of course the case in all sciences, but in some sciences scholars have at least agreed upon certain generally accepted premises. In philosophy of religion, as in other non-natural sciences and arts, however, there are no generally accepted premises! Whatever the difficulties, abstaining from all arguments is an unnecessary capitulation to irrationalism! One has to choose, that is evident. I am prepared to choose for a way that is as rational as possible.

2.8 *Logic of religion. Logical reconstructivism*

We have seen that one of the difficulties for an appeal to religious experience was the multitude of different experiences in this realm. Which one may we trust? Can we trust, without investigation, our own experiences? Certain experiences appeal to one person, other experiences appeal to another. Shall we say that religious experience is a wholly personal matter? Shall we say that in religion one can only give witness to one's faith, and that there are no means of convincing one another? In my view logic of religion can help us to conduct a more rational discussion, although it is evident that we can never come to a universal agreement. One has to choose, as we have seen. But much has been gained already if we realize on what arguments the various religions are founded.

We shall try to find methods that will help us to discover the rational presuppositions of the various religions. The method which I shall employ is not only valid in philosophy of religion, it is a general method of representing philosophical positions as strongly as possible, that is, as interesting as possible and not easily refutable. This method, which we label *logical reconstructivism*, does not give rules for understanding an author; neither does it try to solve definitively the question whether certain statements of the philosopher are true or not. Rather, it tries to make a discussion of these statements as fair and as profitable as possible. Our method concentrates on the arguments and conclusions of a certain author. In order to have a fair discussion with him, logical reconstructivism tries to make his standpoint as strong as possible by improving his arguments, if necessary. Of course, besides this method of logical reconstructivism other methods, e.g. historical investigation, remain valid and useful. But I think that for a fair discussion we should not try to make use of some incidental weak points in the argument of our discussion partner. Though victory would be easy, it will not be very convincing and will not contribute to progress in a philosophical discussion. Let us first sketch the general scheme of our method.

Suppose a philosopher draws a conclusion C from a number of premises p_1, p_2, ...p_n. Now the following cases are possible:

I.   The conclusion C follows from the premises. We accept the premises and therefore also the conclusion.

II.   The conclusion C follows the premises, but we dot not accept one or more premises.

III. The conclusion C does not follow from the premises.

Here a subdivision is possible:

(i) The conclusion C is inconsistent with one or more of the premises; in other words: the contradiction of C (non-C) can be inferred from the premises.

(ii) The conclusion is not inconsistent with one or more of the premises, or in other words: neither C nor its contradiction (non-C) can be inferred from the premises.

Whereas case (I) does not yield any difficulty, the other cases demand our attention. The second case *sub* (III) (III.ii) is the basic one, because the other cases can be reduced to it. In case II we can simply delete the premises with which we do not agree, so that case (III.ii) arises, if the conclusion no longer follows from the premises. The same is true for case (III.i): we can simply delete those premises from which the contradiction of C can be inferred. By doing so we create again case (III.ii). Let us now look at this case more closely. As given, the premises $p_1 \ldots p_n$ do not yield the conclusion C. Now we can always add one or more premises to the number of premises $p_1 \ldots p_n$, so that the conclusion C can be inferred, now from the premises $p_1 \ldots p_{n+1}$ or $p_1 \ldots p_{n+m}$. In doing so we must obey the usual 'principle of economy' by trying to be as strict as possible. That means that:

1. The number of premises added should be as small as possible.

2. The premises added should say as little as possible, for the less the premises say, the less they presuppose and the more chance they have to be true and to be accepted.

For suppose a statement p_i says less than a statement p_j i.e. p_i refers to fewer supposed facts than p_j; then p_i can be more easily inferred from other premises. Therefore, if the addition of both p_i and p_j can render a certain argument correct, p_i is to be preferred to p_j. Of course, what 'fewer facts' and 'saying less' mean in a concrete case cannot always be decided unambiguously. Instead of adding new premises we can also add new and stronger rules of inference, that is, we can make our logical system stronger, i.e. less strict. Here again, however, the 'principle of economy' requires that:

3. Our logical system should be as strict as possible.

Since a rule of inference, however, can very often be transformed into a logical theorem, there is usually no fundamental difference between adding a new rule of inference or adding a new premise. Further it is evident that the premises added must have a maximum of plausibility. This is already implied by what has been said *sub* 2.

The advantage of this method of logical reconstructivism is that a better discussion is possible. It does not, of course, mean that we must accept the premises or the conclusion beforehand. On the contrary. The point is that we present our discussion partner as strongly as possible by attempting to prove his conclusion in a system that is strict as possible.

The same holds for the discussion between the various religions. In principle one can try to prove the truth of certain religious statements with the help of *philosophical* arguments. Such a religious statement can also be founded on revelation, but revelation is not a philosophical concept and such an appeal is philosophically invalid. This does not mean that a statement that is presented as founded on revelation cannot be proved by reason. In principle one can try to bring forward rational arguments for any statement, so why not for statements founded on revelation, provided they are not self-contradictory?

If we extend what we have said so far, we can also try to prove the truth not only of a particular religious statement, but also of a whole religion. In this way the philosophical presuppositions of every religion that claims to be founded on revelation can be investigated. These philosophical premises are thus implicitly, not explicitly, present in such a religion. Of course, we may appeal to religious experiences or dialectical logic in order to prove certain religious statements or a certain religion, if this is necessary. Whether such an argument is convincing or not depends on whether we ourselves, or the readers, etc. are willing to accept its presuppositions or not.

There is a complexity here which should not be overlooked. In order to give our reconstructions we must appeal to what Peirce called abduction and Bocheński reduction. And that means that the discussion remains open, for we can always try to find better arguments. This can easily be shown:

Suppose we want to prove statement p. This can usually be done in various ways:

I	II	III
$q \rightarrow p$	$r \rightarrow p$	$s \rightarrow p$
q	r	s
p	p	p

When argument I turns out to be invalid, some others remain. In this way one never reaches once and for all 'the' presuppositions of a certain religion. Moreover, if one does not want to accept a certain religious statement, one can also try to find a stricter system in which this religious statement cannot be derived as a conclusion. One is never forced to accept particular religious statements. Notice however: if a certain person accepts certain premises from which certain religious statements can be drawn as conclusions, he must accept them too, unless he withdraws his premises. But in that case he must withdraw these premises in the whole of his system. He is not allowed – as is done so often – to reject the views he does not like in a stricter system and prove his own views in another!

From all this it may be clear that no religion can be definitely refuted. I do not claim that the application of this method of logical reconstructivism can definitely settle the discussion between various religions or between religions and atheism. In our fourth chapter I shall discuss various religious convictions and statements in some detail and endeavour to give the strongest possible arguments for the various standpoints. In the rest of this section I shall consider some religions as a whole, and give very broad arguments in favour of each one of them. Again, I do not pretend that in this way the truth of one religion can be proved conclusively, but much would be gained if representatives of the various religions and of atheism decided to enter into a rational discussion instead of offering declarations and confessions of faith or even fighting each other.

Are there any arguments to prove the truth of the Christian faith? Although Barth never pretended to do so in a rational way, he put forward some impressive arguments in favour of Christianity in his main work *Kirchliche Dogmatik* (1932 ff) (Church Dogmatics). He shows that the decisive characteristic of the biblical God is that he, as Lord, can at the same time be a servant. He can be great even in his smallness, he can be majestic, even in his humiliation. In other religions the gods may have many splendid virtues, they cannot be Lord and servant at the same time, they cannot be great and at the same time humiliate themselves, etc. If we take as a premise of God's power (*potentia Dei*): a power which is both extensively and intensively greater than can ever be thought of, then the Christian concept of God follows from this premise. Whether or not God's power should be defined as such is another matter, but if it is done, the Christian concept of God follows from it and other concepts of God do not.

In order to prevent any misunderstandings we must add that Barth himself does not pretend to give proofs in such an abstract way. He gives absolute priority to God's concrete revelation in Christ, which he calls the *reality* of revelation and only after accepting this can one inquire into its *possibility*, i.e. its relations to other human concepts and possibilities; but even here revelation cannot be made plausible. Whatever Barth's official theory was, he is more rational in the actual way he is arguing! In general, however, he had no taste for philosophical arguments, in contrast to his brother Heinrich Barth, a splendid (Christian) philosopher, and his original fellow-traveller in theology, E. Brunner. In a personal conversation he once said that he was prepared to give an impressive eulogy on philosophy, but, he added ironically, it had to be an eulogy at the tomb.

However, it is indeed possible to put forward philosophical presuppositions of the Christian faith. Kierkegaard did so in a masterly way in his *Philosophiske Smuler* (1844). He presupposed – just as a hypothesis – that the moment in time has decisive significance. From this purely philosophical hypothesis he deduced the main dogmas of the Christian faith (*vide* 2.6.2 and appendix 7).

In my view anyone who wants to defend the Jewish or the Mohammedan religion against Christianity does so best by emphasizing the value of a rigorous religion of duty. In (especially Lutheran Protestant) Christianity the gospel has an absolute priority over the law (*vide* Brunner above). In Judaism and Islam, however, the Law has priority over everything else. Both religions emphasize the moral as well as the ritual Law. If one wants a religion which consists in the fulfilling of duties, one must prefer these religions to traditional Christianity. One might object to the various ritual prescriptions which are given in these religions. In that case a more liberal Judaism or liberal Mohammedanism is certainly a way out. Both religions have these liberal variants. It may be difficult to decide between the two religions, for they are closely related. That explains perhaps the vehement struggle between them. But the latter is probably more of a political than of a religious nature; this is also the official version of their present confrontation. On the other hand there are many examples of mutual respect, especially over against Christianity: 'If I meet two Arabs and one of them is drunk, he is, without doubt, a Christian', said an Israelian once to me.

A major difference between the two religions concerns the issue of determinism versus indeterminism. The latter is predominant in Judaism, the former in Islam, though in both religions there are rival views. Of course, there are moralistic tendencies in Christianity too, but there usually other teachings are added. It might be the case, however, that in certain, especially liberal, forms of Judaism, Christianity and Islam, the emphasis on morals has superseded all the other elements in such a way that there is hardly any difference between them. In this case the necessity of choosing has diminished, and we see also that such forms of religion, together with liberal forms of Hinduism and Buddhism, work easily together in practice (for instance in the *International Religious Fellowship*).

If one assumes, however, that that form of religion is true which has the greatest synthetic power, the richest variations in devotion and the best techniques of meditation, Hinduism might be a likely candidate, although Buddhism and (Roman Catholic and Orthodox) Christianity have also made important contributions in this field. A comparison of Hindu and Christian meditation techniques on the one hand and Buddhist techniques on the other brings to light an important difference. The former try to give man a harmonious backing in life, whereas the latter try to teach man resignation. One may defend Buddhism, if one supports a mysticism which teaches experience without thinking, which may lead to the void, the 'full void' of Nirvana, in which both subject and object disappear. In Buddhism it is taught that one should try to reach experience without thinking, i.e. without logic. Therefore especially in certain forms of Zen-Buddhism, the practice of Koan is predominant in which the pupil must learn to think in logical contradictories, that is, learn to give up logic. Only then may he reach experience without logic (thinking). In Western thought this is impossible, but how can we prove that our view is more than a cultural tradition? We shall come back to these and similar views later on in this book.

If one wants to defend the Chinese religion (or better the religion of South East Asia, where we may find the same trend everywhere), I think one should refer to the concept of harmony as a fundamental principle. Chinese philosophy presupposes that two principles, Yang and Yin, which are dialectically opposed to each other, pervade the whole world and that there is no synthesis between the two, but that they must be kept in balance everywhere. Perhaps the Maoist thesis that a synthesis between the various contradictions is impossible, is a remnant of old Chinese tradition, although this view also occurs in Marxism outside China (Stalin, the school of Althusser, etc.). If we accept this dialectic of polarity we could put forward proofs of the truth of the Chinese, Japanese, Javanese or Bali religion. In the latter two there is an official predominance of (respectively) Islam and Hinduism, but these two religions manifest themselves here only in an outward form. Under the surface there remains a kind of religion (or philosophy, world view) of harmony and harmonious opposing forces. Atheism can also be proved in this way.

It might be interesting to point out that it is easier to prove the existence of God than to give a proof of atheism, that is, the proofs of God's existence can be given in much stricter systems than the proofs of atheism. As we shall see, we need 'only' the multiple application of the rule 'ex nihilo nihil fit' and the modal system S_5 (or the modal systems S_4 and some additions) in order to complete the cosmological proof. Atheism, however, is much more difficult to prove. Even if we suppose that in our system the rule mentioned above is not valid, then the conclusion is only that our cosmological argument fails, not that we have proved atheism. Even if one tries to prove dialectical materialism with the help of certain kinds of dialectical logic (and this means that we have less strict system!) we need in addition to it the rejection of the multiple application of the rule 'ex nihilo nihil fir', because otherwise God reappears as the creator of this dialectically structured matter. And even if we presuppose all this we have not yet proved atheism; we have only proved that we can construct a system without introducing God.

The case of atheism may be best defended in the following way. We refrain from any positive proof of the non-existence of God. Instead, we defend a theoretical agnosticism in which the question of the existence or non-existence of God remains undecided. With this theoretical agnosticism we connect a practical atheism, in which it is stated that we need not accept God's existence in practical life. I think that most people are atheists in this way: out of practical indifference, not out of a deep atheistic conviction. In addition, justified objections against the Church as a religious institution may be added. A moral argument against God's existence may also be raised: whence all the evil in the world, if there is an almighty and loving God?

From the fact that theism can be proved in a stricter system than atheism, we are not allowed to conclude that theism is more probable. This follows from the well-known fact that in theism an existential and in atheism a universal statement has to be proved. In theism we have to prove a statement of the form Ex (fx), whereas in atheism the negation of this form has to be proved: $\sim$ Ex (fx), which is equivalent to the universal statement: x ($\sim$ fx). And as is well-known, universal statements that are not analytic are much more difficult to prove than existential statements, because in the latter case showing the existence of one case is sufficient, whereas universal statements can never be proved in a strict sense, but only made more or less plausible.

2.9 *Religious language*

We have seen above (2.4.2) that Van Baaren and other scholars interpret religious experience as ordinary experience which has been put into a religious framework. On the whole I agree with this view, although we should probably make an exception for mystical experience. This kind of experience claims to be a direct experience of God, at least in its highest moments. One of the arguments used by Van Baaren is borrowed from religious language. According to him religious words are words out of the non-religious realm, which have gotten a metaphorical meaning. On the basis of etymological investigations in the Indo-European languages C. Watkins is of the opinion, that there is a whole series of words with an original religious sense. That is the opposite of what Van Baaren says. In a brief investigation I myself came to the conclusion that most of the words Watkins mentioned as being originally religious, had in fact originally a profane meaning. Only some of the words in his list did have an original religious meaning: e.g. *sak-* (cp. Latin *sacer*); *wegh* – (to preach); *sep-el-yo* (to venetrate the dead). The last word is a good example of the reverse movement, *viz.* that a word loses its original religious meaning and gets a profane meaning, for this word led to the Latin *sepelire*, to bury.

The typical religious feature in linguistic usage, however, is due to unusual combinations of words rather than an original religious meaning. Let us consider some representative examples:
1. First of all an example of an unusual word composition. When the Dutch (Netherlandish) mystic Ruusbroec speaks about the contemplation of God he says among other things: '(The souls will rest) ...inder onwisen, daer wij weder in gode sterven in een eewich salich leven...' (The souls will rest... in an 'unmode', for we die again in God in an eternal, blissful life). The word 'onwisen' does not exist in Dutch. It seems to mean something like

unlimitedness, superrational, 'without limiting modes', etc. This quotation is also an example of 3, *viz.* of an unusual semantic combination.

2. In religious literature an unusual combination of an adjective and a substantive very often occurs. For example, the Frisian religious poet Gysbert Japicx, who lived in the 17th century and wrote in the Frisian language of his day, says to God:

'Jôn rjuechterhân to ljeaflijkckheyt on-buwne
Jouwt swiet op swiet, uwt de "ijvigg-swiete" ingruwne'

(Your right hand untied to loveliness gives sweet things to sweet things (gives bliss to bliss) out of the eternal sweet abyss).

Now, an 'eternal sweet abyss' is an unusual combination, but it is understandable in its religious context.

3. We may also find unusual semantic combinations. A certain verb and a certain substantive never occur together in one sentence, unless that sentence has a religious significance. For example, the statement '...has created the world' is only possible in a religious context, possibly also in a religious metaphysical context. Only God can occupy the open space.

It was I.T. Ramsey who did pioneer work in this field. He points out that religious language has its own context and its own 'odd' logic. At first Ramsey seems to introduce the dialectic of infinity again and in a certain sense he does, but he is aware of it and knows that it is not a scientific way of argumentation. It serves only to evoke something in people.

Ramsey employs two key concepts, *viz. disclosure situation* and *qualified model*. Religious states of affairs are always more than empirical situations which can be analysed with the help of instruments and other scientific means. Religious knowledge emerges with the help of an enlightenment and a *disclosure*. There are also non-religious disclosures and Ramsey starts his expositions usually with giving examples of the latter sort. For example: a teacher draws a number of polygons on the blackboard in such a sequence that the number of sides is continuously increasing. What is the result if the number of sides is more and more approaching infinity (or in a mathematically better formulation: if the number of sides becomes greater than any possible number)? Probably, though one cannot be quite sure, a student sees that the structure of the polygon turns into that of a circle. If he does, something has been disclosed to him.

The qualified model is connected with the disclosure. In religious language the disclosure refers to something and has an objective character. The qualified model has the purpose of articulating what has been disclosed. As an example Ramsey gives the model of speaking about God as the *first cause*. The concept of cause is the model with which we speak about God. But God is not a cause in the ordinary sense of the word. Therefore the qualification 'first' serves to attract our special attention. It refers to the fact that God is a cause of a very special sort, even when we have already understood that we use the word 'cause' in an analogous sense. So the unusual combination of 'first' and 'cause' (*vide* above sub 2) may bring about a disclosure in those who have grasped this remarkable connection. In this respect Ramsey makes the important distinction between finite disclosures in ordinary daily life and cosmic disclosures which refer to God. Ramsey wants to be an empirical philosopher in the proper, though somewhat broadened, sense.

Religious language and particularly the word 'God' must have an *empirical fit*. That means that statements in which the word 'God' occurs, are tested to see whether or not they can serve as a comprehensive characteristic of a whole complex of statements, i.e. whether or not many other statements follow from them. The word 'God' shows itself to be a useful elevator- or apex-word. It plays a role in the background of all speaking if we investigate our use of language thoroughly enough. Ramsey also shows that to all our statements, even the most neutral ones, 'I say...' must be added, which means that there is always a personal background in all our scientific work. An apparently objective situation can become a personal one through a disclosure.

Ramsey gives the story of 2 Sam. 12.1-7 as an example. David had Uria killed in order to marry the latter's wife, Bathseba. The prophet Nathan addresses himself to David with a story of a rich man, who had many herds of cattle and sheep, but still took possession of the only lamb of his poor neighbour in order to treat his guests to a good meal. A completely objective story and David reacted to it also in a completely objective and impersonal manner with the words: 'This man has to die'. But then Nathan says: 'You are this man' and now the penny drops: a disclosure takes place. Nathan's logical exercise consists in describing certain events in such a way, that when they are compared with David's deeds a disclosure could follow. David acknowledges his guilt.

In his lectures Ramsey often told stories in order to evoke a disclosure in his audience. If during the discussion someone told him that a certain story did not appeal to him, Ramsey answered laconically: 'Let us take another story'. There have been more analytical philosophers who worked with stories. Braithwaite,for instance, is of the opinion that the gospel is a set of stories, which serve to inspire people to a moral attitude. Ramsey, however, goes deeper. He has not only a moral attitude in view, but also aims at a cosmic disclosure, by which we may see that all our speaking and thinking is sustained by God's speaking. Religious language is descriptive *and more*. Man has to commit himself to God if he wants to adopt a religious attitude.

Thus according to Ramsey, in religious language there is certainly an element of referring to states of affairs (the creation of the world by God, the love of God for man, etc.), but it includes more (confidence, a moral attitude, commitment to God, etc.). Thus, in Ramsey's view religion certainly includes morality, but it is more. It certainly includes belief in facts, but it is more. It is certainly confidence, but it is more...

W. de Pater who introduced Ramsey's ideas in the Netherlands and Germany, continues Ramsey's work in his own way. He combines Ramsey's thoughts with Austin's analyses and with the results of modern linguistic theories. Austin has called the function or role of the speech-act in communication its illocutionary force. What is meant by this may be illustrated with the following example: In the following four sentences the content or meaning (locution) is the same, but the illocutionary force is different, for in the first sentence it is a communication, in the second it is a question, in the third it is a command and in the fourth it is an encouragement.

1. (I say, that) John comes.
2. Does John come?
3. I order that John comes.
4. Let John come!

Obviously the illocutionary force is not always in agreement with the grammatical mode. I once proposed, not yet acquainted with Austin's theories, to speak of a *communicative mode* in contrast to *grammatical modes*. If one of my children leaves the door open, I call loudly: 'The door is open'. Grammatically this sentence is in the indicative mode (mood), communicatively it is in the imperative mode, for it is my intention to say: 'Close the door!' The indicative sentence functions as a part of an implicit argument, because in the language game played the obligation is valid: The door ought to be closed. So we have:

(i)   The door ought to be closed
(ii)   The door is open
_____
(C)   Close the door.

I say only (ii) but have the intention to say (C).

With respect to religious statements it is important to ascertain which operators constitute the illocutionary force of these statements. De Pater shows how in Ramsey's theory of disclosure situations and qualitative models an answer can be given to the problems which may arise here.

De Pater does not only work with the help of Ramsey and Austin and his school (Searle and others), he also applies modern linguistic theories and thus he can show what restriction and admission rules constitute a peculiar utterance such as 'God has created the world' (*vide* appendix 1). 'Peculiar' must be interpreted here in the sense of Ramsey's 'odd': an unusual semantic combination.

Whatever all these linguistic means and techniques may contribute to a better understanding and interpretation of religious language, according to De Pater the attitude of the believers and the act of faith in the religious language still remain fundamental. In the background of all religious language God himself is present. 'The illocutionary force of God's creative words has constituted the situation in which the speaking and the activities of the believers are the appropriate answer. That the believer knows this, is a matter of faith; he is convinced that his activities are in conformity with reality'.

3
The philosophical doctrine of God

3.1 *The arguments for God's existence*

For a long time the arguments for God's existence were considered to be obsolete, because they were said to have been refuted by Kant (2.6.1). It is astonishing that these arguments recently underwent a kind of revival, for our time strongly emphasizes exactness and a scientific attitude. This revival can be traced back to the fact that Kant's refutations are considered dated now. Kant founded his refutations on his epistemology, which was based on Euclidian geometry, Newtonian mechanics and Aristotelian logic. As all these sciences are more or less dated now, Kant's epistemology is no longer sacrosanct.

Even more important are the following considerations. In his epistemology Kant presupposed that the logical relations are always valid and that they are not influenced by the forms of perception and the categories. In Kant's view these forms and categories are, as we have seen, the constituents of human experience. With their help the human mind is able to order the multitude of chaotic sensations. Kant infers these categories from Aristotelian logic, which is therefore presupposed. In other words even for Kant the logical relations must be applied to the Thing-in-itself (*Das Ding an sich*). In this respect Kant agrees with Leibniz.

With the help of modern logic too one can demonstrate that logical statements can be made about the Thing-in-itself, hence about God's world. Logical relations are true in all possible worlds, hence also in God's world.

If one applies the important rule *ex nihilo nihil fit* and interprets this rule timelessly, even a Kantian epistemology cannot overthrow it. Moreover, as I have already indicated, many objections can be raised against Kantian epistemology. In the following pages I shall pay special attention to the two most important arguments for God's existence: the ontological and the cosmological argument. Further the argument from design (the teleological or the physico-theological argument (*argumentum physico-theologicum*)) and some other arguments will be considered.

3.1.1 *Terminology*

Traditionally the ontological argument was understood as a proof that had the *concept* of God as a starting-point. This concept was defined in various ways. From it God's existence was inferred. No use was made of the existence of the world, in contradistinction to some other arguments. The cosmological argument does presuppose the world's existence, but without any further detailing of its content. What is in the world and the relations of the things in the world to each other are not considered. The pure fact that there is something and that this is considered to be astonishing, asks for an explanation. By contrast in the argument from design the content of the world *is* considered. The relations of the things of the world to each other are the starting-point of the argument. In these relations a certain design, a certain plan is discovered, which requires an explanation.

This traditional classification needs further qualification, particularly in respect to the ontological argument. This proof, in which from a concept alone existence was inferred, has always been considered with considerable mistrust and not without reason. I myself am still hesitating whether to accept this argument or not. I am quite willing to accept the cosmological argument, which is more convincing, but proves less. On the whole this is the structure of all argument and the arguments for God's existence are no exception to this rule: the more convincing a proof is, i.e. the less it presupposes, the less it proves.

Traditionally the ontological argument is said to derive existence from a concept without presupposing anything else, not even the existence of the world. This seems to be a magician's trick. As we shall see, a more careful analysis of the proof shows that in its presuppositions there is more taken for granted. If we want a proof of a real, and not a merely mental, existence of God we must presuppose that there is something. We need not presuppose that this world is, but at least something must exist. Of course, the existence of our world implies the existence of something, but the dictum 'there exists something' is weaker than the dictum 'this world exists'. Without accepting at least the former we cannot establish anything. The difference with the cosmological argument is that in the latter use in made of the principle of causality (causa efficiens or the principle of sufficient and/or necessary condition). In the ontological argument the *vis argumenti* (the power of the argument), to use a Spinozistic term, still remains the concept of God and not the existence of anything.

3.1.2 *The ontological argument*

The ontological argument knows many variants of which we shall discuss four. Our attention will be mainly focused on Anselm's argument, which is and remains the most important. The other protagonists to be discussed are Hartshorne, who gives a modern, very interesting re-interpretation which has many advantages, and Spinoza, who presents in my view one of the most interesting philosophies in the world, but whose version of the ontological argument is less interesting than his version of the cosmological argument. Next, we shall discuss a relatively unknown thinker, *viz.* Breedenburg, who opposed Spinoza in his day and who has given an interesting 'cabbalistic' variant of the ontological argument. Finally, we will evaluate the various variants.

3.1.2.1 *Anselm*

The ontological argument is the sublime creation of Anselm. It is, whatever its merits, an ingenious discovery. The other proofs – the cosmological and teleological arguments – have already been known since antiquity. They are also 'natural' in that they occur also in the minds of non-philosophers, though, of course, without the whole technical apparatus. One may very likely hear 'the man in the street' say, even if he does not believe in the God of the churches: 'I am sure that there must be some power who has made this world. It could not have emerged from nothing' (a popular presentation of the cosmological argument) and 'Look at the beauty of these flowers, it cannot have come here in this world spontaneously' (a popular presentation of the argument from design).

Though I have heard such sayings several times I never heard anyone presenting a popular version of the ontological argument. Anselm himself discovered the argument after having presented the other arguments. He was, however, dissatisfied with them, because in his view they made God dependent on the world, or at least on something outside him (*vide* 2.5.2). Hartshorne and Malcolm have pointed out that there are two versions of the argument. Anselm presents them in the second and third chapter of his *Proslogium*:

(2) 'And so, Lord, do thou, who dost give understanding to faith, give me, so far as thou knowest it to be profitable, to understand that thou art as we believe; and that thou art that which we believe. And, indeed, we believe that thou art a being than which nothing greater can be conceived. Or is there no such nature, since the fool hath said in his heart, there is no God? (Psalms xiv. 1). But, at any rate, this very fool, when he hears of this being of which I speak – a being than which nothing greater can be conceived – understands what he hears, and what he understands is in his understanding; although he does not understand it to exist.

For, it is one thing for an object to be in the understanding, and another to understand that the object exists. When a painter first conceives of what he will afterwards perform, he has it in his understanding, but he does not yet understand it to be, because he has not yet performed it. But after he has made the painting, he both has it in his understanding and he understands that it exists, because he has made it.

Hence, even the fool is convinced that something exists in the understanding, at least, than which nothing greater can be conceived. For, when he hears of this, he understands it. And whatever is understood exists in the understanding. And assuredly that, than which nothing greater can be conceived, cannot exist in the understanding alone. For, suppose it exists in the understanding alone: then it can be conceived to exist in reality; which is greater.

Therefore, if that, than which nothing greater can be conceived, exists in the understanding alone, the very being, than which nothing greater can be conceived, is one, than which a greater can be conceived. But obviously this is impossible. Hence, there is no doubt that there exists a being, than which nothing greater can be conceived, and it exists both in the understanding and in reality'.

(3) 'And it assuredly exists so truly, that it cannot be conceived not to exist. For, it is possible to conceive of a being which cannot be conceived not to exist; and this is greater than one which can be conceived not to exist. Hence, if that, than which nothing greater can be conceived, can be conceived not to exist, it is not that, than which nothing greater can be conceived. But this is an irreconcilable contradiction. There is, then, so truly a being than which nothing greater can be conceived to exist, that it canot even be conceived not to exist; and this being thou art, O Lord, our God.

So truly, therefore, dost thou exist, O Lord, my God, that thou canst not be conceived not to exist; and rightly. For, if a mind could conceive of a being better than thee, the creature would rise above the Creator; and this is most absurd. And, indeed, whatever else there is, except thee alone, can be conceived not to exist. To thee alone, therefore, it belongs to exist more truly than all other beings, and hence in a higher degree than all others. For, whatever else exists does not exist so truly, and hence in a less degree it belongs to it to exist. Why, then, has the fool said in his heart, there is no God (Psalms xiv.1), since it is so evident, to a rational mind, that thou dost exist in the highest degree of all? Why, except that he is dull and a fool?'

What has escaped the notice of previous scholars, is that there are two versions in Anselm's argument . The proof in chapter 2 is different from that in chapter 3. By comparing them it can be shown that the variant in chapter 3 is more profound and more convincing from a logical point of view. Remarkably enough, the variant in chapter 2 has drawn most of the attention of the scholars. In chapter 2 Anselm starts from the view that it is meaningful to conceive of a being, of which it is said that nothing greater than this being can be thought of. Taking the concept of 'a being greater than which nothing can be conceived' as meaningful, is already a considerable presupposition. For after all a number greater than which nothing can be conceived is *not* a meaningful concept and why should the concept of a being defined by Anselm in an analogous way be a meaningful concept. Why should it not be self-contradicory? For the sake of the discussion we will for the moment, suppose that it is not and that it can therefore be thought of without contradictions. According to Anselm even an atheist can conceive of such a being.

Now Anselm makes use of the indirect proof, i.e. of the *reductio ad absurdum*. We have seen above that there are stricter systems in logic in which a proof like this is not valid. In intuitionistic logic one is not allowed to start with a negative hypothesis and, after having inferred a contradiction from this, to conclude that the opposite of the hypothetical statement is true. We may only conclude to the negation of the negative hypothesis, not to the positive statement: $\sim (\sim p)$ is not equivalent to p in intuitionistic logic. Therefore Anselm already presupposes classical logic in his argument. Note, however, that classical logic is the usual logic outside pure mathematics!

Anselm hypothetically assumes that God, i.e. a being greater than which nothing can be conceived of, does not exist. Then we may conceive of this being as existing. This is the second premise. And now Anselm makes a third assumption: If two beings A and B have the same properties, but in addition B exists and A does not, B is greater than A. Now, if the being greater than which nothing can be conceived of, did not exist, then this same being would, if it exists, be greater than the being greater than which nothing can be thought of. And this would be absurd, i.e. it would be a logical contradiction. Consequently, the hypothesis that the being greater than which nothing can be thought of, does not exist, leads to a contradiction and that means that this hypothesis is false and that consequently this being greater than which nothing can be thought of, *does* exist. In other words: God exists. We will now present Anselm's argument in a more clearly arranged scheme. As there are more versions of Anselm's argument, we will label this first one: Variant I.

Anselm's ontological argument. Variant I

Premises (presuppositions)

(i)   A being greater than which nothing can be conceived of, is thinkable, i.e. it exists in our mind. We call this being A.
(ii)   This being greater than which nothing can be conceived of, can be thought of as existing in reality. We call this being B.
(iii)   In two beings A and B are the same in every respect, but B exists in reality and A does not, then B is greater then A.

Proof
1. A does not exist (starting-hypothesis);
2. Then B is greater than A (this follows from (1) and the premises (i) and (ii));
3. But (2) contradicts premise (i);
4. Therefore our starting-hypothesis in (1) is false and has to be negated;
5. Consequently A exists.

From a logical point of view, Anselm's argument is correct, at least in classical logic. That means that if one accepts the three premises, one should also accept the conclusion. However, are these premises indubitable? They are certainly not, and therefore we shall consider them more closely. Let us consider first premise (i). Can we be sure that a being greater than which nothing can be conceived of, is thinkable? Of course, we can speak the words, but do they not lead to a contradiction? Anselm did not consider this problem, but some others did, e.g. Duns Scotus and Leibniz.

An objection that immediately presents itself, is that a greatest number cannot be thought of and that consequently such a being greater than which nothing can be conceived of, is also unthinkable, because it is analogous to such a 'greatest number'. In our day especially Plantinga has seen this difficulty. According to him we must make a careful distinction between a being with maximum greatness, like being A in Anselm's argument, and a greatest number. For one can consider 'maximum greatness' as closed, in that nothing can be added to it. This in contradistinction to the sequence of natural numbers which cannot be closed.

In this respect the concept 'maximum greatness' is analogous to the concept of omniscience. It is not self-contradictory to suppose that a being is omniscient, i.e. that it knows everything that there is and might be. Nothing can be added to this knowledge so that one can consider it closed. In the same way I myself once tried to reduce God's perfection to his omniscience. In this attempt I had to add two more premises that are, at least in my view, plausible, namely, that it is possible to establish an objective hierarchy of values and to interpret omnipotence in a certain way. I may refer to appendix 6 here. Perhaps Hartshorne's solution is even better; we shall come to it later.

The objections against premise (ii) seem to be eliminated, if the objections against (i) are removed. Perhaps one might object that in his argument Anselm identifies A and B too quickly, i.e. that he speaks only about the same being, once as non-existent and, next, as existent. He should perhaps also have considered a being that exists, but that is not to be identified with A. This is only a minor point and we shall give an 'improved' version of Anselm's argument, where this objection is eliminated (*vide* p. 98). More important is the objection that Anselm apparently does not distinguish between a *logical* possibility, i.e. a possibility in thought only and a *real* possibility, i.e. a possibility in the real world, also outside the human mind. We shall treat this problem later.

The objections against (iii) are at first sight very strong. It was Kant, who tried to show that existence is not a predicate. Therefore one cannot say that God lacks perfection, if he does not exist. We have to look into this problem more closely, because it is more complex than one would think at first sight. Kant's argument runs as follows: Existence is not a real predicate. A hundred thalers which are thought of have exactly the same properties as a hundred real thalers. If I add 'existence' to the hundred thalers in my mind I do not add a new property. I only say that the hundred thalers which existed until then in my mind only, now also exist in reality. But a counter-objection presents itself immediately: with the hundred real thalers I can pay my bill, at least in the time of Kant, and even now I myself would prefer a hundred real thalers to a hundred thalers in my mind. Kant made the error of considering the things in themselves and not considering their relations to other things. Thus, a hundred real thalers have some properties in addition to the hundred in my mind, for example, that they are a means of payment.

However, a counter-objection against the counter-objection is possible, *viz.* that relations are not properties because they determine only the outward connections with other things. But is this correct? Are relations not properties? This is a difficult problem. It may be evident that the so called external relations are no properties. At this moment my typewriter is in front of me. If I put it behind me, it does not get new properties. One can claim that it has remained the same typewriter. The relation 'being in front of' is an external relation and this is not a property. But are there only external relations? Some scholars say so, e.g. Russell and others. They are obviously impressed by Kant's criticism.

Other scholars maintain that there are also internal relations, which belong to the essence of the things, i.e. the internal relations cannot be removed from the thing without removing the thing itself. Some scholars, as for example the Hegelian Bradley, say that there are only internal relations. Therefore it is not astonishing that in Hegelian circles interest in the ontological argument is still present. However, what are we going to make of the thalers which exist? Is their being a means of payment an internal or an external relation? Obviously, this problem cannot be solved in isolation, i.e. one can only answer this question within a whole philosophical system. I at least am inclined to think that it is an internal relation (i.e. it belongs to the *essence* of the thalers) and therefore a property.

We can also approach this problem from another angle, *viz.* with the help of set theory. Now in set theory sets are constituted (i.e. defined) by means of an unambigous criterion in virtue of which one may decide whether a certain object belongs to a particular set or not. Whether or not the set is empty, is a question which does not belong to the definition of the set. Insofar Kant is apparently right. However, there are also sets in which 'to exist' or 'to be present in reality' belongs to the definition. One might speak about the set of the now living Englishmen. There is nothing contradictory in such a definition. One can operate meaningfully with such a set. Since the definitions of sets mark their properties, should we now say that existence is a property or not?

G.E. Moore gives a famous example in order to show that existence is not a property. Compare:

(i)   Some tigers exist.
(ii)   Some tigers growl.

Now it is obvious that (i) is a senseless statement, and that (ii) is meaningful. But this only shows that there are restrictions in the use of the word 'exist'; it does not show that '...exists' is not a predicate. The predicate cannot be used without restrictions, but does this mean that it is not a predicate?

We can very well say:

(iiia)   There exist tigers in reality or tigers exist in reality.
(iiib)   There have existed dodos in reality, but now they no longer exist

or dodos existed in reality, but now they no longer exist in reality.

(iiic)   There exist no centaurs in reality or centaurs do not exist in reality.

Russell, Moore and others were mistaken in thinking that 'exist' can only be represented by the existential quantifier (in modern symbolic logic) and, consequently, that 'exist' is obviously not a predicate. But we have to translate (iiia) and (iiic) in the following way:

(iiia)   (Ex) (fx & gx)

(iiic)   ~ (Ex) (fx & gx)

It is meaningful in (iiia) to read 'tigers' for f and 'exist in reality' for g. And in (iiic) it is meaningful to read 'centaurs' for f and 'exist in reality' for g. (iiib) is not given in a symbolic formula, because the time constituent introduces a complicating element which is not relevant to our problem. From this it may be obvious that the existential quantifier has another meaning than 'exist in reality'. Further it may be clear that the existential quantifier is not a property. I concede that. But does this mean that 'exist in reality' is not a property, because it must be the value of a variable in a predicate place? Our treatment of the problem seems at least to suggest that existence *is* a property.

However, even if we accept 'exist in reality' as a property, our difficulties are not yet over. For does it mean that 'exist in reality' is greater (or more perfect) than 'not exist in reality', as is implied by Anselm's third premise? Are the living better or greater than the dead? It is difficult to see how to answer this question. Whatever objections may be raised here, they become powerless in the second variant of Anselm's proof. Anselm no longer speaks of existence, but of *necessary* existence. It is obvious that '...exists necessarily' is a property and moreover the statement 'to exist necessarily is greater than to exist contingently' is perfectly meaningful.

Anselm's ontological argument. Variant II

Premises (presuppositions)

(i)   A being greater than which nothing can be conceived of, is thinkable. We call this being A.

(ii)   It is thinkable that the non-existence of this being greater than which nothing can be conceived of, cannot be conceived. We call this being B.

(iii)   If two beings A and B are the same in every respect, but the non-existence of B cannot be conceived and the non-existence of A can be conceived, then B is greater than A.

Proof

1. A does not exist (starting-hypothesis);

2. Then the non-existence of A can be conceived (follows from (1));

3. Then B is greater than A (follows from (2), (ii) and (iii);
4. But (3) contradicts (i);
5. Consequently (1) is false and must be negated;
6. Therefore A exists.

Before evaluating this proof I shall first eliminate the objection mentioned above, *viz.* that in his argument Anselm immediately identifies A and B. For this purpose I shall we give still another variant which is not to be found in Anselm, but which differs from Anselm's variants only in some minor respects.

Anselm's ontological argument. Variant III

Premises (presuppositions)

(i)   A being greater than which nothing can be conceived of, is thinkable. We call this being A.
(ii)   It is thinkable that the non-existence of a certain being cannot be conceived, or in other words, this being exists necessarily. We call this being B.
(iii)   If two beings A and C are the same in every respect, but the nonexistence of C cannot be conceived and the non-existence of A *can* be conceived, then C is greater than A.
(iv)   It is thinkable that there is a being C that has the same nature as the being B of premise (ii) and that in every other respect is the same as the being A of premise (i).

Proof
1. A does not exist (starting-hypothesis);
2. Then the non-existence of A can be conceived (follows from (1);
3. Whether a certain arbitrary being B is greater than A cannot be decided, but it is certain that being C of premise (iv) is greater than A (follows from (2), (ii), (iii) and (iv);
4. But (3) contradicts (i);
5. Consequently (1) is false and must be negated;
6. Therefore A exists.

From a logical point of view this argument is correct. It can no longer be doubted that necessary existence is a predicate. Moreover, to say that a necessary being is greater than a contingent being is meaningful. A necessary being exists in all possible worlds, whereas there are at least some possible worlds in which a contingent being does not exist. So the number of worlds in which a necessary being exists is greater than the number of worlds in which a contingent being exists. And thus it is meaningful to say that a necessary being is greater than a contingent being.

One serious objection must be considered, *viz.* whether the word 'thinkable' includes only a logical possibility in the mind or also a real possibility outside the mind. We have here the old and difficult problem of the relation of a *de dicto* (logical) and a *de re* (real) modality. We shall return to this problem later, when we have discussed the other ontological arguments. Further we should keep in mind that Anselm's argument is only valid in the modal system S_5, which can be seen if we present the proof in a formal way. For this we refer to the appendix 3.

3.1.2.2 *Charles Hartshorne*

Hartshorne, one of the great and profound philosophers of our time, has contributed much to the renewal of the ontological argument. Although he has been inspired by Whitehead his philosophy differs from Whitehead's in many respects. Hartshorne is plainly more theistic and rationalistic than Whitehead. He developed his main concepts of process philosophy before he got acquainted with Whitehead's philosophy. His starting-point is that a perfect being, an *ens perfectissimum*, cannot exist contingently, i.e. his existence is necessary. He calls this fundamental theorem, *Anselm's principle*. Further he assumes that the existence of this perfect being is possible, which is, of course, a considerable presupposition. With the help of these two premises he gives a proof of God's existence in a modern logical presentation (*vide* appendix 3).

The premise that the existence of a perfect being is possible, is considered more extensively by Hartshorne and here he is able to contribute to the discussion in an important way. One of the difficulties of Anselm's proof is to show that the notion of a being greater than which nothing can be conceived of, does not imply a contradiction. To this problem Hartshorne's process philosophy can give a solution. In this philosophy God is not timeless, but participates in the time process. That means that for God the future is open and is not fixed. God knows, of course, the past completely. He knows the future in so far as it is fixed (some events can be predicted), but many events depend on man's choice and one of the main doctrines of process philosophy is that man has a free will. Additionally Hartshorne teaches that certain relational properties belong to God's essence, i.e. they are for God internal relations. The more personal relations are, the more they are internal. Whether I stand in front of my typewriter, or not, does not make any difference, either to me, or to the typewriter. But the relation of love with regard to my wife certainly belongs to my essence.It is an internal relation and any change in this relation means a change in my being also.

Analogously, God's relation to man is also an internal relation and not an external one, as is taught in traditional theology and philosophy. We have seen that the more personal a relation is, the more it is internal. Therefore in God, who is the most personal of all persons, his relations of love are internal and not external. We cannot say that for God it does not matter, how men behave. If mankind would respond to God's call of love adequately, God's relation to mankind would be better than it is now and in this sense one can say that God would have changed. Hartshorne teaches that in this way God can always become more perfect. In his abstract nature, i.e. in his eternal properties, his unity, unchange ability, causality, necessity , etc. God remains the same. But these eternal properties, this abstract nature express themselves in relations and properties in time: love, caring for mankind, etc. And in this concrete nature God can always become more perfect. No being outside God can surpass him in perfection, but he himself can surpass himself; again, not in God's abstract nature (his nature *a se*), but in his relation to mankind or to the world. We can also say: the more people love God, the more God becomes *God*.

3.1.2.3 *Spinoza*

Spinoza preferred the ontological to the cosmological argument, i.e. the a priori proof to the a posteriori one. At least so he says, but in my opinion his contribution to the cosmological argument is at least as important. Of the ontological argument he gave several variants in which he started with the Cartesian arguments. The fundamental idea in Spinoza's philosophy (and Descartes') is that God is a being whose essence involves existence. In this way God's existence can be derived directly from the concept of God. We find this proof in Spinoza's book on Descartes and in his own *Short Treatise*. In his *Ethics* he presents the argument via the concept of *substance*. God is defined as a substance with an infinite number of attributes. Now a substance is defined as a being that exists and may be understood by itself. From this Spinoza can infer that existence belongs to the essence of the substance.

A modern mind will probably not so easily be convinced of the correctness of such arguments. Spinoza goes beyond Descartes, however, by indicating the basis on which the whole argument is built, *viz.* the parallelism between thinking and extension (i.e. the material world), *cogitatio* and *extensio*. If we must necessarily think of certain things, these things have their parallels in the material world. This is only true for things we must *necessarily* think of, and not for products of our imagination. Now the concept of God, a being whose essence involves existence, must necessarily be thought of and therefore God exists. In this connection Spinoza wrote to Jarig Jelles about the ontological argument: 'Descartes' axiom, I concede, is somewhat obscure and confused, as you have already observed. He would have spoken more clearly and truly in the following way: that the power of cogitation to think out things or to understand them is not greater than the power of nature to be and to operate'. Here Spinoza gives a clear indication of the presupposition on which his (and the Cartesian) arguments rest. In short Spinoza has two main presuppositions:

(i)   that we must necessarily think of a being, whose essence involves its existence.

(ii)   that there is a parallelism between thinking and extension (the external world, i.e. the world outside the human mind).

3.1.2.4 J. Breedenburg

This smart merchant from Rotterdam, a friendly opponent of Spinoza, devised an original ontological argument which he cherished, as his opponents derisively said, like a little baby. Still it is an interesting way of reasoning as we shall see. Breedenburg defines God as the 'absolute negation of nothing'. Obviously a vague concept of God like 'plenitude of being' was in his mind. It is not impossible to suppose that Breedenburg devised his definition under Jewish influence, because a similar definition of God can be found in the Cabbala. This definition together with three premises constitutes the following argument:

Definition: God as the most perfect being is the absolute negation of nothing (= complete non-being).

Premise 1:   Out of nothing (= complete non-being) nothing emerges.

Premise 2:   An existing thing can never turn into nothing (= complete non-being).

Premise 3:   There exists something.

Proposition: God exists.

Proof:

1. The proposition is not true (hypothesis).
2. There is a negation of the absolute negation of nothing (follows from 1 and the definition).
3. Complete non-being (= nothing) is possible (follows from 2).
4. There is something (premise 3).
5. Complete non-being (= nothing) is not possible (follows from 4 and the premises 1 and 2).
6. There is a contradiction between step 3 and 5.
7. The hypothesis (step 1) must be negated.
8. The proposition is true, i.e. God exists.

Our bright merchant gives a very nice argument with little material! A weak point seems to be his reference to the fact that there exists something. One might even be tempted not to classify this argument under the ontological arguments. But we shall see in a moment that the other arguments too must refer to the existence of something. A complete proof with the help of a concept alone is impossible. At least, if one wants to arrive at the real existence of God!

3.1.2.5 *Evaluation*

The various proofs contain different definitions of God and they differ also in their presuppositions. Further we must state that the arguments of Anselm and Hartshorne make clearly use of the modal system S_5, if we present their proofs in a formal system (*vide* appendix 3).

Definition of God		*Further presuppositions*
Anselm:	God is a being greater than which nothing be conceived of.	This definition is free of contradictions.
		A beings whose non-existence cannot be conceived is greater than a being – in other respects the same – whose non-existence *can* be conceived.
		S_5
Hartshorne:	God is an *ens perfectissimum*.	Anselm's principle: If an *ens perfectissimum* exists, it exists necessarily.
		The concept of God is process philosophy.
		S_5
Spinoza:	God is a being whose essence involves existence.	We must necessarily think of such a being.
		There is a parallelism between thinking and extension (the external world).
Breedenburg:	God is the absolute negation of nothing.	There is something.
		No thing turns into nothing. Ex nihilo nihil fit.

In our evaluation we should not only look at the plausibility of the arguments, but also at the quality of the concept of God. An argument may be more plausible, but perhaps what has been proved is worth less than what is proved in a less plausible argument.

Let us start by looking at Breedenburg's presupposition that 'something exists'. We shall find this presupposition indirectly also in other philosophies. In Spinoza's thinking this presupposition can be inferred immediately from his doctrine of the parallelelism between *cogitatio* and *extensio*. But Hartshorne and Anselm also have to accept this presupposition if they do not want to abide by a proof of God's existence in which God only exists in our mind and not in reality. As the reader can see, the whole of Anselm's and Hartshorne's argument rests upon the presupposition that something (God) is thinkable. Now an obvious counter-argument is that the whole argument is only *de dicto* (about what can be spoken or thought) and not *de re* (about what is in reality). A *de dicto* possibility is a purely logical possibility, which is only true in our mind. A state of affairs is *de dicto* possible, if it is not logically contradictory. It is *de re* possible, if it is compatible with the other states of affairs in the real world. And it is evident that this is a stronger requirement. In the case of necessity it is the other way round. If something is *de re* necessary, this does not imply that it is also *de dicto* necessary. We can think of another possibility, even if the latter is in reality impossible.

Now Anselm uses the phrase 'It is thinkable that'. *Prima facie* this is nothing more than a *de dicto* possibility, not a real possibility. And the same is true with regard to Hartshorne. He presupposes that the existence of God is possible. Is this more than a *de dicto* possibility? Now Anselm and Hartshorne are in the fortunate position that the distinction between *de dicto* and *de re* is eliminated in S_5. Only in the modal systems S_4 and the stricter systems is this distinction relevant. But even in S_5 there are two possibilities. Every modality is *de dicto*, because there is no reality, or every modality is *de re*, because in S_5 the modalities *de dicto* and *de re* coincide. That means in these proofs reality must be presupposed. In a world in which nothing exists, there is no modality *de re*. In that case one has not yet reached the real existence of God in the proof. Therefore Anselm and Hartshorne must introduce the premise 'there is something' among their premises.

All right, we add this premise 'there is something' to the premises of Anselm and Hartshorne. If we now compare the various premises, it seems that Breedenburg presupposes the least. This does not mean that Breedenburg's argument should have our preference. For ultimately the concept of God proved by him does not contain more than that of an *ens necessarium*, whereas in the thinking of Anselm and of Hartshorne an *ens perfectissimum* is proved. Breedenburg realizes this himself. His concept of God does not transcend that of Spinoza, whom he has opposed in a fair way. The God of his argument acts necessarily and cannot perform miracles. Therefore Breedenburg teaches the double truth: for the Christian faith other states of affairs are true than for the intellect. Breedenburg's opponents accused him of hypocrisy. As was the case with many adherents of the double truth, Breedenburg was not trusted. He was said to refer to the Christian faith only in order to escape the accusation of atheism. Breedenburg was defended by the famous Pierre Bayle, who, a sceptic himself in philosophy and a Calvinist in theology, could appreciate a position like that of Breedenburg. In my view there is not the slightest reason to doubt Breedenburg's sincerity. In his other writings too he makes the impression of being an honest and pious believer, and at the same time a man who seeks for intellectual truth.

Anselm on the other hand is able to derive the whole of Christian dogmatics in his Proslogium. From the ontological argument he derives the principle that we must ascribe to God, in an infinite way, all the properties which are realizations of being and deny to him all the properties which are destructions of being. As, for example, goodness produces being, whereas evil destroys it, we must ascribe infinite goodness to God and deny to him all kinds of evil.

Spinoza's ontological argument presupposes probably the most and proves prima facie not very much. A being whose essence involves existence does not seem rich in content. However, in the development of his doctrine Spinoza succeeds in unfolding a profound doctrine of God. That does not alter the fact that he needs more presuppositions than Anselm and Breedenburg.

In comparing Hartshorne and Anselm it must be said that Hartshorne, better than Anselm, has shown that his concept of God, which is that of process philosophy, is not self-contradictory. Thus this argument has gained in meaning and importance. Still there are disadvantages in his approach, because in the development of his doctrine he needs a reference to the special position of this our world. And that concept belongs to the modal system S_4, whereas Hartshorne works with the system S_5, as we have seen. We shall explain this more fully. Semantically the concept 'necessary' can mean various things. For our purpose the following distinction is relevant. 'p is necessary' may mean that in all possible worlds p is true (or p is the case). And 'possible worlds' may include all kinds of worlds we can think of, also worlds which have no connection with this our world. But one can also stipulate that by 'possible worlds' we understand a world that *does* have a connection with our world. Then our world has a special position.

For example: if we give our world a special position, we must say that it was necessary that Napoleon died in 1821 on St. Helena. All the possibilities that may perhaps be realized in the course of history from this moment on have as their past that Napoleon died in 1821 on St. Helena, or in other words all possible worlds have within their true statements: 'Napoleon died in 1821 on St. Helena'. Now it is obvious that if this our world does not have this special position, we may safely say that a world is thinkable in which there is a course of events different from that of our world. In that world Napoleon did not die in 1821 on St. Helena, so that this is not a necessary event. The concept of a special position of our world belongs to S_4, the other concept to S_5. Now in his philosophy Hartshorne uses the special position of our world. For in his theory God cannot change the past, the past is fixed and even many aspects in the future are fixed, *viz.* those facts that are determined by the facts of our world. Thus Hartshorne uses sometimes S_5 (in his ontological argument) and sometimes S_4 (in his philosophical doctrine of God). Now this is impossible. In my opinion his theory has to be modified in this respect (*vide* appendix 3).

I must refer to yet another presupposition which is tacitly taken for granted, and which may be culturally determined. Here I have in mind premise (iii) in the Anselmian variants II and III. If we interpret 'greater' here in the sense that it means 'having more power of being' (and silently we have done this), then one might contest this presupposition. For in Buddhism non-being is preferred to being. This, at least, was the case in original Buddhism. There one has a negative view of our phenomenal world. This power of being is a false power, a seeming power. We in the West – and of course many people in the East – have a more positive attitude towards life and being. But how to prove this more positive attitude to a Buddhist? Especially in Zen Buddhism a whole doctrine has been developed in which it is shown that we have to mistrust our logical thinking and that we have to strive for 'pure experience'. We may object that in daily life even a Buddhist makes use of logic, and of the positive values of life and being. But he will not deny that, and he will even accept that he has an illogical attitude, but that is just what he is defending, *viz.* that one has to sacrifice logical thinking in order to reach pure experience by means of a special training! It is not my choice, but can I say more than that my position is a choice? This choice convinces me and most people of the West (and East), but it is and remains a choice!

At the background of the ontological argument there is the idea that having more being also means having more perfection. God is interpreted as an *ens perfectissimum*. For example Spinoza identifies *perfectio* and *realitas*. It may be objected, however, that in this way the naturalistic fallacy has been committed, i.e. that a conclusion with respect to some value (perfection) has been drawn from being (reality). But I would defend the ontological argument in this respect. The naturalistic fallacy takes place, where one derives values from pure facts, as we have seen above. The being which is presupposed in the ontological argument is more than purely factual. It involves degrees of being and that means that a concept of being is considered in which the power of being is taken into consideration, the power to maintain being and not to destroy it. This is positively evaluated, as we have seen, and thus on the one hand values (perfection) may be inferred from it, but on the other hand we must realize that we are standing in a certain tradition, because, as we have shown, Buddhists may contest this positive evaluation.

In conclusion we may assert that all ontological arguments meet some objections. Breedenburg meets perhaps the fewest, but he does not prove so much. Spinoza presupposes a great deal more than Anselm. In the development of his system Hartshorne commits a logical error, which is unsatisfactory. Anselm has perhaps presented the best argument, in spite of all its shortcomings.

What did my great teacher in philosophy of religion, G. van der Leeuw, say? 'The original intuitions are the most profound'. In view of all the objections I only hesitatingly accept this ontological argument, as I do not see a satisfactory refutation. Perhaps one should, however, remain with a *non liquet*, i.e. it cannot be decided (*vide* also appendix 11). But I am willing to accept the cosmological argument, as we shall see in our next section.

3.1.3 *The cosmological argument*

3.1.3.1 *General outline of the argument*

As has been said before, in the cosmological argument the world is starting-point and not the concept of God as in the ontological argument. In contradistinction to the argument from design, which takes the supposed order in the world as a starting-point (= its design), the cosmological argument confines itself to the existence of the world as such. Not '*how* the world is' is starting-point, but '*that* the world is'. 'Why is there after all a world and why is there not nothing?', that is the question. The fact that there is a world, asks for a ground (reason, cause). It cannot be there by chance. This argument too experiences a renaissance nowadays, but just as with the other arguments one cannot speak of a definitive proof here. Each proof depends on premises and one can always raise objections to the premises. But it is still a remarkable renaissance, for the argument is now valid in a much stricter system than it was some decades ago.

The term 'cosmological argument' emerges only in the 18th century; previously it was called argument from the first cause, or first mover, or the argument from the contingency of the world. As may be clear from the various names, the argument has many variants. We shall confine ourselves especially to the last (and most interesting) version, since it presents the argument in its strongest form. The argument has a long history and is obviously older than the ontological argument. We find the first well-elaborated form in Aristotle, but the first germs may also be found in the Pre-Socratic Greek philosophers, in Socrates and Plato. The argument has two main variants which we shall discuss:

Starting-point is:

(1)   *There are contingent beings*, i.e. there are beings whose non-existence is possible.

In order to facilitate our discussion of these contingent beings we confine ourselves to only one of them:

(1′)   *There is at least one contingent being.*

Now the principle of sufficient reason, i.e. *ex nihilo nihil fit* (from nothing nothing emerges), demands that for this existence of a contingent being there must be a cause or ground. The difference between cause and ground is that the latter may be timeless, whereas cause is considered to precede its effect. In our reconstruction we will speak of ground, because in that case we avoid a possible criticism of a Kantian epistemology, as we have seen above. A ground is a logical relation and logical relations are also valid for the thing-in-itself, as we have seen. Now for every being the following holds: it finds its ground either in itself or in something else. A contingent being cannot be the ground of itself, because one can think of its non-existence. Something non-existent cannot be the ground of something else and therefore it cannot be the ground of itself. Therefore:

(2)   *This contingent being finds its ground in something else.*

This means that this contingent being is dependent on something else for its existence. Now this ground is either itself a contingent being or a non-contingent, i.e. a necessary, being. If this ground is a contingent being, then the principle of sufficient reason demands again another ground, etc. We must continue this sequence ad infinitum, unless we may stop at a necessary being. Therefore we have:

(3)   *The ground of this contingent being is either an infinite series of contingent beings or it is a necessary being.*

Now we have two main variants of the cosmological argument. One may be found in Thomas Aquinas and others. Here it is argued that such an infinite series of contingent beings is impossible and that we must immediately conclude that a necessary being is the ground of this contingent being. The other variant may be found in Duns Scotus, Spinoza and others. Here it is argued that such a series is certainly possible. The difference between the two is caused by a different interpretation of the infinite. Is an actual infinite possible (as is asserted in variant II) or not? But in variant II also one arrives at a necessary being by seeking the ground of the whole series of grounds. And only a ground that finds its ground in itself can be the ground of such a series. We have now the following steps, starting from the three preceding steps mentioned above:

VARIANT I:

(4)   *An infinite series of contingent beings is an insufficient explanation for the existence of a contingent being.*

Therefore:

(5)   *There must be an ens necessarium, i.e. a necessary being.*

VARIANT II:

(4)   *An infinite series of contingent beings demands for its existence a ground which cannot itself be contingent.*

Therefore:

(5)   *There must be an ens necessarium, i.e. a necessary being.*

Both variants have their advantages and disadvantages. In the first place they differ in being more or less convincing and in the second place they refer to a different concept of God. We will discuss this briefly now. Later in this section we shall put forward the argument of variant II in a more exact form (*vide* also appendix 4).

3.1.3.2 *The convincing power*

The great advantage of variant II is that its convincing power is greater, because we may accept the possibility of an infinite series of contingent beings. *Prima facie* one cannot see why this should be impossible. A disadvantage is, however, that in this variant we seek second order grounds (or causes), i.e. grounds of grounds or causes of causes, and perhaps somebody might raise objections against this multiple application of the principle of sufficient reason. But if one accepts this principle, I cannot see why one should confine its use to first order grounds (or cases). We shall discuss this problem more extensively later in this section. For the moment the following remarks may be sufficient. There are indeed scholars who assert that one should not continue indefinitely looking for grounds (or causes). One has to start with some inexplicable facts. In my view this attitude is completely correct in the various sciences. But in philosophy one has the right (and the duty) to continue asking for the ground of any thing or state of affairs. It is asserted that in quantum mechanics some states of affairs are not yet explained and are perhaps inexplicable. But in the first place our ignorance does not mean that there are states of affairs that have no grounds (or causes). Einstein, for example, always maintained that they are there, but that we only do not know them yet ('God does play with dice'). In the second place, even if we conceded that in quantum mechanics there are some states of affairs which do not have grounds (causes), then at least there would be grounds why these states of affairs do not need grounds (causes), so that in the realm of second order grounds there are no ground-less states of affairs. Therefore variant II is not affected by this kind of objections.

In my view – and we shall come to it later in this section – variant II has more convincing power than variant I, but recently interesting attempts have been made to defend this variant too. The defenders have advanced philosophical as well as empirical arguments. The point at issue is to show that such an infinite series of contingent beings is impossible (*vide* above steps 3 and 4). Aristotle and Thomas Aquinas were of the opinion that such a series could not exist, because the infinite cannot exist in actuality, it can only exist in potentiality. The infinite exists only in our mind in the form of a series that can never be completed. For example, in a sequence of natural numbers we can always add a successor to the last number. The series of natural numbers has no greatest possible number.

Now Spinoza and others did acknowledge the infinite also in actuality and also modern mathematics, at least classical (not intuitionistic) mathematics, operates with the actual infinite. The question remains, however, whether in the concrete world (outside mathematics) the actual infinite is possible. As a counterexample the famous Hilbert hotel has been used in an attempt to ridicule such a concept: Suppose a late guest presents himself to the receptionist of a hotel of which all the rooms are occupied. Of course, the receptionist must send him away. But in Hilbert's hotel there is an infinite number of rooms, all of which are occupied. Now the receptionist, who is a good mathematician, can give the late guest a room. It is always possible to add something to the infinite. Of course, the receptionist cannot give our guest the number infinite, for such a number does not exist, but via the hotel telephone he can order all the guest to move to the next room (the guest in number 1 to room 2; the guest in room number 2 to room number 3, etc.). In this way all the guests receive a new room and our guest can have room number 1! Mathematically there is no problem, but in reality it might be clear that such a solution is impossible, for we have just stipulated that *all* the rooms are occupied! But worse is to follow.

Our receptionist has to give rooms to a bus with an infinite number of passengers. This also is no problem for our receptionist mathematician. He orders the original guests to take the even-numbered rooms. In this way he is able to give the odd-numbered rooms to the passengers of the bus. Mathematically this problem can be solved, but in reality this is and remains a problem, because as is stipulated: *all* the rooms are occupied. Our brilliant receptionist mathematician is even able to bring into his hotel the passengers of an infinite number of buses, each having an infinite number of passengers. The mathematical solution of this problem may be left to the reader! Anyway, it may be clear that there is a difference between the actual infinite in mathematics and in reality. What is said above is only meant as an illustration. We could discuss this problem in a more subtle way, but it may be obvious that even if we concede that the actual infinite is mathematically possible, it may be doubted whether it is possible in reality.

Nowadays even empirical arguments can be brought forward for the thesis that such an infinite series of causes is impossible. Usually it is argued that the world must have had a beginning in time. In that case such a series cannot be continued back in time indefinitely. There are at least two powerful arguments in favour of the thesis that the world must have had a beginning:

(1) In astronomy the hypothesis of the big bang is a well-accepted theory now. And this big bang theory refers to a beginning in time. According to

this theory the world has evolved from a little ball of energy into what it is now. This little ball has exploded with a big bang.

(2) The second law of thermodynamics asserts that in a closed system (which our universe, considered as a whole, certainly is) there is an increase of entropy. This can also be formulated otherwise, *viz.* that our world has the tendency to go from the less probable state to a more probable state, i.e. to go from a state with a greater degree of order to a state with a lesser degree of order. And this proves that the world must have had a beginning with a low degree of entropy (i.e. with a great original impulse to overcome the tendency to chaos) because otherwise it would have died already a hot or cold death (i.e. it would have become a state of complete unordered stability).

All these arguments support variant I. They show that such infinite series of contingent beings cannot suffice as the ground of a contingent being or of the world as a whole (*vide* steps 3 and 4 above).

I myself have constructed a new argument in two fashions, one with the help of set and lattice theory which will be given at the end of this section, because it is rather technical. The other presentation, which is advanced with the help of modal logic, is even more technical and will be given in an appendix (*vide* 4). As a result of the application of these modern techniques it may be said that variant II can be proved with their help, whereas variant I cannot be proved. In discussions about these proofs which I have had in a written or oral form even atheists acknowledged that they are formally correct. If one wants to avoid the conclusion one has to attack the presuppositions. I shall mention the relevant possibilities at the end of this section.

3.1.3.3 *The concept of God*

The concept of God which is proved in the two variants is different. In variant I a God has been proved who stands as first cause in a series of causes or as a first ground in a series of grounds. In the second variant He is a second order cause or ground. In this way the God of variant I has a more immanent character with respect to the world, whereas the God of variant II has a more transcendent character. The danger of variant I is pantheism and that of variant II deism. As theism teaches both the immanence and the transcendence of God it would be a good thing if both variants were valid. They do not exclude each other, provided one accepts with Spinoza that God is *causa sui*. One has to accept this concept anyhow, even if one wants to work with only one variant. From what has been said it may be clear that in my view the convincing power of variant II is much greater than that of variant I. However that may be, the proof of an *ens necessarium* or God as a necessary being does not mean that we have already proved a theistic God, let alone the God of Scripture or Christianity.

Because of this Kant asserted that the cosmological argument needs the ontological argument, because in the latter an *ens perfectissimum* has been proved. Reichenbach, however, has proved that this does not mean that in the cosmological argument itself the ontological argument has been presupposed and the reader may have noticed already that this is not the case. In Reichenbach's view we need the ontological argument to fill in the abstract concept of a necessary being, but not for the proof itself. But it is even far from certain whether we need the ontological argument for the filling in of the *ens necessarium* in order to reach the God of theism. We shall discuss this problem later. Hartshorne has demonstrated that the cosmological as well as the ontological argument need each other without our getting into a vicious circle (*vide* appendix 3).

Anyway, it is still a long way from an *ens necessarium* to the God of theism! For example, could not matter be a suitable candidate for the filling in of an *ens necessarium*? This depends on what should be understood by 'necessary'. Usually this is interpreted as 'being present in all possible worlds' or 'being true in all possible worlds'. Now how broadly can this be taken? If we are allowed to speculate freely about the various possibilities without any restriction, then we can easily imagine a world in which there is no matter. In that case matter is not a possible candidate for an *ens necessarium*. For it is difficult to see how matter can be *causa sui*. Thinking can produce itself. Thinking can enter into a relation with itself. There can be *cogitatio cogitationis*, but not a *materia materiae*, not (in Spinozistic and Cartesian terms) an *extensio extensionis*. But if one subscribes to the opinion that possible worlds must stand in a certain relation to our present world, then a world without matter seems to be unthinkable. Even then some qualifications must be made. For according to the big bang hypothesis, at least in the first moments there was no matter yet, but only forms of energy. But most adherents of materialism have no difficulty with this, because one may see in this energy something like a *protomateria*. Anyway, in this case – if possible worlds must stand in some relation to our present world – this protomaterial energy, which develops into matter, is a candidate for the *ens necessarium* of our cosmological argument.

Still even then there are some difficulties, because we cannot explain the increasing degree of ordering in the world in view of the second law of thermodynamics. But then we are already introducing arguments taken from our next proof (that of design). Of course, materialism has many difficulties which are usually solved by ascribing many unknown properties to matter. The best founded example is *dialectical materialism*, which ascribes dialectical properties to matter so that it can produce something new. This may not, at first sight, seem very plausible, but the question is who contradicts Occam's razor more, he who introduces a new being (i.e. God) or he who ascribes unknown properties to an existing being (matter)? Occam's razor runs as follows: *Entia praeter necessitatem non sunt multiplicanda* (one should not, without necessity, multiply the number of beings).

Even for this dialectically interpreted matter it is and remains a difficulty that it is not a *causa sui* and we must claim this property for the *ens necessarium* of the cosmological argument. Or in the words of John Hick, this *ens necessarium* must be *self-explanatory*. This means that the God of the cosmological argument must have self-reflexion.

3.1.3.4 *Thomas Aquinas*

The great master of the arguments of God's existence was Thomas Aquinas. He gave five arguments, of which the first three belong to the class of what is called the cosmological argument. As they are 'classic' arguments, they will now be mentioned.

'There are five ways in which one can prove that there is a God. The first and most obvious way is based on change. Some things in the world are certainly in process of change: this we plainly see. Now anything in process of change is being changed by something else. This is so because it is characteristic of things in process of change that they do not yet have the perfection towards which they move, though able to have it; whereas it is characteristic of something causing change to have that perfection already. For to cause change is to bring into being what was previously only able to be, and this can only be done by something that already is: thus fire, which is actually not, causes wood, which is able to be hot to become actually hot, and in this way causes change in the wood. Now the same thing cannot at the same time be both actually x and potentially x, though it can be actually x and potentially y: the actually hot cannot at the same time be potentially hot, though it can be potentially cold. Consequently, a thing in process of change cannot itself cause that same change; it cannot change itself. Of necessity therefore anything in process of change is being changed by something else. Moreover, this something else, if in process of change, is itself being changed by yet another thing; and this last by another. Now we must stop somewhere, otherwise there will be no first cause of the change, and, as a result, no subsequent causes. For it is only when acted upon by the first cause that the intermediate causes will produce the change: if the hand does not move the stick, the stick will not move anything else. Hence one is bound to arrive at some first cause of change not itself being changed by anything, and this is what everybody understands by "God".

The second way is based on the nature of causation. In the observable world causes are found to be ordered in series; we never observe, nor ever could, something causing itself, for this would mean it preceded itself, and this is not possible. Such a series of causes must however stop somewhere; for in it an earlier member causes an intermediate and the intermediate a last (whether the intermediate be one or many). Now if you eliminate a cause, you also eliminate its effects, so that you cannot have a last cause, nor an intermediate one, unless you have a first. Given therefore no stop in the series of causes, and hence no first cause, there would be no intermediate causes either, and no last effect, and this would be an open mistake. One is therefore forced to suppose some first cause, to which everyone gives the name "God".

The third way is based on what need not be and on what must be, and runs as follows. Some of the things we come across can be but need not be, for we find them springing up and dying away, thus sometimes in being and sometimes not. Now everything cannot be like this, for a thing that need not be, once was not; and if everything need not be, once upon a time there was nothing. But if that were true, there would be nothing even now, because something that does not exist can only be brought into being by something already existing. So that if nothing was in being, nothing could be brought into being, and nothing would be in being now, which contradicts observation. Not everything therefore is the sort of thing that need not be; there has got to be something that must be. Now a thing that must be, may or may not own this necessity to something else. But just as we must stop somewhere in a series of causes, so must we also in the series of things which must be, and owe this to other things. One is forced therefore to suppose something which must be, and owes this to no other thing than itself; indeed it itself is the case that other things must be.'

In contradistinction to what Thomas Aquinas himself thought, this third way is the most profound way. Thomas Aquinas clearly presents variant I as indicated above, with all its disadvantages.

3.1.3.5 *Modern cosmological argument based on set and lattice theory*

In this section I want to show that the cosmological argument in variant II is valid within certain systems of set or lattice theory (classical set theory, thus presupposing either the axiom of choice or Zorn's lemma or the continuity hypothesis; anyhow, a system including the concept of actual infinity). Even then we must accept some premises in order to establish the proof. From this it might be clear that even a modern approach does not constitute 'definitively' the validity of the cosmological argument. In the first place one can always recur to stricter systems, e.g. intuitionistic set theory, and in the second place the premises from which we prove God's existence may be doubted. On the other hand classical set and lattice theories are respectable systems and the premises have – as we shall see – a certain degree of plausibility, so that on the whole one might say that the cosmological argument might be labelled a respectable argument seen from a logical point of view. We shall start with an informal presentation of the argument using some elementary concepts of set and lattice theory and in the appendix we shall give a more rigorous proof with the help of modal logic.

One of the main counterarguments against the cosmological argument is that it is never necessary to stop the chain of arguments at a first mover, a first cause or a necessary being, as is done in variant I of our argument. Now the main premise of my modern reconstruction of the cosmological argument is to presuppose the a priori principle '*ex nihilo nihil fit*' or formulated otherwise 'for every state of affairs there must necessarily be a ground'. This principle was in some form also presupposed in the traditional cosmological arguments. The novelty consists in the fact that we shall apply this principle not only within the various chains of grounds (causes), but also to the sets of these chains in their relations to each other. That means that we presuppose the multiple application of the principle '*ex nihilo nihil fit*'. I shall explain this in more detail. We can seek the cause of the existence of a human being. It is his parents. We can then seek the cause of the existence of the parents. We must then again refer to a couple of parents, and so on. In this way we remain in a linear line of causality. But we must also seek the cause of the fact that two parents produce a human being. In that case we seek a kind of second order cause, i.e. the cause of a causation.

In this way we acquire the following argument: We presuppose that the set of states of affairs in this world together with the relation 'to find its ground in' (and this is a translation of the principle '*ex nihilo nihil fit*') constitutes an ordered set. This ordered set is a directed set by which we mean the following: If there are two states of affairs within the set, say A and B, and A does not find its ground in B nor B in A, then there is a third state of affairs, say C, which is the ground of both A and B (there might of course be intermediate grounds between C and A/B). In passing: as we shall see, we do not need the directedness of the ordering already here, but it is tempting to start with it from the outset. Now this whole set of states of affairs, which is ordered by the relation 'to find its gound in', has an infinite number of subsets ordered by this same relation. And each of these ordered subsets again has an infinite number of states of affairs as its elements, so that in spite of our assumption that the set is a directed set, we are far from arriving at a last element. And that is the reason why in this modern reconstruction variant I cannot be proved; which does not mean of course that there are no other arguments which might support it, as we have already seen above.

But now we make another assumption, *viz.* that there are subsets of the same type. Such a subset is for example the subset characterized by the relation 'being generated': a child is generated by his parents, who are themselves generated by their parents, and so on. In passing: Perhaps someone will object to the fact that I take persons here as 'states of affairs', but this is common practice nowadays, cf. e.g. Wittgenstein, Hartshorne, Scholz and others. If one does not agree, then the concept 'states of affairs' may be replaced by 'beings'. In that case the proof does not change fundamentally.

We now presuppose that it is possible to recognize types of ordered subsets. All generations of children by their parents constitute one type of a subset. All kinds of things causing heat constitute another type, all kinds of magnetic attraction another, and so on. In this way we can make a partition within the whole set of states of affairs ordered by the relation 'to find its ground in'. We thus get a number of subsets characterized by a certain type of ground-consequence relation. Now the fundamental idea of my reconstruction of the cosmological argument is that this number of subsets is not infinite, in other words, that there is only a limited number of *types* of grounds.

Once more we seek the ground of these subsets. By doing so we apply the principle '*ex nihilo nihil fit*' in a multiple way. That is, we say that the relation 'to find its ground in' is not only applicable within the various subsets, but also to the subsets as a whole, as described above. So this set of subsets is again a directed ordered set and because this directed set has a limited number of elements (the elements are here the subsets, each of different type) this set has a last element according to modern set and lattice theory. I may even weaken my original premise in that the requirement of being a directed set is only needed for the ordering of the subsets (each of a different type). This requirement is not needed for the ordering *within* the subsets themselves. (In the same way Policki weakened the premises of the original argument of Salamucha). Thus we arrive at a last element and this element is a ground that we might interpret as God (last or fundamental ground of all being). In passing one may speak of God as a first or as a last ground. That depends on the direction of the ordering. If we speak of the ordering relation 'to find its ground in', we have to do with God as a last ground. If we speak of the ordering relation 'is the ground of', we have to do with God as a first cause. This direction is, however, a matter of convention and not really important.

As one can see, we have made the following assumptions (premises) in the course of our argument:
(i)   the principle '*ex nihilo nihil fit*' is applied in a multiple way, i.e. it is applied also to the set of subsets, or it is also applied to the causal (grounding) relations themselves, not to the causes (grounds) only;
(ii)   the number of types of grounds is not infinite;
(iii)   the relation 'to find its ground in' constitutes a directed set (as we have seen, this is only needed for the ordering of the set of subsets);
(iv)   we can distinguish various types of grounds.

If one does not want to accept the cosmological argument, one must try to reject one of these premises. And of course this is always possible. One should however consider the price one has to pay for this rejection, because one is not allowed to use one of these rejected premises oneself! In my opinion all the premises are acceptable. Premise (iv) will hardly meet an objection. I do not pretend that we can always give a theoretically exact definition of each type of causation (grounding) but a workable definition can certainly be given here and is given in ordinary science, because we always work with types of causes. Presupposition (iii) in the weak form given here is not likely to be objected to. Premise (ii) cannot be proved exactly, but it is at least plausible. The number of states of affairs might be infinite, the number of *types* of grounds should be taken to be finite. The various sciences also presuppose this premise. They order according to causal principles and in doing so they only presuppose a limited number of them. If they did not do so, if in other words the number of types of grounds are infinite, then one must introduce in one's system a whole series of unknown grounds (causes) and this is implausible and unnecessary.

Premise (i) might be labelled plausible too, but I think that this is the weakest point of the argument. For I am convinced that the following attitude is certainly rational: Good, we admit that if we continue looking for grounds (i.e. if we apply the rule *'ex nihilo nihil fit'* in a multiple way), we finally arrive at a last ground. But why continue seeking grounds? For the construction of science this is certainly not needed. In science we have nothing to do with last grounds or last causes. Naturally we admit that there are boundaries in our science, but we shall remain within these boundaries. Even stronger: it is wrong to transgress these boundaries. Science made its great progress in the 17th century, when thinkers like Galilei and Newton stopped seeking complete explanations, including last grounds. Descartes still made the mistake of building his physics on metaphysics. He was of the opinion that one should first of all know the last metaphysical principles in order to construct a physical system. One should, for example, first know what gravitation essentially is, before one could go on to work with it. This proved to be a wrong point of view. One can very well work with gravitation and make calculations without exactly knowing what exactly caused gravitation and without going further to the last ground, God. Moreover some states of affairs in physics do not seem to fall under the rule *'ex nihilo nihil fit'* or the principle of sufficient ground. For in quantum mechanics some states of affairs escape our possibilities of a causal ordering.

I admit all this readily. I do not claim that modern reconstructions of the arguments for God's existence are relevant to science. However, in my view the problem of the existence of God and other metaphysical questions have their own rights independent of the question whether these problems are relevant to science or not. These are problems that man struggles with and we must try to solve them in the best possible way. And then we must say that presupposition (i) has enough plausibility to be applied. Besides we may even indicate that this principle is silently presupposed in science too.

That this principle is used within science is no problem, asking for causes or grounds is normal procedure there. But in science we presuppose that grounds for explanation do not change. That finds its ground in the fact that we tacitly take it for granted that, if A is grounded in B, this will not change without ground. But if the principle '*ex nihilo nihil fit*' cannot be applied in a multiple way we are never sure of this! And as for the unexplained states of affairs in quantum mechanics, as we have already indicated above, this does not affect our variant II, for in that case there must be a second order ground for this inexplicability, and in variant II only the second order grounds are important. Thus, even if the principle '*ex nihilo nihil fit*' is not always needed in the realm of the first order grounds, we need it in the realm of the second order grounds. And so we can reconstruct our argument of variant II with the help of it.

3.1.3.6 *The modal version of the cosmological argument*

The same proof which we have given above with the help of modern set and lattice theory can also be given with the help of modern modal logic. In this way we prove variant II. This proof has the advantage that it can be formulated exactly, even more precisely than we have done above. The structure is, however, the same, because we have used the multiple application of the rule '*ex nihilo nihil fit*'. As this proof presupposes some (elementary) knowledge of modal logic, we have placed it in appendix 4 to which we may refer now. As one can see, there are various kinds of cosmological argument. If one studies the various proofs, one sees that some proofs in modal propositional logic presuppose the system S_5. In some of the other proofs we have only to presuppose the system S_4 + the Barcan formula. The proof with the help of modal propositional logic runs most smoothly, but it proves least and, moreover, no distinction has been made between grounds on the one hand and sufficient and necessary conditions on the other hand. In the proofs with the help of modal predicate logic this distinction *has* been made. This distinction can easily be grasped by intuition. Therefore I have introduced 'creative ground' as a primitive concept in the proofs with the help of modal predicate logic.

If one does not accept this – and some scholars do not like it – it is possible to work with sufficient and necessary conditions, as is done in the proof with the help of modal propositional logic. To my mind this is not completely satisfactory. Of course, it solves some of the difficulties with the problem of causality. But some other difficulties arise. In the first place one cannot see what the ground is and what its consequence, or what the cause is and what its effect. In the formula $p \rightarrow q$ it is p which expresses the sufficient condition for q, while it is q which expresses the necessary condition for p. The formula may be considered the 'translation' of 'if p, then q'. But what is here the cause and what the effect, or what is the (timeless) ground and what the consequence? For example, we may read for p: 'it is raining' and for q: 'the streets become wet' so that the formula runs:

(i) 'If it is raining, the streets become wet'

Now it may be clear that p is the cause and q is the effect. The sufficient condition is here the cause and the necessary condition is the effect. But the reverse is also possible. If we read for example for p: 'someone has influenza' and for q: 'he has inhaled influenza bacilli' the formula runs:

(ii) 'if someone has influenza, he has inhaled influenza bacilli'.

Here p is the effect and q the cause, i.e. the necessary condition is now the cause and the sufficient condition is the effect. As a translation of the relation cause-effect (or ground-consequence) the scheme of 'sufficient and necessary conditions' is insufficient. Intuitively we know very well which are the causes and which the effects or which are the grounds and which are the consequences, but we cannot express this in the traditional logical language in which we can express sufficient and necessary conditions.

Further with the help of sufficient and necessary conditions one cannot distinguish accidental coincidences from the relation cause-effect. Suppose that someone has the habit of drinking a cup of coffee at 10 a.m. each morning. Now we may read for p: 'it is 10 a.m.' and for q: 'Mr so and so is drinking his morning coffee' so that the formula runs:

(iii) 'if it is 10 a.m., Mr so and so is drinking his morning coffee'.

Now one can hardly assert that the fact that it is 10 a.m. is the *cause* that Mr so and so drinks his morning coffee or the reverse that the fact that Mr so and so drinks his morning coffee, is the *cause* for it being 10 a.m. Intuitively we are able to distinguish such accidental coincidences from real cause-effect or ground-consequence relations. In the latter cases there is an actively working ground, i.e. a ground that really constitutes something. Therefore we have introduced this concept of an actively working ground as a primitive concept in our argument with the help of modal predicate logic. The *ens necessarium* which we have proved with the help of this argument, is therefore itself an actively, creatively working ground. By an actively, creatively working ground we should not immediately think of a consciously working ground, but only of a ground from which some 'power' emanates so that it can produce effects or consequences. And this cannot be expressed by the presentations with the help of sufficient and necessary conditions. If some readers find the introduction of actively working grounds unsatisfactory and still prefer the theory of the sufficient and necessary conditions, in agreement with most philosophers of our time, this does not affect the cosmological argument. We may in that case refer to the proof with the help of modal propositional logic. The only disadvantage is that the proof is in that case only valid in S_5 and not in the stricter system S_4 + Barcan formula.

3.1.4 *The argument from design*

The argument from design is what on the continent is distinguished as (i) the teleological argument and (ii) the physico-theological argument. The difference between the two is that in the teleological argument a design, a plan *in general* is seen in nature. One observes in general that in the behaviour of animals, plants, etc. a certain purpose is served and that these animals and plants cannot consciously try to fulfil this purpose willingly. But the content of the purpose is not considered. The bee seeks the honey of the plant and by this serves the purpose of propagating and generating. One need not look for a deeper content. The physico-theological argument is more ambitious. Here a whole theological message is read into events of nature and a complete theology is built upon it. There was only a very short period in human history in which the physico-theology flourished, *viz.* the 18th century. We may say that today it is given up totally, but it still has interesting features.

The teleological argument is less ambitious and therefore more convincing. It is the fifth way of Thomas Aquinas: 'The fifth way is based on the guidedness of nature. An orderedness of actions to an end is observed in all bodies obeying natural laws, even when they lack awareness. For their behaviour hardly ever varies, and will practically always turn out well; which shows that they truly tend to a goal, and do not merely hit it by accident. Nothing however that lacks awareness tends to a goal, except under the direction of someone with awareness and with understanding; the arrow, for example, requires an archer. Everything in nature, therefore, is directed to its goal by someone with understanding, and this we call "God" '.

Just as the cosmological argument – in contradistinction to the ontological argument – the argument from design is rooted in a long historical tradition and can hardly be called the invention of one man as is the case with Anselm with respect to the ontological argument. The argument even occurs in Scripture, certainly if we include the so-called Old Testament Apocrypha. St. Paul also refers to the argument. Let us listen to the beautiful and clear exposition of this argument in the 13th chapter of the apocryphal book *The Wisdom of Solomon*, in which a distinction is made between two classes of idolaters: 'What born fools all men were, who lived in ignorance of God, who from the good things before their eyes could not learn to know him who really is, and failed to recognize the artificer though they observed his works! Fire, wind, swift air, the circle of starry signs, rushing water, or the great lights in heaven that rule the world – these they accounted gods. If it was through delight in the beauty of these things that men supposed them gods, they ought to have understood how much better is the Lord and Master of it all; for it was by the prime author of all beauty that they were created. If it was through astonishment at their power and influence, men should have learnt from these how much more powerful is he who made them. For the greatness and beauty of created things give us a corresponding idea of their Creator. Yet these men are not greatly to be blamed, for when they go astray they may be seeking God and really wishing to find him. Passing their lives among his works and making a close study of them, they are persuaded by appearances because what they see is so beautiful. Yet even so they do not deserve to be excused, for with enough understanding to speculate about the universe, why did they not sooner discover the Lord and Master of it all?

The really degraded ones are those whose hopes are set on dead things, who give the name of gods to work of human hands, to gold and silver fashioned by art into images of living creatures, or to a useless stone carved by a craftsman long ago. Suppose some skilled woodworker fells with his saw a convenient tree and deftly strips off all the bark, then works it up elegantly into some vessel suitable for everyday use; and the pieces left over from his work he uses to cook his food, and eats his fill. But among the waste there is one useless piece, crooked and full of knots, and this he takes and carves to occupy his idle moments, and shapes it with leisurely skill into the image of a human being; or else he gives it the form of some contemptible creature, painting it with vermilion and reddening its surface with red paint, so that every flaw in it is painted over. Then he makes a suitable shrine for it and fixes it on the wall, securing it with iron nails. It is he who has to take the precautions on its behalf to save it from falling, for he knows that it cannot fend for itself: it is only an image, and needs help. Yet he prays to it about his possessions and his wife and children, and feels no shame in addressing this lifeless object; for health he appeals to a thing that is feeble, for life he prays to a dead thing, for aid he implores something that has not even the use of its legs; in matters of earnings and business and success in handicraft he asks effectual help from a thing whose hands are entirely ineffectual'.

We see that the author of *the Wisdom of Solomon* reasons from the beauty of the things in this world to its Lord and Master. Perhaps one might even call this more an aesthetic argument than an argument from design. But at least in the argument in *the Wisdom of Solomon* there is also the question of the mistake one makes if one does not conclude from the beauty of the things without awareness to the creator of these things who must have awareness.

Paul also refers to this argument in his letter to the Romans (1.18). This is even clearer if one compares the two texts in the original Greek. Many terms used are the same, etc. The fundamental idea also is the same. If one sees the universe, one should conclude to its Lord and Master: 'For we see divine retribution revealed from heaven and falling upon all the godless wickedness of men. In their wickedness they are stifling the truth. For all that may be known of God by men lies plain before their eyes; indeed God himself has disclosed it to them. His invisible attributes, that is to say his everlasting power and deity, have been visible, ever since the world began, to the eye of reason, in the things he has made. There is therefore no possible defence for their conduct; knowing God, they have refused to honour him as God, or to render him thanks. Hence all their thinking has ended in futility, and their misguided minds are plunged in darkness. They boast of their wisdom but they have made fools of themselves, exchanging the splendour of immortal God for an image shaped like mortal man, even for images like birds, beasts, and creeping things'. From this it may be clear that the study of the arguments for God's existence is less unbiblical than some scholars of the Barthian school would have us believe. But we will not go into this theological matter here. There is also a biblical (Rabbinic) logical rule behind the reasoning of the book *the Wisdom of Solomon*, *viz* the rule *a minore ad maius*, or vice versa. It is usually called the rule '*qal wachomèr*'. For a more extensive treatment of this rule one may see appendix 9.

In the 18th century a whole natural theology was based upon the argument from design. A moral message was read from the book of nature. It could be seen from the obvious plan and design, which was so manifest in nature. The great masters of physico-theology were Fénélon, Nieuwentyt, Ray, Derham and Paley. The principles went back to expositions in the works of Boyle, Newton, Leeuwenhoek and Swammerdam. In these writings pure scientific work was achieved and good empirical theories were expounded, but Boyle, Newton, Leeuwenhoek, Swammerdam and others interspersed many remarks about the goodness of God which was manifest from the results of their work. These incidental thoughts were taken up by Nieuwentyt and others, and were worked out more systematically. Nieuwentyt also brought forward good scientific results. His work was clearly set up in two parts. In the first part an exposition was given of the scientific results, while in the second part the moral lessons were drawn from the first part. Others followed him and in this way a theology of the bees, the stars, the stones, etc. originated.

The objections against this argument are obvious. Nobody can dispute the existence of order and beauty in nature, but there is also much disharmony and there are many catastrophes. Especially the great earthquake of 1755 was a great shock to many adherents of this argument in the 18th century. So it was given up after Kant's, Hume's and Darwin's criticism. Perhaps a physico-theological argument based exclusively on beauty (and no longer on the utility of nature for man) may be maintained. We shall discuss this possibility under the argument from aesthetics, for such a kind of reasoning belongs rather to this argument than to pure physico-theology, but the line of distinction is not always sharp here.

The teleological argument, which we found in the thinking of Thomas Aquinas, is more modest and therefore more plausible. In the rest of this section we shall discuss only this version of the argument. In contradistinction to the physico-theological argument it merely states that there is some acting according to purposes in organic nature, and does not pretend that all this acting is of any use for mankind or that man can learn moral lessons from it. The argument is based on the following premises: (i) there is a certain order in nature so that many beings act with a certain purpose, (ii) in the world we know it is only intelligent beings who can construct an order of purpose, i.e. a kind of acting directed by conscious intentions, (iii) by a reasoning through analogy we must conclude that the world as a whole is also created by an intelligent being, i.e. God.

According to Hume there is certainly some kind of order or acting on purpose in nature. He also acknowledges a kind of analogy between artefacts and nature. But he considers all this much too weak to be convincing premises in an argument for the existence of God. If nature is not built on chance, could there not be an inherent process in nature that explains all this acting on purpose? And even if we admit that there must be an intelligent being which orders the world, the way in which he apparently works differs greatly from what could be expected from an omniscient and omnipotent being. In that case all the many disharmonies, catastrophes etc., refer to an architect who makes many mistakes. Hume expected that better explanations could be found, and Darwin with his theory of evolution has long been considered to have fulfilled this expectation. The remarkable order in nature, which even antagonists of the argument from design could not deny, seems to have found a better explanation in the theory of evolution. But even evolution theories have to face many difficulties and leave many things unexplained. To give one example. One can trace the evolution of the many breeds of horse back to one primordial horse, the evolution of the many breeds of elephant to one primordial elephant, but where do these primordial horse, elephant etc. come from? They are suddenly there! On the whole an evolution theory can explain gradual changes and developments in nature, but there are many great leaps in very short periods which are not explained. But these difficulties as such, on the other hand, are insufficient to serve as a full proof for the existence of God.

Tennant and later Swinburne have given cumulative arguments with the help of the argument from design. They claim that in this way it can be shown that theism is a more plausible explanation than atheism, but this can hardly be called a very convincing proof, only a sort of hint. The main argument in Swinburne's thinking is that the normal causal laws must also be explained, and that they cannot be explained on the level of the normal causal explanation. Here one must refer to explanations by intentions. One sees the parallelism with variant II in the cosmological argument. It is in the realm of the second order explanations that the argument begins to work. However, the convincing power is much less, because even as second-order explanation it is not obvious that we should give a teleological explanation of causal laws. Swinburne presents the argument therefore only in a cumulative setting.

An interesting variant of the teleological argument is given by the American philosopher Richard Taylor. He starts his expositions with an analysis of the human cognitive organs and he asserts that it is irrational to accept the two following theorems in conjunction:

(i)   the human cognitive organs are originated purely by chance in a way, which can be explained by the biological laws of evolution;

(ii)   the human cognitive organs are trustworthy in the sense that they may lead us to true knowledge.

For example: suppose we find a set of stones ordered in such a way that they seem to express a message ('Welcome in Wales'). Now it would be strange to say (i) that the stones have this order purely by chance and also (ii) that we have entered Wales. In other words, if we accept (ii) we have to reject (i). From this Taylor draws the following cautious conclusion, *viz* that human cognitive organs, which sometimes discover the truth, seem to be the product of a certain creative being (God). A possible objection could be that the existence of a cognitive organ is useful for survival and that it can thus be explained in the usual biological way. But it may be possible to demonstrate that many discoveries of the truth do not promote this survival. However, a strict argument is not given by Taylor, neither does he claim to do so. His argument may perhaps also be classified under the arguments from knowledge, but he himself classifies it here.

It is even possible to reformulate the argument with the help of modern information theory and cybernetics. It can be proved that the world cannot be the product of chance. This is a well-known idea, but with the help of computer techniques it can be made more plausible. If we imagine nature as a great computer, it works according to a well-conceived programme and this seems to suggest that it has been programmed by an intelligent creator. Here too we have the usual objections that it seems to us that there are mistakes in the programme. Of course, it is always difficult to determine exactly when we may speak of an event caused by chance and when not.

The argument from design misses the plausibility of the cosmological argument. The latter is much more convincing, but the argument from design still has its fascination. Maybe we should regard it as the expression of an aesthetical mental sensation. Perhaps the physico-theologians have made the mistake of working exclusively with moral and utility criteria. Possibly this theological approach to nature has lead to disappointment, because philosophers have applied exclusively moral categories to God. Complementary to the other proofs this argument may have its value. Nature alludes to God, but we must consider it in the right way. Other interpretations of nature are certainly possible, but nevertheless this aesthetic, religious observation of nature may inspire people. Mankind has learned to sing about God's glory, as for instance the poet of psalm 19:

> The heavens tell out the glory of God,
> the vault of heaven reveals his handiwork.
> One day speaks to another,
> night with night shares its knowledge,
> and this without speech or language
> or sound of any voice.
> Their music goes out through all the earth.
> their words reach to the end of the world.

3.1.5 *Other arguments*

Besides the major arguments we have discussed so far, i.e. the ontological, the cosmological and the argument from design, some arguments of minor importance have been devised. We shall discuss them briefly in this section.

3.1.5.1 *The argument e consensu gentium (the argument from the ubiquity of the belief in God)*

One of the weakest arguments is that *e consensu gentium*, i.e. the argument from the ubiquity of the belief in God. We can find this argument in Cicero, but nobody has put it forward as a strong and convincing argument. The startingpoint of the argument is the observed fact that the belief in God is found among all human tribes and races. One may construct the argument as follows:

(i)   The belief in God can be found among all human tribes and races;
(ii)   This refers to the fact that this belief in God is an innate one (inferred from i);
(iii)   This can only be explained if this belief is implanted in man (inferred from ii);
(iv)   Such an implanting can only be made by him who has created man, i.e. God (inferred from iii).

Now (i) is true so far as our experience and investigations go. This does not mean that atheists can nowhere be found. Among all races and peoples there are atheists, or people who have serious doubts about the truth of religious beliefs. On the whole one must concede (i). But to begin with the step from (i) to (ii) is not necessary, for as we have already said, the truth of (i) does not exclude the fact that there are everywhere also atheists and men who doubt. And this again casts some doubt on the truth of (ii). But even if we take the truth of (ii) for granted, the great difficulty remains step (iii), for from the fact that the belief in God is innated it does not follow that it is implanted. Step (iv) from (iii) may be considered to be plausible, but this does not make it a valid argument because of the improbability of step (iii).

A second version of the argument may run as follows:
(i)   The belief in God may be found among all human tribes and races;
(ii)   This refers to the fact that this belief in God is innate (inferred from ii);
(iii)   All innate beliefs are true (premise);
(iv)   Consequently the belief in God is true and therefore God exists (from ii and iii).

Of course, the weak point here is premise (iii) which is not provable. It is not even plausible, because it is certainly possible that the whole of mankind makes a common error, trusting an innate belief.

3.1.5.2 *The argument from the innateness of belief in God*

This argument is, of course, related to the previous one. One starts already with step (ii). The same difficulties arise here.

3.1.5.3 *The argument from morality*

We have met this argument already in Kant's work (*vide* above 2.6.1). We have also seen that according to many scholars the moral attitude precedes the belief in God (the religious stage) (*vide* Kierkegaard, Brunner, and others). The argument may have several variants.

VARIANT I
(i)   Through his moral intuition man knows that he has to do his duty (premise);
(ii)   It is impossible for anyone to fulfil his duties, try as he might (from experience);
(iii)   Justice requires that anyone who has done his utmost to fulfil his duty, but has been prevented from doing it, should be given the opportunity to fulfil his duty (inferred from (i));
(iv)   Therefore there will be this opportunity (from (ii) and (iii));
(v)   As such an opportunity cannot be given in this life, there must be an afterlife in which this is possible (from (iv));
(vi)   As such an opportunity can only be given by God, He must necessarily exist (from v).

I think that I have presented Kant's argument here in its strongest form in that all allusions to possible rewards have been eliminated, so that the usual objection that Kant has fallen back into eudaemonism, is now void. Moreover, I have given the variant in which a reference to moral intuition is

122

made, because in my view this is the strongest variant, for now there is at least a plausible inference from (i) to (iii). This means that in my opinion the argument is impeccable in the steps (i), (ii) and (iii). The main difficulty lies in step (iv). If it had run:

(iv) Therefore there should be this opportunity (from (ii) and (iii));
the inference would be correct, for then we still remain in the realm of what 'should be' and we are not in the realm of what 'is'. And the jump from 'should' or 'ought' to 'is' is still logically incorrect.

Step (v) seems impeccable to me, but step (vi) may also meet serious criticism. It may be possible to defend the view that there is a life after death without inferring from this fact that there is a God. At least many spiritualists, i.e. believers in a life after death on the strength of parapsychological phenomena, are atheists. We shall return to this problem later on.

Another variant is based on the presupposition that (certain) moral prescriptions are objectively valid. In this view morality is not based on human inventions or feelings. It cannot be changed, but has objective validity. And this means that 'Op' or 'O(p → q)' are (moral) facts. ((The sign 'O' stands for moral obligation)). If we now apply the rule '*ex nihilo nihil fit*' also to moral facts, there must be a cause for them. This cause cannot be man, for in this variant we have already taken for granted that morality cannot be a human convention. Therefore it must be a moral creative superhuman being, i.e. God. So the argument runs as follows:

VARIANT II
(i)   'Op' and 'O(p → q)' are moral facts (premise);
(ii)   Every fact needs a ground (cause) (premise);
(iii) Consequently (i) finds its ground in man or in a superhuman being ((from (i) and (ii));
(iv)   Man cannot be the ground of (i) (premise);
(v)   Consequently a superhuman moral being is the ground of man's morality (from (iii) and (iv)).

In my view steps (ii), (iii) and (v) are unobjectionable, but steps (i) and (iv) are doubtful. Probably the main premise is (i), for it might be possible to construct this is such a way that if (i) were true, (iv) may be inferred from it. That is, we may emphasize the objective validity in such a way that it is indeed impossible for man to create it. But, of course, (i) is a considerable presupposition, which will certainly not be generally accepted. We might perhaps even say that most people will reject it.

3.1.5.4 *The argument from religious experience*

This argument has the interesting feature of being subjectively very con-

123

vincing. That means that people who have a strong religious experience, are subjectively completely convinced to its trustworthiness, and that statements based on that experience are therefore true. We have already seen that objectively many objections could be brought forward against it.

3.1.5.5 *The argument from aesthetic experience*

As such, this is a very interesting argument which has not yet been investigated properly. We shall come to an analysis of the characteristics of aesthetics and aesthetic experience later on (*vide* 4.6.3). We shall refer to some of the results of our investigation there. I shall take aesthetic experience as a primitive concept which refers not only to the experience of beauty, but also to the experience of all kinds of phenomena: the sublime, the humorous, the tragic, etc. The experiences of all these phenomena have in common that they lead to an intensifying of life. The argument may have various versions too. One runs parallel to that of the moral argument:

VARIANT I
(i)   'W^a p' and '$W^a(p \rightarrow q)$' are aesthetic facts (premise);
(ii)   Every fact needs a ground (cause) (premise);
(iii)   Consequently (i) finds its ground in man or in a superhuman being (from (i) and (ii));
(iv)   Man cannot be the ground of (i) (premise);
(v)   Consequently a superhuman aesthetic being is the ground of man's aesthetic values (from (iii) and (iv)).

Here 'W^a' is the sign indicating aesthetic values. In (i) it is stated that there are objectively aesthetic values. Now (i) is even more doubtful than its parallel in the moral argument. Usually aesthetic statements are considered to be completely subjective. But one may maintain that *some* aesthetic statements are objective and refer to aesthetic facts without claiming that *all* aesthetic statements are objective and refer to facts. In the same way perhaps the moral argument can be defended, *viz.* that *some* moral statements are objective and refer to facts. In the same way as in the moral argument step (iv) can be defended. Thus it may be considered to be implied by (i) and not to be an independent premise. But on the whole it is weaker than the variant II of the moral argument, and even that was a weak argument.

VARIANT II
    In this variant the emphasis is laid not on the experience of beauty but on the experience of the other features which lead to an intensifying of life. In this way it has value only if it is combined with other experiences. Thus it forms an aesthetic constituent in a whole event of experiences. It may be

combined with religious experience, in which for example the *indirect way* of communication is a plain aesthetic element (*vide* 4.6.3). It may also be combined with modern forms of the physio-theological argument and here it plays an important role. For we have seen that one of the main weaknesses of the latter argument was formed by the obvious disharmonies and catastrophes in nature and human life. Now in the aesthetic realm there is – according to modern views – room for disharmonies, ugliness, etc. How this can be, is, of course, mainly an aesthetic problem which does not concern us here. Suffice it to say that in my view these disharmonies can serve to intensify life and can thus contribute to aesthetic experiences. We shall come to it later (*vide* 4.6.3). If this is true the difficulties of the physico-theological argument are in principle overcome. Combined with the argument from aesthetic experience the disharmonies and the suffering have meaning, and if in a modern view God himself is in some way participating in this suffering a possible inconsistency has been taken away.

Nevertheless it must be said that objectively this argument is not very strong, even if it is combined with other arguments, because it depends completely on certain experiences and the ways in which they are interpreted. All the weaknesses of religious experience return here. But like religious experiences aesthetic experiences are subjectively very convincing, because they transmit deep feelings which inspire man in his totality, and contribute to an intensifying of life. There is a discrepancy here between the subjectively convincing power of the argument and its objective validity.

3.1.5.6 *The argument from truth and knowledge (i.e. the epistemological argument)*

As Augustine is the great propounder of this form of argument, we shall devote a special subsection to him.

3.1.5.6.1 *Augustine*

Nowhere does Augustine speak about the arguments for God's existence in a systematic way. He knows of various proofs: the cosmological argument, the argument *e consensu gentium*, the argument from the human longing for happiness, but he speaks most extensively about the argument from the eternal truths, i.e. the epistemological argument. In the human mind there are eternal truths in morals, aesthetics, logic, mathematics, etc. These truths are objectively given and they could not be present without a truth which includes all these truths, i.e. God.

Augustine gives the following presuppositions of his argument:

(i)   If A includes B and B does not include A, then A is more perfect than B;

(ii)   If A is a criterion of B, or if A has the competence to judge B, then A is more perfect than B.

The argument runs as follows:
(1)   A thinking being includes in his thinking non-thinking beings and is not included by them. Man is the only thinking being in nature (taken from experience);
(2)   Therefore, of all the beings in nature man is most perfect (from (1) and (i));
(3)   In human knowledge reason is the criterion for sensual cognition (taken from epistemology);
(4)   Consequently, reason is more perfect than the senses (from (3) and (ii));
(5)   Of all things in nature human reason is most perfect (from (2) and (4));
(6)   Eternal truths are the criterion of reason (taken from epistemology);
(7)   Consequently, these eternal truths are the most perfect in nature (from (6) and (ii));
(8)   Consequently there is something unchangeable, eternal, most perfect, i.e. eternal truth and this is God (from 7). God, however, may surpass eternal truth.

This argument must not be isolated from Augustine's other epistemological and metaphysical theories. He was for example a forerunner of Descartes in his victory over doubt: Man, who doubts everything, is at least certain that he doubts. But one cannot doubt without existing, *ergo*…

I shall not go into the details of the argument here, but shall confine myself to some critical remarks. Although the two presuppositions have some plausibility, they may also be regarded as not being sufficiently evident. Step (3) presupposes a rational epistemology, which may be doubted also. In step (6) Augustine presupposes that mathematical and other truths are discovered by man and not constructed by him. That means that he presupposes classical logic and mathematics. The weakest point may be the last. The conclusion is that there is eternal, unchangeable truth and that this truth surpasses human reason, but is this eternal truth to be identified with God? In Augustine's view God may surpass this truth, but at least he includes it. But then God is already presupposed.

Concluding, we may say that in Augustine's argument, some transcendent reality is proved (given some premises), but that this does not yet mean that God has been proved.

3.1.5.6.2 *The argument from truth as correspondence*

For a more extensive exposé of the various theories of truth we may refer here to appendix 11. A most commonly accepted view, at least in ordinary language, is that of truth as correspondence. A statement p is true if and only if the fact p exists. This means a statement p refers to a fact p, and this statement is true, if and only if this fact p is really there. If I say: 'My wife is in the drawing-room', this statement is true if and only if my wife is indeed in the drawing-room. If some says 'Winston Churchill was born in 1874', this statement is true if and only if Churchill was indeed born in 1874, etc. There are more complicated cases, but the correspondence theory is a widely accepted theory, at least in common usage. Still we run into difficulties.

If a statement p (let us call it statement A) is true if and only if the fact p exists, how may we then verify this? We must be able to compare in some way the statement p and the fact p and this results in a new statement (let us call this statement B) in which it is stated that statement A is true, or in other words that indeed the fact p exists. But when is this statement B true? Of course, exclusively if and only if the fact to which this statement B refers exists. And this fact is the correspondence between statement A and fact p. How can we verify statement B? Only with the help of a new statement C, in which it is stated that statement B is true, etc. We obviously run into a *regressus ad infinitum*.

In practice this problem is solved, because by convention (*consensus*) it has been settled how we are to verify that, for example, my wife is in the drawing-room. But in a philosophical view there always remain uncertainties here, and if we do claim that the truth by correspondence is objective and not dependent upon human conventions (and this is the case in Augustine's theory of truth) we may look for another solution. One may be tempted to conclude from this, that only God can establish objective truth by correspondence. Even with these presuppositions it is not necessary to accept God immediately as the decisive constituent of truth. In mathematics and logic a certain construction very often plays an important role, i.e. the construction of the so-called ideal observer or ideal mathematician (logician). The theoretical construction is very often important, but we need not ascribe ontological existence to this ideal observer. It is only a means in order to discuss certain problems better. And here it may serve to solve the paradox of the infinite regress in the correspondence theory. We may say that the verification of statement A above is in principle done by an ideal observer.

With the help of this construction one can assert that there is objective truth and that truth is not dependent upon human decisions, although in practice human decisions are needed. Objective truth is in this way constituted by the ideal observer, whereas human truth can be seen as only approaching this objective truth, and here in human truth conventions may play their role, without eliminating objective truth. Nevertheless, as an argument for the existence of God this argument is insufficient. We come to

the same conclusion as in our critical evaluation of Augustine's argument. Only if one does not accept this auxiliary construction and still wants to defend the objectivity of truth, has one to recur to the existence of God. So if one wants to escape the conclusion of God's existence, one has two possibilities at one's disposal:
(i) one may deny that there is objective truth, i.e. that there is truth outside the human mind and/or independent of man;
(ii) objective truth can – in principle – be established by an ideal observer.

3.1.5.6.3 *The argument from the normative theory of truth*

There are more theories of truth than only the correspondence theory. A theory that has fewer adherents, but is still possible, is the normative theory of truth. Here a statement p is true if and only if it fulfils a certain norm or is in agreement with a certain standard. If a certain norm or standard is the criterion of truth and if we claim that it must be an objective norm or standard, then each norm or standard must be evaluated by a higher norm and we shall in this way finally reach a highest norm or standard, which we may call God. In such reasonings one can easily recognize Augustine's way of arguing, and we can also detect the same weaknesses as in the argument from the correspondence theory. Moreover, the two escapes are also possible here.

3.1.5.7 *The argument from parapsychology*

In this argument we presuppose the reality and trustworthiness of the so-called ESP phenomena. These phenomena, the extra-sensory perceptions, are studied in parapsychology and in some hypotheses and views presuppositions may be formulated which can be used in an argument for the existence of God. Of course, the ESP phenomena are not established beyond doubt and moreover, they could be explained in such a way that the presuppositions mentioned above are no longer present. In my view they cannot be accepted scientifically (see also appendix 11), but I think that they are interesting enough to be investigated and discussed. There are many parapsychological phenomena: telepathy, prescience, prophesying dreams, manifestations of ghosts and so on. The latter phenomena are especially important: the manifestations of the dead. There are two main hypotheses to explain them: (i) the so called spiritistic hypothesis in which it is stated that these manifestations, in which remarkable knowledge is sometimes demonstrated, are indeed manifestations of spirits of the dead; but (ii) it is also possible to explain these manifestations otherwise by (the so-called animistic hypothesis). But then a recourse to other ESP phenomena is necessary, i.e. telepathy, prescience, etc. A third possibility would be to reduce all ESP phenomena to 'normal' phenomena.

(i) *The spiritistic hypothesis*

This hypothesis does not automatically include the belief in the existence of God. Many spiritists deny the existence of God, because among the spirits of the dead the discussion does not yet seem to be settled on this point. And indeed the belief in immortality is certainly possible without the belief in God. In the more extended theory of the spiritists it is stated that the spirits of the dead are able to see our world, but are also able to produce worlds of themselves. According to these views there is a possibility of ascending a ladder of perfection. From stage to stage the spirits of the dead learn to think better and thus to create better worlds. Whether they will conceive of God or not, is a matter of their personal conviction, according to 'official' spiritistic theory. Here I think there is an inconsistency, for if these spiritistic theories are true, we have the clue to make the ontological argument valid and also the other arguments such as the moral argument, and the argument from aesthetic experience. For now the difficulty of bridging the gap between thought and reality can be overcome. In this 'official' spiritistic theory the highest concept that can be thought of is both true and the goal of the spiritual ladder and from this it may be concluded that the gap has been bridged! It may be objected that in this spiritistic theory it is the spirits who created their own world every time. That is conceded, but at the same time they may recur to their aesthetic, moral and religious experiences and these are now much more convincing, because powerful thinking creates reality at the same time, and the only thing to be proved is that the concept of God is the highest concept that may inspire man. However, that was not the weak point in the various arguments for the existence of God. The real problem was whether that which was thought of as the highest, which inspired man most, was indeed real.

(ii) *The animistic hypothesis*

This term may be misleading, because the word 'animism' is also used in the science of religion: animists are people who believe that everything is animated and they certainly believe in the existence of spirits. But the term 'animistic hypothesis' originates from parapsychologists and not from scientists of religion. In this hypothesis the ESP phenomena are accepted, but it is denied that the so-called manifestations of the dead are really what they pretend to be. They can be reduced to other ESP phenomena, for example telepathy. Sometimes remarkable knowledge is demonstrated in these manifestations of the dead. For example, the medium through which the dead persom seems to speak tells stories which are only known to the dead person and some of the attendants, at any rate not to the medium. Of course, the medium can unconsciously receive her knowledge through telepathy from those present. Adherents of the first hypothesis indicate that very often the medium knows things which indeed only the dead person could know, so that influence through telepathy is excluded. We will not go into this discussion here, because there are so many ESP phenomena that it seems always possible to give an explanation otherwise than by presupposing real manifestations of the dead. We shall return to this problem later on.

In the whole field of ESP phenomena there are also the so-called 'parakinetic' phenomena, i.e. those phenomena by which the mind can influence matter in a paranormal way. In the so-called 'paragnostic' phenomena the mind knows things in a paranormal way. But the parakinetic phenomena point to the possibility that the mental reality is ultimately not different from the material reality, in conformity with the spiritistic hypothesis. And in that case we could prove the existence of God again with the help of the ontological and other arguments, as we can in the case of the 'spiritistic' hypothesis. However, in the case of the 'animistic hypothesis', the argument is weaker, because then it is only a reasonable possibility that the mental and the material reality will ultimately coincide, whereas in the case of the 'spiritistic hypothesis' this is explicitly stated.

(iii) *All ESP phenomena can be reduced to 'normal' phenomena*

If one accepts this hypothesis, the whole argument for the existence of God by means of parapsychology collapses. Now hypothesis (iii) may be very plausible, but at least one has to prove it in the face of the overwhelming amount of parapsychological material. Still I think it can be done, but the proof must be carried out by means of a scientific programme, and until now we in the West have not taken much interest in such an endeavour. This is, of course, a matter of culture. In the Orient scientific people make much more use of parapsychological results than we do. As long as extensive investigations have not been carried out, we remain with a *non liquet*. And so two kinds of systems are possible: one kind in which the parapsychological data are accepted and one kind in which they are not. In the one in which they are accepted, an argument for God's existence can be given with the help of the argument from parapsychology. And as this argument is combined with that of the ontological, the moral and the aesthetic arguments, the concept of God which is finally proved has much more content than the concept of God which is proved by the cosmological argument only, as happens in the system in which the parapsychological data are not accepted. In this book a system will be developed in which these parapsychological data are *not* accepted (*vide* appendix 11). We have only shown that they help to strengthen the argument for God's existence.

3.1.6 *Final remarks*

We have seen that on the whole the arguments for God's existence are not conclusive, with the exception of the cosmological argument. This is a convincing argument, but its result is not very rich in content. God has only been proved as an *ens necessarium*. The other arguments can, however, in combination with one another constitute a cumulative argument for the existence of God. Swinburne, Mitchell, and (earlier) Tennant have pointed towards this possibility. One should not conclude too quickly that such a cumulation is worthless in the sense that if we add a series of noughts we shall get a nought at the end. For suppose we have four arguments, each of which has a degree of probability of 0.5, which means that they have not a great individual plausibility. But together, provided they are independent of each other, they have a probability of 0.9375 (where 1.0 stands for absolute certainty). And this is a high degree of probability! Even the cosmological argument is not 'definite' as we have seen, but it has at least as such (outside a cumulative argumentation) a high degree of probability, but it does not prove as much as most of the other arguments do.

In the following section we shall try to give a philosophical theology based on what is proved in the cosmological argument only. When we unfold our philosophy of religion further in chapter 4, we shall also refer to religious, moral and aesthetic experience. The reference to these experiences is more plausible now we have proven God's existence.

3.2 *God's attributes (properties)*

In this section we shall deal with God's attributes (properties) in a philosophical way. A complete treatment of the subject is impossible here, because this belongs to dogmatics. In deriving God's attributes we presuppose only the results of the cosmological argument, because the ontological argument is less convincing, although it may function in a cumulative argument. Therefore we have to start with God as an *ens necessarium*. That means that we have to ascribe necessary existence to God; his non-being cannot be thought of. From this fact God's eternity can be derived. In the cosmological argument the *ens necessarium* is at least also a creative ground of all being, because that was already included in the premises. It is proved in the cosmological argument that there must be a creative ground which is an *ens necessarium*. So God must be the creator of the world. This does not necessarily include a creation in time, because we have also taken a timeless ground into consideration. Also Thomas Aquinas was of the opinion that a creation in time was philosophically not necessary. In variant I, however, we have given some arguments in favour of a beginning of the world in time. As the consequences of the creation are probably infinite in number we may in all likelihood ascribe an infinite creative power to God. By infinite creative power we understand the faculty with the help of which God executes his function as active creative ground.

Since in our argument God is a second order ground, i.e. a ground of grounds, the rule must be applied here that in the consequences of this ground there cannot be more creative power than in the ground itself. In contradistinction to what has been very often taught in scholasticism, this rule is not always valid in the relation ground-consequence or cause-effect. If a ground A has as consequence B, it is possible that in B there is more creative power than in A, for other grounds or causes may also have played a role, i.e. other causes can have contributed to the originating of B, and thus have given B some of their power. But with the relation between ground of grounds and consequences this is impossible, because now there are no additional grounds. Therefore we may ascribe to God also those earthly properties which refer to a certain creative power, because all creative activities must finally be traced back to God. One sees how much in the development of the cosmological argument depends on the premise that the relation ground-consequence constitutes a *directed* ordered set. For from this it can be easily inferred that if there is a last element, this element must be unique. Thus the creative power that earthly beings have, pertains also to God in an infinite degree. In appendix 2 we shall give a more exact, modern formulation of this view.

Therefore, if we have the choice of ascribing to God property A or property non-A, we must choose the property which has the most creative power. We may ascribe omniscience, omnipotence, personality (i.e. self-consciousness, cogitation, will, etc.), goodness etc., to God, because in these properties a creative power is manifest while in their opposites there is no creative, but only a destructive power. In other words these properties enable the performance of creative achievements. However, we must concede that God cannot transgress logical laws in spite of his omnipotence. More correctly one must conceive God's omnipotence in such a way that the logical laws cannot be transgressed. In this respect I agree with Leibniz, or better with Spinoza, in contradistinction to Descartes, for I prefer to defend the Spinozistic view that the eternal truths, i.e. the logical laws, etc., are an expression of God and that they are not above God as is the case in the philosophy of Leibniz. We shall return to this concept when we deal with the doctrine of God in the next chapter.

In order to complete my exposition I may add the following hypothetical and speculative reflection, with which I agree for the time being, but which is not necessarily connected with the argument as it is expounded so far and which I am quite willing to give up, if better solutions are available. It is the reflection that God's creative power must also be seen as a kind of self-restraint. In his creative power God would destroy everything, if he did not limit himself, for his power may be compared with an all-consuming fire. So God limits himself and in this self-limitation the world emerges. God bestows a little of his creative power and goodness on his creation. We find this reflection in the Cabbala and in some representatives of German Idealism.

Without doubt a somewhat traditional theologian will find the concept of God in this book, or better the various concepts given here, very 'poor'. He will use this term if he is polite, but if he is not, he will use harsher expressions, for example, that the concept(s) of God in this book falsifies (falsify) the Christian concept of God. One should only compare the rather poor exposition of God's properties in section 3.2 with its parallel in any dogmatic work, or better still let one compare it with Scripture itself, for dogmatics can be boring too. In Scripture we find personal communications between God and man, his people, the faithful. There we meet a God, who loves mankind, who seeks mankind and sacrifices himself in and through Jesus Christ. That is something quite different from an exposition with theses, arguments and objections. But this difference is always present, not only in a philosophical approach, but also in a theological one. Brunner in particular has shown that there is a fundamental difference between revelation and faith on the one hand and theoretical reflection on the other. In revelation and faith we have to do with truth as encounter (*Wahrheit als Begegnung*), i.e. a truth that lies on the level of personal, existential communication. In revelation human factual knowledge is not increased, but the human personality is changed. He becomes a new man in Christ. He sees his former life as a guilty life and he turns to a new life.

In philosophy and science my knowledge is increased, but my personality remains unchanged, my heart is not touched, I do not turn to a new life. In philosophy and science we have to do with an abstract doctrine, where the correspondence between statement and fact is fundamental for truth. The concept of truth in the Bible if quite different. There Jesus Christ is the truth; this means that in the Bible truth is personal, not abstract. Brunner does not disprove abstract science and philosophy. Nor does he deny that such an approach is necessary and useful. Even in theology (dogmatics) we need reflection and abstract thinking. There the concept of truth is mixed: partly it is abstract as in science and philosophy, partly it has the warmth and the personal features of biblical truth. But in theology the error is very often made that the peculiar characteristics of biblical truth are not recognized. It is wrong to think that biblical faith is to hold certain statements as being true, i.e. that they correspond to certain facts.

I agree with Brunner to a certain extent. Philosophy is much more abstract than biblical faith. But in my view philosophy is important enough to be dealt with. There is in man a justified curiosity to try to find out what can be proved and what not. That not everything can be proved in obvious, but an approach such as that of Brunner and Barth is in danger of becoming completely irrational. Barth runs this risk even more than Brunner, who is at least trying to give philosophy some task. And I admit that even Barth, because he himself has personally a great admiration for a good system, is not irrational in his expositions. However, because of the fundamental anti-philosophical doctrine his system does run this risk. It is the right of reason to see how much can be proved, or still better, with the help of what premises the existence of God, human eternal life, etc. can be proved. There must be a legitimate rational approach also to the fundamental questions of life, even though the possibilities for reason to answer them are limited. There are more important things in life than philosophy. In my view philosophy of religion certainly requires a complementary addition coming from religious belief, but with the rational method defended in this book I try to make a rational discussion of religious subjects possible. The fundamental thesis of this book is that every religious statement can be defended. It is the task of philosophy of religion to discover the philosophi-cal (rational and empirical) presuppositions of the various religious beliefs. The latter will only have convincing power, if they can be derived in a rational, sufficiently strict system. I do not deny that the philosophical concept of God is abstract and that the philosophical truth about God does not reach the depth of religious truth, but *abstrahentium non est mendacium* according to a scholastic saying. It is characteristic of abstractions that they are no lies. Philosophical truths are more universally acceptable than religious truths. And if one acknowledges their limits, philosophical truths are certainly legitimate.

Further: Brunner's thesis, that in Scripture 'to believe' always means 'to believe in' and never 'to believe that' is not correct. In Brunner's view biblical truth is always personal and that means that there is no belief that certain statements are true or that certain facts have occurred. However, the expression 'to believe that' is widespread in Scripture:
(a)   to believe that God raised Christ from the dead (Rom. x,9);
(b)   to believe that Jesus died and rose again (1 Thess. iv,14);
(c)   to believe that Jesus has the power to cure someone (Matth. ix,28),
      etc.
And in the Old Testament 'to believe' is also used in this way:
(d)   to believe that God has appeared to Moses (Ex. iv,5);
(e)   to believe that God will destroy Ninive (Jonah iii,5);
      (cp. further Lamentations iv,12; Job ix,16; xv,22; Psalm xxvii,13
      etc.).

The same can be said of the concept 'to reveal' and 'revelation'. It is not correct to assert that in Scripture God reveals only himself as Brunner and others say. Certainly God reveals himself, but he also reveals other things, facts, etc. The design of the Tabernacle is said to have been revealed (Ex. xxv,9; xxvii,9); some facts which play a role in God's plan of salvation have been revealed (1 Sam, ix,15ff; 2 Sam. vii,27). God's promises are thought to have been revealed (Amos ix,13; Hos. xi,11; Isa. lvi,8). Cp. for the New Testament 1 Cor. iv,5; 2 Cor. v,10; 1 John iii,2.

We must remark here that in Scripture the concept of revelation occurs

134

much less than one would expect. It is after all a central concept in dogmatics. Further, Brunner and others are right in saying that the revealed facts are never isolated from God's plan of salvation. They are not revealed for the sake of satisfying the curiosity of man. Here we do not have to do with a communicative indicative (*vide* 2.9). As Ramsey has pointed out: there is a description and more! Revelation is always also appeal, proclamation, promise. It is an appeal to men to change their life, to turn to God and to be redeemed, to love one's neighbour, etc. Man ought to build a new and better world. But this does not eliminate the role played by facts. One cannot reduce the non-descriptive elements in revelation to descriptive elements, but on the other hand one cannot reduce the factual descriptive elements to the non-descriptive.

Even if we took Brunner's existentialist position and regarded biblical truth as completely non-descriptive (non factual), we would, in my view, do wrong to speak of truth as encounter or truth communication (*Wahrheit als Begegnung*). This suggests that revelation and faith, God and man, operate on the same level. If one wants to emphasize the dynamic character of the process of revelation, then one should speak of a truth which consists of preceding and following. In Scripture revelation has absolute priority and human belief is only a response. It is an answer to God's preceding appeal. Through Jesus Christ God draws man to himself (John vi.44; xii.32). For Jesus' first call was: 'Follow me'. The communicatively descriptive mood of biblical revelation is included in the appealing mood of this preceding and following: 'Thy word is a lamp to guide my feet and a light on my path' (Psalm cxix.105).

Another objection against philosophy of religion is that Scripture does not contain philosophy, so that philosophy of religion is an unbiblical activity. This argument does not hold for two reasons. In the first place many scientific activities were unknown in biblical times and were therefore not taken into account. But this does not mean that they are incompatible with the message of the bible. God's commission to man to reign over the earth (Gen. i,28) is at the same time a commission to promote culture, and this includes scientific and philosophical activities. In the second place Scripture, in my view, *does* contain a kind of philosophical literature, *viz* the so-called wisdom literature: Proverbs, Job, Ecclesiastes, Wisdom of Solomon, etc. Wisdom literature may be considered a forerunner of philosophical literature. This wisdom literature is also present in other cultures and is not confined to Scripture. It represents a universal reflection on the important and relevant problems of life and it is remarkable how many parallels we find between the biblical wisdom literature and the extra-biblical wisdom sources. Out of the universal longing for wisdom a philosophy has emerged which is independent of religion. This occurred in Greece, where the 'man of wisdom' Thales was the first philosopher.

Finally we shall face a last objection against the method used here. Some scholars are of the opinion that for a Christian a philosophy which is independent of revelation is impossible. Such an autonomous philosophy is said to be impossible because Christ (God) is Lord and King over our whole life. This kind of criticism rests on a misunderstanding. Even if one acknowledges Christ as Lord and Saviour, this does not mean that all scientific knowledge and philosophy ought to be derived from revelation. According to modern views there are several levels of language and we must not mix them. What is valid on one level does not automatically have to be valid on another level. What is necessary on the level of meta-language has not to be so on the level of the object language. (As a reminder: a meta-language *speaks about* another language). Thus a theory of art speaks about art, but has not to be a piece of art itself. In the same way philosophy of religion speaks about religion, but does not belong to religion itself, nor ought it to have a religious starting point. In other words: what can be said of the set as a whole, may not be true for its members, or vice versa. If we confess Jesus as our Lord, then this has meaning for our attitude in life, for the framework in which we put our activities. This does not mean that we have to infer our philosophical conclusions from this revelation. Whether one chooses intuitionistic or classical logic has nothing to do with belief in Christ. Whether one accepts the arguments for God's existence or not, does not depend on one's faith. I know atheists who accept these arguments theoretically, and I know believers who reject them.

Is just any system of philosophy compatible with the Christian religion? The answer must be negative, if one considers the system as a whole, for this can be atheistic, for example. But every single philosophical thesis can in principle be compatible with Christian belief. Even the thesis: 'God does not exist' is – as a philosophical thesis – compatible with the Christian faith, provided one adds that reason (philosophy) is insufficient for the definite finding of truth. A philosophical atheism, which is the result of a rational argumentation, is not incompatible with religion and religious (theological) theism. But if one asserts that nothing can transcend rational argumentation and in addition one defends a philosophical, rational atheism, then this kind of philosophy is incompatible with Christian theism. The Christian faith may have an influence on one's whole attitude in life, but not on every philosophical thesis.

4
The religious world view and attitude in life

In the preceding chapters and sections we have mainly discussed epistemological questions, i.e. questions of the verification and truth of religious statements, and of the possibilities of proving God's existence. We tried to construct our system on a strict foundation. We have seen that it is possible to give a proof of God's existence, i.e. the cosmological argument, which is valid in a relatively strict system, although it is always possible to remain in a stricter system in which the proof is no longer valid. If we remained within the limits of our standard system in which we could prove God's existence, our philosophical world view would be very meagre. But we have seen above that if it is possible to prove God's existence, an appeal to religious experience becomes much more convincing.

So in my view we are justified in constructing our more complete system of philosophy of religion with an appeal to religious and aesthetic experience. Moral experience also may be referred to, but this was already less problematic. Aesthetic experience also as a subjective experience, which does not evince any truth, is not problematic. But I may now refer to aesthetic experience as a source of truth, because if God exists, not only does religious experience become more convincing, but also aesthetic experience as evincing truth, because it is closely related with religious experience, as we shall see (*vide* 4.6.3). Although we may now refer to religious experience, this does not mean that the truth of the Christian faith has already been proved, for the cosmological argument may also be the foundation of other religious convictions. Even atheism may be combined with religious experience. It is more difficult to combine atheism with the cosmological argument, if this is linked with the complementary additions we have tried to make plausible in section 3.2. Atheism may be defended by giving to the notion of an ens necessarium a content which differs from our exposition. We shall discuss this later on. In this chapter we shall appeal to religious, moral and aesthetic experience, but we shall investigate the various results in a rational way. In this way we may compare the contributions of the various religions. I shall try to offer the strongest possible defence of each point of view, but, of course, my personal predilections cannot always be avoided. The reader may make his own choice. I do not function as an apologist, although I shall regularly indicate my preferences.

From the preceding pages it may be clear that in philosophy also we have to make choices. These choices are not arbitrary: they are convincing enough for me, although obviously not for everyone. In our strict standard system we have chosen for a logical-epistemic approach, for classical logic in contradistinction to intuitionistic logic and for the multiple application of the rule '*ex nihilo nihil fit*'. In the following I shall indicate my choices too. Some of them are of religious nature, some are still philosophical. Sometimes I hesitate and I leave the question undecided. Of course, the reader may make different choices. Our discussion will nonetheless remain friendly, because it must be a characteristic of a logical approach that at least the *rabies theologorum* has disappeared.

In the following sections we deal with some important problems of philosophy of religion by using data from the science of religion. We shall try to give the strongest possible argumentation for the various religious positions. But we have already seen that it is always possible to improve certain argumentations, so that the discussion is never definitively settled.

4.1 *Concepts of God. Man in his relation to God*

When we consider the various religions and philosophical systems we may conclude that there are many different concepts of God. We shall investigate these concepts here in general, schematic traits. What strikes many scholars is the difference between polytheism (the belief in many Gods) and monotheism (the belief in one God). But the difference is less great than it appears to a first superficial investigation. In many polytheistic cultures theologians and 'men of wisdom' have meditated deeply on the phenomenon of the many gods, and after some reflection they have come to the conclusion that these many gods are the manifestations of one unique God. Often the godhead of their own town was considered to be the most important manifestation. 'The Eternal is one, but he has many names' (Indian text). In a Greek-Egyptian text many female names were mentioned and it was said that they were all manifestations of one goddess. Thus the names of Minerva, Diana, Proserpina, Ceres, Juno, and others were proclaimed, but at the end the text runs: '...and the Egyptians, very powerful through their old wisdom, worship me with proper ceremonies and call me by my true name, Isis'.

Sometimes an abstract, impersonal divine principle is taken to be the real substance behind the many divine manifestations (the gods). We find this view not only in religions with written documents, as e.g. in Egypt and Greece, but also in the so-called primitive religions. Anyone who studies the so-called primitive religions is often struck by the profound thoughts developed here. The view that the so-called primitive people, i.e. the people without script, had an odd logic and that they were primordially unintelligent ('*urdumm*', a term coined by Preuss), is completely dated. They have different experiences from ours, but their logic is the same (Van Baaren). Like my teacher Van der Leeuw I use the term 'primitive religion'

138

in a non-pejorative way. Some scholars have proposed to use the term 'people without script', but this circumscription is too diffuse and inappropriate.

A small example may serve to make clear that in primitive religions too polytheism is not simply taken for granted. We have seen in our exposition of the cosmological argument that the set of causes was taken to be a directed set, i.e. if we have to do with two causes, or with two powers, we always look for a common cause or principle from which the two emerge. This is not something which only modern man does, for in the past such endeavours have also been made, and by primitive thinkers as well. Among the Ngadu-Dayaks (Kalimantan, formerly Borneo) there are two main godheads Mahatala and Jata. These two godheads are independent of each other. Mahatala belongs to the higher world and Jata to the lower world. In the various rites they are regarded as two different beings. But in Dayak theology they still form a unity. This is e.g. manifest in the myth of creation. In the ceremonies in which the two godheads play their role they are referred to in the following way: '...the watersnake which forms a unity with the hornbill'. The water-snake is an animal symbol for Jata and the hornbill for Mahatala. This one godhead includes all oppositions: higher and lower world, male and female, good and evil, war and peace. Behind this world view there is certainly a rational principle. But this rational principle does not necessarily function as a unifying principle.

Moreover, many primitive religions know a special high god, who has created the world. He may also be the product of a rational unifying principle, for very often he remains in the background and is not appealed to in the cult, except in times of great need. In the 19th century it was commonly held that the sublime concepts of the higher religions could only have developed out of much simpler notions of primitive religions. In 1898 Andrew Lang protested against this view. He showed that in many primitive religions there is a unique high god. This high god is very often in the background, but not always. Ruhanga the creator-god of the Banyoro (East Africa) is held in high esteem, but he is not worshipped. He is considered to have done his work and does not participate any longer in human affairs, so that it is unnecessary to pray to him. The high god of the Akan (West Africa) has also been regarded as a *deus otiosus* of the same type, but this is not correct. Parrinder has shown that this god was believed to be present in many proverbs, riddles and greetings: he is not only a first cause, he also displays a lasting activity of maintaining the world; he judges the dead and punishes or rewards them.

The fact that we find this type of high god in primitive religions has caused Father Schmidt to devise the hypothesis of an original monotheism, but this idea could not be maintained. Father Schmidt saw in these high gods remnants of an original belief in one God. It was, as it were, a remnant of the belief that existed in paradise! But it is more probable that these high gods are products of more or less rational reflections as we have indicated above. The directedness of the set of causes seems to suggest a highest and ultimate source of causation. Primitive people reflect very deeply about the origin of the world and about the causal connections of the various things. Therefore they know many aetiological myths, i.e. myths about the way in which the things of the world have come into being.

Father Schmidt's hypothesis has been useful, insofar as it has refuted evolutionism. Previously many evolutionistic theories were constructed. According to one theory there was originally animism (the belief in ghosts, or more correctly the belief that everything is animated); out of this animism polytheism emerged and out of this polytheism monotheism origi- nated. According to another evolutionary theory dynamism, that is the belief in an all-pervading, impersonal power, preceded animism. Accord- ing to still another theory the gods first had the features of a fetish, then the features of an animal, then those of human beings, and finally they were considered to be spirits. But we must be very careful with such evolutionary theories. We know practically nothing about prehistoric peoples. We have some archaeological findings and we may construct their original language: primordial Indo-European, primordial Semitic, primordial Malayo- Polynesian, etc., and with the help of such language constructions we may also learn something about their respective cultures. But all this gives us so little knowledge that we cannot draw many conclusions with regard to the original religions. Sometimes interesting hypotheses have been brought forward. For example, it has been said that there were at first only mother goddesses and that father gods appeared later on the scene. This hypothesis was based on archaeological findings, among which there were many distinct female deities. But these 'mother goddesses' could very well have been ordinary female beings accompanying the male being in his tomb, which means that they were not goddesses at all!

Besides the idea of the high gods, some linguistic evidence can be brought forward in support of the theory of on original monotheism. Both in the primordial Indo-European languages and in the primordial Semitic languages there seems to have been one prominent god who occurs in all the languages (Dyauspitar and El respectively). He may have been the original god for all these peoples. But the evidence is too weak to support such a hypothesis, however interesting it may be.

There are some other relevant distinctions. Between monotheism and polytheism there is dualism. Here it is taught that two gods are contending for the hegemony. An example of such dualism is Parsism: Ormuzd and Ariman, the good and the evil god, are fighting with each other. It is man's obligation to help Ormuzd in his struggle. In Judaism, Christianity and Islam this second deity has been reduced to a created being (Satan, devil). In the religions of polarity dualism receives another character. In these religions there are two principles, which do not oppose, but complement each other.

140

A good example of this type of dualism is the Chinese religion, where Yang and Yin are opposites. The famous Chinese sage and poet Lao Tse has expressed this fundamental idea in a beautiful way:

Small determines great;
Weak determines strong;
Going down determines going up;
Void determines plenty.

Here is the principle of thinking about the other world:

Hard is a degree of softness;
Strong is a degree of weakness.
But as a fish does not live outside the dark abyss,
so man ought not to strive after knowledge of the essence of man!
(Saying 36 of his collection of sayings)

Another distinction is that between the role of the individual and the collective (state) in the relation with God. In some religions it is mainly the individual (or a small unit like the family) that has a relation with God. In other religions it is mainly the people or the state functioning as God's partner. But this distinction is not absolute. In his covenant the God of the Old Testament stood in a relationship with the whole people of Israel, but inside this covenant there were also personal relations with God. An example of a religion in which the individual is absorbed by the relation God – State is the Roman religion, where everything which concerns religion is in some way a public affair. But there the family plays its role too, but then as a public institution.

A distinction is also made between a male and a female deity. In the bible the concept of God is dominated by the father symbol. In Christianity, Judaism and Islam the father symbol is appropriate, because it expresses distance and nearness at the same time. The female deities were usually symbols of fertility and the biblical writers did not want to emphasize this element in face of the religion of the Canaanites. The symbol of the Virgin Mary is a remnant of an older worship of a female deity, which was widespread in the Near Orient. Bachofen has advocated the idea that the worship of female deities preceded that of the male deities and in connection with this he taught that matriarchy had a temporal priority over patriarchy. But these two theses cannot be proved and they are even unlikely. The cult of female deities was widespread in antiquity. One may think of Ishtar (Babylon), Isis (Egypt), Durga (India). The female deity was at the same time mother and lover. She had, however, not only amiable characteristics: Ishtar e.g. was the goddess not only of love but also of war. According to the myth she killed all her lovers. The worship of the Indian goddess Durga required bloody sacrifices of human beings and animals on the one hand, but on the other hand she killed the buffalo demon Mahisha and delivered mankind from an evil threat. Moreover, she was able to inspire her adherents to the most sublime ecstasies, for example the famous Ramakrishna.

That in Judaism, Christianity and Islam God is worshipped as a father must, of course, be interpreted symbolically. God is beyond the difference of sexes. For the preference of the father symbol other arguments can be given in addition to those given above. If God were presented as a mother, there would be a danger of comparing the creation of the world with the birth of a child, or in other words the danger that the world could be regarded as *emanating* from God and not as *created* by him. The father symbol emphasizes the distance and is more appropriate to express the idea of a creation. We will return to this later.

The following distinction is also important: there are religions in which God acts in time, i.e. religions in which history is fundamental. In this respect the concept of a history of salvation is important. In these religions history has a beginning, an end and a goal: Creation – Fall – Salvation – Eschatology (the doctrine of the last things, such as death, judgment, heaven, hell, etc.). Examples of this kind of religion are Parsism, Judaism, Christianity, Islam. In other religions God is either timeless or submitted to a cyclic form of time. In many mystical concepts God is timeless. The concept of cyclic time may be found especially in the ancient religions of the state, where God stands in a relationship with a people and a state, e.g. Babylon, Rome, Greece, etc. The cycle of festivals serves either to guarantee the power of the state or to ensure the fertility of the land. By his or her death and resurrection the deity represents the cycle of the seasons in nature. The sacrifices which are presented have the function of helping the deity through a critical phase. One may think here of the death and resurrection of Osiris or of the journey of the sun god Re, who was believed to cross the dark ocean of the nether world every night. The sacrifices were to help Osiris and Re in the fulfilling of their tasks.

Another distinction may be made with respect to the relation God – world. If God remains inside the world and does not transcend it, we speak of *pantheism*. In a literal sense this means that everything is God. But that is not what is really meant by the concept of pantheism. The pantheist believes that the essence, the kernel of all things is divine, not their external appearance. The world has emanated from God and has not been created by him. In contrast to this view *deism* teaches that God has created the world, but having done this, he is no longer active in the world. Nevertheless he is still a guarantee for morality and he rewards the good and punishes the evildoers after death. The philosophers of the Enlightment and also Kant may be called deists. Very often the concept of the high gods, which we have met in the primitive religions, has deistic features. In *theism* it is taught that God is both transcendent and immanent with respect to the world. God has created the world, but He remains active in it. In the great religions a father god is closer to theism or deism while a mother goddess is closer to pantheism. Hence, as we have seen, the preference for the father symbol in Judaism, Christianity and Islam.

Panentheism stands between pantheism and theism. Here the world is seen 'in' God, but God still transcends the world. This concept is, however, not clear in every respect, because in theism also God is both transcendent and immanent, which would imply that the world is *in* God. Here one may think of Paul's saying: '...for in him we live and move, in him we exist' (Acts xvii,28). But insofar as panentheists say that the world has not been created by God but has emanated from him, and still maintain that God transcends the world, they certainly take a middle position between theism and pantheism. It is also possible to assert that a doctrine in which creation is regarded as a self-restriction of God (*vide* 3.2), can be labelled panentheism. For such a view even biblical arguments may be brought forward. One may think of the story of creation in Genesis i. In Genesis i and ii there is no question of a creation out of nothing. That is a later doctrine. On the other hand one may still defend the idea that there is a 'creation out of nothing' in the doctrine of creation as self-restriction, because God has not made use of any matter or power outside himself.

A distinction that is related to the distinction theism – pantheism, etc. is the distinction between a personal God, i.e. God with an ego-structure, and an impersonal God, i.e. a God with a neutrum-structure. In the panentheistic system of the later Schelling, which has an interesting doctrine of potencies in God, God was in the beginning not personal in the full sense of the word, but he becomes personal more and more in the course of history and in relation with man. In the works of many liberal tehologians we find analogous ideas, for example in those of A. Schweitzer, F. Buri, P. Smits, etc. They have expressed this in the following image: God's personality in relation to his impersonal nature is like the warm Gulf Stream in the Atalantic Ocean. In this view God is only partly personal. It is also interesting to note that there are religious systems which are atheistic. Some Hindu systems belong to these, the older Buddhism and Jainism. In later Buddhism, at least in Mahayana-Buddhism, the five Buddhas became personifications of the five aspects of the knowledge of God, and in the Buddhism of China and Japan Buddha is even deified. But here one ought to be careful. Jainism is atheistic, but that does not mean that it is materialistic. It teaches a manifold realism: gods exist, but they are, like human beings, mortal. In Jainistic thought there is an infinite number of imperishable souls. An atheistic system in Hinduism is the doctrine of Samkhya, which is also not materialistic, because it has two principles: the spirit (*puruṣa*) and matter(*prakṛti*). This doctrine has had a great influence on Buddhism.

In the period of the Upanishads an impersonal pantheistic concept of

God is dominant in Indian religion, although in the later parts of the Upanishads there are also theistic sections. Theism is present in the famous *Bhagavadgītā* and in the *purānas*. *Bhagavadgītā* means 'the *song*' (*gītā*) 'of the sacred one' (*bhagavad*), a surname for Vishnu (Krishna) and *purāna* is the Sanskrit word for 'old'. The *purānas* are 18 treatises, written in the Christian era. In Hindu philosophy and mysticism we have both the pantheistic and the non-pantheistic concept of God. The great philosopher Sankara was pantheist. He followed the doctrine of the Vedanta (= the genuine interpretation of the Upanishads) and taught an impersonal God as last principle. In contradistinction to this Ramanuya, Madvha and Manik-kavasagar taught a personal concept of God. Manikkavasagar was a worshipper of Shiva; Ramanuya and Madvha were worshippers of Vishnu from South India, where the Dravids, the original inhabitants of India, live and where the Tamil language is spoken. Some scholars have ascribed these personal concepts of God to this non-Aryan influence, but this is uncertain. Moreover, Sankara teaches the impersonal concept of God only as last principle. He also knows of Isvara, the personal deity, who is, however, ultimately unreal. Real is only the undivided one, *advaita* (a- = the negating a; dvai = two). Sankara teaches a strict monism. Outside the unity of *atman* and *Brahman*, the unity of the individual soul and the impersonal deity, everything is only appearance. This unity is already taught in the Upanishads. The multiplicity of things emerges only through appearance, *māyā*. When Brahman conjures up the world with the help of *māyā*, he also appears as Isvara. This doctrine makes it possible for Sankara to give a place to the traditional Hindu gods in his system. However, they only exist on the level of ignorance, and disappear when a deeper knowledge emerges.

Many Hindus had difficulties with this profound doctrine as is shown in the following anecdote of the elephant: Once there was a king, who became a disciple of Sankara. He was, however, still addicted to the luxury of his palace and the glory of his power. Sankara taught him to consider all this as only appearance, because it belongs to the phenomenal world and not to the real world of the self (*atman*). It was only ignorance (*avidya*) that caused him to take appearance for reality. The king wanted to test the philosopher, and one day when the latter entered the great avenue to the palace a big, dangerous elephant came running in his direction. The king had loosened the animal on purpose. Sankara flew into a tree and in this way escaped the danger. Finally he appeared before the king, from fear sweating from head to foot. The king apologized for the accident, but he could not withhold the remark that he was astonished that Sankara had fled from an elephant which, according to his own view, did not exist and was only a product of ignorance. In Sankara's doctrine the elephant was said only to belong to the phenomenal world. Sankara's answer shows that his doctrine is irrefutable: 'Indeed, Sire, finally the elephant is unreal. But so are we, you and I. We are just as unreal as the elephant. It is only through your ignorance, which obscures this truth through a cloud of appearance, that you saw my unreal body climb into a non-existing tree'.

R. Otto has shown that there are many points of correspondence between Sankara's and Eckhart's philosophy. Eckhart too knows of a deity over and above the personal triune God. This view is not extraordinary or strange in our time. Tillich e.g. teaches a God above God, i.e. an impersonal God above the God of the personal relationship, above the God of prayer. In this respect the views of the Dutch mystics Hadewych and Ruusbroeck are interesting. In their view there is a rhythm of a going in and a going out of the three persons of the Trinity into the one godhead. Man too follows this rhythm in his mystical experience. On the highest level of the mystical elevation the mystic loses himself in God, but then in the following stage he enters again into a personal relationship with the triune God. There is therefore a rhythm of an impersonal ecstasy and a personal relationship. This rhythm is also reflected in the alternation of work and meditation. To return to Eckhart and Sankara: the great difference between the two is that Eckhart does not dismiss the world as mere appearance. Connected with this is Eckhart's view that work is a permanent activity of man. In his interpretation of the famous biblical passage of the meditating Mary and the working Martha (Luke x,38-42) Eckhart unexpectedly takes sides with Martha!

Unlike Sankanra, Ramanuya maintains the unity of Brahman and Isvara. Isvara does not belong to the phenomenal world of mere appearance. Ramanuya does not accept a religion for the great masses and one for the intellectual elite, a distinction which we find in Sankara. He opposes Sankara with religious arguments: he refers to his love for Vishnu, who is a personal God, and so on. But he also refers to rational arguments: Sankara is incorrectly of the opinion, that the senses only transmit seeming knowledge. The purely rational reasoning of Sankara has some reminiscenses of the Greek Eleatic school. Ramanuya is also a rationalist thinker, but by trusting the senses more his system becomes more concrete and he can thus include real individuality, etc. Nevertheless history has no meaning for him either. He too knows only a cyclic time, and in this respect his thought differs from Christianity. He teaches an eternal cyclic course of time. The souls return finally to Brahman, but they emerge from him again, and so on *ad infinitum*. Ramakrishna's doctrine is also interesting. He was a fervent worshipper of the goddess Kali-Durga. In his view man experiences the *unio mystica*, once as a personal communion, another time as an impersonal coalescence. In his view all religions are in principle (partly) true. One may have communion with Jesus as well as with Kali-Durga. His doctrine has been propagated intensively in the West by his disciple Vivekananda.

The contrast 'personal-impersonal' concept of God, theism-pantheism, poses an important problem in philosophy of religion. Both viewpoints have in common that they accept the existence of God. When we compare the two concepts in a philosophical way, we may therefore already presuppose God's existence. Theism may be best defended with the help of the theory of analogy, a variant of which we have given above (*vide* 3.2 and appendix 2). If we presuppose that the consequence cannot have more creative power than the ground, then the eternal, necessary ground must have an ego-structure. A being that has a will, has more creative power than a being that has no will. One can understand this easily, if one considers the fact that a willing being may refrain from using his will. Thus he is able to do everything which a being without a will can do, and in addition to it he can use the power of his will. Therefore we must ascribe the power of will to God. God is a willing being, who may decide certain things, although his will is completely different from ours. In appendix 2 we have shown that, as it were, an unknown multiplying factor is added to it. We have to do here with a transformation, a kind of relation we do not know. But this does not imply that we cannot say anything about God.

In the same way we can prove that God knows self-reflection, because a being who is able to reflect on himself, who can enter into a relationship with himself, has more creative power than a being who is not able to do so. Here too we may use the same argumentation as before. A self-reflective being might refrain from self-reflection, and could thus be equal to a being without self-reflection. He is able to produce the same things. But then, in addition, he is able to produce things on the basis of his self-reflection. Both in the position of willing and in the position of self-reflection a personal being can take a so-called zero position, in which the refrains from all these activities. But this means that he is able to do more, if the performs activities in addition to those of the zero position. In the same way: God is good, because goodness has more creative power than evil. All these arguments point towards a concept of God with an ego-structure. Arguments from religious experience may also play a certain role: theism may appeal to the experience of the love of God, of being a child of God, of knowing of God's commission to take care of the world, and the like.

In my view pantheism may best be defended, if one rejects the doctrine of analogy between God and man and accepts the fundamental identity of all things. The elimination of the analogy has as as consequence either that God is an unknown being about whom nothing can be said, or that he becomes completely similar to worldly things. From the idea that all things are – in principle – identical it may be inferred that they must have something in common. What they have in common may be labelled the divine principle. As has been said above, this may be identified exactly, but it may also be indicated as the deep, unknown essence of all beings. We shall dwell a little longer here on the interesting and inspiring system of Spinoza, who is not a total pantheist in my view, but who certainly has

146

pantheistic tendencies. One of his axioms is that only if two things have something in common, can the one be the cause (ground) of the other. That points towards God as the fundamental substantial ground of all being. But on the other hand there is, according to Spinoza, an infinite difference between God and man. He rejects the doctrine of analogy, but this may be worked out in two ways: either God is completely different from man, or God and man are – in principle – on the same level. Spinoza is able to combine both ideas. God as substance with attributes is totally different from man, but in his infinite modes He is of man's nature, although He remains infinite whereas man is finite.

Not only rational arguments can be brought forward in favour of pantheism, but also religious arguments. One may experience the deep feeling of a fundamental kinship between man and nature. Sometimes the objection is made that although a deep religious feeling may be aroused from seeing flowers and hearing the wind, yet this will certainly stop when one sees the smog, the smoke of the factory chimney and hears the noise of the machines. But I do not think this counterargument is valid. Of course, the latter things will not evoke romantic feelings, but in a broader framework they can certainly be inspiring too. Many modern artists have used them in their work and if they can arouse aesthetic feelings it is not impossible that they evoke religious sentiments also.

It is difficult to choose between theism and pantheism, and perhaps a middle system like panentheism should be preferred. On the whole I prefer theism; its arguments appeal to me more, provided we have a qualified theism. We will come to this in a moment. For even if we accept Spinoza's axiom that consequence (effect) and ground (cause) must have something in common, this ought not to be the essence of these things. In the doctrine of analogy it is taught that the *analogans* and the *analogatum* must be similar in some respects. There must be a partial identity. To my mind an exposition as in appendix 2 is convincing, so that I cannot accept the rejection of analogy. Perhaps the appeal to religious experience may be stronger than the rational arguments. At least the kinship of man and nature will certainly be attractive to the modern mind. The environmental problems of our time may be a sign that we could have learned more from Indian philosophy, Spinoza and others. Christianity has very often favoured an aggressive attitude towards nature referring to the biblical text 'Be fruitful and increase, fill the earth and subdue it, rule over the fish in the sea, the birds of heaven, and every living thing that moves upon the earth' (Gen. i.28). In this view nature is only regarded as an object one has to exploit, not as a fellow creature. But this view is not necessarily implied in biblical faith and theistic philosophy. If we emphasize the fact that we are all created by God, we recognize our fellow creatures as beings that are related to us and that we have to love. Moreover, it would be wrong to blame Christianity alone for this attitude. In the history of human thought we have always had trends that emphasize the love for nature and trends that either neglect nature, or find it irrelevant, or see in nature only an object to exploit. For the latter view point one must think of Socrates, Fichte and others. In contradistinction to Fichte a man like Schelling, influenced by Spinoza, underlined the kinship of man and nature. But at least it may obvious that we may learn much from philosophies like that of Spinoza. In Christianity St Francis, among others, had a positive relationship with nature.

Moreover, in other points I side with Spinoza in that in my view too God expresses himself in the eternal laws and they are not alien to him. They do not stand above him as in Leibniz's, thinking and they are not created by him so that they are a product of an arbitrary will as in Descartes' philosophy. The same holds for the relation between God and what is good, as we have seen above (*vide* 2.5.4). Another important point is Spinoza's making God's will dependent on his thinking. What God thinks good, he must do. There is no independent free will in God. And here too I think Spinoza is right. The conception that God chooses between several worlds and selects the best one as if He could also have chosen another one, which is the view of Leibniz, is wrong. God cannot but choose in the way He does. Not because he would not have, so to speak the 'physical' power to do otherwise, but because his own nature makes it impossible to do otherwise than the right thing. And what is right emanates from his essence! If one considers these things thoroughly, one sees that Spinoza is right, and that the usual objection that Spinoza was a pantheist is not quite correct. He has pantheistic tendencies, but he also knows of God's transcendence so that he may be better labeled a panentheist. I am opposed to Spinoza, however, in his rejection of analogy. This is a weak point in his system (in my view at least)! Still I do not pretend that the discussion between theism and pantheism can ever be settled once and for all. On the ground of a certain criterion, *viz* the principle of analogy, I choose for a kind of theism (or perhaps more correctly panentheism), but this principle is an addition to the concept of an *ens necessarium*. In my view it is a plausible criterion, but it may perhaps be possible, for example, to accept the cosmological argument and to reject the principle of analogy.

Moreover, it is difficult to determine the relation between God and *time*. In the various religions one may find profound thoughts about time and eternity, as also among primitive peoples. For example the Australian aborigines have interesting views on this subject and it was these people who were considered to stand on the lowest level of civilisation in the narrow-minded opinions of (some) Western scholars. This is completely incorrect. They have, for instance, a very complicated system of degrees of kinship and corresponding obligations. For the Western mind all this is hardly conceivable. The Australians have also devised a profound doctrine of time and eternity. The latter, the time of dreams, can also be present in time. As for many theologians, for them time has a beginning. It began, when the supernatural beings woke up from their sleep and were born from eternity. In their view time is continuously surrounded and determined by eternity. All this is explained and told in myths, to which nobody can deny depth and profundity. Where there is time, there is also movement, transitoriness and perishableness. What is subjected to time participates in transitory processes and will finally perish. Therefore many theologians take the view that God and his world are eternal, in the sense of timeless. God and his world are outside the time processes. But this also has its disadvantages. For now in this timeless world nothing can happen and nothing can be done, for every event presupposes time. Suppose a state of affairs A_1 should become state of affairs A_2, then it is impossible that we have both A_1 and A_2 at the same time. We always have a situation in which at a certain point of time t_1 we have state of affairs A_1 and at a later time t_2 we have state of affairs A_2. Therefore if in a timeless eternity no distinction can be made between various moments of time, then equally no distinction can be made between various states of affairs. There can only be one great state of affairs in which nothing can be changed; therefore nothing can happen there. But is this cold and immovable world in agreement with our religious experience of God?

We find ourselves here in a dilemma: either God's world knows time, but then it also knows change and decay; or it does not know time, but then it does not know of events either – nothing can happen. Probably the best thing is to assume that there *is* time in God's world, but another kind if time, a concept of time different from ours. In our concept time has only one direction. What has happened will never return. But God may be able to recall the past and make it present again. So in God's world there can happen something. Processes are possible, but God is the Lord of time and does not participate in its processes of decay. We receive an image of all this if we take *thinking* as an analogy. In thought we may represent the past in our mind, although we can only do it ideally, not really. If, however, we assume that God can do it really and make the past really present (in his world) then we might have an approximate notion of God's time. This may shed a better light on the Christian doctrine of the Eucharist. The real presence of the Lord is celebrated here, i.e. the presence of some past event, *viz* the sacrifice of Jesus Christ. This is possible on the ground of God's promise and his being Lord of time. Although the process philosophy of Whitehead and Hartshorne (appendix 3) teaches that there is time also in God's world, in their view God's time is one-directional only. There is no possibility for God to bring back the past. Against this view philosophical objections may be raised as is shown in appendix 3; but also religious objections are possible. The experience of God redeeming our sins is fundamental. But the presupposition for this is that God may recall our past and we may do the same in faith. Together with this representing of the past there is the possibility of the presence of God's redeeming power in Christ. All this is profound, deep religious experience, which could disappear in Harthorne's view. In my view these ideas may not be given up.

According to Augustine and other theologians time has been created. But in the view of most mystics God's world is timeless, a view which is sometimes shared by theologians too. The concept of God's time, which differs from human time, is also found in Karl Barth's work, although he differs in detail from what has been said above. But it is his opinion that God has time for us and makes time for us every moment, time, in which He looks after us in Christ. In my view this is an appealing concept.

4.2 *The problem of evil*

One of the most difficult problems in theology and philosophy is the problem of evil. How can the presence of evil be compatible with the existence of an almighty and loving God? The Dutch atheistic philosopher Beerling, who has also dealt with religious problems, believes that we must reject God's existence, just because of this fact. In his view God's existence would be a moral scandal. Various solutions have been brought forward. Thus evil is said to be a non-being and therefore it does not belong to creation. This idea may be found in the Neo-Platonist Plotinus and from him it has entered Christian, Judaic and Islamic philosophy. In an image of Plotinus: darkness is destruction of light; it is not something positive. With the help of a source of light one can produce light, but one can never produce darkness in such a positive way. One can only accomplish it by extinguishing the light. Similar to the relation darkness-light is the relation goodness-evil. Evil is not something positive. It can only exist, where there is something good, which it then destroys. Evil is the destruction of what has creative power, but it has no creative power itself.

One may distinguish various kinds of evil. Leibniz mentions three kinds: (i) metaphysical, (ii) physical and (iii) moral evil. What has been said above belongs to metaphysical evil. Physical evil (bodily pain, material dearth, etc.) originates from the fact that human beings are invested with something corporeal, *viz.* the body. Metaphysical and physical evil are based on the finiteness of created things. God could not have made them otherwise, because he has chosen the best of all possible worlds. If they could have been avoided, God would certainly have done so. Moral evil confronts us with the most difficult problems. But this can be explained from the fact that God has created people who were free in their choices. They therefore had the opportunity to choose wrongly and so they did! If, however, we consider the world in its totality, we acknowledge that goodness prevails and that even evil contributes to goodness by giving it more depth, and in this way enhancing it. Evil is unjustly distributed over the world, Leibniz concedes, but it was necessary that every degree of evil and goodness should be represented (also a Spinozistic idea!). Nobody has the right to complain that his portion of evil is too great.

On the whole, I think, Leibniz is right. His doctrine of distribution may be unsatisfactory, but it is difficult to devise a better one on purely philosophical grounds. Another shortcoming in his doctrine is the fact that eschatological constituents are absent. But, indeed, it is especially moral evil that confronts us with the greatest difficulties. Indeed, it should be assumed that God has created man with a free will, because free human beings are better than marionettes. But now these human beings could choose evil (non-being) and God could not prevent this without transgressing the logical laws, which is impossible. Here we also see why we get into insurmountable difficulties if we assert that God is able to transgress the logical laws. Because if this were true, He could do it here, and then it would be possible that human beings are free, can decide to sin and at the same time can be free from sin and thus not sin. All this is logically impossible, but if the logically impossible is still in the reach of God's power, these things are possible and we could blame God for not having prevented sin and evil. But if God cannot transgress the logical laws, and if it is true that a free human being ought to be preferred to a marionette, and if in his freedom this human being chooses for evil and sin, then God cannot prevent evil without destroying man's freedom and making him into a marionette. Now one may object that a world in which, as a result of a free choice, human beings would not sin, is better than a world in which they *do* sin. That is correct. If Leibniz speaks of our world as the best possible world, this is viewed from the possibilities open to God, not viewed from what *realiter* could be. In this view it is man's responsibility to make a better world.

But certainly Leibniz should have integrated eschatological concepts into his system. Then God's power would be shown in his victory over sin and evil. One may also argue in favour of this by asserting that goodness is superior to evil in creative power, and that therefore in the long run evil will be defeated. Goodness produces good things and hence they can form a unity, whereas evil produces only evil and is therefore self-destructive. A tragic feeling of life emerges only if we neither want to nor can see over the boundaries of death. If we accept an eternal destiny for man (*vide* 4.4), the belief in God's final victory over death will also be philosophically established.

As has been said above, another weak point in Leibniz' view is the doctrine of the unequal distribution of evil. Leibniz, Spinoza and others try to solve this problem by asserting that different kinds of distribution are necessary, and that therefore not everyone can have the same share in the quantity of evil. But I do not see how one can prove this. One might perhaps use an aesthetic argument that uniformity has a lower aesthetic value than multiformity. Thus an unequal distribution may prevent a boring uniformity in life. But still such an argumentation might not be completely convincing.

In my view the problem is nowhere dealt with in such depth and profundity as in the biblical book of Job. Its author is not able to give a solution, but after one has studied it, one has, as it were, lived through the problem and, in doing so, one has found spiritual acquiescence. This is a miracle in religious and aesthetic experience that, although one does not receive a rational solution, still by a kind of spiritual intuition or enlightenment one is elevated to such an extent that one is able to face the problems. This is the way in which Job himself lived through it according to its author, and by reading this book the reader may have the same experience. Obviously living through suffering enhances the qualify of life remarkably. I am afraid that our analysis will rather be an obstruction for that experience, but its purpose is only to draw the attention of the reader to this wonderful work.

Before we start our analysis of the book of Job we first want to give a story from another culture which also speaks in a profound way of the problem of suffering and evil and which is very close to the book of Job. It is a story of the Ila from Zambia. They tell a story of an old woman, who had lost her whole family, because the God Leza had taken away all her relatives. When all of them had died, including her grandchildren, the old woman thought that she would soon follow them, and she consented voluntarily to this thought and even hoped for it. But instead of this she became younger and younger and more beautiful. Some members of her tribe believed that she was a witch and that she had taken the power of life out of her relatives. The woman decided to use her new strength to search for the deity and to demand that he should give a justification of his deeds. First she cut down a large number of huge trees and piled them up in order to reach heaven, but the pile tumbled down and all her work was in vain. Then she travelled to the horizon, where the heaven reaches the earth, in order to find the deity there. On her way she told her misfortune to other tribes, and these said to her that her fate was not exceptional, that it was a common destiny of all human beings to suffer, that everything comes from God and that nobody can see into the heart of all the mysteries of life. The same basic themes can be found in Job.

The book of Job consists of two parts. The first two chapters and the final chapter from verse 7ff are written in prose, the other part of the book is in verse. This has been usually interpreted in the following way: the author took an old story, i.e. the part that consists of the prose text. He then wrote a poetical part, and finally he combined the two. There is also a certain contrast between the two parts. In the prose text Job is described as a patient man, who gives all the honour and glory to God. In the poetical part Job gradually revolts against God and against the suffering he has to undergo, because this is unjust. However, the author has combined the two parts and we have to interpret it as a literary unity, because this is how the author has transmitted the book to us. In the conversations with his friends Job becomes more and more rebellious. The friends too become more and more indignant at the impudent answers Job gives. The author brilliantly shows the gradual developments both in the mind of Job and in those of his friends.

The book first tells the background of Job's suffering, which is unknown to Job and his friends. Job was a righteous man, that is one of the promises of the book. The accuser of mankind, Satan, is of the opinion that Job is only righteous because he is wealthy and happy in his family life. According to Satan Job would certainly curse God, if all his wealth were taken away from him. Now Job was delivered into the hands of Satan and his wealth was taken away from him, his children died and finally even his health deteriorated. He was struck by a dreadful illnes. But in all this Job remains unshaken in his faith: 'The Lord gives and the Lord takes away; blessed be the name of the Lord' (Job i,21). When Job's wife revolts and says to him: 'Are you still unshaken in your integrity? Curse God and die!', Job answers: 'You talk as any wicked fool of a woman might talk. If we accept good from God, shall we not accept evil?' (ii,10). Then the three friends come to comfort him and they are so overwhelmed by grief that they cannot speak in the face of such suffering. This is, by the way, a sign of real compassion and a fine trait in the story. Not till later do the friends become harsh and bitter. Then Job starts complaining: 'Perish the day when I was born and the night which said, "A man is conceived"!... Why was I ever laid on my mother's knees or put to suck at her breasts? (if this had not happened) then I should be lying in the quiet grave, asleep in death at rest...' (iii,3,12f).

But now the friends begin to speak and 'comfort' him. They are very careful in the beginning, but in the course of the conversation they reproach Job more and more sharply. Eliphaz, the first speaker, says that Job cannot maintain his claim that he has been punished unjustly. 'For consider, what innocent man has ever perished? Where have you seen the upright destroyed? This I know, that those who plough mischief and sow trouble, reap as they have sown' (iv,7f). Eliphaz wants to assert: I have clearly seen that he who does well receives rewards, and that he who does wrong is punished. This was the traditional view-point of theology in those days: God punishes the godless already in their days on earth, but the pious are given happiness and success. But Eliphaz continues: Even if Job had not committed specific sins he would still not be innocent, because compared with God everybody is guilty: 'Can mortal man be more righteous than God, or the creature purer than his Maker? If God mistrusts his own servants and finds his messengers at fault, how much more those that dwell in houses whose walls are clay, whose foundations are dust, which can be crushed like a bird's nest' (iv,17-19). (In passing: I want to draw the reader's attention to the well-known biblical and Rabbinic rule of inference *qal wachomèr* (how much more) used here (*vide* appendix 9)). These words are in conformity not only with the traditional theology of those days, but also with that of our own time. One can hear such sermons very often in the churches: we are all sinners, nobody is righteous, we all need forgiveness of our sins, etc. What then is wrong with Eliphaz' words? For at the end of the book (xlii,7f) the friends are rebuked by God.

Eliphaz' words were in agreement with the general feeling of his day. As a comparison we quote here a confession of guilt from old Mesopotamia, where the sufferer says: 'I have eaten what is detestable in the eyes of my God... O unknown or familiar God, my crimes are numerous and my sins are great... The crime I have done I do not know; the sin I have committed is unknown to me... O my God, forgive me my sins, although they may be seven times seven...'. Now this is the kind of confession of sins Eliphaz wants to hear from Job's lips, and this is exactly what Job refuses. He will not confess his guilt in general terms, he will not humble himself before God because of sins he has not committed or of which he has no knowledge. He proclaims his innocence, although he is prepared to admit that he has sometimes spoken carelessly. Eliphaz could have considered Job's pain and illness and thus could have understood why Job reacted in this way. 'O that the grounds for my resentment might be weighed, and my misfortunes set with them on the scales!' (vi,2), or in other words: Take my suffering into consideration before you condemn me. 'For my misfortunes would out-weigh the sands of the sea: what wonder if my words are wild?' (vi,3). Job acknowledges that his words had been imprudent, but 'the arrows of the Almighty find their mark in me, and their poison soaks into my spirit' (vi,4). Eliphaz' words might be true, but because of his cold heart they could not comfort a friend. 'He who does not have compassion with his friends, has given up the fear for the Almighty' (vi,14).

But then Job becomes sharper and begins to protest against God as well: 'But I will not hold my peace; I will speak out in the distress of my mind and complain in the bitterness of my soul. Am I the monster of the deep, am I the sea-serpent, that thou settest a watch over me?' (vii,11f). According to ancient Israelite theology God keeps back the big waters and the dragon, so that they cannot destroy the earth. Now, Job asks, am I perhaps this monster of the deep, this dragon, that thou, O God, must act against me? And, Job continues, even if I had sinned unknowingly, why not forgive me? My sin does not diminish thy greatness, does it? 'If I have sinned, how do I injure thee, thou watcher of the hearts of men?' (vii,20) This kind of language arouses the indignation of the friends. Bildad, Job's second friend, supports Eliphaz. He is irritated and calls Job's words 'the long-winded ramblings of an old man' (viii,2). He makes allusions to the fate of Job's children, who had certainly met their death becayse of their sins. He advises Job to implore God that he may have mercy so that the worst can be prevented. But Job answers that God abuses his power. Of course, nobody can really fight against God and nobody can escape God's wrath, but that does not mean that he, Job, is really guilty. 'Indeed this I know for the truth, that no man can win his case against God' (ix,2). Job grows more and more desperate and says to God: 'You know that I am guiltless' (x,7). But, of course, God can always find guilt in someone (x,14ff). Zophar is outraged by these words and speaks of this 'spate of words' that should be answered (xi,1). After all these consolations Job answers sarcastically: 'No doubt you are perfect men and absolute wisdom is yours!'

However, Job shows his greatness in his attitude: in spite of all his protests he still has confidence in God: 'If God would slay me, I should not hesitate; I should still argue my cause to his face. This at least assures my success, that no godless man may appear before him' (xiii,15f). That means that in spite of his despair Job still hopes for God's rescue and still has confidence in him. His friends continuously say: confess your sins, but Job proclaims that he has no guilt, except that God can make anyone arbitrarily guilty. He suffers undeservedly, but he continually pins his hope on God. He says to his friends reproachfully: 'If you and I were to change places, I could talk like you; how I could harangue you and wag my head at you! But no, I would speak words of encouragement, and then my condolences would flow in streams' (xvi,4f). And Job knows, that his redeemer lives (xix,25). Against all appearance Job has confidence in God. This is where Job's greatness and piety lie: not in his patience, because Job was certainly not patient but in the fact that despite his dispute with God he still turns towards him. The message of the book of Job is not: Be humble and confess your sins, even if you do not know them and then God will forgive you, but: in all despair and under all justified protests have confidence in God against all appearance! If we are honest we must admit that it is the false message of the friends that is proclaimed in the current preaching in the Christian churches!

The book has a double ending. I agree with those interpreters who say that both endings stem from the author and that they are complementary to each other. The first ending is to be found in chapters 32-37 in the so-called speeches of Elihu. Elihu suddenly appears in the book without any introduction. Elihu asserts that suffering means purification. Suffering tests and strengthens the faithful. God's majesty is affected neither by human unrighteousness nor by human piety (xxxv,5ff). This was a revolutionary idea in the ancient world. In Babylon, for example, it was thought that the gods had created the world and mankind, because they were bored in their loneliness and needed sacrifices and worship. And in old India the god Indra is introduced with the words: 'Bring me sacrifices, I am hungry!' In this sense the God of Israel does not need human beings (cp. Psalm i,12). Elihu wants to say: Job, look how small and insignificant our little human problems are compared with God's glory and majesty. Are we then allowed to protest against it? Later on this idea was elaborated in philosophy. For example in Spinoza we find the fundamental idea that *sub specie aeter-*

nitatis, viewed from eternity, our little human problems disappear. In the light of God's infinite majesty our questions and problems are naïve and trivial.

Elihu expresses another profound idea: 'Those who suffer God rescues through suffering and teaches them by the discipline of affliction' (xxxvi,15). Just through suffering suffering is overcome. Suffering makes us think of the essentials of life again, which we may have forgotten. If we have no problems and everything goes well in our lives, we *do* care for many things that are unimportant and we neglect the essentials. We do not really see our marriage-partner, our children, our friends, our inspiring books, etc. But as soon as we live in times of war or have to face illness and death, we rediscover what is really important. Anyone who lived through the war, will probably remember how much more intense our lives were. It was as if in one hour we lived more than in a year of peace. It was as if everything had assumed more colour, more light, more depth. And now also, how much nicer the flowers smell, when we have recovered from an illness! Then we live differently, smell differently, hear differently. In times of distress we gain in the intensity and the quality of life what we have lost in its quantity. Prosperity is not only a blessing; it is also a temptation. It can make us forget God, our life, our friends, our love. Among others Nietzsche has pointed towards the positive aspects of suffering. Also Chekhov refers to this in his play: *The three sisters*: 'Lately I read in the diary of a French minister, written in jail, how he described with delight the birds he saw through the window of his cell, birds he had not seen during the time when he was a minister! Now he is free again and he will probably not notice them again...'.

The second ending of the book of Job is to be found in chapters xxxviiff. There God addresses Job. God does not answer Job's questions, but he shows the greatness of creation and the vanity of man. How can man ever understand what God is doing? But if he observes nature correctly he will discover how God takes care of everything. First God demonstrates to Job that his criticism of God's deeds was not justified and that his words lacked insight. This reproach does not refer to everything Job has said. For example Job was perfectly right in proclaiming his innocence. But words like the following are disapproved of: 'But it is all one to God; therefore I say, "He destroys blameless and wicked alike" ' (ix,22). From such sayings one may infer that Job thinks that God does not care for his creation, and that is refuted now.

In his answer out of the tempest God shows Job that neither he nor any other human being can understand God's creation, but that God still cares for every creature, always in its own way: 'Where were you when I laid the earth's foundations? Tell me, if you know and understand.' (xxxviii,4). 'Have you descended to the springs of the sea or walked in the unfathomable deep? Have the gates of death been revealed to you?... Have you

156

comprehended the vast expanse of the world?... Have you visisted the storehouse of the snow?... Has the rain a father?... Did you determine the laws of nature on earth?' (xxxviii,16ff). Many questions about the creation are asked, questions that no man can answer. That means that nature is something incomprehensible to man. But if we look more carefully, we shall discover that God provides for his creatures: 'Do you hunt the prey for the lioness and satisfy the hunger of young lions? Who provides the raven with its quarry? Who has given the wild ass its freedom? Did you give the horse his strength? Does your skill teach the hawk to use its pinions?...' (xxxviii,39,41; xxxix,5,19,26). And in the background of this speech stands unspoken a *qal wachomer* argument (i.e. *a minore ad maius* or from the small to the great things): If God already provides for the animals, how much more will he care for human beings and also for you? And if you cannot see into the heart of some simple details of creation how can you comprehend the whole? Job acknowledges this: 'What reply can I give thee, I who carry no weight? I put my finger to my lips. I have spoken once and now I will not answer again; (xl,4) 'For I have spoken of great things which I have not understood, things too wonderful for me to know. Therefore I admit guilt and repent in dust and ashes' (xlii,3,6). God does not punish Job for his revolt. In the end he blesses him and having reproached Job's friends also God forgives them.

The book of Job does not give a solution to our problem. But by reading it we undergo a certain process of purification and understanding like Job himself. God has the last word, which we cannot understand, but we may trust him and seek him. A life of suffering can be meaningful and through suffering we can be cured of suffering. Suffering can open our eyes for the things we have neglected. But the book of Job does not preach, nor does it have a direct message. Like other great books in world literature it is only through pondering over it that we may learn from it. Its message, as in all aesthetically valuable things, is only indirect!

4.3 *Salvation*

Man does not answer God's call in the right way. He does not correspond to God's or his own ideal. In many religions there is the doctrine of a Fall, the loss of an original innocence (paradise). We find this not only in Judaism, Christianity and Islam, but also in the primitive religions. Alienated from God man seeks salvation and redemption. He will return to the right relationship with God. The various religions indicate different ways leading to this goal.

4.3.1 *Salvation without mediation of a saviour*

4.3.1.1 *Salvation through rites*

In almost all religions there are sacrifices and rites which have the purpose of bringing man into the right relation with God. This ritual is called in Indian religion *karmamārga*. The way of salvation through sacrifices (*karman* = deed, action, work, but also: sacrifice and later ascetic exercises; *mārga* = way). In the old Veda-religion the sacrifice was believed to work automatically. Ancient Israel too knows sacrificial rituals. Here, however, the sacrifice was not thought of as working automatically. In ancient Israel as in most other religions the godhead must be willing to accept the sacrifice if it is to become useful for man. In the mystery religions too rites play an important role. In order to participate in salvation one has to be initiated into the holy rites. In his *Threni for the dead* Pindar says that blessed is he, 'who has seen these things'. We do not know exactly what the rites in the mystery religions include, for it was strictly forbidden to reveal them. It was even a capital crime! So much is certain, that the rites include the seeing of some mystery plays, the knowledge of certain holy symbols and the participating in initiation rites. Also in the Homeric *Hymns to Demeter*, the oldest witness of the mystery religions of Eleusis, it is said: 'Blessed he, who has contemplated these holy rites. But he, who is not initiated and did not participate in the holy rites, will not have the same fate after death...'

4.3.1.2 *Salvation through obedience to the law*

In combination with the observance of the rites there is in Judaism and Islam especially obedience to the (Mosaic of Mohammedan) law, which is important. Of course in the two religions there is also mention of a saviour, and in some sects this belief in a coming saviour may even surpass the observance of the law. Thus in the Judaic Cabbala the sinful predicament of man is more emphasized than in official Rabbinic Judaism and consequently the need for a saviour is greater here. One may also think of the sect of the Chasidim, whose Legends of the Baal Shem have been so beautifully depicted by Martin Buber. But even in official Rabbinic Judaism the belief in a saviour has not disappeared, although there is a saying in the Talmud that the Messiah will come as soon as on one Sabbath day the law has been completely observed! So the coming of the Messiah depends on the observance of the law!

The difference between 'classical' Judaism and 'classical' Mohammedanism is the point of determinism. The latter emphasizes determinism. God directs the course of the world and man has no influence on it. Judaism, however, has stressed the freedom of will in man. I refer to 'classical' Islam, because in some older parts of the Koran determinism is not yet clearly asserted and some modern Mohammedan scholars make a connection here with their own views in which the freedom of will is taught!

4.3.1.3 *Salvation through asceticism*

In all the great religions asceticism has played an important role. *Askèsis* is a Greek word, which means 'exercise'. By asceticism is meant the exercises through which the believer tries to come into direct contact with God. He refrains from many pleasures and sometimes he inflicts bodily and mental pain on himself (fasting, long exhausting prayers, castigation, not moving for hours, etc.). In this way he does penance for his own sins and for the sins of other people. The ascetic exercises are also an appropriate way to the mystical union. Morever here there is a methodical use of the insight referred to in a preceding section (4.2), *viz.* that a decrease in the quantity of life can mean an intensification of life, an increase in the quality of life. Jainism is the religion that lays special emphasis on salvation through asceticism. Since God does not exist in this religion the goal is not the union with God but, as in Buddhism, the liberation from the cycle of rebirths.

4.3.1.4 *Salvation through insight*

In the Indian religions there is besides the way of salvation through rites and asceticism (*karmamārga*) the way through insight (*jñānamārga*) (jñāna = insight; mārga = way). According to the doctrine of the *Vedanta* the central idea in the *Upanishads* is the final identity of *atman* (the self, the soul) and *Brahman* (the godhead). This is expressed in the famous saying 'Tat tvam asi' (That you are). The adherents of the doctrine of the *Vedanta* claim to give the genuine interpretation of the *Upanishads*. *Vedanta* means the end of the *Veda*, and this concept has been extended to the *Upanishads*. Both Sankara and Ramanuya, who had so many different views, were adherents of the doctrine of the *Vedanta*. This doctrine of the final identity of *atman* and *Brahman* is the doctrine of *advaita*, the doctrine of the unity of all beings. Ramanuya taught a qualified unity, *viśiṣṭādvaita*, a unity in which some distinction is still made between God and man. This insight of unity is to be gained by way of mystic contemplation. Buddhism also teaches salvation through insight, *viz.* that all is suffering. Even the obvious pleasures include suffering. This insight leads to salvation. One stops longing for something and comes to understand that there is no permanent pleasure. One should refrain not only from bodily enjoyments, but also from the so-called spiritual goods. In Buddhism the existence of the soul is also denied. What exists is only a stream of loose images and thoughts, which has no *ego* as underlying subject. The belief in the consciousness of an ego is only appearance. The Buddhist appearance discloses illusion and leads the faithful into Nirvana. As nobody has or is an ego, all men are equal. Therefore Buddhism can easily be combined with socialism or communism (Burma, Sri Lanka). The atheistic views of Marxism are no hindrance, because Buddhism itself denies the existence of God. This is at least true for the original Buddhism; in the later developments of Buddhism gods emerge, and the various Buddhas especially are worshipped as gods.

The various ways of salvation do not necessarily exclude each other. Very often we have a combination of the way through asceticism and insight, and also one of the way through rites and observance of the law. But on the other hand there is very often a great contrast between the adherents of the first two and those of the last two. The criterion here is the meaning and relevance of moral activity. In the way of the observance of the law morals consist in obedience to the law, which is only an external attitude in the eyes of the more spiritual adherents of the ascetic way. In this respect in Indonesia the struggle between the offical Islam of the *ulamas* (the authorities in the law) and the mystic Islam of the sages is interesting. On the whole the Indonesian mind has a tendency towards mysticism, so that Mohammedanism adopts a typically Indonesian character here. Philosophically the way through rites is rather weak, if it is not combined with one of the other ways, e.g. the way through observance of the law. For in that case God is completely embedded in a whole of impersonal powers, especially if the sacrifices work automatically. However, if this position is combined with the observance of the law as in Judaism, or with asceticism as in the old mystery religions, this position can be defended more convincingly.

4.3.2 *Salvation through a Saviour*

In many religions salvation, i.e. re-establishment of the right relationship between God and man, is achieved by the work of a mediator or saviour. This is the case especially in Christianity, where Jesus Christ has brought about salvation. This idea has many aspects. By his obedience to the will of God and by his commitment to others (healing of the sick, helping the oppressed, etc.) Jesus Christ fulfilled the law of God and thus he vicariously did what other human beings could not achieve. At the same time by doing this he was an example for the faithful and a model of the true and real man. A second aspect consists in the sacrifice Christ has made in order to rescue mankind. In the biblical view man is submitted to evil powers which live partly within him and partly outside him. He cannot make himself free, but by his sacrifice Christ has liberated him. He has vicariously suffered for him, a suffering which is expressed by the cross, his suffering and dying for the sins of the world. In his resurrection Christ has overcome death, which in Scripture is considered to be a consequence of human sin, at least the death in fear and ignorance. This sacrifice receives a special qualification in the doctrine that Christ has died because of the punishment the human race had to undergo. In this doctrine Christ has undergone this punishment vicariously.

A point of discussion among theologians is still whether God was to be reconciled or whether God was the active subject of redemption, i.e. whether God had to act in accordance with an abstract norm of justice which is apparently above him. We have come across this problem earlier: either justice is an arbitrary product of God or it is above God. We have

160

seen that the Spinozistic solution is the best: justice is a necessary emanation from God. But the whole discussion about such questions as: 'Has Christ paid for our sins?' 'Has he undergone the punishment we deserved?' is superfluous if one does not accept this special qualification of the Christian doctrine of reconciliation. One may also interpret this doctrine in such a way that Christ (or God through Christ) has won the victory over the evil powers. That gives the doctrine of redemption another emphasis.

Salvation through Christ corresponds to the deep human experience of one's own insufficiency. Kierkegaard has formulated this theoretically in a magnificent way. He says that if we presuppose that the moment in time has decisive significance, this would mean that there must have been a radical change in the course of history and in human life. And as no human being can produce such a radical change, it is as it were a new creation. It is more than a mere dialectical change in which the old situation comes back in the new situation, only in other, i.e. partly negative, forms. Then we should not really have a *decisive* moment in time. It would be a moment in time as important as many other moments. It would not be a unique moment in history. From this Kierkegaard is able to infer that such a radical change, which includes a new creation, can only be the moment of Christ's coming into the world, his atonement for our sins, man's becoming a new creature, etc. (*vide* 2.6.2.1 and appendix 7).

Kierkegaard has emphasized the historical character of Christianity. However, if one regards Christianity as an historical religion, one makes it dependent on historical events, which means that it depends on relative, contingent and not on absolute, necessary truths. Ernst Troeltsch has tried to solve this problem in the following way: Even in history there are historical laws which can be known through the method of analogy. Moreover, in history transhistorical values are apparent. Consequently history is not so contingent as it may seem. The great problem to us, however, is that we know these historical laws and transhistorical values only with the help of our relativistic historical sciences. But this means only an epistemological, not a metaphysical relativism. In the U.S.A. the scholars Richard and Reinhold Niebuhr have tried to overcome historical relativism in an analogous way. They were admirers of Troeltsch. But they did not take over Troeltsch' abstract metaphysics. In their view God's revelation is at the same time historical and transhistorical, human and transhuman. It is the personal revelation in Christ that is revealed, not an abstract metaphysical truth. This view is similar to the doctrine of Brunner, with whom they are also in agreement with respect to some other ideas, e.g. the doctrine of the relation between gospel and law.

In his masterpiece *Philosophiske Smuler* Kierkegaard has solved this problem of the historical character of Christianity, which seems to include epistemological relativism, in the following way. First he shows that there must at least be the *possibility* of the Christian revelation, by assuming that there may be a moment in time which has decisive significance. But of course, this does not mean that we can be certain of the truth of this revelation. Now Kierkegaard shows that *all* historical truths are dubitable, and that one can only overcome one's doubt by means of a decision of the will and not by means of abstract reasoning. This is already the case with regard to ordinary historical truths, and consequently *a fortiori* with regard to the truths of the history of salvation. Relativism cannot be superseded by theoretical reasoning alone. In that case every contingent fact could be doubted. One must take the decision to trust either certain communications, or certain documents, or – at least – one's memory. But one can do this only on the ground of a decision and not with the help of mere theoretical considerations. If this is necessary for ordinary historical truths, how much more so for the acceptance of the truths of the Christian faith. We have seen this already in our own exposition: a decision is necessary even for the choosing of logical systems, which Kierkegaard has left out of consideration, because he still thought that there was only one way of logical thinking.

Christianity is not the only religion which knows of a saviour. Buddhism too in its later stages has developed the belief in a saviour, and the same can be said of certain variants of Hinduism. In Mahāyāna-Buddhism, for example, Buddha has made the vow not to be satisfied with his own salvation, but to seek for the salvation of the whole of mankind. Here Buddha becomes a divine mediator of salvation. Hinduism too knows the doctrine of Vishnu's *avatāras* (*avatāra* = 'manifestation'), which is a theology of incarnation. In the *Bhagavadgītā* (iv,7), the significance of the *avatāras* is rendered in the following way: 'Always, when justice decreases and injustice increases in the world, God comes to mankind'. The purpose of the *avatāra* is to present a moral ideal. God manifests himself to human beings in order that they may become divine by following his example. From this we may infer that the incarnation theology in Hinduism has a more limited purpose than in Christianity, where more aspects play a role as we have seen. Nevertheless the doctrine of the *avatāras* is important. It shows that in Hinduism too the personal relation between God and man can be important. This way of salvation is therefore called *bhaktimārga*, the way of love, *bhakti*.

Brunner and others have drawn our attention to the fact that God's revelation in Christ is unique and that other religions, even the *avatāra* theology, do not know this concept, at least not in this form and with this fundamental significance. But uniqueness is no argument for truth! For unique phenomena are present in almost every religion. The doctrine of immortality in ancient Egypt, for example, with its embalmed bodies and special graves, does not occur anywhere else. Buddhism is unique in its negation of being. In Islam and Judaism the belief in a saviour also plays a certain role, in that in some sects of these religions it is believed that a kind of Messiah or prophet will come at the end of time and bring salvation and judgement to the world. But on the whole in these religions the observance of the law is much more important. The primitive religions do not have a saviour in the way Christianity, Buddhism, and other religions do. They know of a great teacher, who has taught them culture, i.e. agriculture and how to build houses, etc. But they do not know a saviour who will liberate them from evil and bring happiness, unless such concepts have originated under the influence of Christianity. This was for example the case in the rise of the cargo cult in Irian Jaya. There it was believed that on a certain day, which was nearing, a great aeroplane would come and bring the power of the white man to the original inhabitants of the land.

Some primitive religions know the belief in a Demagod. This concept has been introduced by A.E. Jensen. It can be found among people who know agriculture, but only that of bulbous plants and not that of cereals. The Demagod is a god, who was sacrificed in primordial time. By means of his sacrifice he created the world and gave the land fertility. As the reader sees this Demagod is to a certain remote extent similar to the saviours in other religions: Christ, Vishnu as Krishna, for example. But there remains a fundamental difference: these saviours have given up their lives voluntarily and this is not the case with the Demagods.

Finally, many religions do not know a salvation at all, especially not those religions in which God does not stand in a relationship with individuals but only with the state or with the people as a whole (cp. for example the Roman religion and many primitive religions). In some other religions there was certainly also a need for salvation, but a tragic sense of life prevented its adherents from believing in a real possibility of salvation. Such a tragic sense of life can be found in ancient Mesopotamia and in the Teutonic religion. The Teutons believed that at the end of time in *Ragnarök* the giants will conquer the gods and consequently the human race also. Still in the Edda sagas a restoration of the reign of the gods is mentioned, to be established by some gods who will have escaped annihilation. But this kind of 'resurrection' may be due to Christian influence.

Philosophical objections against the belief in a saviour, who will bring about salvation, are certainly possible. For this belief is contrary to human autonomy. Instead of taking care of his own salvation man leaves this to another being. Consequently, if we have as premises that in his moral activities man should be autonomous under all circumstances and should be independent of any person, whoever this may be, then we have to reject such a belief in a saviour. On the other hand we cannot be sure that this modern view of life is correct. It may even be incorrect to call this concept of autonomy modern. It originated in the time of the Enlightenment and it was developed during the 19th century. But both modern science and modern experiences in life teach us that man cannot live on his own, without the support of others. This relates not only to his physical needs, but to his spiritual and moral attitudes as well. Man does not believe on his own account; as a moral being, he is not completely autonomous.

Moreover, belief in a saviour does not completely exclude all aspects of autonomy. The believer has to commit himself to Christ, he must take a decision on the ground of which he is united with Christ and only then will he participate in salvation. Without his own activities and without his own more or less autonomous decision man cannot gain salvation. These activities must be continued in a life of gratitude for the salvation received through Christ. Christian faith does not mean passivity!

If one wants to defend or reject a belief in a saviour, one has to bring up arguments which transcend mere states of affairs. Statements about human autonomy, necessary relationship with fellow-men, etc., presuppose value statements. This does not mean that they are irrational. Only if one supposes an absolute autonomy, which may not be true as we have seen, does one have to reject the belief in a saviour. This belief can, however, very well be combined with relative autonomy, in which the faithful make their own decisions. There is no valid command of ecclesiastical authorites to make these decisions.

By committing himself to Christ the believer follows in a certain way Christ himself. For Christ's way is qualified by a certain structure, *viz* gaining the victory by giving in or, in other words, showing strength in weakness. In this way Christ has overcome the evil powers, i.e. by suffering and death. In the same way, by acknowledging his insufficiency, the believer gains the victory through weakness. We shall see in par. 4.6.3 that this view of a victory through weakness is in agreement with aesthetic-religious criteria. A parallel to this 'victory through weakness' may be found in the *Wu Wei* principle of Chinese religion, though it is not connected with a belief in a saviour.

4.4 *Eternal life. Eschatology*

The belief in a life after death is widespread and present in all religions. That does not mean that it is accepted everywhere with the same degree of certitude, nor does it play the same important role everywhere. The Elema (a Papuan tribe) say: 'We do not know exactly of a life after death. Whoever can?' A very sober answer! Sometimes life after death seems to be the privileged destiny of certain groups and persons. Thus among the Hittites only the king is said to be immortal. In the ancient Egyptian religion the immortality of the soul depends on the conservation and maintaining of the body. This explains the building of those splendid pyramids and the refined techniques of embalming. Here too evidently immortality was reserved for privileged groups.

Where a general immortality was taught, this did not always mean that one entered a more pleasant and better existence. Thus the conception was widespread, especially in the ancient Near-East, that the dead in the hereafter had only a ghostly existence, so that a slave's life on the earth was to be preferred to a king's life in the hereafter. We find these thoughts, for example, in Homer, in the Mesopotamian religions and in the Old Testament. The later parts of the Old Testament, however, teach a resurrection of the dead. But in the older parts of the Old Testament and in the other religions mentioned above life after death seems to be a weak parallel to earthly existence. One who was a prince on earth, is also a prince in the hereafter, but it is a bloodless life. It is remarkable how much the Sheol conception of the Old Testament resembles the Hades conception of Homer.

The majority of the primitive religions include a belief in a life after death. Ancestor worship plays an important role in these religions, and this also holds for China (Confucianism) and Japan (Shintoism). In the primitive religions death is not considered a 'natural' phenomenon. Very often someone's death is ascribed to sorcery. And myths tell that death has entered into the world and was not present from the beginning. Thus the Kono in Sierra Leone (Africa) narrate that God has sent to mankind new clothes together with a new life. He trusted these gifts to a dog in order to bring them to the earth. (In passing, in many African myths the dog is the conveyer of death and other bad things!). On his way to the earth the dog came across a festival and joined it. He left the bundle of clothes aside for a moment. A snake saw them and distributed the clothes among its family. Since then it is the snake which receives a new skin regularly, i.e. a new life, and not man. That is why man tries to kill a snake wherever he meets one. The reader who knows the beautiful and famous epic poem of Gilgamesh will recognize a well-known theme here: it is the snake which robs the herb of eternal life from mankind (cf. also Gen. iii). The epic poem of Gilgamesh reveals the tragic sense of life in Babylonian religion. Man's fate could have been different, but nobody can change the current of events, not even the gods. Eternal life is evidently the destiny of the gods, but for human beings there is only hardship and death. The Africans are more optimistic. They believe in a life after death and in a high god, who judges over the good and the evildoers. Not all people believe in a righteous judgment after death, for example *some* Eskimo-tribes do not. Some other Eskimo-tribes believe in reincarnation. The Australian aborigines have a deep faith in eternal life. Earthly time is a part of eternity and consequently life cannot be defeated by death. Only the manifestations in time will perish. It is not necessary for man to wait for his death in order to experience eternal values. They can determine his life here and now. The Australian religion evokes in those who belong to it a deep faith in eternal values with which one can have a personal contact. This motive of eternity and eternal values is a conspicuous constituent of this religion.

In many primitive religions man has more than one soul. Not all these souls are immortal. The concept of a plurality of souls is also present in other cultures, e.g. in the Egyptian religion. Even some philosophers teach this. In Aristotle the *nous poiētikos* is immortal, but not the *nous pathētikos*. In primitive cultures the experiences in dreams are considered to be an argument for the soul's possibility of surviving death. The soul seems to be independent of the body in these dreams and consequently it must be possible for the soul to continue living after the perishing of the body. Death severs the connection between the soul and the body. Some people believe that dancing can restore the contact between the living and the dead. In trance the dancer transmits the answers of the dead to the questions asked by the priest. We can find this *inter alia* in the Shaman religions in Siberia and Korea, in Bali in the Sanghyang dance, in the Javanese religion in the dance of the horse riders (*kuda kepang*). In ancient Persia it was believed that in the hereafter the dead man who had lived well was welcomed by a beautiful girl. This girl was the reflection of his own soul. The dead man who had lived badly had to meet his soul in the image of an ugly old witch.

The doctrine of life after death is also known in the great religions. The assumption of a life after death may be founded philosophically in the doctrine of the immortality of the soul, but this is not necessary. It is also possible to teach that in his goodness God permist the soul to continue to live, without supposing its being immortal by nature. Further immortality of the soul does not necessarily imply its immateriality. The soul may have an astral body, i.e. a body built from finer matter than ordinary bodies. This is at least the view of many primitive people, but it is also a standard opinion among spiritists. In Scripture, especially in the later parts of the Old Testament, the idea of a resurrection of the body is present. 'Many of those who sleep in the dust of the earth will wake, some to everlasting life, and some to the reproach of eternal abhorrence' (Dan. xii.2). This idea was developed in the New Testament. But there we also find the idea that the pious man or woman is united with Christ immediately after death (cp. Phil. i.23). At first sight this conception of a resurrection of the body may seem strange. The underlying idea, however, is certainly meaningful. It stresses the importance of the body and that of material life. The message of Scripture is not that man as an individual would enter heaven, but it preaches the advent of a new heaven and a new earth in which justice prevails. In this new world the individual too will find salvation.

He who rejects God and his law places himself outside the kingdom of God in the view of many religions. In the same way it is unthinkable in the moral consciousness of many people that injustice should not be punished. Consequently, in many religions the idea of a divine judgment after death presents itself. The just enter heaven and the evildoers are sent to hell. Is this a punishment for eternity? That is: does this punishment never end? There is much discussion about this question in the various religions. In Scripture an eternal punishment is very often mentioned, cp. Matth. xxv.46. But there are also texts, from which it may be inferred that God wants everyone to be saved and that Christ will draw everyone to himself (1 Tim. ii.4; 2 Peter iii.9; Rom. xi.32; John xii.32).

The Islamic theologian Ibn Taimiya denied the eternity of infernal punishment on the basis of Sura xi.109: 'Those who are condemned will enter into the fire of hell and remain there as long as heaven and earth exist, unless God wants it otherwise'. Spiritists are passionate defenders of the limitedness of a punishment after death. The concept of an eternal punishment is obviously hardly compatible with a loving and almighty God. If we accept the idea of time developed in 4.1, so that God can always call the past back to the present, then an eternal judgment is compatible with an ultimate salvation of everyone. For although God's judgment may have taken place in the past and the sinner may have been forgiven, this judgment is eternal in the sense that it can always be made present by God. The redeemed too will deplore and regret their sins in eternity, although Christ has saved them. With an appropriate formulation the pietist Johann Albrecht Bengel has called the ultimate salvation of all men (the 'apokatastasis pantōn') God's whispered secret in Scripture.

The doctrine of reincarnation is found especially in India, where the endless sequence of rebirths is experienced as agony, from which man has to be liberated. The mystic union with God is to bring about this liberation. This mystic union may be interpreted in different ways, as we have seen.

The Buddhist concept of Nirvana is difficult to understand. In original Buddhism particularly it was described only in negative terms. In an old characterization it was said: 'There is, O monks, an area where there is neither something fluid nor something solid, neither heat nor cold, neither rest nor movement, neither infinite space nor infinite consciousness, neither being nor non-being, neither imagining nor non-imagining, neither world nor non-world, neither sun nor moon. That, O monks, I call neither a coming nor a going, neither a standing still nor a being born or dying. It is just the end of all suffering'. Elsewhere Nirvana is called the extinction of all passion, anger and spiritual blindness. But also it is said: 'Blessedness, O friends, mere blessedness is Nirvana'.

In the later stages of Buddhism Nirvana is in accordance with the ordinary concepts of heaven. In Zen Buddhism the concept of a 'filled void' has been developed as a characterization of Nirvana. In other trends of Buddhism it is taught that already in this world man can enter Nirvana. This is called a Nirvana with a remainder, because human personality and consequently a residue of suffering (of hunger, thirst, etc.) are still present, but the holy man has the power to liberate himself from these residues.

Very often a parallel was drawn between the concept of God and that of eternal life. The concept of a personal God was said to correspond to the concept of personal eternal life, i.e. an eternal life that consists in a loving commitment to God, in which man is loved by God also. The concept of an impersonal God corresponds to an impersonal eternal life, i.e. an eternal life that consists in the soul's merging in the life of this impersonal God. Atheism corresponds to the denial of any form of eternal life. This parallelism between the concept of God and that of eternal life may be observed very often. Nevertheless it is not always present. There are atheists who believe in a continuation of our personal life after death on the ground of parapsychological investigations. Examples of this view are Tenhaeff (late professor of parapsychology in Utrecht), Broad, Ducasse. On the other hand many members of the church believe in a personal God, but no longer in a personal existence after death.

What arguments can be put forward in favour of existence after death, and what against? An obvious and trivial metaphysical objection against the possibility of a life after death is the simple observation that the human body dies, and after that no sign of life is shown. Moreover, experience teaches us that our thinking depends on the functioning of the brain. On the other hand the parapsychological data are numerous so that one should not neglect them (in my view). Even the socialist countries pay attention to them, which was not to be expected, because here dialectial materialism prevails. The spiritistic hypothesis of a continuation of human existence after death may very well be supported by parapsychological data. Still there is always the possibility of interpreting these data otherwise. In that case, however, it is necessary to appeal to the other paranormal potencies in man, among which especially telepathy and clairvoyance come most into consideration and are the best testified.

Nevertheless, some arguments point towards a greater plausibility of the spiritistic hypothesis. First, even when the investigators try to minimalize the possibility of telepathy, the paranormal phenomena which point towards the spiritistic hypothesis occur in the same quantity and intensity. This seems to indicate that the spiritistic hypothesis explains these phenomena better than the other hypotheses. In the second place there are quite a few phenomena which the telepathy hypothesis cannot explain at all and in the third place, even if we accept the telepathy hypothesis as a sufficient explanation for all these phenomena, then we have, to say the least, discovered a potency in the human mind which differs from those powers which depend on the functioning of the body. This leads to the assumption that human telepathy is founded in something of the human mind which can exist without the human body. This could have its place in the human astral body, as taught by the spiritists. In this way we get our spiritistic hypothesis back by means of an indirect argument. As far as I can see, accepting the parapsychological data means supporting the hypothesis of a personal existence. As we have already indicated above (3.1.5.7), the parapsychological data can also support the arguments for God's existence.

But is it possible to accept the parapsychological data? From the side of philosphy of science some serious, though perhaps not decisive, objections may be proposed. These parapsychological data cannot be repeated or evoked at will, and this is in experiential sciences an important requirement. But there are also other experiential sciences in which this requirement cannot be fulfilled: e.g. medicine, psychology, sociology, etc. In addition, cultural objections can be brought forward. For although in our culture the parapsychological data are not explicitly rejected, they are not really taken seriously. In our eyes they remain strange, and rightly so. This is best understood if we compare our culture with another, say the Indonesian. For example, when in Yogyakarta the European cemetery was taken away, 'one dead person did not want to be removed', i.e. he walked around as a ghost and threatened the workers. Therefore his grave was spared. Nowadays, if one departs from the bus station that has been built in the place of the original cemetery, the buses go in a big arc round the grave.

This strange situation is impossible in Europe. Here the dead body would have been removed; he may walk around as a ghost as much as he likes! Of course, there is some sort of recognition of parapsychology. There are even some professorial chairs for this discipline at a few universities, but altogether it is not taken seriously. The data are simply too strange to be true in our eyes. The objections against the parapsychological data cannot be maintained objectively, i.e. in the tolerant view of the philosophy of science which I defend, these data could be admitted in science. But on the other hand, we as children of our time and culture will have to accept a *non liquet* in this matter. And that means that we must refrain from giving a definitive judgment. Consequently we must take two systems into consideration, one in which the parapsychological data are accepted and one in which they are not. In the system in which the parapsychological data are accepted the belief in an existence after death is rationally relatively well founded. In the other there are strong objections against this belief. Here the doctrine of immortality is still problematic.

But, of course, in philosophy of religion problems are not simply solved with the help of parapsychology. In a system with religious experience and without the parapsychological data the following arguments may be brought forward in order to defend immortality: (i) man experiences a substantial ego as subject of his mental phenomena. This is strictly speaking not a religious, but a metaphysical experience. It is, however, questionable whether man can trust experiences of this kind. Since Hume there has been much doubt about this. But the British philosopher of religion H.D. Lewis still accepts this kind of argument. (ii) The intensity of both the mystical and the ordinary religious experience indicates that they cannot be destroyed by death. Systems in which these experiences are considered a genuine source of knowledge contain therefore a strong argument in favour of the doctrine of immortality. But this argument suffers from the general weakness of the appeal to religious experience and gains strength only by means of the arguments for God's existence. (iii) One may also appeal to revelation. But such an argument is weak because it refers to authority.

A very impressive argument against all belief in immortality is the following. It may be doubted whether the whole belief in immortality has any sense at all. One may say that evil receives a different place in the framework of the world, if there is eternal life. This is supposed to recompense one for injustice suffered during one's lifetime. But is this true? If I suffer injustice, is the moral wrong no longer a moral wrong if I am recompensed in an afterlife? Is the suffering no longer a suffering if it is succeeded by a later happier life? In my view this argumentation is very convincing. It can only be superseded if one accepts the time-concept mentioned earlier, in which God can always recall the past. In that case the moments of suffering, or the evil deeds or any evil thing whatsoever can be made present again and at the same time the redeeming power of Christ's suffering may be made present too. Only such a time concept can make real redemption possible and can make immortality and eternal life meaningful.

4.5 Secularized eschatology

The religious view of an eternal life that already begins in this world has always been inspiring. In our culture religious belief in an eternal life is diminishing. Still many have tried to maintain its positive aspects. So a secularized eschatology emerges, which tries to preserve the inspiring features of Christian eschatology. Therefore in our culture many expectations can be found, which betray their Christian origin, for example, the expectation of a socialist or other ideal state in which everybody will be happy. These expectations are deprived of their typical Christian elements. There is no question of a life after death or of a mystical union with God any longer. However, the belief in a realm in which justice prevails, is still found. The biblical expectation includes the belief in both a new heaven and a new earth, but here only the latter has remained. Marxism is a well-known example of such a secularized expectation of the future.

In this section we shall dwell upon lesser-known examples, which are important all the same, because they are deeply rooted in our culture. Their interesting features are revealed particularly in literature. We find this belief in another, better world especially in the work of the Russian playwright Chekhov. But he has an important predecessor in the Norwegian Henrik Ibsen who has influenced him. An example of Ibsen's belief in another, better world which human beings can arrive at but fail to do so, can be found in *The Masterbuilder*, where the main figure reaches the top of the house, symbol of this better, secularized world, but then falls down. But he has reached the top! So his inspiring and beloved friend Hilde says.

Ibsen is a *Grübler*, a subtle, perhaps over-subtle, brooder who always doubts what he proposes. So on the one hand he even doubts these residues of Christian eschatology, but on the other hand remnants of the Christian faith play an important role in his plays, especially the feeling of guilt and the need for redemption (cp. Rosmersholm). In Chekhov this secularized eschatology is even more obvious. Of course, he knows the ordinary Christian eschatology too, which he subtly secularizes, however. At the end of the play *Uncle Vanya* Sonya, uncle Vanya and some other persons remain behind, disillusioned. Sonya then says: 'What do you want, we must continue living!... we want to work for other persons... and when our hour comes, we shall die committing ourselves to God and we shall say in the hereafter how much we have suffered and then God will certainly have mercy upon us, and we both, you and I, uncle, we will then see a joyous life, a magnificent, splendid life... and we shall have repose'. That is as such a purely Christian expectation of the future. Now this theme 'we shall have repose' is repeated several times, but it is less and less connected with the hereafter. The play ends with a scene in which everybody works quietly and Sonya says again: 'We shall have repose', where the Russian verb used may indeed mean earthly rest. Here we have to do with a purely natural, earthly rest in which heaven has disappeared. Chekhov has subtly changed the Christian eschatology into a secularized one. But I have noticed that some Polish (and even Russian!) stage-managers sometimes shorten the play and let it end with the Christian eschatology! In this way they give Chekhov's play a Christian interpretation!

For Chekhov, however, it is more important that mankind moves towards a better future. So Vershinin, the battery commander in the *Three Sisters*, says: 'How shall I explain this to you? It seems to me as if everything on earth will gradually change, and as if it is changing already. After two hundred, three hundred and certainly after a thousand years a better life will emerge. We, of course, cannot participate in it, but we live and work for it now already and we are in the process of producing it...' And during the scene in which he says farewell to the sisters, he expresses his expectations once again: 'And what shall I, departing, say to you? About what shall I philosophize?... (Laughing) Life is hard. It seems gloomy and without hope to many of us, still one has to say that life will grow light and joyous and that obviously the time is not far away in which it will be all light'.

This theme, that mankind expects a better future and a better world and that it is our task to work for it, plays a great role in Chekhov's work. But to my mind the following conception is even more interesting, i.e. that this better world is already very close to us as a real possibility and that some of us have already reached it, though in an imperfect way. But these people are an exception. Most people grasp at it but fail. Still, this falling short is better than resignation and doing nothing. In this way man shows his greatness and grandeur. To give an example I refer here to the short story *In exile*.

In this story the dreary life in a Siberian exile is depicted. The old Semyon has found rest by giving up all longing and wishing. A Tartar, who works with him, has not yet done so. He still longs for his wife and hopes that she will come one day and share his life. Semyon tries very hard to put this thought out of his mind. He refers to the fate of the rich man Vasili Sergeyitch, whose wife *did* come, but after three years ran away, because she could not bear life in Siberia. Only his sick daughter is still with him. Now he consults all sorts of medical doctors, young and old, real ones and quacks, in order to get his daughter healed. 'Good, good', the Tartar murmured, shivering with cold. 'What is good?' asked the cunning man (a nickname for Semyon). To this the Tartar replied: 'A wife, a daughter... He has forced labour and sorrow, but he has seen at least his wife and daughter... you assert that we do not need anything, but having nothing is bad! He has lived with his wife for three years... God has given him that. Nothing, that is bad, but three years, that is a good thing. Why do you not understand me?'

Then in the deep of the night this Vasili Sergeyitch had himself transported over the river. (For Semyon and the Tartar are ferrymen). He is again in search of a new medical doctor for his incurable daughter. Behind his back Semyon scoffs at him. 'Now, look at him, how he runs to the doctor', says Semyon, his teeth chattering with cold.' Yes, yes, you may seek a good doctor, try to catch the wind blowing over the field. Try to catch the devil by his tail. A pest on you! What strange people there are on earth, God have mercy upon me, poor sinner!' The Tartar approached the cunning man, full of hatred and disgust he looked him in his face and said, shovering and mixing Tartar expressions with his broken Russian: 'He, there, is good... good, but you are bad! You are bad! That man has a good soul, he is a fine fellow, but you are an animal! You are bad! That gentleman lives, but you are dead as a doornail... God has created man in order that he may be a living creature, may have joy, pain and suffering, but you do not want anything, therefore you do not live. You are a stone, a heap of clay! A stone does not need anything and you do not need anything... You are a stone – and God does not love you, but he does love that gentleman'.

To live in expectations, although they may be unfounded, is better than a life of resignation, that makes man into a stone. Perhaps this better world cannot be reached, but it is only by striving for it that we really live. It may even be that this better world is very close to us so that we need only to grasp at it in order to get it. In the story *The great and the little Volodya* the main figure Sophya has married an older man, the great Volodya, but she deceives him with the younger, smarter Volodya. She knows, however, of this better world that is near to everyone of us. This better life is represented by her sister Olya, who lives in a monastery. Sophya also wants to live this better life and she asks both her husband and her lover to teach her this life. But the lover sees in her only on object of lust and not a person to be respected. When Sophya made her request, 'the little Volodya answered, "Yes, yes, so it is enough". He approached her and kissed her hands. Let us leave philosophy to people like Schopenhauer. They may prove what they like, but in the meantime let me kiss your hands'. Sophya remains to him only a little flirtation. She has this better world before her hands. She has only to reach for it in order to grasp it, but she does not have the ability to do so. She remains in a life of regret and penitence.

Nevertheless it is obvious that Chekhov's sympathy is with her and not with the 'pious' Olya. 'Almost every day Sophya visited the monastery, but to Olya she gradually became repugnant because of her lamentations about the unspeakable suffering she had to undergo. Then Sophya wept and she realized that with her something impure, pitiable and worn-out had entered the monastery cell. Olya answered mechanically, in a voice as if she produced a lesson learned by heart, that all this was not important, that everything will pass and that God will forgive her'. Another better world is close to us. Shall we grasp it? Even if we do not reach it, the striving and the longing for it is better than not trying and turning into a passive being of stone.

4.6 Religion and culture

4.6.1 Religion and morals

It is often religion that puts its stamp on the official life of a certain culture. Life in Europe is different from life in Arabia, Indonesia or Japan. When we compare these cultures it is striking how much our lives have changed now that religion has declined. But the reverse is also true. An existing culture transmits certain values and forms of life to a newly introduced religion. For example, in Korea and Japan for a Christian who has lost his honour suicide is a lesser sin than drinking liquor or smoking! And this is totally in contrast to the moral values of Christian Europe.

The hierarchies of moral values of the various religions are different. Humility, for example, is a Christian virtue, but it is absent in most of the other virtue catalogues. In our culture it is also denied by non-Christians (Nietzsche, Spinoza). Generosity as a preparation for meditation is in Buddhism much more important than in other religions. In Confucian China love for one's parents stands in the centre of social life. The fundamental moral principle in Taoistic China is *Wu Wei*, mere passivity. This is also the origin of wrestling according to the method of yielding, *Jou Tao*, Japanese *Judo*! In this way a 'victory through weakness' is gained (*vide* 4.3). In Hinduism the principle of *ahimsa,* abstinence from violence, is essential;

and further *saṁnyāsa*, self-denial, ascetiscism as a stage on the mystical way. According to the Hindu scholar Dandekar this does not mean a refraining *from* action, but a moderation *in* action. In Christianity being available for other persons, serving one's fellow-men, is one of the main principles. In my view this is even more important than the humility mentioned above.

It is important to emphasize that religion is a decisive constituent of the *hierarchy* of values, not of the values themselves. For whether some sort of action, some deed or some moral virtue has a positive value or not, does not depend on religion. In the various cultures the same values are usually held to, but their place on the hierarchical scale is often completely different. In all cultures, for example, bribery is condemned, but the degree in which it is condemned differs remarkably. And the hierarchy of values is for a great part constituted by religion. From the standpoint of a philosopher objections may be raised against the fact that our moral insights are at least partly determined by religion. Is it not characteristic of human beings that they are morally autonomous? Kant protested vehemently against the fact that in their moral actions people are guided by religious traditions in order to receive a reward in the hereafter. A moral prescription is only good if it can be interpreted as a universal rule, irrespective of time and place (and obviously also irrespective of culture and religion!). Man is able to recognize good and evil by means of his own natural insight. He need not receive a special revelation for it, but he may, of course, interpret these natural prescriptions as commands given by God.

In my view too there is no question of moral activity if one performs certain 'moral' deeds against one's own moral conviction, simply on the command of others. Moral activity presupposes freedom and responsibility. Anyone who performs a certain deed because he is threatened does not perform a *moral* deed. And in the same way he does not act morally if he does so in the hope of a heavenly reward or for fear of an infernal punishment. In this consideration it makes no difference whether one acts on the threat of a gun or on that of eternal punishment.

On the other hand it is an illusion to think that man can be morally active in a completely autonomous way. We are connected with our fellow-men, with our culture, our situation, etc. in a thousand ways. Kant's ideas were typically bourgeois liberal on this point and are dated from a modern point of view. We must assert in the first place that religion is more than morals, as Kierkegaard has shown (2.6.2.1). In the second place morality has its own base that is not determined by religion. That means a certain activity is morally good, not because religion prescribes it, but because it is in accordance with moral standards. The question how to discover these standards belongs to ethics and not to philosophy of religion. We shall not enter into this discussion here. Still, religion and morals have to do with each other. For we, human beings, very often lack the power to do the good things.

And when we are asked to bring a sacrifice for a good cause, a religious conviction can motivate us immensely. Moreover religion gives life an all-comprehensive meaning. And it is from this all-comprehensive position that religion influences the hierarchy of values. But it does not have an influence on the values as such.

4.6.2 *Religion and science*

Western culture is deeply influenced by science. Although in the course of centuries there have been many conflicts between religion and science, or, more correctly, between theology and science, the real kernel of religion was not threatened. Well known is the conflict between the church and Galilei. The church did not want to accept that the earth was not the centre of the universe. Another well-known conflict was that between Darwin with his theory of evolution and the church. We can speak of 'the' church without hesitation, for both the Catholic and the Protestant churches were opposed to these new discoveries. An exception may be made, though, for some protestant churches and groups such as the Mennonites, Socians, etc. But the great Calvinist and Lutheran churches were united in this respect with Roman Catholicism in opposing people like Galileo and Darwin. Such an opposition, however, seems to be more detrimental for Roman Catholicism than for Protestantism, since Protestants do not know of an infallible church as the Catholics do. And therefore an error from the side of the church is not fatal for them. At first sight this error seems therefore more detrimental for Catholics, but there is a way out, because the church's infallibility was not meant to have any bearing on the knowledge of worldly facts. The infallibility of the church primarily refers to its guidance on the way to salvation. And for this only an infallible knowledge of morals and matters of faith is necessary.

Today also there are conflicts, as when conservative believers object to the investigation of the space of the universe, for example with the argument that if God wanted man to investigate space he would have created him equipped with wings. Such an argument is not new. In the 17th century there were similar arguments against the use of microscopes. If God wanted man to see in such a subtle way he would have equipped us with the eyes of flies: 'Why has not Man a microscopic eye? For this plain reason, man is not a Fly!'. In the 17th century Robert Hooke complained that no scientific investigations were made with the help of the microscope, with a few exceptions such as Anthony Leeuwenhoek in Amsterdam. It was only used as a curiosity to give demonstrations for one's guests!

Such discussions are dated now and if they occur, they play only a role at the margin of our civilisation. Science and theology have their separate fields of investigation. In science there are investigations of facts; these facts are ordered in a system. In science the laws that govern the various fields are discovered. With their help various new facts can be predicted. Neither in religion nor in philosophy are such first-order facts investigated. There it is important, as we have already pointed out several times, to order these various systems of facts in an overall system. In these fields the *relations* of these systems of facts are investigated. They are second order activities! Moreover they seek the meaning of life, man's destiny, the existence of God, etc., questions which do not arise in the other sciences. Consequently conflicts between natural sciences and theology are, in pinciple, avoidable.

The relationship between philosophy and theology or religion is much more complicated, for here a conflict is always possible. As we have seen above, we can distinguish between scientific philosophy, in which there is only an appeal to classical logic and ordinary experience (our basic system), on the one hand and world-view philosophy on the other hand, in which there may be an appeal to religious experiences, moral intuitions etc. Therefore conflicts especially between religion (theology), on the one hand, and world-view philosophy, on the other hand, present themselves easily. But in scientific philosophy too not only first-order facts are investigated, but greater, meaningful connections as well. For example, how can the data of the various natural and historical sciences be combined and connected together? How can we explain them? From what principles can they best be derived, idealistic or materialistic? Can we prove God's existence? Anyway, it might be obvious that scientific philosophy and theology (religion) move in the same fields of investigation, and then a conflict is always possible. On the other hand if it is clear that philosophy should move within the limits of rational argumentation, it will be clear that, at least in principle, religion and philosophy are complementary.

It is obvious that a conflict between religion and science is avoidable. If there is a conflict here, the limits of either religion or science must have been exceded. In this case either theology has engaged in first-order facts or science has tried to give an overall, total explanation. Theology engages in first-order facts e.g. when it rejects evolution theory with an appeal to the creation story of Genesis. Science enters the field of religion if, for example, it tries to reduce religion to first-order facts. But such attempts certainly belong to the field of philosophy, so that conflicts between philosophy and theology are more likely and more justified than conflicts between science and theology.

4.6.3 *The logic of aesthetics, ethics and religion*

We now want to consider the relationship between religion and art, and especially to consider the logic of aesthetics, morals and religion. It will be shown that the logical structure of aesthetic statements is, at least to a certain extent, similar to that of religious statements. Since there are certain axioms of ethics which are also valid in the logic of religion, but not in that of aesthetics, we may conclude that religion is in a certain sense a synthesis between ethics and aesthetics.

First a terminological explanation. By morals are meant principles of right and wrong, by ethics we mean in the first place the scientific reflection on these moral principles, but then by extension these moral principles are sometimes also included in ethics. Nowadays the logic of ethics is usually classified under meta-ethics. The *adjective* 'ethical' is very often used synonymous with 'moral'. In what follows we shall consider both the direct moral, aesthetic and religious experience and the rational (scientific) reflection on their results. But let us first hear what some 'classic' philosophers have to say on this subject.

In his theory of the various stages Kierkegaard has emphasized that there are fundamental differences between the three stages. If I may simplify Kierkegaard's view a little, he says that in the aesthetic stage man lives exclusively for himself. He is individualistic and hesitates to assume responsibility himself. Kierkegaard depicts aesthetic man in many variations, but we cannot enter into all the details here. The following remarks may suffice: first he describes the man who only seeks mere lust, the ingenious seducer. This kind of man is represented by Don Giovanni (Don Juan) in Mozart's opera 'Don Giovanni'. He enjoys himself directly, although at the expense of others. But he is at least in a certain way still innocent. Another aesthetic man, John the Seducer in 'The Diary of a Seducer', is in contrast to Don Juan, cold and calculating. He reflects on his deeds and stands on a higher level than Don Juan and consequently he has lost his innocence. He enjoys the deceiving more than the sexual seduction. These persons are present in the work *Enten/Eller* (Either...Or). Also in *Stadier paa Livets Vei* (Stages on life's road), in the chapter 'In vino veritas', Kierkegaard depicts a number of variants of the aesthetic life. During a banquet five persons each give a speech about woman and marriage. They do this in various ways, but their conclusion is always the same: One should not marry and pledge oneself. Instead one should enjoy sexual life without taking any responsibility. The aesthetic person does not fulfil general laws; he remains in the sphere of the temporal and does not seek the eternal dimension.

Between the aesthetic and the moral stage there is a deep gap. It is only by a jump that it is possible to pass from the aesthetic into the moral stage. The moral stage is characterized by the general laws that are rejected in the aesthetic stage. A moral person assumes responsibilities and does not try to evade his duties. One reflects on eternity and does not want to stick to temporal values. In marriage a man pledges himself to a relationship with a woman for life. Moreover, one sees no longer in a woman a mere object of lust.

The moral stage is not the final stage. It is followed by the religious stage, and the main difference between the two is that in the moral stage one is always prepared to give a public account of one's activities. Although one is personally responsible, one never has to take decisions completely on one's own responsibility. One has to obey general, i.e. well-known, moral rules. But in the religious stage one has to take decisions, completely on one's own accord. One cannot consult anybody, there are no general rules to obey here, but one has to listen to God's personal call. Kierkegaard has depicted this beautifully in his book *Frygt og Baeven* (Fear and Trembling). Here the example is Abraham the father of the faithful. When God commands Abraham to sacrifice his son, there are no general models which may be taken as an example. Neither Agamemnon's nor Jephtha's sacrifice, although they have both a distant similarity to that of Abraham, transcend the general laws, in a careful consideration. Agamemnon offers his daughter as a sacrifice to the goddess Artemis in order to get a favourable wind. Jephtha has to fulfil a vow. If he refused, the holy covenant between God and his people, Israel, would be broken. In the future no vow or promise would be binding.

Jephtha and Agamemnon can give a public account of their behaviour, but Abraham is not able to do so. He stands alone, he alone knows of God's promise, he alone knows what God asks from him and to what extent this command contradicts God's promises. Abraham, however, believes against all appearance. He believes in the power of the absurd. The religious person is again an individual, he does not obey general laws. In this respect he is similar to the aesthetic person. In conformity with the moral person he assumes responsibilities, but these are responsibilities regarding God, not the general public.

In a certain sense, therefore, the religious stage is a synthesis of the aesthetic and the moral stage. It combines the individualistic features of the aesthetic stage with the sense of responsibility of the moral stage. But it is more than only a synthesis. There is also something completely new in it. Since God gives the condition for faith, man acts as an answering being, who reacts on God's commands and promises and receives everything out of God's hands. He does not find his happiness and salvation in himself, but only in God.

In a certain sense Kant's ethics is similar to that of Kierkegaard, in that for Kant too moral life is founded on general and public laws. Kant's first moral prescription is: Act in such a way that your moral prescription can be at the same time a general public law. With this moral prescription (*Maxime*) the universality and generality of the moral law are clearly expressed. As in Kierkegaard's thinking there is a great difference between the aesthetic and the moral stage. The aesthetic statements and judgments are characterized by the fact that they do not imply practical utility. They have a *Zweckmässigkeit ohne Zweck*, i.e. a structure of appropriateness without having a purpose. Kant characterizes this structure of appropriateness without having a purpose as a unity in the manifold. We shall return to it latter in this section.

Between Kant and Kierkegaard there is, however, a great difference. In Kant's view there is a deep gap between the aesthetic and the moral sphere, but not between the moral and the religious sphere. Religion is the knowledge of our obligations as God's commands. To him religion is, as it were, ethics seen from a special point of view. Religion therefore is not a special matter for the individual, but a public matter for society. If we want to express Kant's position in a modern logical theorem we may say that the following two theorems are valid:

(i) $W^e p \rightarrow Op$
(ii) $W^{ae} p \not\rightarrow Op$

(explication of the signs: $W^e p$ means: 'p has a moral value'; $W^{ae} p$ means 'p has an aesthetic value'; Op means 'p ought to be'; $\rightarrow$ is the sign of implication and $\not\rightarrow$ is the sign of non-implication)

Not only according to philosophers like Kierkegaard and Kant, but also according to many artists and poets it is true that the morally good does not have to be aesthetically beautiful and vice versa.

Some protests have been raised against this view. I think, for example, of the great Russian poet Tolstoy. In his view art had a moral message. Once he even criticized his own earlier work for not being in accordance with moral standards. But here we shall confine ourselves particularly to the relation between art (aesthetics) and religion. Here too we will listen to a 'classic', in this case to Gerardus van der Leeuw, philosopher and scientist of religion, who was also a specialist in aesthetics and art, especially music. He wrote a book *Wegen en grenzen*, which has also been translated into English and German. According to Van der Leeuw art and religion originally formed a unity, as they still do in primitive cultures. This unity is still experienced by us when we think primitively. In Van der Leeuw's view the difference between modern and primitive mentality is not based on chronological or geographical considerations, but is structural. That means that every human being participates both in primitive and in modern ways of thinking. The only thing we may say is that the so-called primitive forms of thinking are predominant in the primitive cultures and the so-called modern forms of thinking are predominant in the modern cultures.

As we have said before, Van der Leeuw does not use the word 'primitive' in a pejorative sense. He is of the opinion that the modern mind has lost much insight into the depth of being and has lost the direct contact with life which the primitive mind possessed. We should therefore try to vitalize the primitive ways of thinking in ourselves, although Van der Leeuw knows very well that this is not completely possible. Some of the points in which modern and primitive thinking differ are: the primitive mind thinks in totalities and does not start with the individual data. To the primitive mind everything is connected with everything. Human beings are able to produce things, because they participate in a supernatural power, *mana*, which pervades the whole world. The modern mind is more logical and analytical, and because of this things are regarded as existing more separately.

It is Van der Leeuw's view that the original bond between art and religion has been loosened in the course of time. Gradually the separation became so great that one may speak of an antagonism between the two. This antagonism is, however, not the only possibility. They have both emanated from the same source; they have the same root. He does not deny that there are boundaries between the two, but there are also ways to connect them; hence the title of the book: *Wegen en grenzen* (= Ways and boundaries). Van der Leeuw regards the religious dimension as represented by the Holy, which he defines with Rudolf Otto as the Wholy Other, if we consider the content of the Holy. Its formal structure is to be defined as that which represents a last, definitive value and appeals to man in his totality. Van der Leeuw borrowed this definition of the formal structure of the Holy from Spranger. Religious values are not values seen from a certain point of view, but they are values before God. The Holy is, compared with the Beautiful or the other aesthetic values, the deeper dimension. But in Van der Leeuw's view all real art is in its final dimension religious. In the first edition of his work Van der Leeuw presents the material in the scheme mentioned above: Unity – Loosening of the ties – Conflict – New Approaching of each other. He brings the various arts into this classification.

In the second and third edition (and this third edition was the basis for the English translation) he used a different scheme. Now he uses a classification according to the arts (dance, theatre, the poetic word, the plastic arts, music) and depicts their historical development with the help of the scheme mentioned above. The final chapter contains his theory of aesthetics, which in Van der Leeuw's thinking has a theological foundation. Van der Leeuw shows how the dance, the use of words, etc. achieve their 'magic' effects. Primitive man dances the rain out of heaven, for example. But gradually this bond between religion and art loosens and turns into antagonism and hostility. Christianity has struggled against the theatre, Mohammedanism has opposed pictorial art.

Van der Leeuw tries to show that this antagonism between religion and art has been universal, i.e. that it has occurred in all religions. But I doubt whether he is right with regard to this point. His remarks with respect to the Greek religion are certainly true. Homer was criticized by various prominent people, among whom even Plato, on religious grounds. But his examples from Hinduism and Buddhism are less convincing. He says, for instance, that on the great Buddhist sanctuary, the Borobudur (Java), the first galleries are built in such a way that the visitor cannot see the beautiful Kedu-plain. The purpose of this is that the visitor in his *pradakshina* (devout walking around the stupa) should turn into himself and not be disturbed in his meditation by his beautiful surroundings. But now, says Van der Leeuw, it is obvious that aesthetics has been sacrificed for the benefit of religion. This cannot be denied, but aesthetics is a very complicated discipline in which dialectic certainly plays an important role. The aesthetic disadvantage of the first galleries enhances the tension and expectation, so that when the visitor finally reaches the top of the building, he will experience and appreciate the beauty of the view even more.

Hinduism and Buddhism have kept more aesthetic elements in their religion than the prophetic religions, Judaism, Christianity and Islam. The same can be said of the religions of harmony which are to be found in South-East Asia. I would even claim that aesthetics plays a more fundamental role there, because Hinduism and Buddhism are ascetic religions in which ultimately all external forms are to be given up. And these external forms include also aesthetic forms. But the religions of harmony (Confuciamism, Japanese religions, the religions of Bali and Java) are religions of polarity and are not ascetic. Consequently the aesthetic values are permanent values. In Buddhist meditation techniques, for example, beauty serves to let one forget oneself in the beauty of a painting. This feeling of life may certainly give aesthetics a place in the whole system of religion, but it is only a temporary one.

Although there are conflicts between religion and art, there are also moments in which man is carried away by art. In this wat he reaches a state that transcends his ordinary frame of mind. This transcendent state need not be the same as the Wholly Other of religion. Van der Leeuw gives a whole set of aesthetic motives that can serve to cause transcendent feelings: large quantities, multitudes, the sublime, the obscure, the Dionysian and Apollonian elements in art. Van der Leeuw shows that very often transitions and changes may be an expression of the Holy, e.g. the modulations in music, blendings in paintings. This is an interesting and remarkable feature. In all these aesthetic moments the transition from aesthetic experience to religious experience is easy.

Art becomes religious when it occupies man totally. Van der Leeuw opposes the idea that it is the religious *theme* that makes a piece of art religious. 'Religious art always originates when we recognize the divine form in human forms, when we recognize a divine creation in a human product'. A piece of art becomes religious when we see in it the Wholly Other or when it occupies us totally. Van der Leeuw agrees with Kant, that beauty is a disinterested pleasure. 'But that art is disinterested means only that art does not participate in the issues of this life. Art does not want to improve the world, nor reform life. It cannot believe. But this disinterestedness does not mean that art is lifeless. The new world which is produced by art is a creation which cannot be traced back in the spiritual life of the artist or of mankind. A work of art emerges neither from human morals nor from human science. It does not emerge from human passion or wisdom. It has its origin in the primordial ground of being'. That means: Every great work of art contains something inexplicable. It is neither a product of art nor of science. This inexplicable dimension indicates a common ground for art and religion.

Another point of contact between art and religion is, in Van der Leeuw's view, the fact that every artist must devote himself lovingly to his work in order to accomplish something really great. In this way he realizes on a small scale something like God's creation. Finally this possibility is founded in Christ's incarnation, so that Van der Leeuw can end his work with a eulogy of Christ's beauty. He does so with the words of the old German folksong:

Alle die Schönheit	All beauty
Himmels und der Erden	of heaven and earth
Ist verfasst in Dir allein	is incorporated in you alone.

In Van der Leeuw's system the step from the aesthetic to the religious is not a long one. If a work of art is more than beautiful in the narrow sense, if it includes also goodness, truth, and other such qualities, it receives the character of totality and hence it becomes religious. It may be obvious that Van der Leeuw differs from Kierkegaard.

We have seen that the great classic philosophers separate the three spheres of life, but that on the other hand they indicate various points of contact. This is in agreement with familiar experiences. We experience the religious dimension as deeper and more profound than the aesthetic or moral dimension. On the other hand religion is not completely separated from aesthetics and ethics. In order to explain the relationship between the three spheres better I shall deal with the logical structure of religion, aesthetics and ethics. I do not intend to give a complete exposition of these three logics, but I shall describe some aesthetic criteria and show that they contain a logical structure which can also be found in the logic of religion.

The logic of ethics, deontic logic, is the best known of the three. In deontic logic scholars have to face some difficult problems, so that for a long time one had to say that modal logic had a better structure. But by incorporating a chronological logic into deontic logic some scholars (e.g. J. van Eck) were able to solve the problems to a great extent. We have seen above that the logic of ethics and the logic of aesthetics differ from each other (*vide* theorems (i) and (ii)). Further, in contradistinction to deontic logic aesthetics has a kind of dialectical logic. If a state of affairs has a positive aesthetic value, then it might be that its negation has a positive aesthetic value too. Or in other words: Two opposing states of affairs can both be beautiful or can at least both affect human beings aesthetically. This is not the case in modal or deontic logic. It makes devising a logic of aesthetics especially difficult, so that I do not even think of constructing a system with the help of symbolic logic.

The use of symbolic logic would be very relevant, for with the help of symbolic logic deontic logic and modal logic can be transformed in such a way that deontic logic presents itself as a subsystem of modal logic. It is self-evident that in such a way our insight into these logics is deepened and that we can work better with them. But as has been said, this way has not yet been open for the logic of aesthetics.

First I shall now give, within the framework of informal logic, a description of the various criteria that play a role in aesthetics. With the help of such criteria people may decide whether something has an aesthetic value or not. I appreciate investigations with the help of empirical methods and this has been excellently done by the Dutch empirical philosopher, Gerardus Heymans. He continued the empirical work of some German professors in aesthetics, G. Fechner and Th. Lipps. I shall add some observations from the analytical and logical-empirical tradition and shall extend the whole system a little more by means of logic.

It is often asked whether there are after all criteria in aesthetics on the ground of which decisions can be made. Is it not true that there is a principle in art: *De gustibus et coloribus non est disputandum* (One should not argue about tastes and colours)? Heymans, who takes a position which is very similar to that of Kant, is of the opinion, however, that there are no discrepancies of opinion with respect to the *elementary* aesthetic judgments, any more than with respect to the elementary moral judgments. I agree with Heymans on this point. Differences of opinion only arise with more complicated judgments, but that is also the case in ethics. In complicated judgments there are always more criteria than only one that play a role, and then these criteria must be compared and chosen according to priority. It is self-evident that then the differences arise. The same is true in ethics. In simple, elementary moral judgments hardly any difficulty presents itself. That lying is morally inferior to speaking the truth is everywhere self-evident. But sometimes there are circumstances in which lying may be morally necessary. The same is true for murdering, stealing, etc. Certain moral values may be superseded by others in a particular situation. Hence there are differences not in the elementary, fundamental moral values, but in their hierarchy.

The same is true for aesthetic values. By experiments it could be shown that a strong straight line was preferred to an irregular, oscillating line. Colours receive a positive aesthetic value, when considered as such. Here too the difficulties arise with the complicated states of affairs. The hierarchy of aesthetic values is even more complicated than that of moral values. And as in moral judgments the differences of opinion may also originate in a difference regarding the relevant facts. Nonetheless, Heymans and Kant can say that there is a universal validity in aesthetic judgments too.

Let us now consider the various sets of criteria more carefully. We shall not discuss all types of criteria, but we must confine ourselves to criteria which are most fundamental, i.e. we confine ourselves to criteria of criteria, i.e. *meta-criteria*. The first group of criteria are of a formal nature and constitute a *unity in variety*. This is still the most important group of criteria to analytical philosophers. We have met this 'meta-criterion' already in Kant's work. A chaos of sensations will not evoke an aesthetic experience. But as soon as we have discovered a certain rhythm or a certain structure in the chaos, the possibility of an aesthetic experience has arisen. This holds for music, painting, a stage-play, etc. But experience of unity without variety is dull and therefore aesthetically uninteresting. A straight line could be aesthetically preferable to a curved oscillating line, but it is not able to keep our attention for a long time. Intervals of the straight line, which have a certain structure, enhance the aesthetic experience.

In all this the following rule holds: The greater the variety combined with unity, the greater the aesthetic experience. This unity need not be experienced immediately. There may be a time interval between the first seeing or hearing and the experiencing of the unity. But this interval has its limits. If the beauty of a book or poem is only recognized by reading long commentaries on it, this will not enhance the aesthethic experience, so that in this case the rule mentioned above does not hold. A joke that is only understood with the help of an explanation is no longer a real joke. So the rule mentioned above must be qualified. It only holds as long as a certain maximum of variety is not exceeded. (In passing, this view that a certain maximum may not be exceeded does not stem from Heymans.) This meta-criterion also plays a role in those aesthetic experiences which are not experiences of beauty, but refer to the sublime, the comical, etc.

A second meta-criterion is an *emotional* criterion, *viz.*, in Heymans' terms, the *richness of associations*. A ruin, which is ugly from a formal point of view, may evoke aesthetic experiences by its richness of associations. It may remind us of an interesting past. Remembering as such is already a pleasant experience. Heymans also classifies the direct sensations experienced as beautiful under this category. There may of course be some dispute about this, but we cannot enter into this question here. It is evident that this meta-criterion is much more solidly founded on experience and is much less of a rational meta-criterion than the preceding one. It is interesting to note that the British aesthetical philosophers of the 18th century, Hogarth and Burke, already worked with this second meta-criterion, whereas originally German aesthetic philosophers preferred the rational meta-criterion. The well-known difference in epistemology between Great Britain and the Continent presents itself here also!

The third meta-criterion in Heymans' theory is that of *typical beauty*. Beautiful is what is in accordance with a certain type. A typical seaman, a typical farmer have an aesthetic effect. Kant also knows this meta-criterion (the second is unknown to him), although he has another name for it, for he calls it *Normalidee* (the normal, standard idea). With the help of this meta-criterion it can be explained why it is more interesting for a painter to depict an old fisherman with his rough but appealing traits than the regular, but unexpressive face of a filmstar.

To us it is interesting that Heymans is able to show that all meta-criteria have something in common and can, as it were, be reduced to one primordial meta-criterion. For, according to Heymans, in all these meta-criteria the application and assimilation of the observing mind's attention play an important role. We can explain this as follows: When we observe something, we must apply our observational attention to it. In doing this we must exert ourselves. Now Heymans shows that we do not have to do this with objects we call beautiful, because by their beauty these objects draw our attention to them as a matter of course and therefore the observation takes place without the usual efforts. This activity of our attention is to be analysed into two constituents. First, our attention has to be attracted and second the observation has to be in some way easy. Therefore we speak of an application and assimilation of our attention.

If the beautiful object draws our attention by its beauty, Heymans speaks of applying our attention and if the observation goes easily through beautiful components he speaks of the assimilation of the attention. This is obvious when we apply the formal meta-criterion of unity in variety. On the one hand the variety attracts our attention and the unity makes the observation easier. Monotony and chaos are both opposed to a fluent process of observation. With the associative beauty it is the associations in the background which make the observation easier. These associations must not stand in the foreground, for in that case they divert the attention from what is to be observed. In the case of typical beauty also, it is obvious that application and assimilation of the attention play their role. In this theory Heymans has taken over some ideas of the German aesthetic philosopher Theodor Lipps, but he has elaborated Lipp's ideas into a consistent theory. Further Lipps placed aesthetics within a whole philosophy of life. This is not done by Heymans; he is too much of a sober scientist to do so.

With the help of Heyman's theory one can very easily understand that there is a variety of judgment about the beauty of an object. It depends very strongly on the criteria that are used. In previous times, for example, it was usual to restore churches in a uniform style. One used criteria which belong to the meta-criterion of the formal kind, i.e. one sought a unity in variety. In today's restorations the unity of style is no longer predominant. Parts of the building which belong to various periods of history are maintained, because now one appreciates the history of the building and wants to show this. That means that now the associative criteria are preferred. Or perhaps the beauty through typical features. Beethoven, for example, is a master in creating beauty through unity in variety, but others, like Grieg and Chopin, may be better in creating lovely melodies. And lovely melodies are to be classified under beauty through association.

When I now go beyond Heymans's theory, this will be the usual criticism by a logical-empiricist of a mere empiricist. Heymans has only taken the observational, i.e. the empirical aspects of aestheticism into consideration and has paid too little attention to the logical aspects. A rational or intellectual meta-criterion must be added to the series of meta-criteria, *viz.* beauty through indirectness. We find this, for example, in Kierkegaard's method of indirect communication, which is attractive from an aesthetic point of view. Indirect communication is aesthetically more valuable than direct communication. Literature, but also film and theatre offer many examples. Heymans takes his examples for the greatest part from the plastic arts.

Can we also present, like Heymans, a common basic structure of aesthetic experience? In my view this is certainly possible and we may take Heyman's theory for starting-point and extend it. The only thing we have to do is to include the rational meta-criterion mentioned above in our considerations. Not only for observation, but also for thinking, is it necessary that one's attention should be attracted and that one overcomes some obstacles. The common ground of all the meta-criteria, which is the logical basis of all the criteria, is that some complicated structures are to be penetrated by our understanding. The structure given by Heymans is a special case of this more comprehensive structure. We may call the *logic* of aestheticism a kind of *logic of victory*. Heymans's application and assimilation of the attention (of observation) is a victory over the difficulties of observation. In the same way the penetrating activity of thinking is a victory over the difficulties of understanding and interpretation. We experience something aesthetically when certain difficulties are overcome. These difficulties could be of an empirical, observational character, but they may also be intellectual. And in the intellectual realm the rule is also valid that the quantity and quality of the aesthetic experience are in conformity with the complexity of the structures that are penetrated by the understanding. And here too there must be a maximum, for if the complexity is too great, then the aesthetic experience will diminish.

Perhaps someone will object that according to this theory victories in sport are to be considered as aesthetic experiences too. I think that this may be defended, but I prefer to regard the ground-structure of the meta-criteria of aesthetics as a necessary condition. We may regard it as a necessary and a sufficient condition, if there are no obstacles which impede seeing a certain event as an aesthetic event. Therefore it is a necessary condition and under certain circumstances also a sufficient condition. Whether or not experiences in sport are to be classified as aesthetic, depends on where one wants to draw the boundary line and this is, of course, culturally determined. One may want to exclude sport from aesthetics and in that case one must declare our fundamental meta-criterion invalid if we have to deal with sporting events. For my part I prefer to take another course and make a distinction between art and aesthetics. In this view a victory in sport would be an aesthetic experience, but not a piece of creative art. Not everything which evokes in us an aesthetic experience is at the same time a piece of art. Experiences of the beauty, sublimity and the overwhelming power *of nature* are without doubt aesthetic, but they are, we might even say by definition, no works of art. In passing I must say that I differ from Van der Leeuw here, because he classifies the contemplation of nature among works of art. By looking aesthetically at nature man is an artist. But then art and aesthetics are synonyms, which is rather artifical.

A further consequence of the theory is that aesthetic experiences contribute to man's joy and happiness in life. This is also in conformity with general experience. Art indeed brings joy in life and is consequently a necessity. Van der Leeuw, Kant and others are right when they think that art does not *necessarily* have to reform life. It is neither art nor aesthetics that has to teach us how to create a better world. But art and aesthetics may give us the inspiring power to work for a better world. They give life another dimension and in doing so they teach us to see, to hear, to smell, to understand better, and that might be a first step towards improving the world's moral situation. Even in bad times one may bear suffering better with the help of aesthetic experience. I might refer here, once again, to experiences in wartime. On the one hand there was a maximum of suffering, but on the other hand there was also a maximum of life's intensity: friends, children, the beloved wife or husband, the smell of flowers, the song of birds mean more than in times of peace. And this more intensive meaning is experienced aesthetically. In some way one may overcome life's difficulties with the help of aesthetics. In this way we may incorporate aesthetics in a philosophy of life.

This logic of victory also plays a great role in religion. For in religious experience it is not the smooth flowing of life's events that produces religious experience, but the border experiences, sorrow, death, marriage, etc. (Jaspers). These border experiences need not only be specimens of suffering, but it must be said that in such moments of intensive suffering or joy God seems to be nearer than in the quiet moments of daily life. In mysticism also depressive moments play an important role. Symbols like 'mystic night', 'dryness', 'sterility' are used to express God's absence. The soul must travel through the dark night in which it learns to purify itself from sins and thus to reach the union with God. '...mi doghen suete hevet gheweest om sine Minne. Mer mi hevet hi wredere gheweest dan mi nie duvel was...' (The suffering for his love has been sweet for me, but further he was more pitiless to me than the devil ever was) (Hadewych, Epistle I). For the devil could not deprive Hadewych of God's love, but God himself could. The way in which God is absent also leads to a (re-)union with God in love. It was John of the Cross who described this mystic night. But now, the mystic, having experienced God's absence, finds even greater joy when God returns. Here too the rule mentioned above is valid that mystic experiences are deeper the more there is to be overcome. Here too the logic of victory applies. This logic of victory is a victory of the cross and resurrection, and should not advocate prematurely an *ecclesia gloriae*, a Christian life of glory only.

On the one hand logic of religion shows as certain similarity to the logic of aesthetics, but on the other hand there is also a great difference. For in contradistinction to aesthetic judgements religious ones are not without practical utility and moral consequences. The following theorem is valid here:

(iii) $W^r p \rightarrow Op$
(Explication: $W^r p$ means 'p has a religious value')

In this respect the logic of religion is in conformity with the logic of ethics. Consequently one may speak of a synthesis of the two. The logic of victory is also important for the problem of theodicy, the vindication of divine justice in the face of the existence of evil. We have probably considered God too much from an exclusively moral point of view (cp. 3.1.4 and 3.3). In that case difficulties are sure to arise. But if we take the logic of victory into consideration then we are able to give sense to a life of suffering. In passing: of course, I do not care about the *term* 'logic of victory'. If someone does not like the term 'victory', another term may do as well. Perhaps 'logic of transcendence' is an acceptable alternative. As long as the logic itself is taken account of!

In many respects Christianity and the other prophetic religions, Judaism and Islam, have had a less positive relation to art than Buddhism and Hinduism. Christianity was hostile towards dance and theatre, Islam was opposed to painting human figures. This in contradistinction to Buddhism and Hinduism. But the latter religions had only provisionally a good relation to art. Through their rejection of the world and their asceticism even art finally disappears. Perhaps the best relation to art is to be found in the 'religion of balance' (Confucianism, Taoism, Japanese religions, the religions of Indonesia, etc.). Here art plays a fundamental role in religion, and there is no rejection of the world here. Consequently there is never an abandonment of the aesthetic attitude as there is in orthodox Buddhism. The logic of victory also has an interesting variant here. Usually the victory of good over evil is never complete in these religions. So, for instance, in the famous barong-dance on Bali the good monster Barong gains an (incomplete) victory over the witch Ranggah. This incompleteness is due to the fact that in this world nothing can really exist unless in a certain balance to its opposite.

188

In the Christian view the victory of good over evil is more complete, although it is only in the representing of the past that the victory is won again and again (cp. 4.1; 4.3). Thus Christianity too can vindicate an aesthetic style, because it is able to give a positive interpretation of suffering. The same can be said of Judaism. The logic of victory teaches us to live life more intensely. This intensity of life is to be interpreted both aesthetically and religiously. Moreover, in this view not only the incarnation, as in Van der Leeuw's thinking, but also the cross and the recurrection must be the foundation of a religious aesthetics.

4.7 *The mystical way*

Several times already we have pointed out the relevance of mystical experience. In order to avoid unnecessary repetitions I shall confine myself here to briefly describing the mystical way by referring to Ruusbroeck. An interesting feature of mysticism is that it shows similar faces in the various religions and cultures. Usually the way to the mystic union has several stages which have quite similar features in the various religions.

In the first stage the disciple is taught to liberate himself from all earthly desires and to open his mind to the spirit of God. In this process of purification moral demands also are usually made, although this is not the case in every mystical system. Ruusbroec, however, points out the dangers of a non-moral life. He warns against seeking a quick way to ecstasy. One should start with moral purification. Sometimes it even seems that he warns the hippies of our time, who seek ecstasy without a preceding moral purification! This stage of moral cleansing and purification is called by him the 'working life'. Here humility is the principal virtue. Then follows the stage of a life seeking God. Ruusbroec describes how the human soul opens itself more and more to the coming of the Lord. The intellect is enlightened and the will submitted. Then a stage follows in which the disciple learns to view the world *sub specie aeternitatis*. Now he realizes the unity in all things, and he sees himself as a member of this great whole. Then finally the moment comes in which he learns to contemplate God. Here we have to do with the *unio mystica* of which there are many variants: (i) a submerging of the soul in God with loss of its own individuality and personality or (ii) an intensive communion of love with God, in which his own personality remains.

We have already seen that Ruusbroec teaches an interesting rhythm of a going into God and a going out of him. The distinction between God and man, however, is maintained in every stage. 'Whant geen ghescapen wesen en mach met gods wesene één sijn ende tegaen in hem selven. Want soe worde de creature god, dat onmoghelijc is' (No created being is allowed to be one with God's essence and go into him, for then the creature would become God, which is impossible). And '...nochtan blijft redene staende sonder werc inder hebbelijcheit ende oec dat sinlijcke leven ende moghen niet vergaen, niet meer dan die natuere des menschen vergaen en mach' (...nevertheless also without work reason remains in its *habitus* and sensory life cannot perish either, any more than human nature can or may...) (*hebbelijcheit* is a translation of the Latin *habitus* and means 'permanent predisposition' a property which is acquired and has, as it were, become a second nature). In this last quotation Ruusbroec wants to say that reason remains also in the stage of contemplation. That it is present in the stage of work is no matter of doubt; hence the formulation which might, at first sight, be a little remarkable: 'also without work reason remains'. From these quotations it may be inferred that in Ruusbroec human nature does not lose its nature, in spite of the fact that it enters the divine being in the *unio mystica*. This going into God means nothing else but participating in God's glory. For a philosophical evaluation of the various mystical concepts I may refer to section 4.1.

In conclusion I refer to the fact that these stages are present in practically all kinds of mysticism, although, of course, its terminology may change. So Hinduism distinguishes between *samprajñāta samādhi* (the conscious ecstasy) and *asamprajñāta samādhi* (the unconscious ecstasy). Buddhism knows various stages before the stage of Nirvana is reached: a stage of reflection and meditation (*vitakka-vicāra*), a stage of joy and satisfaction (*pitisukham*), a stage of mental balance, consciousness and satisfaction (*upekkha, sati, sukham*) and finally the stage of completion of the mental balance and consciousness (*upekkha, sati, parisuddhi*). The Muslim Ghazali knows the stage of concentration of energy, that of deep mental absorption and finally that of the disappearance of selfconsciousness, the submerging into God.

The Javanese *kebatinan* mysticism, again, knows four stages. In the first the (Islamic) commands are fulfilled, in the second (*tarekat*) the deeper, symbolic meaning of these rites and obligations is understood. In the third stage (*hakekat*) the truth of being is learned. The world is seen *sub specie aeternitatis* and the disciple regards himself as a part of the great whole. In the fourth stage (*mahrifat*), which is also called *samadi*, the union between God and man is reached. Javanese mysticism is a synthesis of the indigenous religion, Islam, Hinduism and Buddhism, as can be inferred from the terms used. Pseudo-Jamblichus, a Neo-Pythagorean, also knows of three stages; first we have an introductory stage (*eidos sunagōgon*), then the stage of communion (*eidos koinōnias*) and finally the stage of unity (*henōsis*).

The well-known Spanish mystic Teresa di Jesu knows the stages of concentration (*recogimento*), rest (*quietud*), communion (*union*) and rapture of the soul (*arrobamiento*). And we could continue in this way to give examples from several cultures and religions. Everywhere there is a way to ecstatic union with God characterized by various stages: one of curbing the passions, forsaking the world and concentrating of the soul. Then a stage of seeing the world *sub specie aeternitatis*, seeing oneself as a part of a great whole, and then a final stage which culminates in a mystic union with God.

Finally we shall give a short logical survey of the ecstatic union, the *unio mystica*. We start with the relation (R) of a subject (s) to an object (o):

(i) s R o

In the mystic union 's' is man, and 'o' becomes finally God. The *unio mystica* has various forms, as we have seen. These forms may even present themselves alternatively in one and the same mystic (e.g. Ramakrishna, Ruusbroec). Essentially there are the following possibilities:

(1)   Subject and object maintain, not without qualifications, their independence and individuality. In this case the relation is that of intense love. We find this form especially in Christianity, but also in Judaism, Islam and Hinduism (and even in Buddhism, though perhaps to a lesser extent than in the other religions).

(2)   The subject submerges in the object. That means that the human personality is completely submerged in the deity. The godhead may have an ego-structure or a neutrum structure. We find both forms in the great oriental religions (Hinduism, Buddhism, Taoism, for instance), but also in Christianity, Islam and Judaism.

(3)   The subject becomes a godhead himself and absorbs the object. Here the result is approximately the same as sub (2) in the variant where we have to do with an ego-structure in the godhead.

(4)   Both subject and object disappear and only the pure relationship remains. This position is defended by some Buddhists, especially Zen-Buddhists.

In a scheme we get the following results, where we give the final results of the mystic way, of which the start was the primordial relation: (i) s R o:

(1)   s R o   (esp. Christianity, Judaism, Islam
(2)   o   (esp. Hinduism, Taoism)
(3)   s   (esp. Hinduism, Taoism)
(4)   R   (esp. Buddhism).

4.8 *Myth, sacrifice, symbol, miracle*

Finally we have to deal with some important, but perhaps not central concepts of the philosophy of religion. *Myth* is 'the holy narration of events in original time, which are still the foundation for the present and which give a prospect for the future' (Van Baaren). Myths are very often connected with cult and rites and sometimes it was thought that cult and rites are prior to myth in their origin. But there are many myths that have nothing to do with the cult, e.g. the aetiological myths, which serve to explain why something has come into the world. They are meant to explain the 'how' and 'why' of things. The mythical concept of time is cyclic. Therefore Karl Barth could say that in Scripture there are no myths, because there we do not find a cyclic concept of time. But in Barth's view this does not mean that the biblical narrations are literally true. They are sagas, but no myths. When a man like Bultmann speaks about the necessity of demythologizing, he uses a different concept of myth from Barth's. We shall return to this programme of demythologizing later.

The *sacrifice* is a 'holy activity, by which something from the profane sphere is transported into the sacred sphere. It may also mean a holy activity by which the sacred potency of things that are already in this sacred sphere, are strengthened' (Van Baaren). Why do human beings sacrifice? They do so in order to receive something from the deity, or to show their gratitude, or in order to make the process in nature and society continue, or in view of a redemption for sins. Bloody sacrifices of human beings, such as those of the Aztecs, become understandable, if one keeps in mind that they believed that this was the only way to let the sun continue its course. A special case of sacrifice is that in which God sacrifices himself. We find this in the myths of the Dema-godheads (*vide* 4.1), the various ancient religions of the Near East (Osiris, Tammuz, Adonis, etc.), and in Christianity.

Mystics interpret rites and myths very often symbolically. The same is done by philosophers, for example the Stoics. By a symbolic interpretation of an event (myth, rite) '*a*', we understand that it refers to an event '*A*' (religious mental state, event in the realm of God). If '*a*' is a real religious symbol, it cannot be replaced by something else. This symbolic interpretation is only meaningful if it is more than an arbitrary connection of two concepts, if there is between '*a*' and '*A*' a certain analogy (or formulated in a more modern way: homomorphy, *vide* appendix 2).

Scholars who find it necessary to demythologise biblical narrations are of the opinion that these narrations should be deprived of their miraculous character, i.e. that it should be denied that God interferes in world processes by suspending natural laws. One cannot really raise many objections against this. We do not necessarily want to say that these narrations are not literally true. They might be explained with the help of parapsychology. But in that case too these narrations have been deprived of their miraculous character!

Maybe most biblical narrations cannot hold out against historical criticism. In that case they have not yet lost all sense and value, for they can certainly still have a symbolic meaning in the strict sense given above. Such a narration cannot be replaced by another narration. The best example is the history of Jesus' resurrection: Christ's victory over death and sin, in which also the faithful may participate. In this narration of Christ's resurrection we do not have a literal report of historical events. This may already be obvious from the fact that the accounts of this event given by the various gospels contradict each other. They do not vary, however, in their symbolic interpretation, i.e. in their message that in and through Christ human sin and death are overcome by a divine power, so that man may live in peace with God in all eternity.

The miracle as a literal *miraculum*, in which natural laws have been suspended, is not regarded highly nowadays. However, it may be interpreted as a *sign*, in which there is no question of a suspension of natural laws. In that case a miracle is a wonderful event, which may inspire people religiously and may lead to a 'disclosure' (Ramsey, De Pater). In this view a sign is, in contradistinction to a symbol, something that might be replaced.

Moreover, one could say, the real great miracle is the fact that God has cared for us in Jesus Christ. All other biblical miracles are only signs referring to this fact. But if I start writing in this way I exceed the limits of a philosophy of religion which means that I do not write any longer as a philosopher of religion, but as a theologian or a confessing Christian.

Appendices

1. *Modern linguistic methods in theology*

As an example of a modern linguistic method in theology we give here the treatment of the thesis 'God created the world' by W. de Pater (*Theologische Sprachlogik*, München 1971, p. 130ff). De Pater uses here the theory of semantic restrictions. This theory has been developed by R. MacCormac, 'A New Programme for Religious Language. The Transformational Generative Grammar', in: *Religious Studies* 6 (1970), p. 41-55. Starting-point is the following syntactical description:

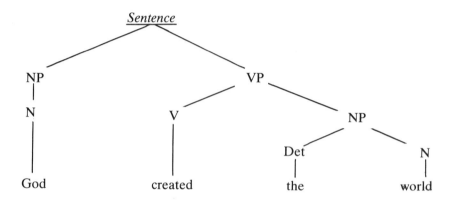

In order to interpret this structural tree semantically we must formulate possible entries for the various words and use suitable rules of projection, by which the entries may be combined in the appropriate way. This is precisely what was done by MacCormac. Because it is only our purpose to show the method we consider only three possible entries for each word:

God... N... 1 (physical object), (with an external form), (human or animal)...
2 (animistic spirit), (connected with nature),...
3 (Spirit), (the most sublime being), (eternal), (creator),...

.
.
.

Created... V... 1 (being the cause that something originates),...

194

```
2  (being the cause that something happens),...
3  (to produce with the help of his imagination)
   .
   .
   .
World... N...   1  (physical object), (planet), (earth),...
                2  (human), (group), (secular),...
                3  (physical object), (universe),...
```

When we interpret the sentence 'God created the world', it is obvious that if we choose meaning 2 for 'created', the three meanings for 'world' are excluded and the same applies if we choose meaning 3, for in this way only ideas can be produced. By this the meanings 2 and 3 for 'created' have been excluded and thus there remains only meaning 1. In the same way one must make selections with the other concepts as well. Thus one gets the following result, *viz.* that the interpretation of the sentence 'God created the world' runs: 'God the most sublime spirit created the originating of the physical universe'. According to De Pater the method of MacCormac has certain advantages. In this way one is able to explain religious statements also to those persons who are of the opinion that they do not experience cosmic disclosures. The structural semantic description given above has a strong intersubjective element, and one may regard it as a preparation for the application of Ramsey's method. For if one wants to explain a sentence with the help of Ramsey's models and qualifiers, it is necessary to know beforehand what kind of sentence one has to explain.

However, one should be aware of the fact that MacCormac's result: 'God, the most sublime spirit, caused the originating of the physical universe' is still insufficient. The proper work of interpretation has still to start. For what is to be understood by 'caused' in this connection? Perhaps it is necessary to construct new semantical descriptions of 'cause' with new semantical restrictions in order to discover the meaning of the sentence. But without something like Ramsey's *disclosures* it is impossible to succeed. According to De Pater this incorporating of Ramsey's method into Mac-Cormac's method could prove to be impossible, because in this method the words have become blocks, which fit more or less into each other. This makes his structural method too static, whereas in Ramsey's theory of disclosures there is more dynamism (and fluency) in the meaning of words, so that sudden disclosures may be evoked.

So far the theory of De Pater/MacCormac. For the most part I agree with De Pater, and also with his criticism. I am only more optimistic about the possibility of incorporating Ramsey's theory into that of MacCormac's. For in my view in this semantic theory one can show in a very clear way the ambiguity of sentences. For only very seldom will the interpretation be unambiguous. And the disclosure very often consists in the fact that the reader or listener suddenly sees another meaning in addition to the one on which he was fixed until then.

One small final remark. The interpretation given by MacCormac is not so felicitous because God has, of course, not only created the physical, but also the spiritual (psychic) universe. The reason of this difference is that MacCormac only considered a limited number of possible interpretations. One should also include the interpretation of the world as physical-psychical universe.

A beautiful example of a combination of modern linguistic methods and logic is the modern logical theory of synonyms. I am, by the way, convinced that logic can contribute much more to the theory of language than has been thought until now. In so-called generative grammar too the logical achievements are not used sufficiently, although particularly in the Montague-grammars there can be no complaints about the neglect of logic.

In the logical theory of synonyms it is possible to formulate the semantical rules of restriction in the form of rules of inference (or in the form of theorems, in which implications are used). In passing: in logic it has been proved that every theorem with an implication can be transformed into a rule of inference and *vice versa*. If we use logical methods instead of the usual linguistic ones, we could make use of the well-elaborated systems of logic. In this way we can see the various meanings better, because we can now also see what can be inferred from certain sentences. In my view the meaning of a sentence does not only depend on its reference, but also on its logical consequences (*vide* appendix 11). In this respect there is a certain parallelism between theories of truth and theories of meaning. Besides the correspondence theory of truth there is also the coherence or consequence theory of truth, and in the same way we have the consequence theory of meaning besides the reference theory of meaning. Of course, in addition to the theories mentioned above, we have also the pragmatic (*consensus*) theory of truth and meaning, in which it is stated that truth and meaning depend on the cultural group to which one belongs or on communicative agreements made in certain circles. But such a theory of truth and meaning (the pragmatic or consensus theory) lies on another level than the other two. It is this cultural group which decides what meaning will be accepted, i.e. what a certain sentence or a certain word refers to and what consequences may be drawn from it. We shall now give some examples of the logical theory of synonyms. Suppose we compare the two English synonyms 'redeem' and 'ransom'. In a logical translation the two concepts have the same logical structure:

(i) a R b

(Here 'R' represents a relation, thus here either 'redeem' or 'ransom'; 'a' is the subject and 'b' is the object of the relation, or in other words: the first and second member of the relation).

Now according to Crabb, *English Synonyms*, London 1966 (^{1}1816), p. 591, the distinction between the two words is: 'Redeem' may have as object both persons and things, whereas 'ransom' can have only 'persons' as object. In a logical theory of synonyms this may be expressed in the following way:

(ii) $(a\ R\ b) \rightarrow (b = a\ person)$

This implication (ii) is only valid, when R = 'ransom', and not when R = 'redeem'. In the semantic field of 'ransom' this conclusion is valid, but not in the semantic field of 'redeem'.

All this might seem at first sight nothing more than an alternative formulation. But it may be very important, especially with respect to the logical evaluation of a system of statements. For if we could translate all the rules of semantic restrictions into logical rules of inference, it would be much easier to check the logical validity of a system of statements.

The following example, however, may be more interesting. This example also shows an alternative formulation of the theory of analogy. (In appendix 2 we give a modern reformulation with the help of set theory):

Suppose we have to translate 'to wish'. Let us use symbols which are customary in intensional symbolic logic:

(iii) $_aW^+p$

($_aW^+$ qualifies the statement 'p' and means 'a wishes'). If 'a' = God or, in other words, if we have to do with a system of God's wishes, then the following theorem is valid:

(iv) $_aW^+p \rightarrow p$

Or in other words, if God wishes that something is the case, it is the case. But if we have to do with human wishes, (iv) is not a theorem. In a system in which theorem (iv) is valid, 'to wish' means something different from 'to wish' in a system in which (iv) is not valid. Thus synonyms may be distinguished by the difference between the conclusions that can be drawn.

By means of the concsons that can be drawn we may acquire a clear insight into the meaning of words or sentences. For partly the same, partly different conclusions may be drawn. Partial identity and partial difference is a characteristic of analogy and thus it may be obvious that with the help of this logical theory of synonymy one may re-formulate the theory of analogy very well. Subtle differences in meaning for which we have no separate words may also be distinguished in this way.

2. *Modern Reformulation of Analogy*

With the help of modern set theory the traditional doctrine of analogy may be reformulated. In the following exposition complicated details have not been considered. We must presume the meaning of 'creating' and 'destroying'. We could have taken these concepts as primitive concepts, but we will try to define them.

Def. (i): *Creating is changing a certain state of affairs A into a state of affairs B, in which B has a more complicated structure than A.*
  We may think for example of a piece of wood which is changed into a figure. The artist creates in this way a statue. But we may also consider a second type of creating:

Def. (ii): *Creating is separating a state of affairs D out of a more complicated state of affairs C in such a way that D is made (relatively) independent.*
  For example: An author takes some ideas out of a complicated set of ideas and put them as a relatively independent whole on paper. Thus he creates a novel or short story. Creating as self-confining (4.1) is a form of creating (ii).
  We may give parallel definitions of 'destroying':

Def. (iii): *Destroying is changing a certain state of affairs B into a state of affairs A in such a way that A is less complicated in structure than B.*
and

Def. (iv): *Destroying is eliminating the relative independence of a state of affairs D in such a way that it is (again) incorporated into a state of affairs C, with which it is now united.*

We may now give the following definition of 'creative property':

Def. (v): *A creative property is a property with the help of which creative activities are performed.*
  Now we will decide (in principle) which properties may be ascribed to God in an analogous way and which not. We will do this with the help of the following recursive function. Here E_i stands for a worldly or human property known to us ($1 \leqslant i \leqslant n$) (This is the usual abbreviation for the fact that we want to consider the sequence of properties, $E_1, E_2, E_3, \ldots E_n$. With E_i we pick out one property from the sequence). The recursive function runs as follows:

(a)   If the property E_i is creative, then we must ascribe this property analogously to God;

198

(b)   If the property E_i destructive, then its negation is ascribed analogously to God.

We may interpret analogy in a modern way as *homomorphy* and that means the following: Each property E_i stands in the relation 'being the ground (cause)' of a whole series of consequences (effects) G_j ($1 \leqslant j \leqslant m$). Now we presuppose a project function F that projects each (creative) worldly or human property E_i and each world (human) consequence or effect G_j in God which results in E_i^+ and G_j^+ respectively. We do not know this project function and consequently we have no exact knowledge of the images of our properties and consequences in God (i.e. what exactly E_i^+ and G_j^+ are). The only thing we know is that there must be an image in God of every property which we ascribe to him. And we are allowed to draw the conclusion that if in our world property E_i has a certain consequence (or effect) G_j, in God's world E_i^+ (= the image of E_i) has a certain consequence (or effect) G_j^+ (= the image of G_j). In other words: Although the project function F has changed E_i into E_i^+ and G_j into G_j^+ and we do not know this project function F and consequently do now know E_i^+ and G_j^+, we *do* know that if there is a certain relation between E_i and G_j (the relation of being the ground (cause)) that same relation also holds between E_i^+ and G_j^+. In other words the logical relations are universally valid, in God's world too. That this is correct according to modern insight, may be seen in Bocheński-Menne, *Grundriss des Logistik*, Paderborn 1954, § 21.4). But, of course, every E_i^+ (in God) is besides being a ground for G_j^+ a ground for an unknown number of consequences G_j^{++}, which are no longer an image of a worldly G_j. Therefore one may only speak of a homomorphic and not of an isomorphic projection of the relation 'being the ground of' in God. God is creative in a completely other sense than that in which the things and human beings in the world are creative. But, of course, the argument would run more easily still if we spoke of an isomorphy instead of a homomorphy.

But things are of course more complicated than we have presented them here. It is possible to create something that is by itself destructive. If we want to determine whether an activity is creative or not, we must take all the consequences into consideration. And even the consequences of the consequences! If we want to get a logical grip on the matter, we must divide all properties nominalistically into a set of properties from which always only one or at least a limited number of consequences follow. Then it is at least theoretically possible to calculate whether or not the total balance of the consequences is positive or negative, in other words whether or not one may label the property as creative or destructive. This should also be done when we apply the concept of analogy. Of course, this is only theoretically possible. Only God himself can understand the analogy completely, but to us only the principle is important. Also the well-known ideal observer or ideal mathematician can see into the heart of the analogy, if it is presupposed that he not only knows all the consequences of a certain deed, but also has a standard to measure the degree of creativity of this deed. But theoretically such a standard may be constructed, as we have seen above.

In this way we must ascribe omniscience, omnipotence, goodness, etc. to God. Also the 'personal' properties such as selfconsciousness and will for, as we have seen (*vide* 4.1), self-consciousness, i.e. an ego-structure, is more creative than a neutrum-structure. But if we apply our theory of analogy correctly, then we must analyse out worldly properties until we reach the simple elementary properties mentioned above, the producers of a limited number of consequences. Only then can we apply our recursive function correctly:

(a)   If the elementary property E_i is creative, it must be ascribed analogously to God;
(b)   If the elementary property E_i is destructive, its negation must be ascribed to God.

The construction of the analogy proceeds as shown above. But from the complexity of the nature of creativity, i.e. because of the fact that a certain deed may inevitably have good and bad consequences, it follows that even God cannot be creative without at the same time bringing about the possibility of destruction. In this view, of course, it is supposed that God cannot transgress the laws of logic. But if he could, things would be even worse, for in that case he could have avoided evil, which in this view is impossible.

3. *Hartshorne's contribution to the ontological argument and the relevance of process philosophy*

One of the first scholars who called our attention to Anselm's ontological argument in a modern way, was Charles Hartshorne in an article in the *Philosophical Review* (May 1944, Nr. 3, p. 225-245) under the title 'The Formal Validity and Real Significance of the Ontological Argument'. Also in a book he has written together with W.L. Reese, *Philosophers Speak of God* (Chicago 1953), Anselm's argument was considered in a new way. Still these attempts remained relatively unnoticed. On the other hand Norman Malcolm's fine and interesting article aroused everybody's attention immediately: 'Anselm's Ontological Arguments' (*The Philosophical Review*, January 1960, nr. 1) (The article is also included in the volume containing Malcolm's collected articles, *Knowledge and Certainty*, Englewood Cliffs, 1963, ²1964.)

In this article the Wittgenstein disciple Malcolm clearly shows that Anselm's argument in Proslogion 2 is not valid, but that the argument in Proslogion 3 is indeed valid. In the history of the Anselmian arguments all the attention had been focussed on the argument in the second chapter. We have seen above (3.1.2.1) that the difference between the two arguments is that in chapter 3 the mere existence of God is no longer the focus of interest, as in chapter 2, but God's necessary existence. Then Hartshorne published his famous reconstruction of the Anselmian argument in his book *The Logic of Perfection* (1962), in which he used modern modal logic. We shall discuss this argument later on in this section. The quintessence of the reconstruction consists in the fact that Hartshorne shows that for God (i.e. for a perfect being) the following theorem is valid: either he (it) exists necessarily, or necessarily he (it) does not exist, i.e. his existence is self-contradictory. I call this theorem Hartshorne's central thesis or simply *central thesis*, abbreviated CT. This CT is very important, for if we could show that God's existence is at least possible, i.e. that it is not self-contradictory, then we may prove his existence with the help of CT, in the following way:

(1)   CT: Either God exists necessarily or he necessarily does not exist.
(2)   God's existence is possible (by hypothesis)
(3)   It is not true that he necessarily does not exist (from 2)
(4)   God exists necessarily (from (1) and (3) by *modus tollendo ponens*)

Now Hartshorne is of the opinion that from the cosmological argument it at least follows that God's existence is possible. But is this correct? Kant tried to show that the cosmological argument presupposes the ontological argument; do we not get into a *circulus vitiosus* in this way? Hartshorne has solved this problem by pointing out that Kant's analysis should have shown that what the other arguments for God's existence borrow from the ontological argument are not the steps towards the conclusion, i.e. the steps which in the argument follow the demonstration of CT (i.e. the steps 7, 8 and 9 of the argument (see p. 218)). What is borrowed from the ontological argument is the exclusion of contingency from perfection, i.e. the proof of CT, and this again is a logical transformation of Anselm's Principle, to which we come in a moment. According to Hartshorne in this way there is no *circulus vitiosus*, if we use both arguments together. They are both complex and when one is weak the other is strong, and *vice versa* (cp. *The Logic of Perfection and Other Essays in Neoclassical Metaphysics*, Lasalle 1962 (abbr. LP), p. 52). In other words the ontological and the cosmological argument together form a cumulative argument. In the argumentation above premise (1) (= CT) is proved by the ontological argument independently of the cosmological argument. The latter argument proves premise (2), totally independently of the ontological argument. Put together they form as a result a valid argument for God's existence.

Various objections have been raised against the ontological argument. Hartshorne, however, is of the opinion that these objections only hold true if we use the classical concept of God, but that they fall short, if we accept the neoclassical concept of God, developed in process philosophy. We have already referred to this concept. Here we have to distinguish between two fundamental aspects in God, namely his primordial or abstract nature, which is eternal and unchangeable, and his consequent or concrete nature, which realizes itself in the concrete divine states of affairs. These concrete states of affairs may also include contingent elements, which are excluded from God's abstract nature.

Moreover, Hartshorne teaches the *law of inclusive contrast*. That means, that in the world there are always two pairs of oppositions, eternity-time, necessity-contingence, being-becoming, unchangeable-changeable, cause-effect, abstract-concrete, unity-variety, etc. These oppositions are not separated from each other, but those mentioned first are included in the second, i.e. the abstract in the concrete, the necessary in the contingent, what is in what becomes, the unchangeable in the changeable, and so on. Thus God's primordial nature is included in his consequent nature. Also for God the future is open and not determined by him. But still he knows all abstract things as abstract and he knows all possible things as possibilities. Hartshorne does not deny that *finally* the future is in God's hands, and that his love will lead everything to a good future. But God's creatures, at least the human beings, are free in their choice. Therefore we, human beings, decide our future partly by ourselves. God's relation to us is not an exclusively external relation, as we have seen already.

Besides the philosophical arguments which may be put forward (*vide* 4.1), one may also point out that Hartshorne's interpretation is closer to the biblical concept of God than to that of classical metaphysics. In the biblical view the history of God and his people is not an apparent history, in which human decisions do not play an important role, because everything is already decided beforehand. No, this history is a real history in which God tries again and again by means of new covenants to lead mankind on the right track. First there was a covenant with Adam, then with Noah, Abraham, Moses, the whole people of Israel, etc. When everything goes wrong, he tries to reach his goal with a remnant of the people, and only when that also fails does he send his Son. This account of biblical history is much more in harmony with Hartshorne's (and Whitehead's) concept of God than with that of classical metaphysics. In the latter God is completely unchangeable, which is something that differs totally from the biblical presentation of God's activities. Many theologians have rejected philosophy on this ground, because theology is not compatible with (classical) metaphysics. In my view it is better to replace this classical metaphysics by a better one in order to surmount the schism between philosophy and theology.

To Hartshorne the temporal interpretation of modalities is important. Here, however, I go in another direction. In Hartshorne's view time is an objective modality, and eternity should not be interpreted as timelessness.

Hartshorne sees the relation between future and past as asymmetrical. The modality of the past is actuality, that of the future is potentiality, and that of eternity is necessity. The past cannot be changed. Hartshorne's position is a very common one. But there are also thinkers, who teach a symmetrical relation between past and future, in which case there are again two possibilities: in one trend (Spinoza, Hegel, and others) the past is determined, and consequently also the future; in the other trend (Kierkegaard) the future is open, and consequently also the past. Kierkegaard has defended this standpoint quite impressively in his *Mellemspil* (Interlude) in the *Philosophiske Smuler* (Philosophical Fragments). Kierkegaard does not contend that what has happened can be changed as far as it is a fact, but he asserts that the past is only fixed in its 'that', not in its 'how'. We will come back to this immediately.

Hartshorne weakens the distinction between logical and real possibility (cp. his article: 'Necessity' (*Review of Metaphysics*, Dec. 1967, p. 290-296); and his article: 'Real Possibility' (*Journal of Philosophy*, Oct. 1960, p. 593-605)). This distinction is only a consequence of our insufficient knowledge. For the rest Hartshorne maintains the usual distinction: Logically possible is what does not contain a (logical) contradiction and what is consequently logically meaningful. Really possible is what is compatible with actuality, i.e. with the world's past until the present moment. But according to Hartshorne logical possibilities must refer to something real in order to be meaningful, so that in the last analysis they must refer to real possibilities. This contradicts his view that the past is fixed and only the future is open, for it is certainly *logically* possible that e.g. Napoleon did not die on St. Helena in 1821, but this is *really* not possible. Therefore the set of real possibilities is still a subset of that of logical possibilities. In Hartshorne's temporal interpretation of the modalities our actual world appears as a specially indexed world. Possibilities outside the actual course until the moment we live, are not considered: the past is fixed.

This position presupposes the so-called Kripke-semantics (*vide* G.L. Goodwin, *The Ontological Argument of Charles Hartshorne*, Missoula Montana 1978). But in Kripke-semantics the Barcan-formula (see next appendix) is not derivable, whereas it is derivable in S_5. And Hartshorne needs S_5 in order to prove his ontological argument! Even Goodwin refrains from mentioning this contradiction. I myself take as my foundation the semantics of Hughes and Cresswell, in which the Barcan-fomula is derivable and, as the reader may see, I need this formula in my proof (or I use S_5, but there the formula is derivable!). In other words Hartshorne uses in his philosophy a system that is too strict for his arguments for God's existence. This difficulty may be eliminated by not giving a temporal interpretation of the modalities. One may assume (with Kierkegaard) the openness of future and past. Of course, what has happened has happened and nothing can change that. That Napoleon died on St. Helena in 1821 (in the course of our history) is unchangeable. But in that case we consider past events in isolation. The past events have, however, their relations with innumerable other events, and by means of these other events, which may lie far in the future, these past events may change in their objective and subjective meaning. That is, the *objective* meaning of an event in the past may change insofar as its consequences may become different.

Its subjective meaning also may change: we can experience an event in the past differently. Did there in 1821 on St. Helena die a criminal, a dictator, a victim of unjust vengeance or a misunderstood genius? To use Kierkegaard's terminology, of past events, the 'that', not the 'how' is fixed. Moreover, God has another time. He may call back the past and make it real again (*vide* 4.1). With all this not only have philosophical objections been eliminated, there are now greater possibilities for theology. For now a classical doctrine of redemption and of the sacraments becomes possible (*vide* 4.1).

A second objection that I may raise against Hartshorne is that in his system the necessity to make choices, even in logic, is not taken into consideration. That means that also in a rational philosophy such as ours choices are necessary. But for the rest Hartshorne's process philosophy is able to give satisfactory answers to many objections that have been raised against the ontological argument in the course of time.

1. The best-known objection is that existence is not a predicate. We have dealt with that objection already above (p. 96ff.).

2. Another very important objection is that the concept of a being 'greater than which nothing can be thought of' is not conceivable, because something like a greatest possible number is not conceivable either. But in process philosophy God is perfect in the sense that he cannot be surpassed by any other being outside himself. But he may surpass himself! A God, who at the end of time has a mankind before him that responds to his love in a loving way is more perfect than a God in which this is not the case. We have shown that in process philosophy God's relations to people belong to his essence.

3. Another objection is that of logical type. A universal like 'perfection' cannot be instantiated in an actual individual. An individual cannot represent a universal. Humanity is not human and why should the universal 'perfection' be perfect? According to Hartshorne, however, we must distinguish between *existence*, and *actuality*. God *is* indeed perfect but, strictly speaking, only in his primordial nature, i.e. in his abstract, eternal unchangeable being. But the concrete divine states of affairs (with respect to God-now) *have* perfection. They include perfection, which may be abstracted from it, as we have seen. Now, what has perfection (the *de facto* state of affairs), is *per definitionem* perfect and cannot be surpassed by the state of affairs of another individual, but only by the future states of affairs of that same individual. God-now and God-tomorrow can only be the states

204

of affairs of the same individual. 'God is the one individual in respect of whom the line between property and instance falls only between individual and state, not also, as it usually does, between individual and some broader class property such as humanity. Perfection is not a class of similar individuals, but only a class of similar and genetically related states of one individual' (LP, 67). What the ontological argument proves is not the false conclusion that there is a necessary instantiation of perfection, but that the set of instantiations of perfection is not empty and that this set must necessarily belong to one individual.

4. Related to the preceding objection is that of the *paradox of the abstractness of the necessary*. Logical analysis is said to teach us that the meaning of necessary is what all possible contingent alternatives have in common. In this view God as an *ens necessarium* can only be interpreted as abstract, without concrete contents. But here too the neoclassical view can solve this problem by making a distinction between God's primordial and consequent natures. God's primordial nature is an *ens necessarium*, but this is never without concrete instantiations.

5. One of the arguments that has been raised against the ontological argument in its modal form was that in this way one has to accept an Aristotelian essentialism. It is supposed that a certain individual may be the same in all possible worlds. And at first sight this essentialism leads to insurmountable difficulties. Suppose that Eisenhower had been born in the Middle Ages, how would he have acted? How could we have recognized this individual as Eisenhower? Such questions are not meaningful! And if they are not meaningful, then this means that there is no individual with an identical essence that can be identified in all possible worlds.

But Hartshorne can answer this question very easily. With the help of the distinction between existence and actuality mentioned above, it is certainly possible to speak of an existence that remains the same in all possible worlds, and to speak of instantiations (actualities) which include this existence that is everywhere identical. This holds both for the course of this world and for the various possible worlds. For we have seen that Hartshorne gives a temporal interpretation of the modalities. The past is fixed. Therefore questions about Eisenhower in the Middle Ages cannot be asked meaningfully, for there is no continuous stream of experience which makes it possible to speak of a set of actualities which includes the existence of 'Eisenhower in the Middle Ages'. But this does not mean that there cannot be an existence which remains the same in all possible worlds, for such a continuous stream of actualities is indeed, in principle, possible.

For us, who have rejected this temporal interpretation of the modalities, the question is more difficult, for in our system asking for 'Eisenhower in the Middle Ages' is indeed possible as our concept of logical possibility is much wider (but therefore in this respect also free of inconsistencies, which Hartshorne's system is not, as we have seen). But I think the problem can be solved in my system too. We may also make Hartshorne's distinction between existence (in the Hartshornian sense) and instantiations (actualities). But in our system reincarnations are, at least logically, not excluded and then it is possible to speak of an abstract existence, which remains the same in changing instantiations. Thus it is possible to think of a person Y in the Middle Ages, who is later reborn in the 20th century as Eisenhower. Both this Mr. Y and Eisenhower may have an abstract personality in common. In passing: I will not defend a *real* possibility of reincarnation, but I do not want to exclude it *logically*, as Hartshorne does.

6. A usual distinction is that between logical (*de dicto*) and real (*de re*) modalities. Now a frequent objection against the ontological argument is that it has shown the *de dicto* possibility and necessity of God's existence, but not that of a *de re* modality. But we have seen that for Hartshorne this distinction vanishes, although here there was a weak point in his argument. We have it easier here, in contradistinction to the preceding objection. For the distinction between a *de dicto* and a *de re* possibility is only important if we have to do with a situation in which our actual world is specially indexed. In that case all possibilities must be related to this world and we do not have 'free' possibilities. We have, however, as we have seen, a system with 'free possibilities', so that this distinction finally collapses. Moreover, even if the distinction were relevant, the *de dicto* necessity of God's existence would include its *de re* necessity. This may be self-evident, but we can also prove it easily by supposing (which might be more self-evident) that a *de re* possibility includes a *de dicto* possibility. Let me introduce the following signs:

$\mapsto$ = the sign for strict implication
$M^r p$ = p is *de re* possible, i.e. is really possible;
$M^d p$ = p is *de dicto* possible, i.e. is logically possible;
$L^r p$ = p is *de re* necessary, i.e. really necessary;
$L^d p$ = p is *de dicto* necessary, i.e. logically necessary.

Now it is selfevident that:

(i) $M^r p \mapsto M^d p$
   For if some state of affairs is really possible it is certainly logically possible.
(ii) $\sim M^d p \mapsto \sim M^r p$ (from (i) by ordinary propositional logic.: the falsity of the consequence includes the falsity of the antecedens)
(iii) $L^d \sim p \mapsto L^r \sim p$ (from (ii) rewriting of the modality 'possibility' into that of necessity)

But in (iii) we have proved that a *de dicto* necessity includes a *de re* necessity! (Negation signs are irrelevant!). Thus, if in the ontological

206

argument a *de dicto* necessary existence of God has been proved, this includes also a *de re* necessary existence.

We will now give Hartshorne's argument in its original form and in some later simplified forms.

1. *Hartshorne's reconstruction of the ontological argument* (LP, 50f)

'The logical structure of the Anselmian argument in its mature or 'Second' form, may be partially formalized as follows: 'q' for '(Ex)Px' there is a perfect being, or perfection exists:

1. $q \mapsto Lq$	'Anselm's Principle': Perfection could not exist contingently
2. $Lq \lor \sim Lq$	Excluded Middle (only valid in classical logic!)
3. $\sim Lq \mapsto L \sim Lq$	Form of Becker's Postulate: modal status is always necessary (This is Hartshorne's formulation. I would indicate that this step is only valid in S_5)
4. $Lq \lor L \sim Lq$	Inference from (2, 3)
5. $L \sim Lq \mapsto L \sim q$	Inference from (1): the necessary falsity of the consequent implies that of the antecedent (Modal form of *modus tollens*)
6. $Lq \lor L \sim q$	Inference from (4, 5)
7. $\sim L \sim q$	Intuitive postulate (or conclusion from other theistic arguments): perfection is not impossible
8. Lq	Inference from (6, 7)
9. $Lq \mapsto q$	Modal axiom
10. q	Inference from (8, 9)

(Here the sign '$\mapsto$' stands for strict implication).

Given Anselm's principle (step 1) the proof runs unobjectionably until step 6. This step 6 may be considered as the central thesis (CT) in Hartshorne's proof. It is a major achievement of Hartshorne to have proved this important proposition (thesis). The modal system S_5 is presupposed as is classical logic, but classical logic and S_5 usually go together. Step 7 is the weakest step in the argument, also acknowledged as such by Hartshorne. We have discussed this already above.

2. *Purtill's simplified version of the Proof*

In his article 'Hartshorne's Modal Proof' (*The Journal of Philosophy*, 1966,

p. 397-409) Richard L. Purtill gave the following shorter and simplified version of Hartshorne's proof (again as in Hartshorne 'q' stands for 'there is a perfect being, or perfection exists'):

1. $(q \mapsto Lq) \to (Mq \mapsto q)$ Theorem in modal logic.
2. $q \mapsto Lq$ assumption (Anselm's Principle)
3. $Mq \mapsto q$ 1, 2 Modus Ponens
4. Mq assumption (perfection is conceivable, i.e. logically possible)
5. q 3, 4 Modus Ponens.

The advantage of this version is that it shows directly and neatly the two assumptions in step 2 and 4, the one being Anselm's principle, the other step 7 in Hartshorne's proof that may be assumed or proved by the cosmological argument. Step 1 is a theorem of S_5, the proof of which is rather complicated.

3. *Hartshorne's simplified version of the Proof*

In a letter to me Hartshorne himself proposed the following simplified version of his proof (the explanations are mine):

1. $\sim L \sim q$ Assumption. God is possible
2. $L (\sim q \vee Lq)$ Transformation of Anselm's Principle
3. $L \sim q \vee LLq$ From 2 by theorem T 29 of Hughes and Cresswell, *o.c.*, p. 51 (valid only in S_5)
4. $L \sim q \vee Lq$ From 3 In S_5 (and S_4) LLq is equivalent with Lq.
5. Lq By 1 and 4
6. q From 5

Indeed, Hartshorne once more showed his genius in constructing a simpler proof. Here one can see the two fundamental presuppositions immediately (steps 1 and 2).

4. *Reconstruction of Anselm's proof with the help of symbolic logic*

In order to show that in Anselm's argument we also have to do with the system S_5 I will give this argument here with the help of a formal reconstruction using symbolic logic. For the sake of simplicity I give here a reconstruction of variant II, using the system of natural deduction and the tabular forms of Fitch.

208

1. ((Ex)(y) (x>y)) & (x =A)		This is a formalized description of axiom (i)
2. M (~M ~B)		This is a formalized description of axiom (ii)
3. L((~M~B & M~A) → (B>A))		This is a formalized description of axiom (iii)
4.	~A	Starting hypothesis (= step 1 of the informal presentation)
5.	M ~A	From 4 by modal logic (= step 2 of the informal presentation)
6.	L B	repetition of 2 and re-description according to modal logic (only in S₅!)
7.	L(B>A)	From 3, 5, 6 (= step 3 of the informal presentation)
8.	~M(A>B)	From 7
9.	M(A>B)	From 1 with re-description
10. A		From 4, 8, 9 (*reductio ad absurdum* (= steps 5 and 6 of the informal presentation)

4. *Modal reconstruction of the cosmological argument*

Several reconstructions of the cosmological argument with the help of modal logic are possible. We shall discuss two, one with the help of modal predicate logic in which a primitive concept 'active working ground' is introduced, referred to by the symbol G (G𝑥 means now '𝑥 is an active working ground') and the other, in which modal propositional logic is used. Here we do not need this primitive concept, for now the relation ground-consequence is expressed by the implication or equivalence relations. Here we have to do with the concepts of sufficient and necessary conditions.

Proofs with the help of modal predicate logic

We may prove God's existence here in a system stricter than the system S_5 and, as we have seen, this is a great exception. The difference is, however, not so great, for we have to use the Barcan-formula, which is provable in S_5, but not in S_4. But still we have in this way proved God's existence in a system stricter than S_5, for we have proved it in S_4 + Barcan-formula! But, unfortunately we have to 'pay' for this stricter system with a less probable premise. If we introduce a second variant in which this premise is replaced by a more probable one, we are in S_5 again! Further we shall consider some other translations of the relation 'being the ground of'. But we shall see that then the proofs go more easily.

For a technical exposition of the Barcan-formula and for some other technical details of the argument I may refer to the standard work on modal logic: G.E. Hughes and M.J. Cresswell, *An Introduction to Modal Logic*, London 1968. The Barcan-formula is treated on pages 142-145. It may be represented in the following way:

(i) (x) Lfx → L(x)fx

As is well known, the reversal is without problems and is valid in all modal systems:

(ii) L(x)fx → (x) Lfx

We use the symbol system of the book of Hughes and Cresswell, and some well-known symbols for propositional logic. L(→) stand for strict implication, etc. The structure of the proof is the same as in set theory, i.e. here too we need to recur to a multiple application of the principle '*ex nihilo nihil fit*'.

VARIANT A

1. (x) L (fx ⟷ Gb)   *Premise*: There are states of affairs which have necessarily a certain ground, i.e. that in all worlds in which fx occurs also b, its ground, occurs. For the proof it is irrelevant whether we take this ground as a necessarily necessary condition L (→) or as a necessarily sufficient and necessary condition L (⟷). Here b is a constant parameter and G a constant predicate-symbol 'ground'. The domain of interpretation of f is limited, i.e. the premise is not necessarily valid for each predicate. (If it were, this would be the better for the proof!)

2. (Ey) L ((x) L (fx ⟷ Gb) ⟷ Gy) *Premise*: There is a ground for pre-

210

mise 1 and as the state of affairs in 1 is necessary, the functor that expresses this ground must also be necessary $L(\longleftrightarrow)$, because something that is necessary cannot have a contingent ground. Here too it is irrelevant whether we take this to be a necessarily necessary ground or a necessarily sufficient and necessary ground. This premise expresses the multiple application of '*ex nihilo nihil fit*'.

3. L (x) (fx $\longleftrightarrow$ Gb)

from 1; application of the Barcan-formula.

4. L(Ey) ((x) L(fx $\longleftrightarrow$ Gb) $\longleftrightarrow$ Gy)

from 2; application of thesis T4 in Hughes and Cresswell, *o.c.*, p. 144.

5. L (L (x) (fx $\longleftrightarrow$ Gb) $\longleftrightarrow$ Gc)

from 4; Existential Instantiation and again application of the Barcan-formula.

6. L(x) (fx $\longleftrightarrow$ Gb) $\rightarrow$ Lgc

from 5; Derivation of the strict implication from the strict equivalence. Further application of the distribution axiom (A6) (Hughes and Cresswell, *o.c.*, p. 31) and T19 (*o.c.*, p. 46).

7. LGc

from 3 and 6 (modus ponendo ponens)

8. (Ex) LGx

from 7; Existential Generalisation.

We may interpret this conclusion (Ex) LGx as 'There is a necessary ground, i.e. a ground in all possible worlds, an *ens necessarium* and a *causa necessaria*'.

Perhaps not everybody will consider premise 1 given above plausible. We may, however, weaken it by considering it only as a possibility and as this premise is not logically contradictory, it is then very convincing. The proof now runs as follows:

VARIANT B

1. M(x) L (fx $\longleftrightarrow$ Gb)   Premise

2. M L(x) (fx $\longleftrightarrow$ Gb)   From 1; Barcan-formula

3. L (x) (fx $\longleftrightarrow$ Gb)   From 2; Hughes and Cresswell,

o.c., T 25 (p. 25), which theorem is
only valid in S_5.

And this is again step 3 of the proof above. Together with premise 2 (step 2) the rest of the proof is the same as the proof above. But this second variant is, however, less strict, for we have to do here with the system S_5 and no longer with the system S_4 to which the Barcan-formula has been added.

VARIANT C

The translation of the rule '*ex nihilo nihil fit*' in step (premise) 2 of variant A is not necessary. It is also possible to translate it in a weaker way, i.e. in such a way that the premise says (presupposes) more. Step 2 in variant C now runs:

1. $L((x) L(fx \longleftrightarrow Gb) \longleftrightarrow (Ey) Gy)$

This translation says more than the translation in variant A, for now it is already presupposed that this active working ground is in all worlds the same. It is no wonder that now the proof runs a little bit more easily, for we may make the same steps as in variant A, but step 4 can now be inferred without an appeal to theorem T4 of Hughes and Cresswell.

VARIANT D

Not only can step 2 be translated differently, but step 1 as well. In a personal communication G.I. Mavrodes and A. O'Hear required that the translation should be done in the language of *Principia Mathematica*, i.e. so that all existential expressions should be translated with the help of the existential quantifier (Ex). I do not think this is necessary, what is more, I think that one should distinguish between the expressions 'there is...' and 'some...'. That we may do so, has been demonstrated sufficiently by the Polish logician Leśnievski. But on the other hand I have no objection to using the language of *Principia Mathematica*. In this way step 1 is translated (Ex) L (fx $\longleftrightarrow$ Gb) instead of (x) L (fx $\longleftrightarrow$ Gb). This has the advantage that the proof can now be given in S_4 even without using the Barcan-formula. The proof now runs:

1. (Ex) L (fx $\longleftrightarrow$ Gb)   1st premise in the new translation
2. L(Ex) (fx $\longleftrightarrow$ Gb)   From 1; Hughes and Cresswell, *o.c.*, p. 144 (T4), (valid in S_4).
3. (Ey) L (L(Ex) (fx $\longleftrightarrow$ Gb) $\longleftrightarrow$ Gy) 2nd premise. There is necessarily a ground for the state of affairs mentioned in step 2 (and 1).

212

4. L (L (Ex) (fx $\longleftrightarrow$ Gb) $\longleftrightarrow$ Gc)	From 3; existential instantiation.
5. L(Ex) (fx $\longleftrightarrow$ Gb) $\longleftrightarrow$ LGc	From 4; derivation of the implication from the equivalence. Further Hughes and Cresswell, *o.c.*, p. 31 (A6) and p. 46 (T19). Both the axiom A6 and the theorem T19 are valid in S_4.
6. LGc	2,5. *Modus ponendo ponens.*
7. (Ex) LGx	From 6; Existential generalization.

The great difference with the proof in variant A is, that the whole argument is now valid in S_4, which is an advantage.

Proofs with the help of modal propositional logic

We can also give the proof by using modal propositional logic only. From the premises 'there is a state of affairs' and 'for the possibility of this state of affairs there is necessarily required a necessary (or necessary and sufficient) ground' we may infer that there must be an *ens necessarium*. The multiple application of the principle '*ex nihilo nihil fit*' is introduced here when we formulate in our second premise 'for the *possibility* of this state of affairs' and not simply 'for this state of affairs'. Since we may represent beings as states of affairs (*vide* 3.1.3.5), we can formulate an *ens necessarium* by Lq. So we have to prove the following thesis:

$(p \ \& \ L(Mp \rightarrow q)) \rightarrow Lq$

We do this by using a system of natural deduction, for the technical details of which we must again refer to Hughes and Cresswell, *o.c.*, p. 331ff.

1. p & L (Mp $\rightarrow$ q)	premise
2. p	from 1; elimination of the conjunction
3. L (Mp $\rightarrow$ q)	from 1; elimination of the conjunction
4. Mp	from 2; thesis T1 of Hughes and Cresswell, *o.c.*, p. 33
5. □ | MP $\rightarrow$ q	from 3, strict reiteration
6. | MP	from 4, strict reiteration (only admissible in S_5)
7. | q	from 5 and 6, elimination of the implication (= *modus ponendo ponens*)
8. Lq	from 7, introduction of necessity.

By inferring Lq from the premises p & L(Mp → q) we have proved our thesis.

5. *Is it possible to reduce religion to non-religious constituents?*

Of course, I do not deny that all kinds of circumstances and conditions influence human beings in their choices and consequently also in their religious convictions. But it would be incorrect to state that if it is possible to prove that there is a correlation between a religious conviction and a non-religious constituent or condition, we have proved that religion can be reduced to these non-religious constituents or conditions. This is sometimes attempted. Religion is said to be nothing else than a compensation for sexual or economic frustrations. In that case the following error is made:

Suppose, q_i $(1 \leqslant i \leqslant n)$ is a variable having as semantic field of interpretation a set of statements which refer to social and economic states of affairs.

Suppose, r_j $(1 \leqslant j \leqslant m)$ is a variable having as semantic field of interpretation a set of statements which refer to religious convictions or attitudes.

Suppose that it has been proved that with each q_i there corresponds a r_j. We assume this for the sake of discussion, for until now this has not yet been proved!

Thus we have the following premises:

(1) $q_i \rightarrow r_j$
(2) $\sim q_i \rightarrow \sim r_j$

May we conclude to $q_i \longleftrightarrow r_j$ from these two premises? Naturally, if we are sure that only q_i and r_j are relevant. But there are always other constituents, so that the two premises mentioned above reflect the actual states of affairs insufficiently. Let us for the sake of discussion simplify the whole set of constituents that may be relevant to one variable, which we give in the statement p_k. The premises are in that case:

(1') $(p_k \, \& \, q_i) \rightarrow r_j$
(2') $(p_k \, \& \, \sim q_i) \rightarrow \sim r_j$

And now the reader may easily see (with the help of the truthtables for example) that the conclusion $q_i \longleftrightarrow r_j$ is incorrect. The correct conclusion is:

$$p_k \rightarrow (q_i \longleftrightarrow r_j).$$

This means: It is only through the constituent p_k that this correlation between q_i and r_j exists. Therefore it is very well possible that a constituent such as revelation or religious intuition may produce this correlation and that without it this correlation would not exist. Therefore one has to be very careful in drawing reductionist conclusions from certain correlations!

6. *Possible reduction of the concept of God's perfection (as a primitive concept) to the concept of God's omniscience (as a primitive concept)*

One of the objections against the ontological argument was that the idea of God as a perfect being is difficult to conceive. Can we indeed give sense to such a concept? In this appendix we will try to do so, by reducing the concept of perfection to that of omniscience to which some other presuppositions are added. In my view the concept of omniscience is less dubitable than the concept of perfection.

We presuppose that, at least in principle, all complex states of affairs can be reduced to elementary (simple) states of affairs that cannot be further reduced. We ascribe to these elementary states of affairs degrees of desirability. Now every state of affairs may be the cause of several other states of affairs. Therefore we must not only ascribe to each state of affairs its own 'intrinsic' degree of desirability, but also its derived degree of desirability which may be computed with the help of the D-calculus. For this I may refer here to my article 'Zijn ethische uitspraken wetenschappelijk fundeerbaar? Enkele opmerkingen over de wetenschappelijkheid van de ethiek' (*Tijdschrift voor Filosofie*, 33, (1973), (p. 41-65), p. 60ff) and to appendix 12. This D-calculus is a system of deontic logic, in which there are degrees of desirability which run parallel to degrees of probability in modal logic. Now as has been said above, each state of affairs has its 'intrinsic' degree of desirability, but it also has derived degrees of desirability which it receives, because its effects also have degrees of desirability. Now with the help of the D-calculus it is, at least in principle, possible to compute for each state of affairs its 'absolute' degree of desirability, which is composed of its 'intrinsic' and its derived degrees of desirability. From the D-calculus it is obvious that the intrinsic degree of desirability of a state of affairs and the intrinsic degree of its negation taken together will give the degree 1. That is, if a certain state of affairs has the intrinsic degree of 1, its negation has 0, if it has 0.9 its negation has 0.1, etc. We work here with a scale running from 0 to 1. But the absolute degrees do not necessarily show this symmetry, because of their complicated effects. But of course, it is possible to compare the absolute degree of each state of affairs with its negation: $D_\alpha p$ and $D_\beta \sim p$, where the indices under D (α and β) represent the absolute degrees of desirability of respectively p and $\sim p$.

Now we define a perfect being in the following way:
A being is perfect if it produces state of affairs p if $\alpha > \beta$, and state of affairs $\sim p$ if $\alpha < \beta$, presupposing that it is in his power to produce both p and $\sim p$. If we identify this perfect being with God, it is necessary to add the

restriction 'if it is in his power to produce etc.' for even God cannot produce what is logically contradictory. All this may seem plausible at first sight, and I shall not deny this, but we have tacitly taken the following presuppositions for granted:

(1) that there is a hierarchy of desirabilities (or as an alternative: a hierarchy of values);
(2) that there is a complete knowledge of all causal relations between the various states of affairs;
(3) that our D-calculus is correct.

If these presuppositions are correct it is possible to substitute God for perfect being. By this we have reduced the concept 'perfect being' to a being which has omniscience or at least knowledge of the hierarchy mentioned above and of all the states of affairs together with their effects.

However, are these presuppositions plausible?

Now (3) will not give insurmountable difficulties, because the system which has been constructed is purely logical. Should any insufficiencies, however, be discovered in the system, they may easily be eliminated. The system can be improved.

Supposition (1) is more difficult. It is not generally accepted by philosophers. A special additional difficulty for us here is that of the relation between God and what is good (desirable). Is something good, because it is God's will or does God produce something, because it is good? Or is the good an emanation from God? I subscribe to the view that the good is an emanation from God, but this reconstruction also holds with the view that God produces something, because it is good. But even if one holds the first view, *viz.* that something is good (desirable) because it is God's will, an analogous reconstruction is possible. In that case, however, perfection is not reduced to omniscience, but to omnipotence as a primitive concept. Our reconstruction is somewhat simpler, because omnipotence is a more complicated concept than omniscience.

Although (1) may not be generally accepted, it is in my view plausible; even atheistic philosophers have accepted it, for example N. Hartmann. An additional difficulty is that the hierarchical order of desirabilities is not a total linear order, but only a half-order, i.e. a non-linear order. In other words, there are incomparable values of desirabilities. We know this problem from our moral praxis. Must I spend my time in service of a certain social issue or do I have to spend it with my family? Shall we build a school or a hospital?

Now the problem may be theoretically solved in the following way. We may suppose that there is a function which projects the original hierarchy of desirabilities, which was non-linear, on to a new hierarchy which is linear. In our daily life we have to do this frequently, for we have to choose between incomparable desirabilities. The only thing is that we make this

216

choice without being sure that we make the right choice. But by making this choice we use a project function which projects the non-linear hierarchy on to a linear one, without knowing whether this function is the correct one. But we may presuppose that an omniscient being knows the correct project function.

In this way (1) and (3) are reduced to omniscience and (2) refers by itself already to omniscience. In this way from the concept of an omniscient being that of a present being may derived, and from this concept the other properties. With the help of the hierarchy of values, the project function and the D-calculus the concept 'perfection' may be understood by means of the concept 'omniscience'. And the concept 'omniscience' is less problematic than the concept 'perfection'. The 'ideal observer' or the 'ideal mathematician' are familiar models in mathematics and natural science. One should, however, take this reconstruction as a possibility of understanding the ontological argument for the concept of God better. I do not claim that we are able to construct an absolute hierarchy of God's properties or that in God his property of omniscience is ontologically more fundamental than his property of perfection. The only thing I want to state is that we understand omniscience better than perfection and that it is possible to interpret the latter concept with the help of the former!

7. Logical reconstruction of Kierkegaard's argument from the decisive moment in time

In the first chapter of his book *Philosophiske Smuler* (Philosophical Fragments) Kierkegaard puts forward a kind of argument for the truth of the Christian religion. He starts with the presupposition that there is a decisive moment in time. From this purely philosophical premise he derives very convincingly the truth of some main dogmas of the Christian faith. But Kierkegaard does not claim to have given a proof, he presents his proof only as a project. He does not claim that the premise given above is a plausible one. But in my view his argumentation as such is brilliant. Let us look more closely into Kierkegaard's argument, which at least shows the great relevance of history for the Christian faith.

Evidently Kierkegaard emphasizes the word 'decisive' in the expression, 'decisive significance' (*afgjørend*; modern Danish: *afgørend*; *gøre* = to do, to make; the prefix *af-* corresponds to the Dutch *af-* and the Latin *per-*; af-gøre = Dutch *af-doen*; Latin *per-ficere* = to finish, to complete something). In order to speak more conveniently about such a decisive moment in time, let us introduce the following terminology. Let us call the situation before this decisive moment S(a) and the situation after that moment S(b). Now if this moment should be really decisive, the situation S(a) before this decisive moment should be *totaliter aliter* (completely different) from the situation S(b) after this moment. There may not be a continuous change from S(a) to S(b). It is necessary that we have a completely sudden change. Now, if 'decisive' has this strong meaning, then Kierkegaard is right that man is not able to establish such a radical change and that only God can do it. Of course, this is a new hypothesis. But if change has such a radical character as Kierkegaard presumably presupposes, *viz.* that something completely new must come into existence, then in my view this hypothesis has a great plausibility. At first 'God' has in this connection no other meaning than that of a being that is able to produce such radical changes as Kierkegaard presupposes. If, however, a continuous change is meant so that there is a continuous connection from a situation S(a) to a situation S(b), we have not to do with such a moment as Kierkegaard obviously presupposes.

Other philosophers, Hegelians, Marxists, and others also speak of decisive changes, but here the situation S(a) includes negative elements so that there is an inner antagonism in this situation. Therefore the situation S(a) develops gradually towards its own elimination (*Aufhebung*). The final stage in this process of elimination might be of a radical charachter: the change might develop from a quantitative gradual change into a qualitative radical change. But here situation S(b) is still in a complicated way related to situation S(a). The laws and rules that govern this relation are those of dialectical logic, whereas Kierkegaard uses classical logic here.

As far as I can see, it is not necessary for Kierkegaard to state that situation S(b) is different from S(a) in every respect. That would of course be impossible. Every change presupposes at least some elements that remain the same. But from his point of view it is essential that some facets of situation S(b) should be completely new with respect to situation S(a). Let us formulate this more sharply: Let S(a) be considered as a set of elementary facts $(P_1, P_2, \ldots P_n)$ and S(b) as a set of elementary facts $(Q_1, Q_2, \ldots Q_m)$; then in Kierkegaard's radical change at least some elementary facts $Q_i \ldots Q_k$ have no connection (relation) with any member of the set $(P_1, P_2, \ldots P_n)$, although some members of the set $(Q_1, Q_2, \ldots Q_m)$ are also members of the set $(P_1, P_2, \ldots P_n)$, i.e. as we have seen above, some 'facets' remain unchanged. In a dialectical change, however, all elementary facts of the new situation S(b) have some relation with the old ones. Some are the same and the others are the (dialectical) negation of their counterparts in S(a).

Or, in a set-theoretical formulation: in a dialectical change there must be a function of the set S(a) *on to* the set S(b) and in Kierkegaard's radical change the function is not on to the other set. A function of a set that is *on to* another set relates all the members of one set – in our case S(a) – to all the members of another set – in our case S(b) –, so that each member of the first set S(a) is correlated with at most one member of the other set S(b) and that no member of this other set remains unrelated.

Let us summarize Kierkegaard's argument:

1. There is a moment in time that has decisive significance. (The situation before this moment is called S(a); after this moment: S(b)) (There is no function of S(a) on to S(b))   Premise 1
2. No natural being can produce radical changes from S(a) to S(b) as is meant sub 1. Neither can a subnatural being do it.   Premise 2
3. Every change must be produced by some being.   Premise 3
4. If a being is not a natural being it must be either a subnatural or a supernatural being.   Premise 4
5. There is a radical change from S(a) to S(b).   Analytically deduced from 1
6. There must be a being that produces the radical change from S(a) to S(b).   From 1 and 3
7. The being that produces the radical change from S(a) and S(b) must either be a natural being or not be a natural being.   Law of classical logic
8. The being that produces the radical change from S(a) to S(b) is not a natural being.   From 2 and 7, modus tollens
9. The being that produces the radical change from S(a) to S(b) must either be a subnatural or a supernatural being.   From 4 and 8
10. The being that produces the radical change from S(a) to S(b) must be a supernatural being.   From 2 and 9

In my view this argument is logically correct and the premises 2, 3 and 4 are without doubt sound. The weak point is premise 1, because its plausibility is not beyond doubt, but nor was it for Kierkegaard.

Having proved in this way God's existence Kierkegaard goes on and proves the other truths of the Christian faith: man's guilt, the necessity of a redeemer, etc. They can all, and in my view correctly, be derived from premise 1. But whether this premise is true is, as has been said, another matter.

8. *Argument that the dialectic of the infinite is not universally valid*

The dialectic of the infinite certainly has a flavour of plausibility. It contains the validity of the rule of inference from the finite to the infinite, or from the relative to the absolute. It is quite understandable that during many centuries this rule was practised without any doubts. The reasoning goes for example as follows: 'there are degrees of certainty; then we must postulate a degree of absolute certainty in order to measure the various degrees of certainty' Or: 'there are many different forms of loyalty. There is the relation of a human I to a human you. Now the loyalty of human relations is only relative. Therefore there must be a source of absolute loyalty from which the relative human forms of loyalty derive their strength'. A classical example of this way of reasoning we may find in the fourth way of Thomas Aquinas: 'The fourth way is based on the gradation observed in things. Some things are found to be more good, more true, more noble, and so on, and other things less. But such comparative terms describe varying degrees of approximation to a superlative; for example, things are hotter the nearer they approach what is hottest. Something therefore is the truest and best and most noble of things, and hence the most fully in being; ...There is something therefore which causes in all things their being, their goodness, and whatever other perfection they have. And this we call 'God''? Now, in my view it would be permissible to draw this conclusion as a regulative idea (Kant) without ontological pretensions. But the examples mentioned above are meant to be ontological conclusions (by Augustine, Gabriel Marcel, Thomas Aquinas respectively). And, again, even as an ontological conclusion it may have a certain tempting plausibility. Still it is not universally valid. The late Amsterdam professor of logic and philosophy of science, E.W. Beth, formalized this rule and in doing so he clearly showed its limits ('Historical Studies in traditional philosophy' (*Synthese*, 5 (1946-1947), pp. 258-270); 'The Prehistory of Research into Foundations' (*The British Journal for the Philosophy of Science*, 3 (1952-1953), pp. 58-81)). We shall give his formalisation in a slightly simplified way.

Let there be given a set of elements: a_1, a_2, ... and let there also be an ordering relation R. This means that a_1 stands in the relation R to a_2, a_2 stands in the relation R to a_3, etc. In symbolic notation: $a_1 \ R \ a_2$, $a_2 \ R \ a_3$, etc. We shall ignore the various technical aspects of set theory here, for they are, although interesting, of no relevance to our purpose here. Now according to the rule of inference in the dialectic of infinity there must be a last element with certain characteristics.

For with respect to this last element the following is valid: there is no longer any element to which this last element stands in the relation R, except possibly to itself; and all other elements stand in the relation R to this last element. In other words: let us call this last element a_n, then the following two theorems are valid:

(i) $a_i \, R \, a_n$
(ii) $\sim (a_n \, R \, a_i)$

where a_i stands for any arbitrary element in the ordered set of elements different from a_n and '$\sim$' is the sign for negation.

Let us give some concrete examples: Let a_1, a_2, a_3, ... be various periods of time with their various social systems and let R mean 'is succeeded by' then in orthodox Marxism the following conclusion is valid: there must finally be a communist period which will be the last period in history. Any period succeeding it, would still be the period of communism and this period will make an end to all class struggle. In other words a_n is the period of communism.

Another example: let a_1, a_2, a_3 ... be the facts in the world and let R be the relation 'being caused by', then a_n is God. Here we have formalized the second way of Thomas. We have seen in our expositions of the cosmological argument that this is the first, and in my view, an inferior variant of this argument.

Thanks to Beth's formalisation, however, we can show in a rather trivial way that this rule of the dialectic of infinity is not universally valid. Let for example a_1, a_2, a_3 ... be the row of natural numbers (starting with number 1) and let R be the ordering relation 'smaller than', then we get the following sequence: '1 smaller than 2', '2 smaller than 3', etc. Should the rule of the dialectic of infinity be valid, then we should be allowed to conclude that there must be a number a_n, of which it could be said that no number a_{n+1} can be found of which can be stated:

$a_n \, R \, a_{n+1}$

In other words there could be found a greatest possible number. Now it is clear that this is not true.

On the other hand it is clear that the rule is sometimes valid. Let for example R be the relation 'greater than' and let a_1, a_2, a_3 ... be a set of natural numbers beginning with 100, i.e. a_1 is 100. Now we get the sequence '100 is greater than 99', '99 is greater than 98', etc. Is there now a number a_n for which no number can be found, of which can be said

$a_n \, R \, a_{n+1}$?

This is certainly true, If we do not count '0' among the natural numbers, this number is 1.

Furthermore in classical set theory (not in intuitionistic set theory!) a certain theorem, Zorn's lemma, is known, in which the rule of inference of the dialectic of infinity is valid, provided that special conditions are fulfilled: 'Let A be a non-empty partially ordered set in which every totally ordered subset has an upper bound in A. Then A contains at least one maximal element' (vide e.g.: S. Lipschutz, *Set Theory and Related Topics*, New York 1964, p. 180).

We mention Zorn's lemma here only because of its curiosity. It would take us too far to explain this lemma and to point out its philosophical implications. But it may be clear that it means that the inference rule of the dialectic of infinity may be drawn, provided one has proved that the conditions of Zorn's lemma are fulfilled. For the first variant of the cosmological argument this would for example mean that if it could be proved that every sequence of causes must have a first (or last) element, then the argument would be valid, inspite of the fact that there may be an infinite number of such sequences.

9. *The biblical rule of inference a minore ad maius and a maiore ad minus (Qal waḥomer)*

In biblical and rabbinic logic an interesting rule of inference is used, which is called by the rabbinical scholars *qal waḥomer* and by the scholastic authors the *conclusio a minore ad maius* and *a maiore ad minus*. In literal translation the expressions mean respectively 'the light and the heavy' (qal waḥomer) and 'the conclusion from what is small to what is great (large)' and 'the conclusion from what is great (large) to what is small'. The reader of Scripture will recognize this rule in the expressions: 'if... how much more...' or 'if... how much less...'. In Biblical Hebrew we often find in that case the expression' '... אֵיךְ ... הֵן (or הִנֵּה (see ... how)' and '... אַף כִּי ... הֵן' *(aph ki)* (*aph* means: 'also, even, the more so', and after negative clauses 'how much less', *vide* L. Koehler, *Lexicon in Veteris Testamenti Libros*, Leiden 1948, p. 74, *sub voce*). In Greek we may find (the New Testament): πόσω μᾶλλον (how much more).

Now according to L. Jacobs the Midrash (Gen. R. 92:7) traces its use to the Bible. The following cases are mentioned: Gen. 44.8, Ex. 6.12, Num. 12.14 (not explicit), Deut. 31.27, I Sam. 23.3, Jer. 12.5, Ezek. 15.5, Prov. 11.31, Esth. 9.12. There are many more *qal waḥomer* arguments in the bible, some of them unspoken: II Sam 4.10f; 16.11; I Kings 8.27; Jonah 4.10f; Job 9.13f; 38ff (*vide* 4.2). The rabbinical scholars made use of this way of arguing. It already appeared as one of the rules of R. Hillel. Thus we may read in the Talmudic Tract *Sanhedrin* (6.5) that it is stated in Deut. 21.23 that the corpse of a criminal executed by the court must not be left on the gibbet overnight, which R. Meir takes to mean that God is distressed by the criminal's death. Hence R. Meir argues: 'If God is troubled at the shedding of the blood of the ungodly, how much more (*qal waḥomer*) at the blood of the righteous!' In this example the minor and the major of the argument are readily apparent. It might be termed a simple *qal waḥomer*.

The following example might be termed a complex *qal waḥomer*. 'If priests who are not disqualified for service in the Temple by age, are disqualified by bodily blemishes (Lev.21.16-21) then levites, who are disqualified by age (Num. 8.24-25) should certainly be disqualified by bodily blemishes' (*Hullim* 24a) (A Talmudic Tract). Here an extraneous element (disqualification by age) has to be adduced to indicate which is the minor and which the major. Symbolically the two types can be represented as:

SIMPLE: If A has x, the B certainly has x.

COMPLEX: If A which lacks y, has x, then B, which has y certainly has x.

For what has been said above we have made use of L. Jacobs's exposition in the *Encyclopaedia Judaica*, Jerusalem, Tome VIII, s.v. 'Hermeneutics', p. 366-372 and also of his work *Studies in Talmudic Logic and Methodology* (1961).

This inference rule is quite interesting, because it belongs neither to Aristotelian logic nor to ordinary symbolic logic. But still intuitively we see at once that it gives a correct conclusion. That it is not a part of Aristotelian logic has already been pointed out by Jacobs. This in contradistinction to A. Schwarz, *Hermeneutischer Syllogismus in der talmudischen Literatur* (1901). Schwarz erroneously identifies the Aristotelian syllogism with the *qal waḥomer*. But Jacobs, referring to Kunst in the *Bulletin of the School of Oriental and African Studies*, 10 (1942), p. 976-991, rightly remarks first that the element 'how much more' is lacking in the syllogism and second that the syllogistic inference concerns *genus* and *species*: All men are mortal; Socrates is a man; hence Socrates is mortal. That is, since Socrates belongs to the class 'man' he must share the characteristics of that class. However, in the *qal waḥomer* it is not suggested that the major belong to the class of the minor, but that what is true of the minor must be true of the major.

Another interesting point in this logic, to which Jacobs draws our attention, is the principle of *dayyo* (it is sufficient). It says that the conclusion advances only as far as the premise and not beyond it. It is said to be a qualification of the *qal waḥomer*. It must not be argued that if A has x, then B has x + y. The *qal waḥomer* suffices only to prove that B has x, and it is to go beyond the evidence to conclude that it also has y. R. Tarfon, however, rejects the *dayyo* principle in certain instances (Bava Kamma 25a).

In my view it must further be emphasized that in Scripture the inference is very often also present in a hidden way, i.e. that the reader is being led to use it without the formula 'how much more' actually being used. The rabbis also have suggested this occasionally. We have given examples in our text (*vide* 4.2).

Further, it would in my view be interesting to compare this inference with modern symbolic logic, into which it does not fit very well. If we may present the argument in a somewhat simplified form we may distinguish four argumentation-schemes which are used here

I	II	III	IV
$W_x (p \rightarrow q)$	$W_x (p \rightarrow \sim q)$	$W_x (p \rightarrow q)$	$W_x (p \rightarrow \sim q)$
$W_y (r \rightarrow q)$	$W_y (r \rightarrow \sim q)$	$W_y (r \rightarrow q)$	$W_y (r \rightarrow \sim q)$
$(x > y)$	$(x > y)$	$(x > y)$	$(x > y)$
$p \rightarrow \sim q$	$p \rightarrow q$	$r \rightarrow q$	$r \rightarrow \sim q$
r	r	p	p
_____	_____	_____	_____
$\sim q$	q	q	$\sim q$

($W_x (p \rightarrow q)$ expresses the degree of probability that the implication is true. 'x' and 'y' are indices which express this degree of probability).

In ordinary language it is said in scheme I, that one should expect that p, rather than r would 'produce' q and that in spite of that p produces the opposite, how much more would r produce the opposite! In the same way the other schemes may be read.

The inference-schemes are self-evident and of all the possible inference-schemes that may represent *qal waḥomer* these are closest to what is usual in modern symbolic logic. But they are a little simplified. For we have only used propositional logic. But for an inference-scheme this may suffice. For a full classification we need predicate logic, relational logic, etc. It would be certainly worthwhile to represent the various biblical uses of *qal waḥomer* in an elaborated classification-system, but this would exceed the purpose of this book. The schemes III and IV are the most usual in the Bible, e.g. Jerm. 12.5, Prov. 11.31, 2 Kings 5.13, Deut. 31.27, I Sam. 23.3, etc.(scheme III) and Ex. 15.5, Job 15.16, Job 35.14, etc. (scheme IV). But occasionally the other schemes also occur: Ex. 6.11, Job 25.6 etc.

10. *Logical analysis of the concept of revelation*

In this appendix we want to give an example of a logical analysis in the style of the logic of religion, and we have chosen a central concept of philosophy of religion, *viz.* the concept of revelation. First we ask what phenomena are revelatory? The anwer to this question may seem trivial at first sight, but on further consideration many problems arise which we will discuss in connection with an analysis of the concept of revelation proper. Here we shall give, to begin with, a linguistic analysis of the concepts of 'revelation' and 'reveal'. We will also look for the meaning of this concept in the Old and New Testament. Then we shall go on with a logical analysis proper of this concept using the results of our linguistic analysis as a starting-point. The problem of truth will not be dealt with in this appendix.

When we consider the question 'What phenomena are revelatory?' the answer might seem trivial. In principle everything can be a means for revelation: dreams, visions, prophesies, but also ordinary things: mountains, lakes, trees, food, drinks, all kinds of events, etc. (cp. Th.P. van Baaren, *Voorstellingen van openbaring phaenomenologisch beschouwd*, (D) Utrecht 1951). It is, of course, not true that in every religion everything has been a means of revelation: we all know that in Christianity revelation is mainly concentrated on Christ and the events of his life and resurrection. But if we consider the various things that have been vehicles for revelation in all the religions, this series might be inexhaustible. Perhaps a computer investigation should be carried out, in which a list of all things that have been a means of revelation is checked against a list of all possible things. We might discover a phenomenon that has never been a means of revelation. This may satisfy our curiosity and besides it may be interesting to see whether this phenomenon has special features that make it unfit as a vehicle for revelation. But even then we cannot be absolutely sure, for in the first place we are not exactly acquainted with all religions of all times and places and in the second place since revelation did not only happen in the past, but also happens in the present and will happen in the future, what has not yet been a vehicle for revelation can become so at any time.

Still we cannot get rid of this question so easily. Let us begin by putting forward the truism that it is not true that everything is everywhere and at all times a vehicle for revelation, so that we must at least presuppose that there are some constituents that make a certain phenomenon a means of revelation. Our problem is, of course, what are these constituents. But investigating this problem would exceed the scope of this appendix. So I will concentrate on the 'logic of revelation', i.e. on the question what the logical structure of revelation is, what elements could be distinguished in the revelatory event, etc. The problem why a certain event is a revelation and another event is not, although this other event might have, at least at first sight, an analogous structure, will not be analysed in this appendix. Even the logic of revelation is so complicated and comprehensive that I will give only some broad outlines.

Let us begin by investigating the various meanings of the words 'reveal' and 'revelation'. In *The Shorter Oxford English Dictionary on Historical Principles* we read *sub voce* 'REVEAL 1. trans. To disclose, make known (*to* a person) in a supernatural manner. 2. To disclose, to divulge, make known (to a person) by disclosure or communication. late ME † To betray – 1657.3. To display, show, make clear or visible, exhibit 1494. ...' (I omit the examples).

'REVELATION 1. The disclosure of knowledge to man by a divine or supernatural agency. 2. Something disclosed or made known by divine or supernatural means. late ME b. A striking disclosure of something previously unknown or nor realized 1862. 3. The R. (of St. John), the last book of the New Testament; the Apocalypse. So in pl. *(the) Revelations*. late

ME. 4. Disclosure of facts made by a person; exposure of something previously disguised or concealed 1475. ...' (again I omit the examples). And in the *Concise Oxford Dictionary* we find: *'Reveal* 1. (Esp. of God) make known by inspiration or supernatural means (-ed religion opp. natural). 2. Disclose, divulge, betray; display, show, let appear (-itself, come to sight or knowledge).'

As can be inferred from the quotations, both the verb 'reveal' and the substantive 'revelation' are used not only in a religious context referring to disclosures in a supernatural way but also in a non-religious context. Moreover, we may notice that there are two main shades of meaning, *viz.* the *disclosure* of something (heretofore unknown) and the *showing* of something (which need not have been hidden before). The verb can also be used reflexively: God, a person (or even a thing or an event) may show himself (or itself).

The same features are to be found in other European languages, e.g. in Dutch (*vide* C. Kruyskamp, *Van Dale Groot Woordenboek der Nederlandse Taal*), in German (*vide* G. Wahrig, *Deutsches Wörterbuch* and R. Klappenbach & W. Steinitz, *Wörterbuch der deutschen Gegenwartssprache*) and in French (*vide Le Petit Robert*).

It could be useful to study the meaning of a word in its *Wortfeld* (i.e. in the scope of its synonyms). The word and the method stem from the school of Weisgerber. In our case this brings a confirmation of what we have already discovered above: Crabb gives in his list of synonyms 'unveil', 'disclose', 'remove' and 'show' characterizing 'reveal' as follows: 'reveal... signifies to divulge something known to ourselves but not to others, to lay bare a mystery or a secret purpose; in a special sense, to make known something which could not become known without divine or supernatural instruction' (Crabb's *English Synonyms*, London 1966, p. 694, s.v. 'unveil'). Crabb also places 'reveal' in another category. Here the synonyms are 'publish', 'promulgate', 'divulge', 'reveal', 'disclose' (o.c., p. 581).

Webster (*Dictionary of Synonyms*, Springfield, Mass., USA, p. 708) gives 'discover', 'disclose', 'divulge', 'tell' and 'betray' as possible synonyms. About 'reveal' he writes: 'Reveal implies a setting forth or exhibition by or as if lifting a curtain that veils or obscures. In its earliest and still not uncommon sense, it implies supernatural communication by means of vision, inspiration, or the like, of truths beyond or above the range of human sight or reason... But the term may also imply an imparting by a human being such as a seer or a poet whose vision penetrates into that which cannot be seen or understood by the ordinary man... or as a person in possession of a secret... In somewhat less strict, but nevertheless correct use, *reveal* may carry no suggestions of an intentional communication, but rather an affording of signs or other evidence from which the truth may be inferred...' (I omitted again the many quotations).

226

In French the following synonyms are mentioned: 'dévoiler', 'démasquer', 'découvrir', 'vendre la mèche' (fam.), 'déceler', 'trahir' (H. Bénac, *Dictionnaire des synonyms*, Paris 1956, p. 221) and 'montrer' (o.c., p. 603). Another dictionary of synonyms gives the following rather different list of synonyms: 'prouver', 'témoigner de' (R. Bailly, *Dictionnaire des synonyms de la langue française*, Paris 1947, p. 518) and also: 'divulger', 'publier', 'proclamer', 'ébruiter', 'trompeter', 'trahir' (*o.c.*, p. 210). Further 'reveal' is characterized as follows: 'Révéler, retirer de dessous le voile ce qui était inconnu pour en faire connaître l'existence ou faire savoir en quoi cela consiste, se dit spécialement de la pensée divine' (Bénac) (reveal, to pull down the veil of what was unknown in order to make known its existence or its nature; is especially said of the divine mind) and 'Révéler, c'est faire connaître par quelque signe extérieur ce qui est inconnu, secret ou comme voilé' (Bailly) (reveal, i.e. to make known, by means of an outward sign, what is unknown, secret or as it were veiled). We see that the dictionaries of synonyms confirm what can also be inferred from the 'ordinary' dictionaries. We may perhaps also remark that they give a great variety of synonyms and do not agree with each other at all (cp. especially the French quotation!). This may of course cast, considerable doubt on this method. But we shall not go further into this matter. We shall also pass over other points that do not interest us now, e.g. that the SHOED marks 'reveal' in the meaning of 'betray' as obsolete, whereas the other English dictionaries do not do so, or that the French 'révéler' also has the special meaning of 'to develop the film', a meaning lacking in the other languages. In connection with what follows it is important to consider the question whether there can be revelation without assent or understanding. I think the answer is affirmative. I may say:

(i) 'Mr. A revealed the true meaning of B (a piece of music, a cryptic saying, etc.) to Mr C. but the latter did not believe (understand) it'.

I think that (i) does not involve a logical contradiction. But I know of some people who claim that this use of 'reveal' is illogical. As one can infer from the end of the quotation from Webster, one may even say in a general way:

(ii) 'Mr A revealed the true meaning of B' (without Mr A's having a special communication to a Mr C in mind).

The same people who claim that (i) is logically inconsistent also consider (ii) illogical, for if there are no possible receivers, then there is no revelation. Now, although I claim that (i) and (ii) are logically possible (and with Webster backing me I am fairly safe), still I admit that the words 'reveal' and 'revelation' carry the strong suggestions with them, that if it is said 'Mr. A revealed the true meaning of B to Mr. C' one would normally expect Mr. C to believe (understand) B. If this should not be the case it might be more elegant to say:

227

(iii) Mr. A *tried* to reveal the true meaning of B to Mr. C, but the latter did not believe (understand) it'.

We will take this point up again later in this appendix.

Summarising, we may say that 'reveal' and 'revelation' originally had a purely religious meaning, which they still have, but that the terms are now also widely used in non-religious contexts. Further 'reveal' may be used reflexively, both in the religious and in the non-religious sense. God reveals himself, but also a person may reveal himself as an artist, and even things may do so: a piece of music may reveal itself as a piece of art. The Dutch dictionary (*Van Dale*) especially underlines this, but as far as I can see the other languages too have this use.

Further there is in 'reveal' and in 'revelation' (i) the notion of unveiling (hidden, secret) things and (ii) the notion of showing things, which ought not necessarily to be hidden or kept secret to this extent. Then there is also (iii) the notion of 'promulgating', 'publishing'. The notions (ii) and (iii), however, are closely related. If a person A reveals (= shows) a certain fact (or thing) B that has not been hidden or kept secret until now, but has not yet been widely known, he evidently promulgates or publishes B.

We shall now investigate the use of the concept 'reveal' and 'revelation' in the Bible. On the whole we shall meet the same features as in 'ordinary language'. The two main concepts in the New Testament are: ἀποκάλυψις ('ἀποκαλύπτειν') and φανέρωσις ('φανεροῦν'). Also γνωρίζειν (to make known) may be classified under 'reveal'. In the word ἀποκαλύπτειν we easily recognize the notion 'unveil,', 'disclose', etc. and in the notion φανεροῦν the notion 'show'. The Old Testament word for 'reveal' and 'revelation' is גלה (Hebrew) or גלא (Aramaic). Further the nif'al of ראה (to appear) and also the hiphil of ידע (to make known) among others are used. (See E. Jenni and C. Westermann, ed., *Theologisches Handwörterbuch zum AT*, s.v. gālā, etc., and H. Ringgren and G.J. Botterweck, ed., *Theologisches Wörterbuch zum AT*, s.v.).

In Scripture the word 'reveal' is also used in a non-religious sense, e.g. Ruth 4.4, I Sam. 20.2,12, etc. St. John 7.4, etc., but in the majority of cases the word is used in a religious sense. Some scholars think that God only reveals himself and not facts or objective truths to believe in, cp. Brunner, mentioned in our text. Some biblican scholars also do this e.g. A. Oepke. According to them God reveals himself and there is no communication of truths and knowledge in Scripture. 'In the NT, too, revelation denotes, not the impartation of knowledge, but the actual unveiling of intrinsically hidden facts, or, theologically, the manifestation of transcendence within immanence. ...In brief, revelation in the NT is the self-offering of the Father of Jesus Christ for fellowship.' (A. Oepke, *Theological Dictionary of the New Testament*, edited by G. Kittel, Grand Rapids, Michigan, 1965, Vol. III, p. 591, s.v. 'apokaluptoo' (in the original German, Vol. III, p. 595f).

Strictly speaking, however, this view cannot be correct, for on closer inspection of the biblical texts it will be evident that 'reveal' and 'revelation' are also used with respect to a communication of knowledge. We must admit, however, that this knowledge of some states of affairs has, in the majority of cases, to do with God. What else should one expect in Scripture? But as we have seen in our text (*vide* 3.3), it is not true that in Scripture God reveals only himself. He certainly also reveals facts, although Brunner and others are right when they maintain that Scripture does not contain revelations of purely neutral and uninteresting facts. The facts revealed always have moral and religious overtones. The communication of the revelatory facts is in the (communicatively) indicative *modus*, but they always contain some (communicative) *modus* in addition!

In dogmatic theology a distinction is made between 'general revelation', given to all men, although the majority of them do not accept it, and 'special revelation', given to the faithful. This special revelation is to be found in Christ, in the history of the Jewish people, in short, in the Bible, whereas general revelation is given in nature, certain religous experiences, in short outside Scripture. Now some scholars have objected to this distinction by stating that there is no revelation without response in belief. We have come across this position already in our exposition of the word 'reveal' in ordinary language. Man answers God's revelation with belief, or to use a wider concept, with religious experience. But there is a problem here: can there be any revelation without belief or some sort of answer from the part of man? Is it true that in Scripture there is no revelation without belief? We must admit that usually revelation seems to imply belief. But in the *locus classicus* of the doctrine of general revelation (Romans 1.18ff) revelation is mentioned without the corresponding belief. A revelation in secrecy occurs also (cp. Numbers 12.18), and a revelation that is disobeyed, because it is not recognised (I Sam 2.27), Scripture speaks many times of God's revelation in nature (his creation): Psalms. 8, 19, 24, 29, 33.6ff, 65, 97.6, 96.11f, 104, 135.7, 136.25, 139, 147, 148; Amos, 4.13, 5.8, 9.6, Jeremiah, 5.22, 10.12ff, 27.5, 31.35, 32.17, 33.25, 51.15; Isaiah, 40.12ff, 42.5, 44.24, 45.8ff; Job, 28, 38-40; Proverbs, 8.22ff, etc. Now this revelation in nature might be recognized by believers. Non-believers, however, do not usually see God's hand in nature, but is this revelation not present for them? In my view this revelation is, according to Scripture present for everyone, regardless of whether they see and accept it or not.

Still there remains a problem here, for in Scripture the normal situation is that revelation is believed. As we have seen in our short analysis of the use of these words in ordinary language, 'reveal' and 'revelation' carry the strong suggestion that something is revealed to somebody, when at the same time this 'somebody' believes it. In our following analysis we shall return to this problem.

We shall now continue this appendix with an analysis of the logical structure of revelation. Of course, we shall concentrate on the religious aspect of revelation, but it may be useful to compare the revelation in a religious context with that in a nonreligious one. Since there is a tendency to compare religious language with aesthetic language (*vide* 4.6.3), we shall also consider revelation in aesthetic contexts. In the following we shall introduce some variables, A, B, C, D, E in an abstract scheme (propositional form) which are not the usual variables of a logical calculus. In a logical calculus variables may replace each other, but here we have to do with so-called place-variables within an abstract scheme, which represents a revelatory structure. The domain of the variables are all kinds of beings that may have a place within a certain revelatory context. The abstract scheme that is the starting-point of our logical analysis is:

(I) *A reveals B by means of C to D.*

If we now speak of the *values* of the variables, we introduce the signs A^+, B^+, C^+, D^+ and E^+. These values can be God, certain persons, things, events, etc. As has been said above, these values may be all beings that play a role in a revelatory context. They can be mentioned *in concreto*, e.g. 'my dog', 'I', 'myself', but they can also remain unindicated (e.g. 'a certain person'). In the latter case A^+, B^+, etc. function as dummies or ambiguous names. By giving values to the variables we transform the abstract scheme (propositional form) to a proposition. For example, if we fill in:
A = God; B = God's love (his love); C = Jesus Christ; D = mankind
we get the proposition:
God reveals his love by means of Jesus Christ to mankind
It might be that in giving values to the variables a certain variable does not get a value, i.e. it does not occur in the proposition. In that case we say that the variable is void or that the value is the null-class. The revelatory structure in its most abstract form is thus represented by the following scheme (propositional form):

(I) *A reveals B by means of C to D.*

It may already be evident from our preliminary analysis that the four variables do not necessarily have different values: A^+ may reveal himself (i.e. $B = A^+$); A^+ may also reveal something to himself (i.e. $D = A^+$), i.e. he may realize that something is the case, etc.
Now revelation is answered by man in belief (religious experience) i.e.:

(II) *D believes (understands, accepts in religious experience) that (I).*

Now it may be possible that not D^+ but another person accepts the revelation. Therefore it is necessary to introduce (II) in a modified form:

(II') *E believes that (I).*

(II') is the standard form for our investigation in addition to (I), because (II) can be constructed out of (II') simply by filling in D^+ for E. But it is also possible that $E^+ \neq D^+$.

Now for our purpose it is interesting to investigate the structure of revelation in its religious context, but in order to get a better view of this structure it is better to begin by investigating the logical possibilities in an 'ordinary' context. Since the various possibilities are numerous, and not all of them are interesting for our purpose, we shall give only some of them.

A normal (standard) possibility in an 'ordinary' context is that A^+ and D^+ are human beings, that B^+ is some message (the content of revelation) and that C^+ is some means by which this message is communicated. As we have already seen, there might be an identity of B^+ and A^+ or/and of B^+ and D^+. In the latter case we have:

(1) A^+ reveals A^+ by means of C^+ to A^+.

i.e. through certain means A gets to know himself. He reveals himself to himself. We might even have the interesting borderline case:

(2) A^+ reveals A^+ by means of A^+ to A^+.

This may be interpreted as the logical structure of narcissistic activity! It is important to notice that the domain of the variable A is not restricted to human and divine beings. Also animals reveal something to other animals and even man.

(3) A^+ may be my dog and D^+ may be myself. B^+ may be his wish for food and C^+ may be some growling or some other means of communication.

(3') *My dog reveals his wish for food by means of growling at Hubbeling (myself).*

It took some time before my dog and I could communicate with each other, but in the long run we have learned to build up some ways of communication.

Much more interesting, however, is such a case as the singing of birds. In this case A^+ = one bird and D^+ = another bird. Usually the singing of birds is interpreted by biologists as a way of claiming a certain territory. Now musicians (and also *some* biologists) tend to see more in the singing of the birds than only a way of claiming a certain territory. There is a spontaneous joy in singing and we cannot deny birds a certain musical feeling. This is at least the view of E.T.A. Hofmann, the great German poet and musician, who could also give some (circumstantial) evidence for it. His theories are continued by the well-known philosopher Charles Hartshorne, who besides being a great philosopher of religion is also known for his ornithological works. He has developed interesting views on this subject which we cannot discuss here in detail. We will only point out some logical problems. According to this theory birds have a spontaneous joy in singing and the higher singing-birds even follow and develop certain aesthetic rules, such as avoiding monotony. In this case the singing not only serves to claim a certain territory, it also reveals a joy in music.

So in the case of the majority of the biologists we have:

(4) $A = A^+$ (a certain bird); $B = B^+$ (the claiming of a certain territory); $C = C^+$ (a certain way of singing); $D = D^+$ (another bird) i.e.

(4')   *A certain bird reveals his claiming of a certain territory to another bird by means of a certain way of singing.*

But in the case of Hartshorne and others we have: A^+ is a certain singing bird. It is doubtful whether there is a D^+. There might be a singing-competition among birds; at least the dominant birds, which have the best territories, also sing best! But in this case we are back again with our biologists who say that the singing serves only to claim a certain territory. Let us assume for the sake of the discussion that there is indeed something more in the singing of the birds. Then there might be a D^+, or D may be void. We may leave this open for the moment. It is more important to say what other values of the other variables are. C^+ is of course the singing, but what is B^+? In the analysis of the logical structure of revelation the determining of B^+ is always very difficult. We might fill in the joy of singing, but then the content C^+ is part of B^+, and this must be expressed in the value. The best thing to do, in my view, is to give B the value 'A^+ R C^+', i.e. A^+ stands in a certain relation to C^+, i.e. A^+ enjoys its singing. So we get:

(5) $A = A^+$ (a certain bird); $B = (A^+ R C^+)$; $C = C^+$ (a certain way of singing); $D = D^+$ (may be the null class or another bird).

(5')   *A certain bird reveals its joy in its singing by means of a certain way of singing (to another bird).*

(5")   *A certain bird reveals that it enjoys its singing by means of a certain way of singing.*

232

So we see that it is very complicated to assess exactly such a simple thing as the singing of a bird, if we assume the hypothesis that it is singing for joy! There are even more logical difficulties here, but we must return to the revealing processes among human beings.

Is it possible for D^+ to believe the revelation (i.e. to understand it and accept that A^+ reveals something to him) and still not to accept the truth of B^+? I think this is quite possible: D^+ may understand that A^+ reveals to him that B^+, but he may also believe that B^+ is not true. There is no logical contradiction in this position. It is in agreement with what we have already seen before. So we get:

(6) $A = A^+$ (a certain person) $B = B^+$ (a certain message); $C = C^+$ (a certain means of revelation); $D = D^+$ (a certain person).
Here it is no contradiction for D^+ to accept the revelatory situation and still deny that B^+ is true.

But there is a difference in a religious context, where A^+ is God. I do not think that D^+ can accept the revelatory situation, i.e. that A^+ (God) has revealed to him that B^+ and still not believe it. If he does not believe that B^+, he would refuse to accept the revelatory situation. The foundation of this is the great revelatory power of God. So we have:

(7) $A = A^+$ (God); $B = B^+$ (a certain message); $C = C^+$ (a certain means of revelation); $D = D^+$ (a certain person).
Here it is contradictory for D^+ to accept the revelatory situation and still not to believe that B^+ is true.

Let us now consider aesthetic contexts. In ordinary language the terms 'reveal' and 'revelation' are used quite frequently here: 'Her performance of Chopin was a revelation'; 'His playing of Beethoven revealed the true beauty of the symphony'; 'Rembrandt's paintings reveal the aesthetic sense of the contrast of light and dark (*chiaroscuro*)'. In this human context the giving of values to A, C, and D is no problem, but what is the value of B? Of course, in art many things may be communicated. A painter may present certain scenes, religious themes, even moral lessons. There is programme music in contradistinction to absolute music. But are these things the real value of B? At least they do not constitute a work of art. There must be an aesthetic value added to them. So B^+ may be a piece of information about things, but this is not necessary, there is absolute music, abstract painting, etc. Anyway B^+ must also contain something else. How shall we denote this? I propose to call this value simply 'aesthetic value'. In passing I must remark that in the term 'aesthetic value' the term 'value' has, of course, another meaning than in the combination 'the value of a variable'. The latter term 'value' belongs to standard logical theory, whereas the first term 'value' belongs to value theory.

It certainly sounds Platonic to speak about 'aesthetic value' (and we shall speak about 'religious value' as well!). I myself am quite prepared to accept values in their 'Platonic sense' in my philosophy. In logic and mathematics too I am a 'Platonist', but, of course, one is not allowed to smuggle a whole philosophy into a particular piece of logical analysis. It might be obvious from our analysis, however, that logic by its nature has Platonic tendencies, so that many logicians are Platonists or have sympathy for this position. But here I only want to propose 'aesthetic value' as a term for the sake of the discussion and I should like to leave a further analysis of this term aside. A non-Platonist might succeed in reducing this 'aesthetic value' to other constituents of an aesthetic event. For example he might reduce it to activities of A^+, or even to activities of A^+ and D^+ together, for modern reception theory asserts that something is only a work of art, when the receiver makes it a work of art in his interpretation!

Now it is possible that D^+ accepts a certain piece of work as a work of art, i.e. he may attribute an aesthetic value to it in the terminology used above, without his accepting it as containing truth, i.e. he may accept the aesthetic value and still state that it is not true. We may admire a novelist without accepting his views. So we have:

(8) $A = A^+$ (a certain person; the artist); $B = B_1^+$ (aesthetic value) and B_2^+ (some piece of information; may be void or $= C^+$); $C = C^+$ (a certain artistic performance or product); $D = D^+$ (a certain person or group of persons).

Here it is possible for D^+ to accept B_1^+ and still deny that B_2^+ is true.

Here too we have the problem: Can an aesthetic value be revealed without anybody accepting it? Can there be a work of art which is not accepted as such? Here different positions may be taken. For modern art it would be a bad thing if aesthetic value were dependent on general acceptance! Modern composers like Karl Heinz Stockhausen, Berio, and others have lost contact with the general public, quite in contradistinction to the composers in preceding centuries, and the same is true for painters like the American expressionists (Rothko, Riley and others). At first sight it would seem that according to reception theory there is no work of art without a receiver, without someone recognizing it as such. So it seems that D^+ cannot be the null class! But even here is a way out. The creator of the work of art is at the same time also its receiver! But what is the position where even the composer or painter does not acknowledge his work as a work of art? And this position is not exceptional. If e.g. Brod had obeyed Kafka, the works of the latter would have been destroyed! Now very often later generations *do* recognize certain works as works of art, which were in the time of their origin not acknowledged as such. To these later generations the aesthetic value, which had been hidden in these works, was revealed. But what is the

234

position of the aesthetic value hidden in a work that until now nobody, not even the artist himself, has discovered? According to reception theory there is no aesthetic value in a work of art as long as nobody has discovered it. I, being a Platonist, should certainly maintain that there is indeed an aesthetic value in it. But am I justified in stating that it is revealed? Here we have the old problem again of something that might be revealed without anybody acknowledging it as such. We might, however, introduce God or the angels as beings who see the aesthetic value. But I prefer to introduce the ideal observer, a well-known figure in logic and mathematics. But then there is a value for D: God, the angels, or the ideal observer. However, it may be even better to state that we need scheme (II') here and it is the variable E that is to be given the values. So we have:

(9) $A = A^+$ (the artist, who does not know he is one here); $B = B_i^+$ (the aesthetic value); $C = C^+$ (the work of art); $D = D^+$ (is the null class); $E = E^+$ (the ideal observer).

So my solution is that there is revelation of aesthetic value in a work of art that until now has not been recognized as such by anyone, but this is so because there are values for E, although these values are not ordinary people.

Let us now turn to religious contexts. There are many possibilities here and we shall not treat them all, because this would exceed the purpose of this appendix. First I want to consider the 'standard situation':

(10) $A = A^+$ (God); $B = B^+$ (a communication or God himself); $C = C^+$ (the means of revelation); $D = D^+$ (the receiver of the revelation).

In scheme (II') we have:

(10a) $E = D^+$ (if D^+ accepts the revelation).

or

(10b) $E = E^+$ (another person). This is the case, if D^+ does not accept the revelatory situation, but someone else does.

or

(10c) $E = E^+$ (the ideal observer).

We have already seen (*vide* (7)) that it is impossible for D^+ to accept the revelation and not to accept B^+ as true. So there is at first sight no need to introduce a specific religious value B_3^+. Now we have the following possibility: there are persons who claim to have religious experiences and still remain atheists. I may refer here to the interesting school of Ghent (L. Apostel, Vandamme, Thibau and others) ('Mr Hubbeling, we are all atheists here, but we cannot get rid of religion! It has such qualities!'), but there are others too. We might try to prove that this position is impossible and logically contradictory, but I do not think that we can succeed. And what is even more important, it is not the task of a logical analysis to exclude such a position in advance; in this appendix we are dealing with the logic of religion. So what are the values of the variables in this position? A^+ cannot be God, of course, but what is it then? The best thing to do, in my opinion, is to accept two possibilities here. The atheist may have certain religious experiences caused by some events. In the school of Ghent, however, they even evoke such experiences by using traditional mystic techniques, expecially the *Exercitia Spiritualia* of Ignatius of Loyola! Now if a certain event or thing causes religious experience, there might be nothing else but this event or thing besides the religious value that is revealed. So we have:

(11) $A = A^+$ (this thing or event); $B = B_3^+$ (the religious value); $C =$ void (or $= A^+$); $D = D^+$ (the person who has this religious experience)

There may, of course, also be a piece of information, but just as in the case of the aesthetic value, this is not necessary. But then we have:

(12) $A = A^+$ (this thing or event); $B = B_3^+$ (the religious value) and B_4^+ (some piece of information); $C =$ void (or $= A^+$) and $D = D^+$ (the person who has this religious experience)

(11) and (12) are the cases in which a certain person happened to have religious experiences. When we evoke them, we must have other values, e.g.:

(13) $A = A^+$ (the person who has this religious experience); $B = B_3^+$ (the religious value) and B_4^+ (some piece of information, might be the null class); $C = C^+$ (some events or things evoked by A^+) and $D = A^+$.

There are more possibilities, but anyone who is willing to use this logical apparatus can construct them for himself.

Let us now for a moment return to the 'standard position' (10). It might be better in view of our analysis to introduce also B_3^+ (the religious value) here. So we get:

(14) $A = A^+$ (God); $B = B_3^+$ (the religious value) and B_4^+ (some piece of

information); $C = C^+$ (the means of revelation); $D = D^+$ (the receiver of the revelation).

In this view a revelatory event has some quality that constitutes it as a revelatory event, i.e. the religions value. In my view this is a plausible position. Otherwise there is no explanation for the 'revelatory power' of the event. But here too it might be possible to reduce this religious value to something else. Logical analysis as such does not exclude such a possibility beforehand, although I do not think that this is possible.

When God reveals himself, a difficulty arises. Where must we place him in the giving of values? We may put him as value B_3^+. Then God *is* the religious value or better coincides with the religious value, which does not imply that he is absorbed by it. Religious value may be considered to emanate from God. This would be a more or less 'Spinozistic' position. We may also put him as value B_4^+. In this case God *has* religious value. I hesitate to decide here. At the moment I would prefer the first ('Spinozistic') position, provided that God is not absorbed by the religious value. But of course this is a philosophical position and not a logical one. So we have:

(15)   The same values as in (14) and in addition: God *sub* B_3^+ or *sub* B_4^+.

Now it is easy to indicate the logical position of a revelation that is not accepted by anyone. In this case we have (cp. the aesthetic position (9)):

(16) $A = A^+$ (God); $B = B_3^+$ (the religious value) and B_4^+ (some piece of information); $C = C^+$ (the means of revelation) and $D = D^+$ (men for whom the revelation is meant). God may be *sub* B_3^+ or *sub* B_4^+ and $E = E^+$ (the ideal observer) (in scheme (II')).

In (16) nobody accepts the revelation, i.e. no one *sub* D^+ believes in it. In this position the ambiguity of revelation is solved, in that there is general revelation although perhaps nobody accepts it. Even in this case we can speak of revelation.

With the help of this apparatus we may formulate the difference between (i) the physico-theological variant and (ii) the teleological variant of the argument from design (*vide* 3.1.4). In (i) the argument tries to show that God wants to teach people something in nature. There are moral lessons hidden in natural events. So if we accept this revelation we understand a certain message. In other words we find this message *sub* B_4^+, which here cannot be the null class. So we have:

(17) $A = A^+$ (God); $B = B_3^+$ (the religious value) and B_4^+ (a message

expressed in nature); C = C⁺ (some events or states of affairs in nature); D = D⁺ (the person(s) who received the revelation).

There may even be a modern reconstruction of this variant of the argument, when it is held that aesthetic values are revealed in nature. In that case we also have B_1^+ in our formula. So we have:

(18)   A = A⁺ (God); B = B_1^+ (the aesthethic value) and B_3^+ (the religious value) and B_4^+ (a message expressed in nature, but might be the null class here); C = C⁺ (some events or states of affairs in nature); D = D⁺ (the person(s) who received the revelation).

There might even be a revelation of moral values (B_5^+) and this moral value may even appear in other contexts too. The reason why I did not refer to B_5^+ earlier is that it is not my purpose to give a *complete* logical analysis of the concept of revelation. For that we should need a fuller analysis of the relation between B_1^+, B_3^+, and B_5^+, or between aesthetic, religious and moral values (*vide* 4.6.3). But in the physico-theological variant of the argument from design we may have the following position:

(19)   A = A⁺ (God); B = B_3^+ (the religions value), B_4^+ (a message in nature) and B_5^+ (the moral value); C = C⁺ (some events or states of affairs in nature); D = D⁺ (the person(s) who received the revelation).

In the teleological variant of the argument from design there are no lessons revealed in nature. Only God's presence is revealed in the order of nature. So B_4^+ might be the null class, and at least it does not contain any message. It may, however, contain God's presense. So we have:

(20)   A = A⁺ (God); B = B_3^+ (the religious value) and B_4^+ (may be the null class or may contain God's presence); C = C⁺ (some events or states of affairs in nature); D = D⁺ (the person(s) who received the revelation).

Of course, moral values can be revealed otherwise than only in nature with the help of the physico-theological variant of the argument from design. We may have:

(21)   A = A⁺ (God); B = B_3^+ (the religious value), B_4^+ (a piece of information) and B_5^+ (the moral value); C = C⁺ (a means of revelation, in this case not exclusively nature otherwise we have (19)); D = D⁺ (the receiver of the revelation).

But as has been said before, for a complete analysis of the logical structure of revelation we need an analysis of the difficult relation between moral, aesthetic and religious values which would take us beyond the scope of this appendix.

There are many other logical possibilities in a revelatory event. God, for instance, is not necessarily the value of A. In a revelation somebody else can also reveal him, for example Jesus Christ. We may have:

(22) $A = A^+$ (Jesus Christ); $B = B^+$ (God); $C = C^+$ (some means of revelation); $D = D^+$ (the person(s) who received the revelation).

Sometimes the person who received the revelation does not recognize it as such. Then another person must tell him. One may think of I Sam. 3 or of the first revelation to Mohammed who did not understand the revelation either. His uncle told him that what he experienced was a revelation. Now in I Sam. 3 we have:

(23) $A = A^+$ (God); $B = B^+$ (God's message to Samuel, only given when Samuel understood the revelatory situation); $C = C^+$ (the calling of Samuel by name); $D = D^+$ (= Samuel) and now in (II') $E = E^+$ (Eli).

Until now we have considered only the possibility of God's revealing himself or something to man. It is also possible that God reveals himself to himself as this is stated in the doctrine of the trinity. Various positions are possible, which may be formulated clearly with the help of the apparatus:

(24) $A = A^+$ (God); $B = B^+$ (God, the Father); $C = C^+$ (God, the Holy Ghost); $D = D^+$ (God, the Son).

The position given in (24) is the view of scholars like Eckhardt, who taught a *Deitas*, a divine being, above the Trinity. If one does not accept his view and wants to adhere to the more orthodox position of *Pater fons totius trinitatis*, we have:

(25) $A = A^+$ (God, the Father); $B = A^+$ (God, the Father); $C = C^+$ (God, the Holy Ghost); $D = D^+$ (God, the Son).

It may be immediately obvious that for God a totally narcissistic position as in (2) is impossible. The triune God is a loving God, going out of Himself, revealing himself permanently.

Of course, with the help of such logical analyses alone we cannot solve philosophical problems. We may formulate certain problems in such a way as to give us a greater insight. That is important enough, though!

11. *Some epistemological remarks*

In this appendix we shall make some remarks on a few epistemological problems which play a certain role in the main text, but which lie outside the scope of the philosophy of religion.

I. *Parallelism of truth and meaning*

It is not my intention to deal here with the various theories of truth (abundancy, semantic, non-descriptive, correspondence, coherence, pragmatist theory, etc.) or with theories of meaning. The only thing I want to do here is to show that there is a certain parallelism between the main theories of truth and those of meaning. Further I want to demonstrate that various theories are compatible with each other; this at least holds for what I want to call the four main theories.

a. *The correspondence theory of truth and the reference theory of meaning*

In ordinary language the reference theory of meaning is usually tacitly presupposed. If I say 'My house has seven rooms' this statement is meant to refer to something in reality, *viz.* a certain building of which it is said that it is mine (i.e. that it stands in a certain relation to a certain person) and that there are seven rooms in it and this statement is true, if we look in the house mentioned, count the rooms and find seven. I do not claim that the reference is the only constituent of meaning, but that it is undeniable that it plays a certain role. However, I do not think that one can subscribe to a reference theory of meaning and refuse to use a correspondence theory of truth. I also admit that the theory has certain difficulties. For example we run into a *regressus ad infinitum* (vide 3.1.5.6.2). But since in this appendix it is our main purpose to emphasize a point that is much neglected, *viz.* that there is a certain parallelism between truth and meaning, and because a full treatment of the theories of meaning and truth would exceed the scope of this appendix, I shall not go further into this matter. The only other thing I want to point out is that even moral statements may have their reference. In a modern logical view they refer to an ideal world. It may be said of statements with other modalities too that they refer to something: a statement with the word 'possible' may refer to a 'possible world', a statement with an epistemic word like 'I believe' may refer to a world that exists in my mind, and so on.

b. *The consequence theory of truth and meaning*

Even if we extend the reference theory of meaning and the correspondence theory of truth, there is still another constituent and that is with respect to the theories of truth the coherence theory or the consequence theory. A statement is true if it is compatible with a system of true statements (coherence theory), or if it is derivable from that system (consequence theory). There is not much difference between thse two theories (coherence theory and consequence theory). For our purpose the consequence theory is more suitable, and therefore I shall henceforth only speak of the consequence theory.

Now even adherents of this theory do not claim that it is the only possible theory. It always occurs in addition to other theories, usually the correspondence theory. As I said before, a statement is true, if it is derivable from a system of true statements. But what is the foundation of the truth of the statements of that system? They may also be derived from a true system, etc. But finally one must refer to another foundation which may be the correspondence with reality. So the consequence theory is never isolated. I am prepared to subscribe to this consequence theory but never as an isolated theory.

All this is well known and hardly worth mentioning. But what is very often overlooked is that besides a consequence theory of truth we also have a consequence theory of meaning. Two statements in the same words, spoken at the same time and place and referring to the same reality, mean something different from when they are placed in different systems of inference rules. In a system where 'p → q' is valid the statement p means something different what it means in a system where 'p → ~q' is valid. To give an example. If a captain of industry and a labour union man both say 'Mr A works hard' they refer to the same state of affairs, but they may still mean something different, because their systems of inference rules are different. Another example (*vide* appendix 7): Kierkegaard's statement that there is a decisive moment in time has a different meaning from the same statement spoken by a Marxist. In deontic logic the statement 'Op' means something different in a system where the axiom 'Op → OOp' is valid from what it means in a system where this axiom is not valid. The word 'necessary' means something different in S_4 and in S_5! All this is self-evident but very often overlooked. Moreover, it goes without saying that a whole system of inference rules lies at the basis of every indirect communication! Hence it is often the basis of art. And just as the consequence theory of truth cannot be valid in isolation from the other theories, so the consequence theory of meaning needs the reference theory as supplement. Without some statements that refer to something the consequence theory of meaning cannot hold.

c. *The consensus theory of meaning and truth*

This theory is known by this name in Germany and the Netherlands, in England the term 'non-descriptive' (pragmatic) theory is used. According to this theory it is the consensus between the members of a certain community which gives words and statements their meaning and which also decides which basic statements are true and which are not. I think the theory is right in claiming that there is no meaning and no truth without a deciding community. However, it would be totally wrong to suppose – as is very often done – that this theory stands in opposition to the two theories mentioned above. This theory lies on another language level. For it is the language and cultural community which decides to what a statement refers and it is this community that decides which meaning and truth inference rules are valid. One cannot say 'I oppose the correspondence theory, for I am an adherent of the consensus theory!' The three theories do not contradict each other.

d. *The normative (standard) theory of truth*

A less known theory, but in the days of German idealism quite generally accepted, is the normative theory of truth. Here it is held that a statement p is true, if it is in accordance with a certain standard of truth. The great advantage of this theory is that now also moral, aesthetic and other 'modal' statements can very easily be said to be true, which is in accordance with ordinary language. It is, however, still a little difficult to fit this into the existing theories. But it may be obvious that statements such as: 'It is true, that one ought to love one's neighbour' are not unusual and that consequently a theory of truth must also contain the truths of moral statements. Also this theory does not compete with the first two theories. It contains them. For certain statements their agreement with reality is the standard of truth. A moral statement has to be in conformity with certain moral standards, etc. The third theory, the consensus theory, applies here too on another level. Either the community sets up these standards or it is held that the standards are ideal, and that the community must strive to live up to them. In the latter case the normative theory is usually combined with the model of the ideal observer or logician, we have already referred to. In that case we must try to live up to the standard set by this ideal observer. In practice this ideal observer may seem superfluous, but now it is possible to assert that there is an objective truth, although we do not know this (exactly). But even those who adhere to the standard (normative) theory of truth cannot get rid of the consensus theory.

At first sight is might seem that the parallelism between truth and meaning is broken here, but this is not the case. Only here too the standard theory of meaning cannot replace the others. This theory only says that a statement must reach certain standards in order to fulfil its purpose. And these standards are different. When the communicative mode is indicative, i.e. the statement is meant to refer to something or to describe something then the standard is not the same as when it is meant to express a moral judgment. In the first case clarity must be the main standard, whereas in the

242

second case it might be meant to be inspiring and/or provocative, etc. It is self-evident that a poetic statement has other standards. A treatment of this standard theory of meaning would take us too far. We only want to offer some clarifications with regard to the use of truth theories and meaning. It was not out purpose to give an exposition of these theories with all their merits and disadvantages.

II. *The concept of intuition*

In the second place I want to offer some clarifications with respect to the concept of 'intuition'. By intuition usually two completely different things are meant:

(i)   a kind of vague feeling that something is true or right, which we cannot formulate directly in the clear language of logical-empirical systems.

(ii) a kind of deep conviction, that some religious, aesthetic or moral insight is right. This too is difficult to formulate in the usual logical-empirical language.

These two concepts are often confused. Spinoza for example gives his famous three ways of knowledge. The first is the empirical way, which gives by itself only vague and confused knowledge. The second way is the way of rational, or rational-empirical thinking which may lead to truth, but which sometimes fails. The third way is the way of infallible truth and is directly available. It is, however, rare according to Spinoza.

Now it seems as if Spinoza uses the word 'intuition' in the sense of meaning (ii), but his examples are from meaning (i)! To Spinoza, however, it is important that in a *final* analysis rational or rational-empirical thinking may arrive at the infallible truth of intuition.

For the meaning of (i) we may think of the many cases in which we vaguely feel that something is correct of incorrect. We may hear an argument of which we immediately 'feel' that it is incorrect, but which we cannot refute immediately in a rational way. Or we may 'feel' that something is true without being able to prove it. In scientific discoveries man makes very often use of this kind of intuitions. We may refer here e.g. to the concept of 'tacit knowledge' of Polanyi.

Now it is very difficult to distinguish between the two, or, more correctly, it is difficult to identify intuition (ii), because it participates in all the difficulties of religious experience. He who has experienced it, i.e. he who knows this 'deep intuition', is convinced of its truth, but it is difficult to convince others. For the rest I am convinced – with Spinoza – that in a final analysis the way of rational(logical)-empirical thinking and the way of intuition (in its two meanings) must coincide. But this also is based only on intuition and cannot be proved rationally, for at the moment there are many discrepancies! I will not go into the relation between intuition (ii) and rational thinking, for that has been dealt with sufficiently in our section on religious experience. But here we will make some remarks on the relation between intuition (i) and rational thinking. Very often there is a discrepancy between the two, and the question arises which source of knowledge do we have to follow? I do not think that for this problem it is easy to give generally valid strategic rules. I myself, have a vague intuition that the ontological argument is not valid (even with the accepted presuppositions), but rationally I cannot deny that it is valid! I am also vaguely convinced intuitively that the parapsychological data and the theories built on them are not true, but if I am honest, I must confess that there are strong empirically arguments in favour of them. What to do? This vague intuition is not infallible. A man like Polanyi emphasizes this very strongly. Of course, sometimes a further logical-empirical investigation shows its truth. For example, long before I discovered how to prove the correctness of the cosmological argument, I had the strong 'intuitionistic feeling' that it must be correct, although at that time hardly anybody believed in it. In contradistinction to the ontological argument my intuition (i) always accepted the cosmological argument!

A chess player meets this difficulty very often. His calculations before the chess board may invite him to play a move which his intuition forbids! What to do? On the whole I think in scientific investigation two provisional strategic rules are sensible.

(i)   If the problem or argument is purely rational, or practically completely rational (logical) and your intuitive feeling is in opposition to your rational thinking, follow your rational thinking provisionally. But if the problem is purely or to a great extent empirical, follow your intuition (i), because it usually functions as a set of unconscious experiences.

(ii)   Your intuition may tell you (a) either to accept something or (b) not to accept something. If your rational thinking says otherwise, follow in case (a) your rational thinking and in case (b) your intuition, for the burden of proof rests on the side that intends to extend the number of assumptions.

I think in case of a conflict rule (i) should be preferred to rule (ii). In this way I accept the ontological argument *provisionally*, but for the time being I do not accept the parapsychological data.

On the whole, however, this problem of a (provisional) conflict between rational thinking and intuition (i) has not yet been sufficiently discussed.

244

Some scholars would object to my idea that the conflict is in principle only provisional, but if one is convinced that one has to do here with a permanent conflict, the necessity of devising a strategy is even more urgent!

12. *The Desirability Calculus*

The purpose of this calculus is to quantify moral arguments, given a certain hierarchy of values. This scale of values runs from 0 to 1. The following symbolic presentation is proposed to express this scale:
$/p/ D_x p$, where $0 \leqslant x \leqslant 1$.
   This expresses the intrinsic desirability of p, where x stands for the degree of desirability.
$/q/ D_y p$, where again $0 \leqslant y \leqslant 1$.
   This expresses the desirability of p, as far as p causes q, or as far as p has q as a consequence. Now the following rule of inference is valid:

(i)
$$p \rightarrow q$$
$$/q/ D_x q$$
___
$$/q/ D_y p$$
(where x = y)

That means that the desirability of p insofar as it has q as a consequence is identical with the intrinsic desirability of q.

   $D_z p$ stands for the absolute desirability of p. Of course in the use of the symbolism it is not the variables that are important, but the question whether there is something before the desirability functor D. If nothing precedes D, then we have to do with the absolute desirability of the variable that follows D. If the propositional variable that precedes D is the same as the one that follows D, we have to do with the intrinsic value of that proposition and if it is different, we have to do with the desirability with respect to this proposition as a consequence. The propositional variables refer to states affairs which received a degree on the scale of values.

   Now $D_z p$, i.e. the absolute desirability of p, is found as the average of the intrinsic value of p and all the other desirabilities. Let us suppose for the sake of simplicity that p has only q as a consequence. Then the absolute degree of desirability of p, i.e. $D_z p$, given $/p/ D_x p$ and $/q/ D_y p$ is the average of x and y. I.e. $z = \dfrac{x + y}{2}$

Further the following rule is valid.

(ii) $/p/ D_x p \longleftrightarrow / \sim p/ D_{1-x} \sim p$.

That means that for the intrinsic value p and its negation are together 1. The more desirable p is, the less desirable is its negation.

I think all this is self-evident. But in their absolute degree of desirability we do not have the situation that the more desirable p is the less desirable is its negation and vice versa, for now both have consequences and these can be very different. For example if p has q as a consequence, it does not follow that its negation has the negation of q as a consequence. If we want to know whether Op or O ~p is true, then the absolute degree of desirability has to be computed. If the absolute degree of desirability of p is greater than that of its negation, then p is to be performed, i.e. we have Op. But if the degree of desirability of its negation ~p is greater then we have O ~p. If they are both equal, then we have Ip, i.e. p is indifferent. Thus we have:

(iii) $D_x p$
         $D_y \sim p$
         _____

        (a) if $x > y$ we have Op
        (b) if $x < y$ we have O ~p
        (c) if $x = y$ we have Ip.

To give a simple example: Let us assume for the sake of simplicity that p has only q as its consequence, and that ~p has only ~q as its consequence. Let there further be given /p/ $D_{0.6}p$ and /q/ $D_{0.1}q$. Then the absolute desirability of p:D_z p is:

$$\frac{0.6 + 0.1}{2} = 0.35$$

and the absolute desirability of its negation is:

$$\frac{0.4 + 0.9}{2} = 0.65.$$

Consequently we have: O ~p.

That means that as such p is more desirable than its negation, but it has an undesirable consequence. Therefore we have to try to prevent p.

It is self-evident that the computing of the absolute desirability of a certain state of affairs to which a certain proposition refers is usually not so simple. A certain state of affairs has more consequences, but the computing occurs in principle in the same way.

246

DW-calculus

The calculus mentioned above has, of course, been kept very simple. In practice one cannot be sure of a particular consequence. There is only a certain probability that a particular consequence may follow. Now one may introduce a probability functor W with an index W_x indicating its degree of probability. Thus $W_{0.8}$ (p → q) means that the degree of probability that p has q as its consequence, is 0.8 (again our scale is from 0 to 1).

Now, it is possible to set up a calculus in order to compute the desirability of p. Suppose we have /q/ D_xq (the intrinsic value of q) and W_y (p → q), then the degree of desirability of p with respect to the chance to have q as a consequence, i.e. /q/ D_zp, is:

$$z = \frac{y - 0.5}{0.5} \times (x - 0.5) + 0.5$$

The derivation of this formula is beyond the scope of this appendix. But its correctness may be evident from the following consideration. For y = 1, we have z = x. For y smaller than 1, but greater than 0.5 and 1 > x > 0.5 z becomes smaller than x but is still greater than 0.5, which means that it is still desirable to realize p as far as it has q as a consequence. Because if x is greater than 0.5 then it is desirable to realize p as far as it has q as a consequence proportional to the degree of probability that it has q as a consequence. If y becomes smaller than 0.5, then z becomes smaller than 0.5, which means that it is no longer desirable to realize p insofar as it has q as a consequence, because now the chance that it has the negation of q as a consequence is greater.

An example: suppose we have /q/ $D_{0.8}$q and $W_{0.6}$ (p → q) than the desirability of p insofar as it has q as a consequence is: 1/5 × 0.3 + 0.5 = 0.06 + 0.5 = 0.56. Consequently /q/ $D_{0.56}$p.

The calculus serves only to show the computability in principle of moral arguments. Of course an ideal observer can do this, for only he knows the hierarchy of values and the exact probability of all consequences. This is something we can only approach.

Bibliographical references

1.1 The approach in the present work is characterized by the use of modern logic, although in the text itself references to logical systems have been avoided. Moreover, the book uses the empirical data of the various concrete religions more than most others in this field. Aesthetic experiences are also taken into account, and this too is not a common practice. As for the use of logic, the approach which is closest to that of the present work may be found in the works of A. Plantinga: *The nature of Necessity* (Oxford, 1974); *God, Freedom and Evil* (London, 1974) and *Does God have a Nature?* (Milwaukee (Wis.), 1980). Plantinga, however, has a more 'semantic' approach in logic, whereas the present author bases himself on the axiomatic approaches and on those of natural deduction.

The late bishop I.T. Ramsey has done pioneering work in the field of analytical philosophy of religion. He has opened the discussion with logical positivism already in an early stage. Of his numerous works I mention: *Religious Language* (London, 1957); *Models and Mystery* (London, 1964); *Christian Discourses. Some Logical Explorations* (London, 1965). The late W.F. Zuurdeeg, *An Analytical Philosophy of Religion. A Treatment of Religion on the Basis of the Methods of Empirical and Existentialist Philosophy* (New York, etc., 1958) also worked in this spirit. The title of this work already expresses his programme, *viz.* to give a synthesis between analytical philosophy and existentialism. A disadvantage of Zuurdeeg's book is that he gives insufficient consideration to modern logic. Another pioneer in this field has been John Hick in his book *Faith and Knowledge* (London, 1957). He also deals extensively with the dialogue between Christianity and the other religions. He wrote a book on this subject *God and the Universe of Faiths* (London, 1973), but tried in practice also to join in a concrete dialogue with the immigrants in Birmingham, the town in which he teaches. He is of the opinion that all religions reveal a part of God's truth (*vide* 2.4.2): *God has many Names* (Philadelphia (Pa.), 1982). His well-known *Philosophy of Religion* has received its third edition (Englewood Cliffs, 1983). B. Hebblewaite also enters into a discussion with the other religions and theologies in his book *The Problems of Theology* (London, 1983). For him the Christian revelation has no longer an unquestionable authority. He tries, however, to show that it makes greater sense of the world and of life than any other worldview can do. In his book *The Justification of Religious Belief* (London, 1973) B. Mitchell has made the attempt to justify the Christian faith with the help of a so-called cumulative argumentation. R. Swinburne did the same and included an impressive amount of empirical data in his works: *The Coherence of Theism* (Oxford, 1977) and *The Existence of God* (Oxford, 1979). He stands, however, in an older tradition. One may read the excellent book by F.R. Tennant, *Philosophical Theology* (Cambridge, 1928), where many empirical data can also be found, but, of course, Swinburne is more modern. The spirit of the later Wittgenstein appeared in the following works: W.D. Hudson, *A Philosophical Approach to Religion* (London, 1974); T. McPherson, *The Philosophy of Religion* (London, 1965); D.Z. Phillips, *Faith and Philosophical Inquiry* (London, 1970); idem, *Death and Immortality* (London, 1972); idem, *Religion without Explanation* (Oxford, 1976). There are, however, differences among them. Phillips maintains that religion has its own language game, and he is less interested in trying to give rational arguments in favour of it. Hudson does not try to prove religious convictions either, but he at least tries to show that the language game of religion is reasonable, e.g. that it is free of inconsistencies and that it has explanatory power. Process philosophy (*vide* appendix 3) has given an important stimulus to new approaches in philosophy of religion: S. Ogden, *The Reality of God and other*

248

Essays (London, 1967); idem, *Christ without Myth. A Study Based on the Theology of Rudolf Bultmann* (New York, 1961); idem, *Faith and Freedom. Toward a Theology of Liberation (Nashville, 1979); J.B. Cobb, and D.R. Griffin, Process Theology. An Introductory Exposition* (Philadelphia (Pa), 1976); Keith Ward, *Rational Theology and the Creativity of God* (Oxford, 1982). This process theology and philosophy is opposed by P.T. Geach, *Providence and Evil* (Cambridge, 1977), who combines Catholicism and analytical philosophy.

Logical positivism was introduced into philosophy of religion by the pioneering work of A. Flew and A. MacIntyre (ed.), *New Essays in Philosophical Theology* (London, 1955), but not all the articles were written by logical positivists. It was more a book of discussion, but it definitely had a logical positivistic flavour. K. Nielsen's book *Contemporary Critique of Religion* (London, 1972) is based on logical positivism too. Much more based on logic and more theistic is the collection of articles: J. Donally (ed.), *Logical Analysis and Contemporary Theism* (New York, 1972). This book is meant to be a critical continuation of the book edited by Flew and MacIntyre. Modern readers are: S.A. Matczack (ed.), *God in Contemporary Thought. A Philosophical Perspective* (Louvain/Paris, 1977); S.M. Cahn and D. Shatzy (ed.), *Contemporary Philosophy of Religion* (Oxford, 1982); Stuart C. Brown (ed.), *Reason and Religion. A Royal Institute of Philosophy Symposium* (Ithaca/London, 1977) (topics like the rationality of belief, the problem of evil, immortality, etc. are discussed here). An introduction on a historical basis is: M.J. Charlesworth, *Philosophy of Religion. The Historical Approaches* (London, 1972). Introductions from a Roman Catholic and Reformed view point are respectively: J.F. Donceel, *The Searching Mind: An Introduction to a Philosophy of God* (Notre Dame, 1979) and N.L. Geisler, *Philosophy of Religion* (Grand Rapids (Mi.), 1974).

Some German handbooks and introductions are: W. Trilhaas, *Religionsphilosophie* (Berlin, 1972), who bases himself on Kant and Schleiermacher. N.H. Søe writes interestingly on the relation of Christian faith to natural sciences, taking Karl Heim as his starting-point: *Religionsphilosophie. Ein Studienbuch* (München, 1967). A well-known modern Catholic book is: H. Küng, *Existiert Gott? Antwort auf die Gottesfrage der Neuzeit* (München, etc., 1978). The work has also been translated into English: *Does God Exist? An Answer for Today* (New York, 1980). Another Catholic book, which stands more in a traditional line, is: W. Brugger, *Summe einer philosophischen Gotteslehre* (München, 1979); the book has an excellent bibliography. Catholic, but starting with anthropology, is: H. Ogiermann, *'Es ist ein Gott'. Zur religionsphilosophischen Grundfrage* (München, 1981); it can be proved philosophically that we must attribute personal attributes to God, but that God is a person *for mankind* cannot be proved in this way. In Karl Jaspers's spirit Karl Albert shows that philosophy needs the inspiration from the side of religion: *Vom Kult zum Logos. Studien zur Philosophie der Religion* (Hamburg, 1982). E. Wölfel's book is closer to the approach in the present book: *Welt als Schöpfung. Zu den Fundamentalsätzen der chrislichen Schöpfungslehre heute* (München, 1981); Wölfel stands in the logical tradition of H. Scholz. The same can more or less be said of the works of Härle and Herms: W. Härle, *Systematische Philosophie. Eine Einführung für Theologiestudenten* (München/Mainz, 1982); W. Härle and E. Herms, *Rechtfertigung. Das Wirklichkeitsverständnis des christlichen Glaubens* (Göttingen, 1979); E. Herms, *Theologie – eine Erfahrungswissenschaft* (München, 1979). Härle is a disciple of Wölfel and Herms stands in the tradition of semiotics. He tries to show that religious experience is a necessary element of the total experience of life.

Philosophers of religion in an analytical tradition are: W. de Pater, *Theologische Sprachlogik* (München, 1971); idem, *Das Reden von Gott. Reflexionen zur analytischen Philosophie der religiösen Sprache* (Bonn, 1974) (De Pater, by the way, is a Dutchman); A. Grabner-Haider, *Vernunft und Religion. Ansätze einer analytischen Religionsphilosophie* (Graz, 1978). H. Hofmeister, *Wahrheit und Glaube. Interpretation und Kritik der sprachanalytischen Theorie der Religion* (Vienna, etc., 1978) bases himself on Wittgenstein. In contradistinction to most British 'Wittgensteinians' he underlines the unity of Wittgenstein's thought, i.e. that there is a continuity between the *Tractatus* and the *Investigations*. Methods based on linguistics have been introduced by E. Güttgemans and his school, which is concentrated in the journal *Linguistica Biblica*. W. Pannenberg started a discussion with modern

249

theories of science, *Wissenschaftstheorie und Theologie* (Frankfurt a.M., 1973). M. Gatzemeier opposes approaches like those in the present book, i.e. the giving of modern rational reconstructions of the arguments for God's existence, etc.: *Theologie als Wissenschaft?* (Stuttgart, etc., 1975). Modern readers are: S. Moser and E. Pilick (ed.), *Gottesbilder heute. Zur Gottesproblematik in der säkularisierten Gesellschaft der Gegenwart* (Königstein, 1979). A reader in the phenomenological tradition is: B. Caspar (ed.), *Gott nennen. Phänomenologische Zugänge* (Freiburg/München, 1981). A series of popular talks for the radio is given in: J. Schultz (ed.), *Wer ist eigentlich Gott?* (München, 1977).

In the Netherlands various traditions are represented. In a modern Catholic spirit was written: U. Dhondt, *Hedendaags denken en christelijk geloof* (Antwerpen/Amsterdam, 1981). H.J. Heering (Leiden) emphasizes the Jewish tradition: *Inleiding tot de godsdienstwijsbegeerte* (Meppel, 1976).The present work emphasizes the logical tradition combined with aesthetics and science of religion. Some of its thoughts may already be found in the more introductory works: *Denkend geloven. Inleiding in de wijsbegeerte van de godsdienst* (Assen, 1976) and *Einführung in die Religionsphilosophie* (Göttingen, 1981) as well as in *Language, Logic and Criterion. A Defence of Non-Positivistic Logical Empiricism* (Amsterdam, 1971). But the present work is more extensive and does not have a purely introductory character. A religious philosophy on a basis of logical empiricism has been produced by H.J. van Unen, *Pro-deonisme. Eerste deel: De wijsbegeerte van grond en zin* (Muiderberg, 1984).

In the analytical tradition the following works have been written: W.A. de Pater, *Taalanalytische perspectieven op godsdienst en kunst* (Antwerpen, 1970) (*vide* also his German books above); W. Brümmer, *Wijsgerige begripsanalyse. Een inleiding voor theologen en andere belangstellenden* (Kampen, 1975); this book has also been translated into English: *Theology and Philosophical Inquiry. An Introduction* (Philadelphia (Pa.), 1982).

In the Scandinavian countries several works have been written in the analytical tradition: L. Bejerholm and G. Hornig, *Wort und Handlung. Untersuchungen zur analytischen Religionsphilosophie*; G.R. Bråkenhielm, *How Philosophy Shapes Theories of Religion. An Analysis of Contemporary Philosophies of Religion with Special Regard to the Thought of John Wilson, John Hick and D.Z. Phillips* (Diss. Uppsala, 1975); T. Simonsson, *Logical and Semantic Structures in Christian Discourses* (Oslo, etc., 1971); U. Forell, *Wunderbegriffe und logische Analyse. Logisch-philosophische Analyse von Begriffen und Begriffsbildungen aus der deutschen protestantischen Theologie des 20. Jahrhunderts* (Göttingen, 1967). An interesting synthesis of analytical and phenomenological methods can be found in Z.J. Zdybicka, *Czowiek in Religia* (Man and Religion) (Lublin, 1977) (with an extensive summary in English). The analytical tradition is almost absent in France. An interesting existentialistic work on philosophy of religion was written by R. Mehl: *Vie intérieure et transcendance de Dieu* (Paris, 1980).

An extensive bibliography on philosophy of religion (until 1974) can be found in: IJ. Galama and A.F. Sanders, *Logic, Epistemology and Analysis of Religious Language. A Select Bibliography* (University of Groningen, 1974). The work has been continued until the beginning of the 80's by F. Blaakmeer, N. van der Plas and P.J. Huiser, *Philosophy of Religion. An Extensive Select Bibliography* (University of Groningen, 1987). Both works can be ordered from the administration of the theological faculty.

The present book is based on logic. An alternative basis could have been modern systems theory; G.J. Klir, *An Approach to General Systems Theory* (New York, etc., 1969); idem, *Trends in General Systems Theory* (New York, etc., 1972).

1.2 For K.L. Bellon cp. his book: *Godsdienstwijsbegeerte* (Nijmegen, 1934). My book is not in conflict with this tradition insofar as it also comprehends the results of science of religion.

For the logic of religion, cp. J.M. Bocheński O.P., *TheLogic of Religion* (New York, 1965) and the collection of articles: H.G. Hubbeling, L. Apostel and F. Vandamme (ed.), *Logic and Religion* (Studies in Culture) (Ghent, 1982). This collection includes articles by both positive Christians and atheists. There are also articles in which the axiomatic or purely deductive approaches are used as well as articles using semantical methods. The work of Bocheński is discussed in: W.A. Christian, 'Bocheński on the structure of schemes of doctrines' (*Religious Studies*, 13 (1977)), 203-219; M. Kämpfert, 'Logik und Linguistik der Religion. Zur Diskussion mit Bocheński (*Linguistica Biblica*, 1 (1971)), 17-27.

Some other works on the logical structure of religious language are: M. Durrant, *The Logical Status of 'God' and the Function of Theological Sentences* (London, 1973); P. Helm, *The Varieties of Belief* (New York, 1973).

For E. Brunner cp. *Religionsphilosophie evangelischer Theologie* (München, 1927; 2nd edition, 1948). Also translated into English: *The Philosophy of Religion from the Standpoint of Protestant Theology* (London, 1937). Further: idem, *Offenbarung und Vernunft. Die Lehre von der christlichen Glaubenserkenntnis* (Zürich, 1941). This book has also been translated into English: *Revelation and Reason. The Christian Doctrine of Faith* (London, 1947). There is, however, a certain difference between the two works. In the 1927 work Brunner takes a more or less Neo-Kantian position, whereas in the 1941 book he has been strongly influenced by personalistic movements (M. Buber, F. Ebner); (cp. for a critical description of Brunner's theology and philosophy and the various stages of his thought: H.G. Hubbeling, *Natuur en genade bij Emil Brunner* (Assen, 1956, Diss. Theol. Groningen).

For the important works of W. de Pater, cp. his works mentioned *sub* 1.1.

1.4 The 'usual' approach can be found in any handbook of the philosophy of religion. Charlesworth's approach can be found in his book mentioned *sub* 1.1.

2.1 For my approach which considers the many possible starting-points in philosophy, cp. also my contribution to the volume of R.C. Kwant and S. IJsseling (ed.), *Filosoferen. Gangbare vormen van wijsgerig denken* (Alphen a/d Rijn, 1977) pp. 102-120 ('Analytisch filosoferen') and my book (1981) mentioned *sub* 1.1. In his book mentioned *sub* 1.1 (1982) W. Härle has taken over this approach (pp. 45-52), but in an interesting way he tried to find a kind of superposition by taking a semiotic standpoint: All approaches presuppose semiotics. He is right, but only from a semiotic standpoint!

For H. Scholz, cp. his *Metaphysik als strenge Wissenschaft* (Cologne, 1941; reprinted Darmstadt, 1965) and *Mathesis Universalis* (edited by H. Hermes, F. Kambartel and J. Ritter) (Basel, etc., 1961).

The Lindenbaum Algebra may be studied in L. Rieger, *Algebraic Methods of Mathematical Logic* (Prague & New York, etc., 1967), pp. 105ff, 116ff.

Kripke's semantic approaches can be found in: S.A. Kripke, 'Semantical Analysis of Modal Logic I, Normal Propositional Calculi' (*Zeitschrift für mathematische Logik und Grundlagen der Mathematik*, vol. 9, 1963, pp. 67-96) and 'Semantical Considerations on Modal Logics' (*Acta Philosophica Fennica*, 1963): *Modal and Many-valued Logics*, pp.83-94).

Further: S.A. Kripke, *Naming and Necessity* (2nd edition) (Oxford, 1980). Here Kripke's well-known theories of the rigid designator, his possible worlds theory (or it may be better to speak of the possible states of the actual world), his theory of the possibility of a posteriori statements which are necessarily true, etc., can be found.

2.2 Expositions on logic may be found in the various textbooks on logic, e.g. H. de Swart and H.G. Hubbeling, *Inleiding in de symbolische logica* (Assen, 1976), in which also an abstract all-comprehensive system of intensional logical systems can be found.

For Gödel's theorem, cp. K. Gödel, 'Über formal unentscheidbare Sätze der *Principia Mathematica* und verwandte Systeme I' (*Monatshefte für Mathematik und Physik*, 38 (1931), 173-198). Authorized translation in the collection of articles: J. van Heijenoort, *From Frege to Gödel. Source Book on Mathematical Logic* (Cambridge (Mass.), 1966), 595-617.

For dialectics, cp. J. McTaggart, *Studies in the Hegelian Dialectic* (Cambridge, 1896, 2nd edition New York, 1964); K. Kosik, *Dialectics of the Concrete* (Dordrecht, 1976) (Originally in Czech, *Dialektiske konkrétního*, 1961); W. van Dooren, *Dialektiek* (Assen, 1977); J. Zelenỳ, *The Logic of Marx* (Oxford, 1980) (gives an analysis of the logic used in *Das Kapital*, a logic that is strongly influenced by Hegelian dialectic. According to the author Marx does not have a universal dialectical theory that can be abstracted from the object studied); W. Becker and W.K. Essler (ed.), *Konzepte der Dialektik* (Frankfurt a.M., 1981) (This volume includes also articles in English. It presents historical investigations (studies in Kant, Schiller, Marx, Neo-Marxism and especially Hegel) and systematic investigations (dialectics as a scientific theory, as a means of clarifying ordinary language, as a scheme for formalising discussions, etc.); W. Viertel, *Eine Theorie der Dialektik* (Königstein, 1983).

The fourth way of Thomas can be found in: *Summa Theologiae* I, qu. 2, art. 2, resp.

A more extensive exposition of the various systems of logical empiricism can be found in Hubbeling, the work mentioned *sub* 1.1 (1971).

2.3 For the model of language systems, which has been inspired by the later Wittgenstein, cp. H.G. Hubbeling, 'Theology, Philosophy and Science of Religion and their Logical and Empirical Presuppositions' in: Th.P. van Baaren and H.J.W. Drijvers (ed.), *Religion, Culture and Methodology* (The Hague, etc., 1974), 9-33, in which other references also can be found. In this section there are further references to H. Albert 'Theorie, Verstehen und Geschichte. Zur Kritik des methodologischen Autonomieanspruchs in den sogenannten Geisteswissenschaften' (*Zeitschrift für allgemeine Wissenschaftstheorie/Journal for General Philosophy of Science*, 1 (1970), 3-23); J.G. Droysen, *Historische Vorlesungen über Enzyklopädie und Methodologie der Geschichte* (München, 1960); W. Stegmüller, *Probleme und Resultate der Wissenschaftstheorie und Analytische Philosophie*, Band I, *Wissenschaftliche Erklärung und Begründung* (Berlin, 1969); Th.S. Kuhn, *The Structure of Scientific Revolutions* (in: O. Neurath, R. Carnap and Ch. Morris (ed.), *Foundations of the Unity of Science. Toward an International Encyclopedia of Unified Science*, Vol. II, 53-273 (Chicago/London, 1970)); W. Pannenberg, *Grundfragen systematischer Theologie. Gesammelte Aufsätze* (Göttingen, 1967); cp. for the latter book also: H.G. Hubbeling, 'Einige kritische Fragen an Pannenberg' (*Kerk en Theologie*, 24 (1970), 246-259).

Before Kuhn Polanyi had already shown that factual progress in science does not follow the ideal concepts of Popper and logical positivism: *Personal Knowledge – Towards a Post-Critical Philosophy* (Chicago/London, 1962 (1st edition 1958)). For the finding of fruitful hypotheses a kind of intuition ('tacit knowledge', 'personal knowledge') is needed. About Polanyi: T.F. Torrance (ed.), *Belief in Science and Life. The Relevance of Michael Polanyi's Thought for Christian Faith and Life* (Edinburgh, 1980); R.L. Hall, 'The Role of Commitment in Scientific Inquiry. Polanyi or Popper? (*Human Studies* 5 (1982), 45-60).

Imre Lakatos tried to take a mediatory position between Kuhn and Popper. He developed the idea of research programmes in which a distinction can be made between the hard kernel of the theory that need not be tested and the hypotheses that should be tested by experience. And also in the latter a distinction must be made between the hypotheses that need not be tested directly (the protective belt) and the hypotheses that are the proper subject of the investigations. Thus Lakatos can claim that there is an internal logical structure of scientific investigations, although it cannot be denied that external progress in science has often been made by means of accidents, brilliant intuition, etc. *Vide*: I. Lakatos, 'Falsification and the Methodology of Scientific Research Programmes' (in: I. Lakatos and A. Musgrave, *Criticism and the Growth of Knowledge* (Cambridge, 1970, 91-196); idem, *Proofs and Refutations. The Logic of Mathematical Discovery* (London/New York, 1976); idem, *Philosophical Papers. Vol. I, The Methodology of Scientific Research Programmes. Vol. II, Mathematics, Science and Epistemology*, (London: New York, 1978). About him, Kuhn and others: I. Hacking (ed.), *Scientific Revolutions* (Oxford, 1981); C. Dilworth, *Scientific Progress. A Study Concering the Nature of the Relation between Successive Scientific Theories* (Dordrecht, 1981). Important for the relation of religion and the theory of knowledge are: J. Margolis, *Knowledge and Existence* (New York/Oxford, 1973); J.E. Smith, *Purpose and Thought* (New Haven, 1978); G. Sauter (ed.), *Kritik der Theologie. Die Theologie und die neuere wissenschaftstheoretische Diskussion* (München, 1973).

2.4.1 The various references to Schleiermacher can be found in his *Über die Religion. Reden an die Gebildeten unter ihren Verächtern* (Berlin, 1799), p. 50, 251, 281, 48 (also translated into English: *On Religion: Speeches to its Cultured Despisers* (London, 1893; New York, 1958) and *Glaubenslehre* (Berlin, 1821/2), Section 3.11 (also translated into English: *The Christian Faith* (Edinburgh, 1948; New York, 1963).

An account of the central ideas in Schleiermacher's theology against the background of his philosophy can be found in Richard R. Niebuhr, *Schleiermacher on Christ and Religion* (New York, 1964). The most detailed examination of Schleiermacher's philosophy in English can be found in R. Brandt, *The Philosophy of Friedrich Schleiermacher* (New York, 1941). A more recent study against the background of the German Romantic movement is: J. Forstmann, *A Romantic Triangle. Schleiermacher and Early German Romanticism* (Missoula (Mont.), 1977). Further: A.L. Blackwell, *Schleiermacher's Early Philosophy of Life. Determinism, Freedom, and Phantasy* (Chico (Calf.), 1982); J.E. Thiel, *God and World in Schleiermacher's Dialektik and Glaubenslehre. Criticism and the Methodology of Dogmatics* (Bern, etc., 1981); H.R. Reuter, *Die Einheit der Dialektik Friedrich Schleiermachers. Eine systematische Interpretation* (München, 1979) (gives a modern *werkimmanente* analysis (= approximately: close reading) of the main sections of the *Dialektik*, in which the author shows that the work can be interpreted as a unity). As it is always interesting to listen to Karl Barth I may refer to his lectures on Schleiermacher: K. Barth, *The Theology of Schleiermacher. Lectures at Göttingen, Winter Semester of 1923-1924* (Ed. by D. Ritschl) (Grand Rapids (Mi.), 1982). My interpretation can be found more extensively in 'Logical Reconstructivism as a Metaphilosophical Method of Interpretation and Discussion' (*Philosophy* (Ghent), 13 (1975), 51-64. In this article I discussed especially Kierkegaard and Schleiermacher.

2.4.2 References have been made to: C.B. Martin, 'A Religious Way of Knowing' (in: A. Flew and A. MacIntyre (ed.), *o.c.* (mentioned *sub* 1.1 (1955)), 76-95: F. Ferré, *Language, Logic and God* (New York, 1961), 110; J. Hick, 'Religious Faith as Experience-as' (in: G.N.A. Vesey (ed.), *Talk of God* (New York, 1969), 20-35; G.I. Mavrodes, 'God and Verification' (*Canadian Journal of Theology* 10 (1964), 187-191 (cp. also, idem, *Belief in God: A Study in the Epistemology of Religion* (New York, 1970)); R. Oakes, 'Is "Self-Validating" Religious Experience Logically Possible?' (*Thomist*, 34 (1972)), 256-266; K. Nielsen, *Contemporary Critics of Religion* (London, 1971, 49f; idem, ' "Christian Positivism" and the Appeal to Religious Experience' (*Journal of Religion*, 42 (1962), 248-261; J. Hick, *God and the Universe of Faith. Essays in the Philosophy of Religion* (London, 1973); A. Hofstadter, *Truth and Art* (New York, etc., 2nd edition, 1968), 162.

Some recent works on the justification and verification of religion statements and experiences are *inter alia*: D. Cupitt, *The Leap of Reason* (London, 1976); T.V. Litzenburg and M.L. Diamond (eds.), *The Logic of God: Theology and Verification* (Indianopolis, 1975); W. Beinert, 'Das Problem der Verifikation theologischer Sätze' (*Catholica*, 32 (1978)), 177-187; D.H.M. Brooks, 'Confirmability and Meaningfulness' (*Philosophical Papers*, 9 (1980)), 41-44; H.G. Hubbeling, 'Die Logik der Religion. Probleme der Verifikation der religiösen Aussagen auf Grund der religiösen Erfahrung' (*Neue Zeitschrift für systematische Theologie und Religionsphilosophie*, 21 (1979)), 1-19; K.H. Klein, *Positivism and Christianity. A Study of Theism and Verifiability* (The Hague, 1974); K. Nielsen, 'On the Rationality of Radical Theological Non-Naturalism. More on the Verificationist Turn in the Philosophy of Religion' (*Religious Studies*, 14 (1980)), 193-204; D.F.Sullivan, 'Vagueness and the Verifiability of Ordinary Faith' (*Religious Studies*, 14 (1978)), 459-467; H.J. Cargas and B. Lee (eds.), *Religious Experience and Process Theology* (New York, 1976); P. Donovan, *Interpreting Religious Experience* (London, 1979); P. Masterson, 'Experience and the Affirmation of God' (*Neue Zeitschrift für systematische Theologie und Religionsphilosophie*, 22 (1980)). 17-32; R.A. Oakes, 'Religious Experience and Rational Certainty' (*Religious Studies*, 12 (1976)), 311-318; H. Lyttkens, 'Religious Experience and Transcendence' (*Religious Studies*, 15 (1979)), 211-220; V. Brümmer, 'Lyttkens on Religious Experience and Transcendence' (*Religious Studies*, 15 (1979)), 221-225.

Some recent works on mystical experience and mysticism are: H. Coward and T. Penelhum (eds.), *Mystics and Scholars* (Waterloo, 1976); W. Earle and E. Freeman (eds.), *The Philosophy of Mysticism* (= The Monist 59 (1976), no. 4) (La Salle (Ill.), 1976); W. Earle, *Mystical Reason* (Chicago, 1980); R.S. Ellwood, Jr., *Mysticism and Religion* (Englewood Cliffs (N.J.), 1980); S.T. Katz (ed.), *Mysticism and Philosophical Analysis* (London, 1978); B.A. Scharfstein, *Mystical Experience* (Oxford, 1973); F. Staal, *Exploring Mysticism. A Methodological Essay* (Berkeley (Calf.), 1975).

Hick in his book mentioned *sub* 1.1 (1957) proposed the possibility of an eschatological verification as a means to claim empirical meaningfulness for religious statements. This has led to an extensive discussion. We mention only: R. Audi 'Eschatological Verification and Personal Identity' (*International Journal for Philosophy of Religion*, 7 (1977)), 391-408; L.H. Cox, 'Does John Hick's "Eschatological Verification" commit a Logical Mistake?' (*Personalist*, 55 (1974)), 95-105; H. Craighead, 'John Hick's After Life' (*Thomist*, 43 (1979)), 653-665; idem, 'Audi's Critique of Hick. An Evaluation' (*International Journal for Philosophy of Religion*, 9 (1979)), 51-60; V.C. Hayes, 'Beyond Eschatological Verification' (*Interchange*, 4 (1974)), 221-228; J. Hick, 'Eschatological Verification Reconsidered' (*Religious Studies*, 13 (1977)), 189-202. For the sake of curiosity I may mention that in the 19th century two Dutch scholars discussed the possibility of using the argument of an eschatological verification, *viz.* J.H. Scholten and A. Pierson. Some of today's arguments were then put forward: that it was not a real empirical argument, for instance. J.H. Scholten, by the way, may be an underestimated scholar: he developed a Bultmannian programme before Bultmann, partly in the same terms: 'demythologizing', 'kerygma' as the central kernel of the gospel, etc. About him: H.G. Hubbeling, 'Synthetisch modernisme. J.H. Scholten als wijsgeer en theoloog' (*Nederlands Theologisch Tijdschrift*, 1961/2), 107-142.

For the relation of aesthetic and religious experience, cp. also W. de Pater, the book mentioned *sub* 1.1 (1970), 135-174; F. Sparshott, 'Religious Experience and Aesthetic Experience' (in: J. King-Farlow (ed.), *The Challenge of Religion Today* (New York, 1976)), 96-114.

A philosophical evaluation of the concrete religious experiences in the various religions (a kind of continuation of James' *The Varieties of Religious Experience*), has been given by Alister Hardy, *The Spiritual Nature of Man. A Study of Contemporary Religious Experience* (Oxford, 1979): In religious experience there is an awareness of the divine presence, which we may feel as transcendent but with which we also have a mystical communion. God is transcendent and all-embracing at the same time.

For Van Baaren and his school, cp. Th.P. van Baaren and H.J.W. Drijvers, op.cit. (mentioned *sub* 2.3 (1973)).

2.4.3 Cp. L. Feuerbach, *Das Wesen des Christentums* (Leipzig, 2nd edition, 1843); also translated into English: *The Essence of Christianity* (New York, 1957); W.B. Chamberlain, *Heaven Wasn't His Destination: The Philosophy of Ludwig Feuerbach* (London, 1941); K. Marx, *Zur Kritik der Hegelschen Rechtsphilosophie* (in: Werke (Cotta) (Stuttgart, 1962)), 488ff; F. Engels, *Herr Eugen Dührings Umwälzung der Wissenschaft* (Leipzig, 1878); also translated into English: *Herr Eugen Dühring's Revolution in Science*.

Some recent works on Marxist critique of religion: L.A.R. Bakker and H.P.M. Goddijn (eds.), *De godsdienstkritiek van Karl Marx* (Baarn, 1983); P. Frostin, *Materialismus, Ideologie, Religion: die materialistische Religionskritik bei Karl Marx* (Lund, 1978); G.M.M. Cottier, *L'ateismo del giovane Marx. Le origine hegeliane* (Milan, 1981); H. Steussloff, *Einführung in Engels' Schrift 'Ludwig Feuerbach und der Ausgang der klassischen deutschen Philosophie'* (Berlin, 1981); M. Seliger, *The Marxist Conception of Ideology. A Critical Essay* (London, 1979, 2nd edition); H. Monz, *Karl Marx. Grundlagen der Entwicklung zu Leben und Werk* (Trier, 1973) (studies Marx' youth in Trier in which also Marx' anti-religious views have been formed). See also the literature mentioned *sub* 2.2.

S. Freud, *Die Zukunft einer Illusion* (Vienna 1927). Cp. also: E. Fromm, *Beyond the Chains of Illusion. My Encounter with Marx and Freud* (London, 1980); idem, *Greatness and Limita-*

tions of Freud's thought (New York, 1980); A. Plé, *Freud e la religione* (Rome, 1978); Th. Pfrimmer, *Freud, lecteur de la Bible* (Paris, 1982).

Some recent works on the critique of religion and atheism in general: G.H. Smith, *Atheism. The Case against God* (Buffalo, 1979); G. Stein (ed.), *An Anthology of Atheism and Rationalism* (Buffalo, 1980); K.H. Weger (ed.), *Religionskritik. Beiträge zur atheistischen Religionskritik der Gegenwart* (München, 1976) (enters into a discussion with various opponents of religion. According to Weger himself, atheism neglects a fundamental constituent of human being, *viz.* hope).

2.5.2 The English translation of the ontological argument and other important works of Anselm may be found in: Anselm, *Basic Writings* (La Salle (Ill.), 1962²).

The new insight into Anselm's ontological argument can be found in: C. Hartshorne, *Anselm's Discovery. A Re-examination of the Ontological Proof for God's Existence* (LaSalle (Ill.), 1965); G. Schulfreider, *An Introduction to Anselm's Argument* (Philadelphia (Pa.), 1978). Barth's 'theological' interpretation may be found in his book: *Fides quaerens Intellectum. Anselms Beweis der Existenz Gottes im Zusammenhang seines theologischen Programms* (München, 1931). For Anselm's philosophy cp. A. Schurr, *Die Begründung der Philosophie durch Anselm vom Canterbury* (Stuttgart, etc., 1966). Anselm's cosmological argument is characterized by a modern proof of God's unity with the help of what are nowadays called recursive functions. One may also consult: A.P. Martinich, 'Scotus and Anselm on the Existence of God' (*Franciscan Studies*, N.S. 37 (1977)), 139-152.

2.5.3 Good introductions to Thomas Aquinas are: J. Konecsni, *A Philosophy for Living. A Sketch of Aquinate Philosophy* (Washington D.C., 1977); J. Pieper, *Guide to Thomas Aquinas* (Translated from the German) (New York, 1982); A. Kenny, *Aquinas* (New York, etc. 1980) (shows that analytical philosophy rediscovered many fruitful Aquinate distinctions and in this way the author shows Thomas' relevance for today's philosophy); B. Delfgaauw, *Thomas van Aquino. Een kritische benadering van zijn filosofie* (Bussum, 1980) (emphasizes the various Platonic elements in Thomas' philosophy); J.A. Aertsen, *Natura en Creatura. De denkweg van Thomas van Aquino* (Diss. Vrije Universiteit, Amsterdam, 1982) (emphasizes that Thomas thinks in two lines: nature and creature (grace). The author himself criticizes Thomas' doctrine of the relation of God to man, which is only an accidental relation, whereas the author asserts that all being is relational. This criticism brings him in the vicinity of process philosophy, see appendix 3); L. Elders, *de metafysica van St. Thomas van Aquino in historisch perspectief. I. Het gemeenschappelijk zijnde* (Brugge, 1982) (A very learned modern defence of the thesis: Thomas sui verus interpres. We should not go beyond Thomas); F. van Steenberghen, *Le problème de l'existence de Dieu dans les écrits de S. Thomas d'Aquin* (Louvain-la-Neuve, 1980); idem, *Le thomisme* (Paris, 1983) (defends quite the opposite: Ultraconservative Thomism compromises the real and true Thomism, because thus it is pushed back into a truly intellectual ghetto). M.F. McLean, *An Exposition and Defense of St. Thomas Aquinas' Account of the Rational Justification of Religious Belief* (Diss. University of Notre Dame).

On the occasion of the 700th anniversary of Thomas Aquinas' death some collections of articles appeared, which give an excellent survey of modern Thomism: S. Kamiński, M. Kudzialek and Z.J. Zdybicka (eds.), *W 700-Lecie Śmierci Św. Tomasza z Akwinu. Proba uwspócześniene jego filosofii* (Lublin, 1976) (with many articles in French, German and English); G. Verbeke and D. Verhelst (eds.), *Aquinas and Problems of his Time* (Louvain, 1976); A. Parel (ed.), *Calgary Aquinas Studies* (Toronto, 1978).

2.5.4 An introduction to Spinoza's thought (with an extensive descriptive bibliography): H.G. Hubbeling, *Spinoza* (Freiburg i.Br., 1978); also translated into Spanish: *Spinoza* (Barcelona, 1981). Spinoza's methods are treated in: idem, *Spinoza's Methodology* (Assen, 1964; 2nd edition, 1967) (asserts that there are two ways to salvation: an absolute and a relative one). Spinoza may also be seen as an early representative of the method of logical reconstructivism, used in the present book: idem, 'Spinoza comme précurseur du reconstructivisme logique dans son livre sur Descartes' (*Studia Leibnitiana*, XII/I (1980)), 88-95. A recent very interesting

255

work is: J. Wetlesen, *The Sage and the Way. Spinoza's Ethics of Freedom* (in a different way here too it is maintained that there are two ways to liberation in Spinoza's thought: a relative and an absolute way. The author also emphasizes structural similarities between Spinozism and Buddhism). A good orientation in Spinoza's philosophy is offered by the following collections of articles: J.G. van der Bend (ed.), *Spinoza on Knowing, Being and Freedom* (Assen, 1974); S. Hessing, (ed.), *Speculum Spinozanum 1677-1977* (London, 1977); J.B. Wilbur (ed.), *Spinoza's Metaphysics. Essays in Critical Appreciation* (Assen, 1976); J. Wetlesen (ed.), *Spinoza's Philosophy of Man. Proceedings of the Scandinavian Spinoza Symposium 1977* (Oslo. 1978); R. Kennington (ed.), *The Philosophy of Baruch Spinoza* (Washington D.C., 1980); K. Gründer and W. Schmidt-Biggeman (eds.), *Spinoza in der Frühzeit seiner religiösen Wirkung* (Heidelberg, 1984); C. de Deugd (ed.), *Spinoza's Political and Theological Thought. International Symposium under the Auspices of the Royal Netherlands Academy of Arts and Sciences Commemorating the 350th Anniversary of the Birth of Spinoza, Amsterdam 24-27 November 1982* (Amsterdam, etc., 1984). In France and Italy especially there is a lively interest in Spinoza's philosophy. A standard work is: M. Gueroult, *Spinoza, Dieu* (*Ethique*, 1) (Paris, 1968); idem, *Spinoza, L'Âme* (*Ethique*, 2) (Paris, 1974). For the historical background the translation of the following work is important: K.O. Meinsma, *Spinoza et son cercle* (Paris, 1984). The editors of this work, H. Méchoulan and P. Moreau, in collaboration with J. Ogier, G. van Suchtelen and H.G. Hubbeling added 200 pages of notes to the original work, in which a summary has been given of present-day Spinoza research. In 1984 an extensive bibliography appeared on Spinoza research, compiled by Th. van der Werf, H.J. Siebrand, and C. Westerveen, in the well-known series: *Mededelingen vanwege het Spinozahuis* (Leiden): *A Spinoza Bibliography 1971-1983.*

2.5.5 Hegel's view on the relation between philosophy and religion may be found in his *Vorlesungen über die Philosophie der Religion*, in his *Phänomenologie des Geistes* and in his *Enzyklopädie der philosophischen Wissenschaften im Grundrisse* (in the volumes 15/16, 2 and 6 of the Jubilee-edition of Hegel's *Works*, ed. by H. Glockner (Stuttgart, 4th edition, 1961ff). These works have also been translated into English: *Lectures on the Philosophy of Religion* (London, 1895), *Phenomenology of Mind* (London, 1910; 2nd edition, 1931), *Encyclopedia of Philosophy* (New York, 1959), *The Berlin Phenomenology* (Dordrecht, 1981) (this is the part of the subjective mind, with excellent explanatory notes and introduction by M.J. Petry).

For Hegel's philosophy of religion the following works are important: J.M.E. McTaggart, *Studies in Hegelian Cosmology* (Cambridge, 1901); G. Lasson, *Einführung in Hegels Religionsphilosophie* (Leipzig, 1930); R. Garaudy, *Dieu est mort. Étude sur Hegel* (Paris, 1962); B.M.G. Reardon, *Hegel's Philosophy of Religion* (London, etc. 1977); W. Jaeschke, *Die Religionsphilosophie Hegels* (Darmstadt, 1983) (gives a survey of Hegel research with respect to philosophy of religion); G. Planty-Bonjour (ed.), *Hegel et la Religion* (Paris, 1982); E.L. Fackenheim, *The Religious Dimension in Hegel's Thought* (Chicago (Ill.), 1982).

Some general introductory works: C. Daniel, *Hegel verstehen. Eine Einführung in sein Denken* (Frankfurt, etc., 1983); P. Singer, *Hegel* (Oxford, 1983).

On Hegel's dialectic one may see (cp. also the literature mentioned *sub* 2.2): J.M.E. McTaggart, *Studies in the Hegelian Dialectic* (Cambridge, 1896, 2nd ed., 1922); M. Rosen, *Hegel's Dialectic and its Criticism* (Cambridge, 1982); D. Punter, *Blake, Hegel and Dialectic* (Amsterdam, etc., 1982); W.R. Beyer (ed.), *Die Logik des Wissens und das Problem der Erziehung.* Nürnberger Hegel-Tage 1981 (Hamburg, 1982); J. Naeher, *Einführung in die idealistische Dialektik Hegels* (Opladen, 1981); P. Günter, *Der Schritt in die Dialektik. Band 1: Hegel – Der Bruch mit der Metaphysik* (Hegel's dialectic is social and historical and thus a destroyer of traditional metaphysics); L. de Vos, *Hegels Wissenschaft der Logik: Die absolute Idee. Einleitung und Kommentar* (Bonn, 1983); G. Maluschke, *Kritik und absolute Methode in Hegels Dialektik* (Bonn, 1974) (there is no purely abstract dialectic in Hegel; it is constituted by a concrete stream of concepts); W.N.A. Klever (ed.), *Hegel omstreden. Boedelscheiding na 150 jaar* (Bussum, 1983) (in this work there is *inter alia* a discussion of Hegel's dialectic).

H. Thielicke has shown that Hegel took over the formula 'God is dead' (*Gott ist tot*) from a positive Christian hymn, which shows that the expression was originally not atheistic: 'O, grosse Not! Gott selbst liegt tot'. This song was written by Johann Rist (1641), cp. *Der evangelische Glaube. Grundzüge der Dogmatik*, Bd. I (Tübingen, 1968); cp. also E. Jüngel, *Gott als Geheimnis der Welt. Zur Begründung der Theologie des Gekreuzigten im Streit zwischen Theismus und Atheismus* (Tübingen, 2nd ed., 1977), 84ff.

For the 'God is dead' theology cp.: G. Vahanian, *The Death of God. The Culture of our Post-Christian Era* (New York, 1957); T.J.J. Altizer and W. Hamilton, *Radical Theology and the Death of God* (New York, 1966); D. Sölle, *Stellvertretung. Ein Kapitel Theologie nach dem 'Tode Gottes'* (Stuttgart, etc., 1965). A survey of this movement was given in H.G. Hubbeling, 'Enkele aspecten en figuren van de "God is dood"-theologie' (*Kerk en Theologie*, 18 (1967)), 14-33.

2.6.1 The three Critiques are fundamental for the understanding of Kant. The *Kritik der reinen Vernunft* (Riga 1781, 2nd ed., 1787) has been translated several times into English. N. Kemp Smith's version (London, 1929) is the most reliable: *Immanuel Kant's Critique of Pure Reason*. The *Kritik der praktischen Vernunft* (Riga, 1788) has been best translated by L.W. Beck (New York, 1956): *Critique of Practical Reason*. The *Kritik der Urteilskraft* is also available in English: *The Critique of Judgement* (Oxford, 1952). *Die Religion innerhalb der Grenzen der blossen Vernunft* (Königsberg, 1793) is also important for our subject. It too has been translated into English: *Religion within the Limits of Reason Alone* (Chicago, 1934; 2nd ed., 1960).

For Kant's philosophy of religion the following works are important: C.C.J. Webb, *Kant's Philosophy of Religion* (Oxford, 1926); F.E. England, *Kant's Conception of God* (London, 1929); A.W. Wood, *Kant's Rational Theology* (Ithaca (N.Y.), 1978); Th. Auxter, *Kant's Moral Teleology* (Macon (Ga.), 1982).

In my view one of the best works on Kant is E. Cassirer, *Kant's Life and Thought* (New Haven (Conn.), 1981), which interprets him primarily as a moral philosopher. In owe my admiration of Kant's *Critique of Judgement* to Jaspers's lectures at the university of Basel, where I heard him on this subject in the Winter Semester 1952/53.

An interesting collection of articles, which gives a survey of the various interpretations, is: P. Laberge (ed.), *Proceedings of the Ottawa Congress on Kant in the Anglo-American and Continental Traditions*, held Oct. 10-14, 1974 (Ottawa, 1976).

2.6.2.1 The standard edition of Kierkegaard is the 2nd edition: *Samlede Vaerker*, 14 vol. (Copenhagen, 1920-1931). Practically all his works have been translated into English (Princeton, 1936ff). A good introduction to Kierkegaard's doctrine of the stages is: G. Malantschuk, *Indførelse in Kierkegaards Forfatterskab* (Copenhagen, 1979). In his *Der komische Kierkegaard* (Stuttgart, etc., 1982) F.W. Korff shows that in the religious stage some aspects of the aesthetic stage reappear. He underlines the fact that Kierkegaard very often uses cryptic sayings and that his whole attitude may be called ironic. The same is done by H.B. Vergote, *Sens et répétition. Essai sur l'ironie Kierkegaardienne* (Paris, 1982) (with an emphasis on the Copenhagen background in Kierkegaard's thinking) Vergote says that it was not Kierkegaard's intention to demonstrate anything. He tried to make it possible that the reader sees himself in the right way and thus might become his real self.

An interesting attack on Kierkegaard has been undertaken by the great Lutheran theologian K.E. Lögstrup, *Opgör med Kierkegaard* (Copenhagen, 1968): According to him the gap between Christianity and humanity in Kierkegaard is too great. Lögstrup was critized by Vera Plougmann, *Sören Kierkegaards Kristendomforstaaelse* (Copenhagen, 1975): the world and the inner soul are not separated to the extent that Lögstrup thinks. That there is, in Christian belief, a kind of complex synthesis between direct and indirect communication has been shown by P. Müller, *Meddelelsesdialektiken i Søren Kierkegaard's Philosophiske Smuler* (Copenhagen, 1979). N. Thulstrup and M. Mikulova Thulstrup are the editors of a series of collections of articles: *Bibliotheca Kierkegaardiana* (Copenhagen, 1978ff). For our subject the following volumes are especially interesting: *Kierkegaard's View of Christianity* (Vol. 1)

(1978); *The Sources and Depths of Faith in Kierkegaard* (Vol. 2) (1978); *Theological Concepts in Kierkegaard* (Vol. 5) (1980). S. Salladay wrote an interesting dissertation on Kierkegaard's religious language: *A Study of the Nature and Function of Religious Language in Relation to Kierkegaard's Theories of Subjective Truth and Indirect Communication* (Ph.D. Diss. Boston College, 1974).

I have defended my own interpretation in the article mentioned *sub* 2.4.1 (1975).

2.6.2.2 For a more extensive interpretation of Brunner see the work mentioned *sub* 1.2 and further my contribution to the collection of articles: H. Vorgrimmler and R. van der Guchte (eds.), *Bilanz der Theologie im 20. Jahrhundert. Bahnbrechende Theologen* (Freiburg i.Br., etc., 1970) (also translated into French).

Brunner's works on philosophy of religion are mentioned *sub* 1.2. The following works are also important for our purpose: *Der Mensch im Widerspruch* (Berlin, 1937; 3rd edition, Zürich, 1941); English translation: *Man in Revolt. A Christian Anthropology* (London, 1939); *Wahrheit als Begegnung* (Berlin, 1938; 2nd ed., Zürich, 1963); English translation: *The Divine-Human Encounter* (London, 1944); later: *Truth as Encounter* (London, 1964); *Dogmatik* (3 vol. (Zürich, 1946-1960); English translation: *Dogmatics* (London, 1949-1962).

2.7.1 For Karl Barth *vide* the article by W. Fürst in the collection edited by Vorgrimmler and Van der Gucht, mentioned *sub* 2.6.2.2 (1970); further: W. Härle, *Sein und Gnade. Die Ontologie in Karl Barths Kirchlicher Dogmatik* (Berlin, 1975). Barth's position is best studied in his *Kirchliche Dogmatik* (Zürich, 1932ff) (13 volumes appeared). The work has also been translated into English: *Church Dogmatics* (Edinburgh, 1936ff).

2.7.2 For Wittgenstein's philosophy of religion the following works are interesting: J.G. Møller, *Wittgenstein og Religionen* (Copenhagen, 1969); K. Studhalter, *Ethik, Religion und Lebensform bei Ludwig Wittgenstein* (Innsbruck, 1973); J. Poulain, *Logique et Religion. L'atomisme logique de L. Wittgenstein et la possibilité des propositions religieuses* (The Hague, etc., 1973); W.D. Hudson, *Wittgenstein and Religious Belief* (London, etc., 1975); A. Keightley, *Wittgenstein, Grammar and God* (London, 1976); Ch. Gudmunsen, *Wittgenstein and Buddhism* (London, 1977).

The similarities between Wittgenstein and Zen Buddhism are a central topic in a number of studies: H. Hudson, 'Wittgenstein and Zen Buddhism' (*Philosophy East and West*, 23 (1973)), 471-481 (Hudson shows the similarities and differences); C.H. Cox and J.W. Cox, 'The Mystical Experience: with an Emphasis on Wittgenstein and Zen' (*Religious Studies*, 12 (1976)), 483-491; J.V. Canfield, 'Wittgenstein and Zen' (*Philosophy*, 50 (1975)), 383-408; D.Z. Phillips, 'In Wanting to compare Wittgenstein and Zen' (*Philosophy*, 52 (1977)), 338-343 (discusses Canfield's article). R. Goodman thinks that there are some similarities between Wittgenstein and Taoism, for in both ways of thought the reader is given a new insight in the world, in both ways philosophy is an activity, both ways have a dialectical structure and for both ways peace is the ultimate goal: 'Style, Dialectic, and the Aim of Philosophy in Wittgenstein and the Taoists' (*Journal of Chinese Philosophy*, 3 (1976)), 145-157.

In philosophy of religion the followers of Wittgenstein II are very often called Wittgensteinian fideists (D.Z. Phillips, and others, cp. *sub* 1.1). This kind of philosophy has been discussed in several articles. We mention: A. Brunton, 'A Model for the Religious Philosophy of D.Z. Phillips' (*Analysis*, 31 (1970)), 43-48; L.B. Keeling and M.F. Morelli, 'Beyond Wittgensteinian Fideism. An Examination of John Hick's analysis of Religious Faith' (*International Journal of Philosophy of Religion*, 8 (1977)), 250-262; K. Nielsen, 'The Coherence of Wittgensteinian Fideism' (*Sophia*, 11 (1972)), 4-12; A. Olding, 'D.Z. Phillips and Religious Language' (*Sophia*, 16 (1977)), 23-28; T.B. Ommen, 'Wittgensteinian Fideism and Theology' (*Horizons*, 7 (1980)), 183-204; P. Sherry, *Religion, Truth and Language-Games* (London, 1977).

Besides the mystical passages in the *Tractatus*, Wittgenstein's view on religion is best studied by reading his 'Lecture on Ethics' (*Philosophical Review*, 74 (1965)), his *Lectures and Conver-*

sations on Aesthetics, Psychology and Religious Belief (ed. by C. Barrett) (Oxford, 1966) and his *Remarks on Frazer's Golden Bough* (Retford, 1979).

In my introduction to Wittgenstein *Inleiding tot het denken van Wittgenstein* (Amsterdam, 1965, 2nd. ed., 1969) I emphasized the religious trend in Wittgenstein's thought. The same was done by C.A. van Peursen, *Ludwig Wittgenstein* (Baarn, 1965). This was vehemently contradicted by W.F. Hermans, *Wittgenstein in de mode* (Amsterdam, 1967). Later documents affirmed Van Peursen's and my position!

2.7.3 Van der Leeuw's main works (for our purpose) are: *Phänomenologie der Religion* (Tübingen, 1933; 2nd extended ed., 1956; 4th ed., 1977); English translation: *Religion in Essence and Manifestation. A Study in Phenomenology* (London, 1938); *Wegen en Grenzen. Studie over de verhouding van religie en kunst* (Amsterdam, 1932; 2nd extended and revised ed., 1948; 3rd ed. revised by E.E. Smelik, 1955); also translated into English: *Sacred and Profane Beauty. The Holy in Art* (London, 1963); *Inleiding tot de theologie* (Amsterdam, 1935; 2nd ed., 1948); *Sacramentstheologie* (Nijkerk, 1949). About him cp: J. Waardenburg, *Reflections on the Study of Religion, Including an Essay on the Work of Gerardus van der Leeuw* (The Hague, etc. 1978); H.G. Hubbeling, 'Das Heilige und das Schöne. Gerardus van der Leeuws Anschauungen über das Verhältnis von Religion und Kunst' (*Neue Zeitschrift für systematische Theologie und Religionsphilosophie*, 25 (1983)), 1-19 (with a summary in English); H.G. Hubbeling, 'Divine Presence in Ordinary Life. Gehardus van der Leeuw's Twofold Method in his Thinking on Art and Religion' (*Mededelingen der Koninklijke Nederlandse Akademie van Wetenschappen, afd. Letterkunde*, Nieuwe Reeks, Deel 49 – No. 1, 1986).

2.8 For Kierkegaard cp. Appendix 7 and my article mentioned *sub* 2.6.2.1 (1975). That Spinoza may be considered a forerunner of my method of logical reconstructivism may be seen in the article mentioned *sub* 2.5.4 (1980). A defence of Islam along similar lines as given in the text may be found in: I.R.Al Fārūqī, 'On the Metaphysics of Ethics in Islam' (*Listening*, 14 (1979)), 25-43. For Zen Buddhism one may see: F. Vos and E. Zürcher, *Spel zonder snaren* (Deventer, s.d. (= prob. 1964)). A brilliant (logical!) defence of the possibility of a pure mystical experience without (logical) thinking has been given by J. Debrot in her lecture: 'Zelf-Verifiërende ervaring is objectloze ervaring' (Archives of the section 'Systematic Theology', Faculty of Theology, University of Groningen). For Hindu mysticism, cp. among others M. Eliade, *Patanjali et le Yoga* (Paris, 1962) and H. Zimmer, *Philosophies of India* (New York, 1957).

2.9 Van Baaren's argumentation is beautifully expounded in his lecture 'Religieuze ervaring' (Archives of the section 'Systematic Theology', Faculty of Theology, University of Groningen).

A list of concepts which had originally a religious meaning can be found in the article of C. Watkins, 'Indo-European and the Indo-Europeans' in: W. Morris (ed.), *The American Heritage Dictionary of the English Language* (Boston, 1973), 1502ff. I myself compared this with the standard work by J. Pokorny, *Indogermanisches Etymologisches Wörterbuch* (Bern, etc., 1959) with the result mentioned in the text.

The quotation from Jan van Ruusbroec has been taken from (*Vanden Blinckenden Steen*, published in *Werken* III (Mechelen, etc., 1932), 32. The quotation from Gysbert Japicx has been taken from *Wurken* (Bolsward, 1966), 109.

The works of Ramsey and W. de Pater are mentioned *sub* 1.1. The relevance of modern linguistics for the analysis of religious language is treated by De Pater in (1971), 109-184. The quotation can be found on p. 175.

An outstanding work on religious language is: A. Jeffner, *Study of Religious Language* (Bristol, 1972). The study of the language of stories is important in order to understand biblical language. In his article 'Story Shapes that tell a World. Biblical, Homeric and Modern Narrative' (*Christian Schol. Review*, 9 (1980)), 291-316, P. Borgman shows that the shape of narratives reveal a world view. The narratives of David give an 'open' world view, but those of Homer have a 'closed' world view. T.P. Burke, 'The Theologian as Storyteller and Philosopher' (*Horizons*, 4 (1977)), 207-215 is of the opinion that theology translates biblical stories into philosophy. But in this way both the stories and philosophy are mutilated. A better task for theology is to evaluate the stories in the light of our modern religious experience.

The language of prophets and prophecy is treated in A. Lascaris, 'Profetisch spreken' (*Tijdschrift voor Theologie*, 11 (1971)), 3-29. He is critically towards modern linguistic analysis. N. Rotenstreich, 'On Prophetic Consciousness' (*Journal of Religion*, 54 (1974)), 185-198 shows that the prophets teach that God is uncognizable, which refers to God's numinosity. He is nevertheless understandable, which refers to God's pathos, his love towards us.

The language of prayer has been dealt with in: E. Stump, 'Petitionary Prayer' (*American Philosophical Quaterly*, 16 (1979)), 81-91. Stump defends petitionary prayer. At first sight petitionary prayer is impossible, because either man asks for something good, and then God will give it to him anyhow, or he asks for something wrong and then God will not give it to him. But Stump shows that we need to use personal language and that this is meaningful also in the case of petitionary prayer. R. Young, 'Petitioning God' (*ibidem*, 11 (1974)), 193-201 is of the opinion that a petitionary prayer is possible both in a deterministic and in a non-deterministic world view.

3.1 Literature on the arguments for God's existence may be found in the bibliographies mentioned *sub* 1.1. An historical survey has been given by H. de Vos, *De bewijzen voor Gods bestaan. Een systematisch-historische studie* (Groningen, 1971). A recent work is: J.L. Mackie, *The Miracle of Theism. Arguments for and against the Existence of God* (Oxford, 1982). A special issue of *Wijsgerig Perspectief op maatschappij en wetenschap*, 24 (1983/1984) (H.G. Hubbeling (ed.), *Godsbewijzen*) had the arguments for God's existence as its subject.

Some studies of the nature and relevance of the proofs of God's existence are: D. Burrell, 'The Performative Character of the "Proofs" for the Existence of God' (*Listening*, 13 (1978)), 20-26; D.M. Holley, 'Should Believers Be Interested in Arguments for God's Existence?' (*American Philosophical Quarterly*, 20 (1983)), 383-389; F.B. Dilley, 'Are Conclusive Proofs Irrelevant to Religion?' (*Thomist*, 39 (1975)), 727-740; idem, 'Fool-Proof Proofs of God?' (*International Journal of Philosophy of Religion*, 8 (1977)), 18-35. Dilley's opinion that the proofs are relevant to philosophy of religion, because if they are valid and sound a reference to religious experience is no longer subjective, is also defended in the present book.

3.1.2 Anselm's ontological argument can be found in his *Proslogion*, chapters 2 and 3; Hartshorne's argument in his *The Logic of Perfection and Other Essays in Neoclassical Metaphysics* (LaSalle (Ill.), 1962). 50ff. For Breedenburg cp. my article 'Zur frühen Spinozarezeption in den Niederlanden' in: K. Gründer and W. Schmidt-Biggeman (1984) mentioned *sub* 2.5.4. For Spinoza cp. my book mentioned *sub* 2.5.4 (1964); 2nd ed. 1967), 86-102. The quotation has been taken from his letter to Jarig Jelles, *Epistola* 40 (*Opera*, ed. C. Gebhardt, Heidelberg, 1924), IV, 198. Spinoza's identification of *perfectio* and *realitas* may be found in *Ethica*, II, def. 6.

The ontological argument has also been given a new stimulus by Plantinga, cp. his work mentioned *sub* 1.1 (1974). He shows quite convincingly that the concept of a being greater than which nothing can be thought of is not self-contradictory. In Plantinga's spirit A. Vos wrote his excellent dissertation *Kennis en noodzakelijkheid. Een kritische analyse van het absolute evidentialisme in wijsbegeerte en theologie* (with a summary in English). There was a lively discussion of this book in *Nederlands Theologisch Tijdschrift* in 1982 and 1983. W. Stenfert Kroese is writing a dissertation on Anselm's argument in which he uses the Quine system of logic, which is stricter than the one used in the present book (and in Hartshorne's and Plantinga's expositions!). He is able to show that Anselm's argument is valid in that system too. H.J. Siebrand writes a dissertation on the reception of Spinoza in the Netherlands, in which he also deals with Breedenburg: *Spinoza and the Netherlands. An Inquiry into the Early Reception of his Philosophy of Religion* (Assen, 1987). See further Vos's article 'De ontologische argumenten' in (1983/1984) (mentioned *sub* 3.1), 158-163. W.L. Rowe wrote an interesting article which provoked a lively discussion: 'The Ontological Argument and Question-Begging' (*International Journal for Philosophy of Religion*, 7 (1976)), 425-432. He argued that if Anselm says that God is a possible being, then he says more than only that the concept of God is not self-contradictory. And thus he presupposes already an existing being that is supremely great, but this he had to prove so that his argument is question-begging. In my view— see the text – there is a great difference between the concept of God as non-contradictory (= a modality *de dicto*) and that of God as a possible being (= a modality *de re*) in S_4. But this no longer applies to the system S_5, a system that Anselm must presuppose anyhow. Rowe's article was given a lively discussion. cp.: S.T. Davis, 'Does the Ontological Argument Beg the Question' (*idem*, 7 (1976)), 433-442; idem, 'Anselm and Question-Begging. A Reply to William Rowe's 'Comments on Professor Davis "Does the Ontological Argument Beg the Question" ' (*idem*, 7 (1976)), 448-457; P.J. Lopston, 'Anselm, Meinong, and the Ontological Argument' (*idem*, 11 (1980)), 185-194; W.L. Rowe, 'Comments on Professor Davis' "Does the Ontological Argument Beg the Question" ' (*idem*, 7 (1976)), 443-447; W.J. Wainwright, 'The Ontological Argument Question-Begging and Professor Rowe' (*idem*, 9 (1978)), 254-257; S.T. Davis, 'Lopston on Anselm and Rowe' (*idem*, 13 (1982)), 219-224.

In *Ratio*, 18 (1976), 85-89 R.J. Richman argued that Anselm's ontological argument is incoherent: 'A Serious Look at the Ontological Argument'. Existence *in intellectu* and existence *in intellectu et in re* are both different and identical and thus incoherent. W.J. Wainwright, 'On an Alleged Incoherence in Anselm's Argument. A Reply to Robert Richman'(*idem*, 20 (1978)), 147-148 defends Anselm: Richman confuses logically equivalent states with identical states. Moreover, he does not distinguish between the statements 'God exists *in intellectu*' and 'God exists *only in intellectu*'.

Other recent studies of Anselm's ontological argument include: G. Schulfreider, *An Introduction to Anselm's Argument* (Philadelphia (Pa.), 1978); J. Hopkins, 'On an Alleged Definitive Interpretation of Proslogion 2-4. A Discussion of G. Schulfreider's *An Introduction to Anselm's Argument*' (*Southern Journal of Philosophy*, 19 (1981)), 129-139. A. Poppi, 'La struttura elenctica dell' argomento anselmiano' (*Verifiche*, 10 (1981)), 195-203; H.J. Oesterle, 'Karl Barths These über den Gottesbeweis des Anselm von Canterbury' (*Neue Zeitschrift für systematische Theologie und Religionsphilosophie*, 23 (1981)), 91-107; W. Rentz, 'Die Analyse und Interpretation des *argumentum Anselmi* von Heinrich Scholz' (*idem*, 21 (1979)), 71-91; P.E. Devine, ' "Exists" and Saint Anselm's Argument' (*Grazer Philosophical Studies*, 3 (1977)), 143-168 (some people think that if we speak of God's existence and thus refer to it we have already presupposed this existence and that therefore Anselm's argument begs the question. This is, however, not true, for we can very well speak about and refer to non-existing objects); C. Diamond, 'Riddles and Anselm's Riddle' (*Aristotelian Society*, 51 (1977)), 143-168 (treats Anselm's argument as a Wittgensteinian riddle).

Recent studies on Spinoza's argument are: J.N. Chubb, 'Spinoza's arguments for the Existence of God' (*Indian Journal of Philosophy*, 17 (1968)), 116-125: Spinoza concludes incorrectly from a proven mathematical (logical) existence of God to a real existence. This is exactly the same objection that had been raised by Nieuwentyt against Spinoza (see *sub* 3.1.4). D. Garrett, 'Spinoza's Ontological Argument' (*Philosophical Review*, 88 (1979)), 198-223: Although Spinoza claims that he has given an ontological proof, many scholars say that he indeed bases himself on a private rational perception. According to Garrett the four proofs are interrelated variants of one argument. All four are a priori, but they are cosmological proofs, because they make use of the principle of sufficient reason. The proofs are valid. J.M. Humber, 'Spinoza's Proof of God's Necessary Existence' (*Modern Schoolman*, 49 (1972)), 221-233: Spinoza's proofs are in reality one proof and this is more empirical than ontological. C.E. Jarrett, 'Spinoza's Ontological Argument' (*Canadian Journal of Philosophy*, 6 (1976)), 685-692: Spinoza's argument has two fundamental presuppositions: (i) It is possible that God exists; (ii) It is necessary that if God exists, then He exists necessarily. Now, according to Jarrett, (ii) can be proved in S_5. But (i) is still to be proved and Leibniz had already drawn our attention to this fact. The reader may see that these two presuppositions are exactly

Hartshorne's presuppositions too, (ii) being 'Anselm's principle' and (i) his 'central thesis' (*vide* appendix 3).

Hartshorne's ontological argument has also been discussed in various ways: R. Brecher, 'Hartshorne's Modal Argument for the Existence of God' (*Ratio*, 17 (1975)), 140-146: Hartshorne concludes incorrectly from a modal state to a real state or in other words, he does not distinguish between modality *de dicto* and *de re*; but Hartshorne has faced this objection (see appendix 3). Brecher has been opposed by J.R. Baker, 'What is not Wrong with a Hartshornean Modal Proof?' (*Southern Journal of Philosophy*, 18 (1980)), 99-106; H. Craighead, 'Non-Being and Hartshorne's Concept of God' (*Process Studies*, 1 (1971)), 9-28: the God that has been proved by Hartshorne can only be the God of process philosophy and moreover: the argument presupposes the cosmological proof. In my view Hartshorne has faced this latter objection sufficiently (*vide* appendix 3) and the first objection is irrelevant to Hartshorne. G.A. Johnston, 'Hartshorne's Arguments against Empirical Evidence for Necessary Existence. An Evaluation' (*Religious Studies*, 13 (1977)), 175-187: it is certainly possible to refute God's existence in an empirical way and moreover it is also possible to prove empirically a necessary existence. W.A. Lenhardt, 'Hartshorne's Presuppositions' (*Canadian Journal of Philosophy*, 4 (1974)), 345-349: if we give a semantical interpretation of the necessary operator, the argument becomes either trivial (and superfluous) or invalid. In my view one must be very careful in semantical interpretations. Several interpretations of the necessary functor are possible: logical, physical, metaphysical, historical, etc. In my view the necessary functor in the arguments for God's existence must be given an interpretation of metaphysical necessity. And then Hartshorne's argument is valid and non-trivial (see appendix 3 and our expositions in the present book). Further on Hartshorne: C.W. Lewis, Jr., *Sense and Nonsense. The Ontological Argument for the the Existence of God in the Thought of Charles Hartshorne* (Diss. Ph.D., University of Georgia, 1973); R.D. Schoener, *Anselm Revisited. A Study of the Role of the Ontological Argument in the Writings of Karl Barth and Charles Hartshorne* (Leiden, 1974); G.L. Goodwin, *The Ontological Argument of Charles Hartshorne* (Missoula Montana, 1978); P. Grim, 'Plantinga, Hartshorne and the Ontological Argument' (*Sophia*, 20 (1982)), 12-16; K. Surin, 'The Self-Existence of God. Hartshorne and Classical Theism' (*idem*, 20 (1982)), 17-36. For Plantinga one may see: M. Corrado, 'Plantinga on Necessity "De Re" ' (*Logique et Analyse*, 17 (1974)), 445-452 (Plantinga operates with proper names with necessary properties. This is doubtful); P. Grim, 'Plantinga's God and Other Monstrosities' (*Religious Studies*, 15 (1979)), 91-97 (Grim wants to play the role of Gaunilo and demonstrate the existence of a maximal uniformed being, special Gryphons, etc.); R.A. Oakes, 'God, Electrons and Professor Plantinga' (*Philosophical Studies*, 25 (1974)), 143-146 (the being of electrons, although they exist from eternity, is a contingent truth and does not refute Plantinga's argument) (according to modern astronomy, the 'big bang theory', even electrons do not exist from eternity, but I think Oakes is right in the other respects of his argument. W.B. Johnston, *Plantinga's Modal Argument for the Existence of God* (Diss. Ph.D., State University of New York at Albany, 1980).

For a semantical approach cp. also: J.I. Friedman, 'Kripkean Necessity and the Ontological Argument' in H.G. Hubbeling, *et alii* (1982) (mentioned *sub* 1.2), 173-183.

3.1.3 The cosmological arguments of Thomas Aquinas can be found in his *Summa Theologica*, I, qu. 2, art. 2. One may further see: H.G. Hubbeling, 'A Modern Reconstruction of the Cosmological Argument' in H.G. Hubbeling *et alii*, (1982) (mentioned *sub* 1.2), 39-46; P.K. Policki, 'Zum Problem des Beweises *ex motu* der Existenz Gottes' (*idem*, 185-189) (gives a modern reconstruction and improvement of the famous proof *ex motu* of the 'father' of modern logical reconstructions of the arguments for God's existence: J. Salamucha. The article of Policki was originally in Polish. I received it in an inadequate German translation, but corrected it in accordance with the Polish original); H.G. Hubbeling, 'Het kosmologisch Godsbewijs' (1983/1984) (mentioned *sub* 3.1), 163-167. J. Hick, *Arguments for the Existence of God* (London, 1970) gives a survey of the modern discussions. His important exposition on the 'self-explanatory and the non-self-explanatory' may be found on p. 46ff. In his *The*

Cosmological Argument. A Reassessment (Springfield, 1972) B.R. Reichenbach gives a defence of the two variants. His refutation of Kant's reduction of the cosmological to the ontological argument can be found on p. 125ff, although he admits that one may possibly need to refer to the ontological argument in order to fill in the concept of an *ens necessarium*. A defence of the first variant with the help of mathematics and natural science has been given by W.L. Craig, *The KALAM Cosmological Argument* (London, 1979). W.L. Rowe, however, is of the opinion that the cosmological argument is, considered as a proof, insufficient. But it may function as a justification for the belief in God, because it is reasonable to *believe* in the cosmological argument: *The Cosmological Argument* (Princeton, 1975).

Swinburne's plea for a cumulative argumentation by which the theistic concept of God is more probable than the other alternatives can be found in his work (1979) (mentioned *sub* 1.1). He also proves the probability of the principle of sufficient reason (ground). For Hartshorne's contribution one may see appendix 3. The nice example of the Hilbert hotel is to be found in G. Ganow, *One, Two, Three... Infinity* (London, 1946), 17. The theorem that a directed ordered set with a finite number of elements must have a last element, has been proved by H. Gericke, *Theorie der Verbände* (Mannheim, 1967), 38.

Also the cosmological argument has been energetically discussed during the past 15 years. I may refer here to the extensive bibliography on this subject in T.L. Miethe, 'The Cosmological Argument' (*New Scholasticism*, 52 (1978)), 185-305. The author says correctly: 'The era is past when all metaphysical statements or arguments for God's existence can simply be dismissed as silly or senseless, because they do not meet a preestablished criterion of verifiability'. We may call the reader's attention to the following discussions: R.B. Edwards, 'Another Visit to the "Third way" ' (*idem*, 47 (1973)), 100-104, reasons critically with respect to the argument: If each of the parts of nature is contingent, then the whole of nature is contingent. Now, each of the parts of nature is contingent, therefore the whole of nature is contingent. There are no counter-examples of a necessary whole with contingent parts. This is exactly Breedenburg's critique of Spinoza! (see *sub* 3.1.2.). The critique, if valid, only affects a God who is identical with nature. L.H. Cox opposes Edward's reasoning in 'Composition and the Cosmological Argument' (*idem*, 48 (1974)), 365-370. He rightly states that from the contingency of the parts one is not permitted to conclude to the contingency of the whole. H. Craighead, 'Edwards, Cox and Cosmological Composition' (*idem*, 45 (1976)), 122-124, takes the side of Edwards: In his view it is true that the contingency of the parts leads to the contingency of the whole. Of course, if the parts of a whole have a certain property, we may not infer from this fact, that the whole has the same property. But with existence the case is different. Here contingency of the parts leads to the contingency of the whole. I do not think that this argumentation is convincing. It is at least thinkable that something exists necessarily (i.e. in all possible worlds) and that all or some parts of it are contingent. J.F. Knasas, ' "Necessity" in the Tertia Via' (*idem*, 52 (1978)), 373-394, argues that Thomas indeed saw the difference between a modality *de re* and one *de dicto*. A logically necessary being is not logically absurd, if what the proposition is designating is subsistent existence. Furthermore, it is not necessary to divide factual (real) necessary existence and logical necessary existence in watertight compartments. In this I think the author is right. It depends on the modal system (S_4 or S_5)! L. Leahy, 'Contingency in the Cosmological Argument' (*Religious Studies*, 12 (1976)), 93-100, combats Russell's argument: The cosmological argument is said to run parallel to the argument: 'every being has a mother, therefore the human race has a mother' and this is obviously invalid. According to Leahy, however, the world is not only a class of particulars. It is a *system* of particulars including their relations. And this system is infected by the contingency of the parts. The universe as a whole is not a self-sufficient reason for the being of any of its parts. Cp. further: J.D. White, *God and the World. An Essay on the Cosmological Argument* (Diss. Ph.D., Syracuse University , 1978); H.A. Meynell, *The Intelligible Universe. A Cosmological Argument* (Totowa, (N.J.), 1982); W.L. Rowe, *Philosophy of Religion. An Introduction* (Encino (Calf.), 1978); C. Dore, 'Rowe on the Cosmological Argument' (*International Journal for Philosophy of Religion*, 14 (1983)), 25-31.

3.1.4 For this argument cp. A.F. Sanders 'Cumulativiteit en redelijkheid: het teleologisch argument' (1983/1984) (mentioned *sub* 3.1), 167-172. Some classical works in the field of Physico-Theology are: J. Ray, *The Wisdom of God Manifested in the Works of the Creation* (London, 1691); W. Derham, *Astro-Theology or a Demonstration of the Being and the Attributes of God from a Survey of Heavens* (London, 1714). A standard work that gave a survey of the whole of empirical science of his day and in addition proofs so that we may read God's hand in this whole fabric, is: B. Nieuwentyt, *Het regt gebruik der Wereldbeschouwingen ter overtuiginge van ongodisten en ongelovigen* (Amsterdam, 1715). The book has been translated into English: *The Religious Philosopher* (London, 1718; 4th ed. 1730). Another important work of Nieuwentyt is: *Gronden van Zekerheid of de regte betoogwyze der wiskundigen, so in het Denkbeeldige als in het Zakelyke: Ter Weerlegging van Spinozas Denkbeeldig Samenstel. En ter aanleiding van eene sakelyke Wysbegeerte* (Amsterdam, 1720). This is a very modern book. Nieuwentyt defends the fundamental distinction between pure and applied mathematics, the principal unity of logic and mathematics, the gap between logic and mathematics on the one hand and empirical sciences on the other hand, etc. Cp. on him: E.W. Beth, 'Nieuwentyt's Significance for the Philosophy of Science' (*Synthese*, 9 (1955)), 447-453; C.B. Boyer, *The History of Calculus* (New York, 1959), 213; J. Bots, *Tussen Descartes en Darwin. Geloof en Natuurwetenschap in de 18e eeuw in Nederland* (Assen, 1972), 16-48; M.J. Petry, *Nieuwentyt's Criticism of Spinoza* (Mededelingen XL vanwege het Spinozahuis) (Leiden, 1979).

Taylor's proof may be found in his *Metaphysics* (Englewood Cliffs, 1963), 99ff. See also: R.J. Glass, 'Taylor's Argument from Design' (*Personalist*, 54 (1973)), 94-99.

Rightly the teleological argument caught less attention than the ontological and cosmological ones. Still it would be impossible to mention all the articles written on this argument. I think that the following are important: B.L. Clarke, 'The Argument from Design. A Piece of Abductive Reasoning' (*International Journal for Philosophy of Religion*, (5 (1974)), 65-78; M. Kraft, 'Thinking the Physico-Teleological Proof' (*idem*, 12 (1981)), 65-74; B.L. Clarke, 'The Argument from Design' (*American Journal of Theology and Philosophy*, 1 (1980)), 98-108; G. Doore, 'The Argument from Design. Some Better Reasons for Agreeing with Hume' (*Religious Studies*, 16 (1980)), 145-161; R. Hambourger, 'The Argument from Design' in: C. Diamond (ed.), *Intention and Intentionality* (Ithaca, 1979), 109-131; K.V. Nelson, 'Evolution and the Argument from Design' (*Religious Studies*, 14 (1978), 423-443; G. Schlesinger, 'Probabilistic Arguments for Divine Design' (*Philosophia* (Israel), 3 (1973)), 1-16; G. Priest, 'The Argument from Design' (*Australian Journal of Philosophy*, 59 (1981)), 422-431.

3.1.5 For the various arguments: *vide* H. de Vos (1971) (mentioned *sub* 3.1). See further for the moral argument: H.J. Adriaanse, 'Het morele Godsbewijs, in het bijzonder bij Kant (1982/1984) (mentioned *sub* 3.1), 173-180. A common objection against Kant's argumentation is (cp. especially Adriaanse's article) that if it is impossible to know God along speculative lines (in a theoretical way), it must also be impossible to know him via a moral argument. We find this objection again in: P. Byrne, 'Kant's Moral Proof of the Existence of God' (*Scottish Journal of Philosophy*, 32 (1979), 333-343. I do not think that this objection is correct. If certain factual states of affairs are necessary in order that valid moral propositions are possible and if we accept the validity of these propositions, we have to conclude to certain factual states of affairs. This is not impossible a priori and therefore there is no a priori inconsistency in Kant's reasoning. One may see further: C.R. Kordig, 'A Deontic Argument for God's Existence' (*Nous*, 15 (1981), 207-208; P. Grim, 'Against a Deontic Argument for God's Existence' (*Analysis*, 42 (1982)), 171-174 (Criticizes Kordig's article); J.B. Stearns, 'The Moral Argument' (*Idealistic Studies*, 8 (1978)), 193-205.

For the arguments from religious experience, *vide* the literature mentioned *sub* 2.4 and 2.4.2. A. Vos gave a new version of the epistemological argument (1981) (mentioned *sub* 3.1.2).

4. The various results of science of religion have been taken, among other works, from C.J. Bleeker and G. Widengren (ed.), *Historia Religionum. Handbook for the History of Religions* (2 vol.) (Leiden, 1969-1971); J. Asmussen and L. Laessnøe in cooperation with C. Colpe (ed.), *Handbuch der Religionsgeschichte* (3 vol.) (Göttingen, s.d. (= 1971-1974)); G. van der Leeuw (ed.), *De godsdiensten der wereld* (2 vol.) (Amsterdam, 1940/41).

For the primitive religions the following works are – among others – very important: G. van der Leeuw, *De primitieve mens en de religie. Anthropologische studie* (Groningen, 1937); idem, *L'homme primitif et la religion. Etude anthropologique* (Paris, 1940); idem, *Der Mensch und die Religion. Anthropologischer Versuch* (Basel, 1940); Th.P. van Baaren, *Wij mensen. Religie en wereldbeschouwing bij schriftloze volken* (Utrecht, 1960).

4.1 The details of the Ngadu-Dyaks can be found in Van Baaren (1960) (mentioned *sub* 4), 59; also in H. Schärer, 'Die Vorstellungen der Ober- und Unterwelt bei den Ngadju Dajak von Süd-Borneo' in: H. Hoogenberk, *Cultureel Indië* (Leiden, 1948), 221-231. References to the high Gods in Van Baaren, *o.c.*, 60ff. Parrinder's observations are found in the work (1969-1971) (mentioned *sub* 4), II, 557. Father Schmidt defended an original monotheism in his work, which comprehended many volumes: *Der Ursprung der Gottesidee* (Münster, 1921ff). Ramanuya's personal mysticism is explained by A.M. Esnoul, *Ramanuja et la mystique vishnouite* (Paris, 1964). The thesis that this personalism is rooted in a Dravidian background is to be found on p. 13ff. Cp. further: S.S. Raghavachar, 'Concept of Moksha According to Sri Ramanuja' (*Vedanta Kesari*, 65 (1978)), 384-391.

The story with the elephant can be found in H. Zimmer (1957) (mentioned *sub* 2.8), 19f. The comparison between Sankara and Eckhart stems from R. Otto, *West-Östliche Mystik* (Gotha, 1926). Tillich's concept of a 'God above God' can be found in his *The Courage to Be* (New Haven, 1952).

For Ruusbroec, cp. H.G. Hubbeling, *Logica en ervaring in Spinoza's en Ruusbroecs mystiek* (Mededelingen XXXI vanwege het Spinozahuis) (Leiden, 1975). The concepts of time and eternity in the Australian religion can be found in T.G.H. Strehlow (1969-1971) (mentioned *sub* 4), II, 606-627, especially 610-615.

See further: J.E. Caraway, *God as Dynamic Actuality* (Washington, 1978); B.Z. Cooper, *The Idea of God. A Whiteheadian Critique of St. Thomas Aquinas' Concept of God*, The Hague, 1974; N. Kretzmann, *Eternity*, (Cornell University, 1975); J.Y. Lee, *God Suffers for Us. A Systematic Inquiry into a Concept of Divine Passibility* (The Hague, 1974); C.R. Michael, *A Comparison of the God-Talk of Thomas Aquinas and Charles Hartshorne*, (Diss. St. Mary's Seminary and University, 1975); G.S. Nordgulen, *The Reality of God. A Study of the Arguments for the Relational Existence of God* (Diss. Ph.D., Claremont Graduate School, 1966); N. Pike, *God and Timelessness* (London, 1970); C. Stead, *Divine Substance* (Oxford, 1977); K. Ward, *The Concept of God* (Oxford, 1974); E.E. Harris, *Atheism and Theism* (New Orleans, 1977) (defends a kind of Spinozistic theism); G. Keil, *Gott als absolute Grenzüberschreitung* (2nd ed., Marburg/Lahn, 1982); L. Kolakowski, *Religion. If there is no God... On God, the Devil, Sin and other Worries of the so-called Philosophy of Religion* (London, 1982) (Even if there is no God, philosophy still needs religion); F. Sonntag and M.D. Bryant, *God. The Contemporary Discussion* (New York, 1982); J.C. Eaton and A. Loades, *For God and Clarity. New Essays in Honor of Austin Farrer* (Allison Park (Pa.), 1983).

4.2 The story of the Ila of Zambia can be found in Parrinder (1969-1971) (mentioned *sub* 4) II, 569. For the analysis of *Job* one may see the various commentaries and also: Ph. Nemo, *Job et l'excès du mal* (Paris, 1978). For suffering in Buddhism cp. I. Schoegl, 'Suffering in Zen-Buddhism' (*Theory to Theory*, 11 (1977)), 217-277. Reichenbach has pointed out, that in a theodicy it is always the problem that we do not have generally accepted criteria to decide which world is better or to identify a 'best possible world'. It is always possible to look for a world with more beings, or better beings or more optimistic beings, etc. Moreover, God is primarily ontologically good and not morally good, cp. B.R. Reichenbach, *Evil and a good God* (Bronx (N.Y.), 1982); cp. also his articles: 'Natural Evils and Natural Laws. A Theodicy for Natural Evils' (*International Philosophical Quaterly*, 16 (1976)), 179-196; idem, 'Must God create the Best Possible World?' (*idem*, 19 (1979)), 203-212; B.R. Reichenbach, 'Why is God good?' (*Journal of Religion*, 60 (1980)), 51-66. Cp. further: A. Plantinga, *God, Freedom and Evil* (New York, 1974); D.L. Ratsch, *God, Freedom and Plantinga* (Diss. Ph.D., University of Massachusetts, 1975); T.R. White, *God and Evil. A Study of the Problem of Evil* (Diss. Ph.D., New York University, 1979); J.S. Feinberg, *Theologies and Evil* (Washington D.C., 1979); P.T. Geach, *Providence and Evil* (Cambridge, 1977); D.R. Griffin, *God, Power and Evil. A Process Theodicy* (Philadelphia (Pa.), 1976); W. Sparn, *Leiden, Erfahrung und Denken. Materialien zum Theodizeeproblem* (München, 1980).

4.3 The quotations from Pindar and the Homeric hymn to Demeter stem from the contribution by A.W.H. Adkins (1969-1971) (mentioned *sub* 4), I, 433. The theory of the Dema deity is devised by the German scholar A.E. Jensen, *Mythus und Kult bei Naturvölkern. Religionswissenschaftliche Betrachtungen* (Wiesbaden, 1960); idem, *Die getötete Gottheit. Weltbild einer frühen Kultur* (Stuttgart, etc., 1966). The Avatāras of Vishnu are described by R.N. Dandekar (1969-1971) (mentioned *sub* 4), II, 302ff.

Cp. further: H.D. Lewis, *Jesus in the Faith of the Christians* (London, 1981); T. Moretti-Constanzi, *La fede sapiente e il Cristo storico* (Assisi, 1981); G. Puente, *Messianisme et Idéologie* (Paris, 1983).

4.4 The story of the Kono from Sierra Leone can be found in Parrinder (1969-1971) (mentioned *sub* 4), II, 570; cp. also: W. De Mahieu, *Structures et Symboles* (Louvain, 1980) (where the Kono culture is treated). The quotation from the Australian religion stems from Strehlow (1969-1971) (mentioned *sub* 4), II, 615. The idea that a dead person may meet his soul in the figure of a beautiful young girl can be found in the younger parts of Avesta: Hadokt Nask, 2.1. A biblical defence of the universality of salvation has been given by W. Michaelis, *Versöhnung des Alls. Botschaft von der Gnade Gottes* (Gumligen, 1950). The Mohammedan discussion on the eternity of the punishment in hell can be found in A. Schimmel (1969-1971)(mentioned *sub* 4), II, 187. Buddha's speech about Nirvana is in Udama VIII, 1-4. Cp. further A. Waymann (1969-1971) (mentioned *sub* 4), II, 449f.

The hypothesis of spiritism has been defended in a scientific way by the late Utrecht professor for parapsychology, W. Tenhaeff, *Het Spiritisme* (The Hague, 3rd ed., 1965). A classical work in this field is: W.H. Myers, *Human Personality and its Survival of Bodily Death* (New York, 1961; 1st ed., 1903). A good survey can be found in: H. Bender (ed.), *Parapsychologie. Entwicklung, Ergebnisse, Probleme* (Darmstadt, 1966), 543-604. For C.D. Broad, cp. his *Lectures on Psychical Research* (London, 1962). For Ducasse, cp. his *A Critical Examination of the Belief in a Life after Death* (Springfield (Ill.), 1961). For H.D. Lewis cp. his *Philosophy of Religion* (London, 1965) and his *Persons and Life after Death* (London, 1978).

For our problem the view of the relationship between mind and body is also relevant. Here we have various theories: materialism (which bluntly denies a possibility of life after death; e.g. Büchner, Vogt, Moleschott), dialectical materialism (Marx, Engels, Lenin *et al.* Here also this possibility is denied), qualified materialism (spiritism is of this kind. The soul is a finer sort of matter and can survive bodily destruction, dualism (Descartes), panpsychism (Fechner, Heymans, Hartshorne), idealism (Schelling, Fichte, Hegel), parallelism (Spinoza, Leibniz), Occasionalism (Geulincx, Malebranche). To all this a new hypothesis may be added: dualistic interactionism (Eccles (and Popper)). Eccles argues that mind and body act upon each other, but that there also remain some independent regions. Moreover he argues that the mind has a superior position. It is the conscious mind that observes the brain processes! Eccles does not give his view as a definite theory, but as a hypothesis with the greatest explanatory power. In this view a survival of the mind after death is certainly possible: J.C. Eccles, *The Human Mystery* (The Gifford Lectures, 1977-1978) (Berlin, etc., 1979); idem, *The Human Psyche* (The Gifford Lectures, 1978-1979) (Berlin, etc., 1980); idem & K.R. Popper, *The Self and its Brain* (Berlin, etc., 1977; 2nd ed. 1981), cp. also: L. Gabriel, 'Neue Sicht des Leib-Seele Problems. Die Eccles-Hypothese' (*Wissenschaft und Weltbild* (Vienna), 30 (1978)), 178-186.

Cp. further: T. Penelhum, *Survival and Disembodied Existence* (London, 1970); R. Young, 'Professor Penelhum on the Resurrection of the Body' (*Religious Studies*, 9 (1973)), 181-187; J. Hick, *Death and Eternal Life* (London, 1976) (defends the possibility of eternal life, but shows the logical difficulties of remaining the same person); W. Rorarius, *Seele, Tod, Unsterblichkeit* (Gütersloh, 1979) (defends also the possibility of reincarnation besides the traditional Christian possibility of the resurrection); H. Thielicke, *Leben mit dem Tod* (Tübingen, 1980) (death as a human limit is a sign of God's wrath. Man behaves himself too presumptuous); also translated into English: idem, *Living with Death* (Grand Rapids, 1982); E. Kübler-Ross, *Living with Death and Dying* (New York, 1981) (refers to the heavenly experiences of people who have been nearly dead; in this she continues the well-known theories of R. Moody, *et alii*; cp. also the same theories in: J.V. Teunissen, *Paradijselijke visioenen* ('s-Gravenhage, 1971); H. Schwarz, *Wir werden weiterleben. Die Botschaft der Bibel von der Unsterblichkeit im Lichte moderner Grenzerfahrungen* (Freiburg i.Br., etc., 1984) (gives a critical evaluation of these theories); P. Badham & L. Badham, *Immortality or Extinction?* (London, 1982); B.R. Reichenbach, *Is Man the Phoenix? A Study of Immortality* (Lanham (Md.), 1983). An excellent historical survey can be found in: W.A. de Pater, *Immortality. Its History in the West* (Louvain/Amersfoort, 1984, 2nd. ed. 1984) (a systematic study will follow!).

4.5 Cp. also: E. Castelli (ed.), *Herméneutique de la sécularisation* (Paris, 1976) (includes also articles in English); A.J. Nijk, *Secularisatie; over het gebruik van een woord* (Rotterdam, 1968) (also Diss. Amsterdam, 1968); P. Smits, *De onttoverde wereld. Geschiedenis, sociale verschijningsvormen en culturele problemen van het secularisatieproces* (Amsterdam, 1972); *Modernità. Storia e valore di un'idea* (ed. by the Centro di studi filosofici di Gallarate) (Brescia, 1982); H.H. Schrey, *Säkularisierung* (Darmstadt, 1981).

4.6.1 Cp. also: W. Pannenberg (1973) (mentioned *sub* 1.1); A.R. Peacocke, *Creation and the World of Science* (Oxford, 1979); R.J. Pendergast, *Cosmos* (Bronx, 1973); W.A. de Pater, 'Wissenschaftstheoretisches zu Theologie und Glauben. Neuere Entwicklungen' (*Linguistica Biblica*, 37 (1976)), 69-102; R. Schlegel, 'Quantum Physics and the Divine Postulate' (Zygon, 14 (1979), 163-185). S.L. Jaki, *The Road of Science and the Ways to God* (Gifford lectures) (Edinburgh, 1978).

4.6.2 Some recent studies on the relationship between ethics and religion are: P. Helm (ed.), *Divine Commands and Morality* (Oxford, 1981); A. Babolin (ed.), *Etica e filosofia della religione*. Vol. I (Perugia, 1980); Vol. II (Perugia, 1981); J. Ansaldi, *Ethique et sanctification* (Geneva, 1983).

4.6.3 For the relationship between religion and aesthetics cp. especially H.U. von Balthasar, *Herrlichkeit. Eine theologische Ästhetik* (3 vol.) (Einsiedeln, 1961-1969). Kierkegaard's observations on Mozert's opera *Don Giovanni* can be found in *Enten-Eller* I (*Samlede Vaerker*, Anden Udgave, Første Bind) (Copenhagen, 1920), 35ff.; *The Diary of the seducer*, o.c., 317ff. The fragment 'In vino veritas' is in *Stadier paa Livets Vei* (*Samlede Vearker*, Anden Udgave, Sjette Bind) (Copenhagen, 1924), 21ff.
  Kant's first moral principle can be found in his *Grundlegung zur Metaphysik der Sitten* (Leipzig, 1904), 55. The thesis that the aesthetic judgments of taste are without any practical utility is in *Kritik der Urteilskraft* (ed. K. Vorländer) (Hamburg, 1954), 64 (1st ed., 40). Cp. also R. Eisler, *Kant Lexikon* (Hildesheim, 1964), 626ff. (s.v. 'Zweckmässigkeit'). Kant's idea that religion is knowledge of our obligations as God's commands in: *Kritik der Urteilskraft*, 357 (1st ed., 477).
  The quotations from the work of Van der Leeuw can be found in *Wegen en Grenzen* (Amsterdam, 1932), 4, 185, 209, 217, 210; or (2nd ed., 1948), 4, 175, 457f, 472, 458; or (3rd ed.,1955), 3, 316ff, 306f, 376, 307.
  The combination of deontic logic and chronological logic can be found in my pupil's

dissertation: J. van Eck, *A System of Temporarily Relative Modal and Deontic Logic and its Philosophical Applications* (Diss. Ph.D., Groningen, 1981); the main body of the dissertation also appeared as article in *Logique et Analyse*, 25 (1982), 249-290, 339-381. I devised a comprehensive abstract system in which deontic logic is a subsystem of modal logic: H.C.M. de Swart and H.G. Hubbeling, *Inleiding tot de symbolische logica* (Assen, 1976), 113ff. Heymans's aesthetic theory has been published in various articles: H.G. Hubbeling, 'De fundamenten van Heymans' esthetica' (*Algemeen Nederlands Tijfschrift voor Wijsbegeerte*, 72 (1980)), 174-192; idem, 'Heymans' theorie van het verhevene, het tragische en het komische' (*idem*, 73 (1981)), 44-57; *idem*, 'Heymans' filosofie van de kunst' (*idem*, 73 (1981)), 168-186. See also H.G. Hubbeling, 'Heymans' esthetica' in D. Draaisma *et alii, Gerard Heymans. Objectiviteit in filosofie en psychologie* (Weesp, 1983), 53-64. A classical handbook for aesthetics, in which some of the criteria mentioned may also be found is: M.C. Beardsley, *Aesthetics. Problems in the Philosophy of Criticism* (New York, 1958; 2nd ed. 1981). The criteria on p. 462ff. Instead of typical beauty Kant speaks of the normal idea (*Normalidee*), cp. *Kritik der Urteilskraft*, 76f (1st ed., 58ff). The thesis that contemplation of nature is a kind of art has been defended by Van der Leeuw, *o.c.*, 5; (2nd ed.), 5; (3rd ed.), 5.

A survey of the two main trends in present day aesthetics (analytical and structural aesthetics) is given in: J. Zimmerman, *Sprachanalytische Ästhetik. Ein Überblick* (Stuttgart/Bad Canstatt, 1980) and J. Mukarovski, *Structure, Sign and Function* (New Haven/London, 1978). For a systematic approach to the history of aesthetics one may see: W. Tatarkiewicz, *A History of Six Ideas. An Essay in Aesthetics* (The Hague/Warsaw, 1980) (the six main ideas are: art, beauty, creativity, imitation, form, aesthetic experience). Cp. further: E.H.J. Gombrich, *Ideals and Idols. Essays on Values in History and in Art* (Oxford, 1980); A. Plebe (ed.), *Semiotica ed estetica. Semiotik und Ästhetik* (Rome/Baden Baden, 1981); W. Oelmüller (ed.), *Ästhetische Erfahrung* (Paderborn, etc., 1981); G.K. Kaltenbrunner, *Was aber schön ist... Rechtfertigung des Ästhetischen* (Freiburg i.Br., etc., 1983).

4.7 For Ruusbroec *vide* H.G. Hubbeling (1973) (mentioned *sub* 4.1), in which an extensive analysis of the mystical terms may be found.

Cp. further: M.M. Davy (ed.), *Encyclopédie des Mystiques* (4 vol.) (Paris, 1977-1978); J.M. van der Lans, *Religieuze ervaring en meditatie. Een godsdienstpsychologische studie* (Deventer, 1980); L. Dupré and E. Cardoen, *Terugkeer naar innerlijkheid* (Antwerpen/Amsterdam, 1981); R. Mehl, *Vie intérieure et transcendance de Dieu* (Paris, 1980); J.R. Horne, *Beyond Mysticism* (Waterloo (Ont.), 1978).

4.8 The quotations from Van Baaren stem from his work (1960) (mentioned *sub* 4), 185, 187. De Pater's expositions on miracles can be found in (1977) (mentioned *sub* 1.1), 51-100. The modern theories of religious symbols and symbolism have been treated in a special issue of the journal: *NeueZeitschrift für systematische Theologie und Religionsphilosophie*, 27 (1985), edited by H.G. Hubbeling and H.G. Kippenberg, 77-193. (Also published as: *On Symbolic Representation of Religion. Groninger Contributions to Theories of Symbols* (Berlin, 1986)). Here it is taught that a (religious) symbol refers in some indirect way to a religious object. Thus it plays a role in religious epistemology. But it may also make the religious object present in reality. Thus it becomes a sacrament and it is a part of the way to salvation. Moreover, symbols play a role in every culture as a means of self-identification: national flag, national anthem, etc. One understands a symbol only in its relations to other symbols. One may describe this in a structural, but also in a logical way. The meaning of a symbol depends also on what can be inferred from it, on what consequences it has, etc. In a community where it is believed that unbaptized persons cannot enter heaven baptism means something different from baptism in a community where no such belief exists, although in all other respects the interpretation of the symbol may be the same. Further a symbol can be abstract or concrete and that to which it refers can also be abstract or concrete. A symbol can be natural or conventional, institutionalized or not, but without symbols no culture can survive!

Cp. further: T. Peters. 'The Problem of Symbolic Reference' (*Thomist*, 44 (1980)), 72-93 (religious symbols refer in another way than ordinary signs) (cp. also the text in the present book!); E.C. Banchi, 'A Holistic and Dynamic Development of Doctrinal Symbols' (*Anglican Theological Review*, 55 (1973)), 148-169 (symbols are expressions of a religious intuitionism. They change from culture to culture); R.N. Bellah, 'Christianity and Symbolic Realism' (*Journal of Scientific Study of Religion*, 9 (1970)), 89-96 (symbols express a real religious reality. They cannot be reduced to something non-religious); A.P. Martinich, 'Sacraments and Speech Acts' (*Heythrop Journal*, 16 (1975)), 289-303 (written under the influence of Austin); J. Skorupski, *Symbol and Theory. A Philosophical Study of Theories of Religion in Social Anthropology* (Cambridge, 1979); Cl. Geertz, *The Interpretation of Cultures* (New York, 1973); S.K. Langer, *Philosophy in a New Key* (Cambridge (Mass.), 1960); E.R. Leach, *Culture and Communication: The Logic by which Symbols are Connected* (Cambridge, 1976).

In his *The Concept of Miracle* (London, 1970) R. Swinburne points out that there are two main possible interpretations of miracles: (i) God intervenes in physical causality and (ii) we have insufficient knowledge and therefore there is only a seeming intervention from the side of God. Today the latter position is the most usual. Spinoza had defended this position. Sometimes a more traditional view on miracles is defended, e.g. P. Byrne, 'Miracles and the Philosophy of Science' (*Heythrop Journal*, 19 (1978)), 162-170, who states that the classical doctrine of miracles stands in conflict with strong scientific determinism only. If we accept a weak scientific determinism exceptions are possible and thus this kind of scientism can be brought into harmony with a more traditional concept of miracles. R. Young too in his article 'Miracles and Physical Impossibility' (*Sophia*, 11 (1972)), 29-35 defends a more traditional concept while at the same time trying to avoid the violation model of miracles. God changes the surrounding conditions of some event so that it appears as a miracle. As an event it remains, however, inexplicable. According to T.T. Wei 'Mr. Young on Miracles' (*Religious Studies*,10 (1974)), 333-337, this attempt has not been successful. Our so-called rational culture is not only determined by symbols, but is also pervaded by magical thinking: J.J. Oosten, *Magie en rede. Een onderzoek naar de invloed van magische denkwijzen binnen onze op het verstand georiënteerde cultuur* (Assen, 1983).

Appendix 1: Besides the literature mentioned in the text cp.: H. Fischer, *Glaubensaussage und Sprachstruktur* (Hamburg, 1972); A. Grabner-Haider, *Semiotik und Theologie. Die religiöse Rede zwischen analytischer und hermeneutischer Philosophie* (München, 1973); E. Herms, 'Die Einführung des allgemeinen Zeichenbegriffs. Theologische Aspekte der Begründung einer reinen Semiotik durch Ch.W. Morris' (*Neue Zeitschrift für systematische Theologie und Religionsphilosophie*, 20 (1978)), 16-38; J.J. Katz, *Semantic Theory* (New York, 1972); M. Polanyi and H. Prosch, *Meaning* (Chicago, 1975); G.H.R. Parkinson, *The Theory of Meaning* (London, 1968); A. Kasher and S. Lappin, *Philosophical Linguistics. An Introduction* (Kronberg, 1977) (defends a formal pragmatic theory); H. Parret, *Filosofie en taalwetenschap* (Assen, 1979) (an epistemological approach to linguistics); M.J. Cresswell, *Logics and Linguistics* (London, 1973) (presents a semantical logical approach to grammar); J. Simon, *Sprachphilosophie* (München/Freiburg i.Br., 1981) (on a neo-existentialistic basis); M. Geier, *et alii, Sprachbewusstsein. Elf Untersuchungen zum Zusammenhang von Sprachwissenschaft und kulturhistorischer Psychology* (Stuttgart, 1979) (emphasizes the connection between language and the history of culture, referring to the Sovjet school of cultural psychology).

Appendix 2: Cp. also R. Swinburne (1977) (mentioned *sub* 1.1) (categories as 'personal', 'necessary', etc. can only analogically be applied to God. Swinburne rejects, however, the Thomistic doctrine of analogy. According to Swinburne a word is used analogically, if its meaning differs from its literal use, and if it is closer to this literal meaning than to its opposite. I myself have defended a modern reinterpretation of Thomistic analogy); J.M. Bocheński, O.P. (1965) (mentioned *sub* 1.2), 156ff (my dealing with analogy stands in the line of this tradition!); T. Chapman, 'Analogy' (*Thomist*, 39 (1975)), 127-141; K. Nielsen, 'Analogical Talk of God. A Negative Critique' (*idem*, 40 (1976)), 32-60; W.N. Clarke, 'Analogy and the Meaningfulness of Language about God. A Reply to Kai Nielsen' (*idem*, 40 (1976)), 61-95; R.

Attfield, 'Religious Symbols and the Voyage of Analogy' (*International Journal of Philosophy of Religion*, 11 (1980)), 225-238. J.J. van Es, *Spreken over God: Letterlijk of Figuurlijk? Analogie en metafoor in het spreken over God* (Diss. V.U. Amsterdam, 1979).

Appendix 3: Besides the literature mentioned in the text and *sub* 1.1 and 3.1.2 one may consult: H.J. Cargas and B. Lee (eds.), *Religious Experience and Process Theology* (New York, 1976); J.B. Cobb, *God and the world* (Philadelphia, 1969); J.B. Cobb and D.R. Griffin, *Process Theology. An Introductory Exposition* (Philadelphia, 1976); P.A.Y. Gunter and J.R. Sibley, *Process Philosophy. Basic Writings* (Washington, D.C., 1978) R.C. Neville, *Creativity and God* (New York, 1980); J. van der Veken *et alii*, *Proces Filosofie* (Louvain, 1980); P. Jonkers and J. van der Veken (eds.), *Whitehead's Legacy* (Louvain, 1981); G. Hélal, *La philosophie comme panpsychisme. La philosophie des sciences de A.N. Whitehead* (Montréal, 1979) (Whitehead's philosophy is constituted by his empiricism, rationalism and growing subjectivism. They lead to several discontinuities in his works); R.L. Fetz, *Whitehead. Prozessdenken und Substanzmetaphysik* (Freiburg: München, 1981); E. Herrmann, *Die logische Stellung des ontologischen Gottesbeweises in Charles Hartshornes Processtheologie und neoklassischer Metaphysik* (Lund, 1980) (criticizes the connection between Hartshorne's modal variant of the ontological proof and the main theses of process philosophy); J. van der Veken, *Proces denken en orientatie* (with extensive bibliography) (Louvain, 1984); J. Leclercq, *Whitehead between Empiricism and Rationalism* (Louvain, 1984) (both Leclercq and Fetz gave an Aristotelian interpretation of Whitehead against the usual Platonic one); H. Holz and E. Wolf-Gazo (eds.), *Whitehead und der Prozessbegriff/Whitehead and the Idea of Process* (Proceedings of the first International Whitehead-Symposium 1981) (Freiburg/München, 1984).

Appendix 10. In the next text we have given a structural-logical analysis. We could also have given a more consequential-logical analysis by making use of the consequences that may be drawn from the various concepts of revelation. E.g. if $_aRp$ may mean 'a reveals that p', than, if a = God, the following axiom is valid:

$_aRp \rightarrow p$

i.e. if God reveals that p than p is true (or p is a fact). This axiom is, however, invalid if *a* is a human being. And that means that a calculus in which this axiom is valid is related to modal logic, whereas the other calculus is related to deontic logic, (see the abstract scheme of logics in my book: H. de Swart and H.G. Hubbeling, *Inleiding tot de symbolische logica* (Assen, 1976). In this way these calculi fit in the well-known calculi.

Cp. further: J. Astley, 'Revelation Revisted' (*Theology*, 83 (1980)), 339-346; L.T. Howe, 'Revelation. A Conceptual Analysis' (*Theology Today*, 33 (1977)), 329-340; J. Keller, 'Revelation and the Test of Language' (*Encounter*, 41 (1980)), 353-363; J.J. Shepherd, 'The Concept of Revelation' (*Religious Studies*, 16 (1980)), 425-437.

270

Index of Names

274

Index of Subjects

Buddhism, 3, 37, 41f, 80, 102, 162, 167, 180f, 188, 191
–, Mahayana –, 143, 162
–, Zen –, 80, 102, 167, 191

Cabbala, 158
cargo cult, 163
Cartesianism, 51
category, 56, 87
cause
–, difference between – and ground, 104
Ceres, 138
Chassidim, 158
Christ, 41f, 160, 163, 166
(*see also* incarnation of Christ; resurrection)
Christian
– religion, 136
– –, argument for the truth of – –, 216
–, faith, 164
– –, argument for the truth of – –, 32
Christianity, 37, 42, 44, 62, 80, 140ff, 147, 157, 160, 174, 180f, 188f, 191f
–, historic character of –, 161f
church, 67
(*see also* authority, ecclesiastical)
combination, unusual semantic – in religious language, 83, 85
communication
–, extential –, 133
–, (method of) indirect –, 186, 241
communism, 159
complementary of theories, 10
conclusio a minore ad minus and *a maiore ad minus*, see *Qal wahomèr*
Confucianism, 165, 173, 188
contingency, 103f
cosmological argument, Ch. 3.1.3. *passim*; 47, 81, 87ff, 97, 116, 125, 130, 132, 137, 201
–, modal reconstruction of, Appendix 4. *passim*
create, to, 194f,
creative
– power, see power, creative
– property, 198ff
culture, religion and –, see religion and –
cumulative argument, 28, 45, 119f, 131, 201
cybernetics, 120

dance, 180, 188
dayyo, principle of, 223
D-calculus, 215, 217, 245f

deduction, 25
deism, 107, 142f
Deitas, 239
Demagod, 163, 192
Demeter, 158
demythologizing, 192
design
–, argument of –, Ch. 3.1.4 *passim*; 87f, 103
(*see also* physical-theological argument; teleological argument)
determinism, 65f, 158
deus otiosus, 139
devotion, 32
dialectic
– materialism, 81, 168
– of the infinite or the absolute, see logic, dialectical
– of polarity, 19
– of synthesis, 19, 30f
Diana, 138
disclosure, 83f, 192, 225f
– situation, 83
dogma, 5
–, Christian –, 55
dogmatics, 3, 5, 47f, 68, 72, 133
– order of topics in –, 47
dualism, 140
Durga, 141f
duty, see religion of –
DW-calculus, 247
Dyauspitar, 140
dynamism, 71, 140

economy in science
–, principle of –, 22f, 77
Edda, 163
El, 140
Elema, 164
elephant, anecdote of –, 144
elevator-word, see apex-word
emanation, 142
empirical
–, fit, 84
–, method in the study of religions, 34
empiricism, 13, 56
–, logical –, 12
Enlightenment, 52, 54
epistemology, 12, 47, 65, 87, 126, 137, 240
– and aesthetic experience, 42
– and metaphisical questions, 39
– and religious experience, 35, 45
– as foundation of philosophy, 8, 11

–, consequence theory of – and meaning, 241
–, correspondence theory of –, 240
–, non-descriptive (pragmatic) theory of meaning and –, 242
   –, normative (standard) theory of –, 242

ulama, 160
unio mystica, 37, 39, 159
Upanishads, 1, 143, 159

values
   –, aesthetic –, 238
   –, ethical –, 3
   –, moral –, 238
   –, religious –, 238
Vedanta, 144, 159
Veda-religion, 158
verification
   – of aesthetic statements, 68
   – of moral statements, 68
   – of religious statements, 35, 68
Vienna Circle, 68
Vishnu, 145
   –, *avataras* of –, 162
viśiṣṭādvaita, 159
vitalism, 72
void, filled –, 38

Weisgerber, school of, 226
will, 55
world
   – as startingpoint for philosophy, 7
worship, 155
Wortfeld, 226
Wu Wei, 164, 173

Yang, 19, 81, 141
Yin, 19, 81, 141

DATE DUE

HIGHSMITH   #LO-45220